TAKING RISKS

TAKING RISKS

The Management of Uncertainty

Kenneth R. MacCrimmon
and Donald A. Wehrung

with W. T. Stanbury

THE FREE PRESS
A Division of Macmillan, Inc.
NEW YORK

Collier Macmillan Publishers
LONDON

The Free Press
A Division of Macmillan, Inc.
866 Third Avenue, New York, N.Y. 10022

Collier Macmillan Canada, Inc.

First Free Press Paperback Edition 1988

Printed in the United States of America

printing number

1 2 3 4 5 6 7 8 9 10

Library of Congress Cataloging in Publication Data

MacCrimmon, Kenneth R.
Taking risks.

Bibliography: p.
Includes index.
1. Risk management. I. Wehrung, Donald A.
II. Stanbury, W.T. III. Title.
HD61.M23 1986 658 85-16275
ISBN 0-02-919563-2

To the memory of
Jacob Marschak
who provided the
inspiration for the study,
and to Marilyn and Linda,
who helped to keep it going.

Contents

Preface

Risks are an important part of everyone's life. A decision being made today by someone you do not even know can create risks for you. For example, a takeover of your firm may jeopardize your job security. Likewise a decision you make today can create risks for other people. For instance, a drug that you decide to introduce to the market may have unknown side effects. Thus you should learn more about your own willingness to take risks, as well as the risk inclinations of those making decisions that can affect you. Yet, to date little has been known about the risk dispositions of top-level executives. There has been no standard way for managers to assess their willingness to take risks.

Taking Risks has three major objectives. First, it develops a framework for understanding risk taking and uses this framework to determine what we know about managerial risk taking. Second, it presents a Risk Portfolio that you can use to assess your own willingness to take risks. Third, it reports on a comprehensive study of the willingness to take risks of senior business executives.

The Risk Portfolio consists of several questionnaires relevant to the risk disposition of managers. These questionnaires, and the associated measures of risk, are based on theories of risk in economics, finance, management, and psychology. Thus they are managerially oriented and have solid underpinnings. Answers to the Risk Portfolio questions can be summarized into an Individual Risk Profile that helps a manager understand his own willingness to take personal and business risks, and an Organizational Risk Profile that helps a firm compare the risk dispositions of its managers.

The Risk Profile was used in a comprehensive study of the risk taking of over 500 top-level American and Canadian managers. From this study we have answered questions such as:

- Are managers generally risk takers or risk averters?
- Are managers more willing to take risks in their business decisions than in their personal decisions?
- Are risk takers in one situation willing to take risks in other situations?
- Are older managers more risk-averse that younger managers? Does willingness to take risks depend on other personal factors such as nationality and education?
- Are CEOs more willing to take risks than more junior managers? Do other business factors such as firm size and industry affect inclination towards risk?

Taking Risks is intended for managers, students, and researchers. Managers who want to assess their own willingness to take risks should begin by following the directions given in Chapter 12. Those who wish a brief description of our main results should read the summaries in Chapters 7 and 11. Further details may be found where these key results are highlighted throughout the text in Chapters 3 to 6 and 8 to 10. Managers and students who want a thorough, but nontechnical, discussion should read the main text of the whole book but may skip the technical notes set in smaller type. The research details have been put into 70 technical notes, interspersed throughout each chapter, to allow researchers to understand and extend the study.

Acknowledgments

Our greatest debt is to the 509 top-level executives who participated in the study. They took several hours out of their busy schedules to answer questions about how they have handled risk and how they would handle risk in a variety of situations. They also supplied considerable information about their personal and business status for which we promised anonymity. Thus we regretfully cannot list the participants but we are grateful to each of them.

Several organizations provided crucial financial support. The initial funding by the Department of Industry, Trade, and Commerce of the Canadian Government was instrumental in financing the design of the study, the data collection, and early analyses. The Social Sciences and Humanities Research Council of Canada provided two grants that were indispensable for conducting the analyses and preparing the manuscript. They also awarded leave fellowships to both co-authors that allowed for the necessary work on the book. We are especially grateful to both DITC and SSHRCC for their support of us and their general funding of research on important management issues.

Other financial support was provided by the University of British Columbia through the President's Research Grants, the E.D. MacPhee Chair, and miscellaneous funding of the Faculty of Commerce and Business Administration as well as by the Associates' Program of the University of Western Ontario.

This project was a group effort by a number of people over the past twelve years. We are indebted to all our co-workers and assistants and apologize to those whom we are not able to mention individually. We are especially grateful to our families. They endured countless evening and weekend sessions devoted to the planning and evaluation of analyses and the redrafting of chapters. Their encouragement and support reduced the overall risk.

Our colleague Bill Stanbury was a major contributor to this study from the outset. He helped to get the initial funding, to conduct the pilot studies, to organize the sample design, to conduct the personal contact part of the data collection, and to specify variables of interest. His contributions were invaluable. Unfortunately other commitments precluded his participation in the analysis and manuscript preparation of recent years.

John Bassler also made important early contributions. He helped on the design of the questionnaires, on the data collection for both the pilot and main studies, on the coding of the data, and on some preliminary analyses. Geographical remoteness and other commitments forced him to leave the project midway through.

Alfred Kwong helped with the early design of questionnaires and pilot testing as part of his master's thesis. Russel Quinn did coding, collected data, and conducted interviews. Vinay Kanetkar kept track of our very large database and he both suggested and performed voluminous and useful analyses of the data. Brad Cousins did analyses, made preliminary write-ups, and kept us moving forward on the project.

Other assistants who deserve special mention are Michael Leung, Hazel Ramsey, Jay Siegel, Carolyn Arnold, Rosemary Carter, Peter Coates, Barb Doyle, Cathy Giles, David Ing, Karyn MacCrimmon, Genaro Matute, Maureen McGeough, Darlene Osterlin, Peter Ross, Gail Taylor, Peg Tittle, Andrena Welch, and Grace Wong.

We are grateful for the administrative help of Dean Peter Lusztig and Gail Robertson of the Faculty of Commerce, U.B.C., as well as the secretarial efforts of Evelyn Fong, Harriet Noot, Sharon Parent, Linda Stewart, Mabel Yee, and the staff of the Word Processing Center.

Various colleagues made helpful comments on the study. We are grateful for the noteworthy contributions of David Bell, Kent Brothers, Morrie DeGroot, Jim Dyer, Peter Fishburn, Mike Gibbins, Duncan Luce, Jacob Marschak, John Payne, Larry Phillips, Paul Slovic, Ron Taylor and Amos Tversky.

Other colleagues whose suggestions are particularly appreciated were Cris Banks, Max Bazerman, Hilly Einhorn, Haim Falk, Peter Farquhar, Baruch Fischhoff, Howard Kunreuther, Sarah Lichtenstein, Rakesh Sarin, Carl Sarndal, Tom Wallsten, and Stan Zionts.

With so many people contributing to this project we would like to be able to share the risks of any errors with them. Alas, we cannot do so. We must bear the risks ourselves.

The original conceptualization for the study, its research design, and the development of the instruments are due to MacCrimmon. The design of the analyses was equally shared although primary responsibility for the conduct of analysis is due to Wehrung. We have shared the responsibilities for preparing the many drafts of the manuscript and the book is truly a joint product. We willingly share the risks equally.

PART ONE

Introduction

Chapter 1

Essence of Risk

A life without adventure is likely to be unsatisfying, but a life in which adventure is allowed to take whatever form it will, is likely to be short.

—Bertrand Russell

INTRODUCTION

Some risks such as natural disasters are dramatically obvious, and they affect many people. Hurricanes, volcanoes, and earthquakes can destroy entire communities in minutes. Malaria, smallpox, and sleeping sickness can devastate populations. Other risks are more personal. Crossing busy streets, working in a polluted environment, borrowing money, or failing to contain our anger are everyday risks that most of us face.

Consider getting food from the supermarket. We jump in the car and run a risk of being hit by a careless or drunk driver, even if we are cautious ourselves. Once inside the store we are faced with goods that may have been tampered with or tomorrow may be declared carcinogenic or environmentally harmful. On a more minor level, we may discover that the meat we bought was on sale at a competing supermarket.

If everyday choices present us with a shower of risks, our major choices are immersed in a virtual downpour. Think of what can go wrong in getting married, changing jobs, or taking a trip to a foreign country. In many of these situations, our choices do not just affect us, they affect many other people. Business and government decisions can influence the risks faced by thousands or millions of others.

Risk is a pervasive part of all actions. While eventual death may be certain, every day we engage in activities—even just crossing the road to mail a letter—that carry a risk of death. Although death is the ultimate risk, the economic and social risks that we face can be more oppressive. Seemingly secure jobs may disappear in economic hard times. Seemingly stable marriages may shatter for many possible reasons.

Life requires choices; choices require risks. While you can choose to minimize the risks you face, you cannot avoid risks completely. Along with death and taxes, risk is one of the certainties of life.

Proust-like, we may decide to isolate ourselves in the safety of our homes to avoid risks. However, we still may fall down the stairs, have a plane crash into the roof, be electrocuted in the bath, be assaulted by a burglar, be blown away by a tornado, or be downwind of an unsafe nuclear power plant. We may move to an isolated mountain region to escape from the risks of a city's polluting factories, traffic congestion, and racial tension only to expose ourselves to the risk of inadequate emergency medical services in the event of a heart attack. That many risks are hidden and not foreseen may mean greater peace of mind, but it does not reduce our exposure to their possible negative effects.

Primitive man had little control over his environment. The daily activities of acquiring food and shelter were fraught with risk. While modern man has gained some control over his environment and may experience fewer risks in acquiring the basic necessities, a more complex environment has brought new risks. In this century, technology and collective action fill our lives with man-made hazards such as nuclear war or acid rain. Gaining control over some risks has led to different types of risks that may even be more dangerous than the ones that have been mitigated. In general, avoiding one kind of risk will introduce some other risk. By not building nuclear powered energy plants, we run risks of impairing our economic structure by running short of fuel, increasing coal-related disease, and so forth.

Some actions appear to be free of risk. We invest our life savings in a "risk-free" savings account insured by the federal government instead of buying mutual funds or we marry our childhood sweetheart whom we have known for twenty years instead of marrying the seductive stranger. Although these actions seem to have predictable outcomes, they have risks of their own. Several years after putting the money into the savings account, it provides little security because of rampant inflation. Investing in mutual funds would have provided better security against changes in the price level. After marrying the childhood sweetheart and building a family, the marriage crumbles because the partners no longer find each other stimulating.

Thus even apparently riskless actions have risks associated with them due to unforeseen events or changes in perspective. Nonetheless it is often a useful fiction to think of some particular action as riskless so that other risky actions can be judged against it.

We sometimes think that by not taking an action we can avoid risks. You are approached by the chief executive of a multinational firm who wants you to leave your current position to assume the presidency of a small subsidiary. You delay responding so that you can think about the offer and its implications for yourself and your family. A week later another executive is made president of the subsidiary which grows into a multi-million dollar enterprise. By not accepting the risks of changing jobs, you missed an opportunity.

Not only can risks not be totally avoided, but most individuals seek risks in at least some aspects of their lives. Uncertainty about outcomes of virtually all important activities provides the excitement that stimulates as well as creating the anxiety that worries. People engage in hazardous recreational activities such as hang gliding and rock climbing, they play the stock market, and they gamble partly because of the stimulation that accompanies the risk. Success itself increases risks as we discover whether we can handle the new opportunities that become available.

We must face risks in all aspects of our lives and in the many roles we play. The risks we confront as a business executive or community leader are not the same risks we deal with as spouse or parent. We face personal risks that are financial, physiological, medical, social, and so forth. Risks also affect our careers and the organizations that employ us. Most human endeavors bring major risks. To set high goals of success is to run high risks of failure.

We expose ourselves to personal *financial risks* in several ways. We can live beyond our means when we spend more than our income and wealth can support. We can hold too many of our assets in investments that have a chance of major losses. We can hold too great a share of these assets as highly levered investments that are subject to the control of creditors. In each case loss of credit, loss of an asset, or personal bankruptcy are possible outcomes. During hard economic times unemployment rises and savings dwindle. Individuals with prudent financial investment and expenditure strategies do not suffer the same wide swings in economic well-being as those who sought greater gains with their associated financial risks.

Risks to one's physical *health* can take many forms—accidents, disease, violence, heredity, diet, exercise (or its absence), personal habits, and so forth. Some physical risks have only minor consequences such as temporary mild discomfort or inconvenience whereas others have more major consequences such as permanent physical disability, severe suffering, or even death.

If you are an average American male under age 55, the number of days you lose from your life expectancy has been estimated to be more than ten times as high from motor vehicle accidents as from fires (195 days to 14 days). While indulging in regular coffee drinking will only shorten your life by an expected six days, being 30% overweight will cut your life expectancy by more than three and a half years! Even worse than being overweight is smoking more than 20 cigarettes a day; the risks involved (primarily lung cancer) can be expected to shorten your life by almost seven years. The ultimate risk (among normal activities), though, seems to be the risk of remaining single. It has been estimated that being unmarried shortens a man's life expectancy by nine and a half years (Cohen and Lee, 1979)!

Setting high goals can also involve *social risks* which result in negative consequences if we fail to meet them. The social risk that perhaps affects us most personally is the loss of self-esteem that we sometimes experience in the face of repeated failures. Social risks occur when parent-child relationships within the family undergo change. The normal process of dating exposes the participants to social risks as they experiment with their interpersonal relationship. Joining and participating in any organization or group may lead to social rejection if one fails to be accepted as a contributing member. In its extreme form social rejection can take the form of imprisonment or death when a society imposes its harshest penalties on those convicted of taking antisocial criminal risks.

The choice of one's *career* has many inherent risks. A career as wife and mother has different financial, physical, and social risks than a career as banker or lawyer. The attainment of a chosen career depends upon satisfying its educational and apprenticeship requirements as well as overcoming any other barriers to entry that have been set up. Once a career is established, will it provide the envisioned opportunities and stimulation that are needed for maintaining interest in the career? Will one's performance on the job lead to success and career advancement? One of the greatest risks is changing careers in midlife when we may be less adaptable to change and when there is less time available for adequate career development before retirement.

Although everyone makes daily decisions involving risks, not all of us make decisions that result in risks for thousands or even millions of people. Managers of business firms or political leaders, however, continually face such risks. Government officials decide whether to commit us to military ventures and trade wars. They decide on traffic speed limits, drug testing requirements, disposal of hazardous wastes, and so forth. Business managers oversee the building of the cars, production of the drugs, and running of the factories that are the objects of such political decisions.

Not all managers, however, are fully accountable for their decisions. While politicians are subject to review by the electorate every few years, many of the decisions are made in a bureaucracy that is well buffered from detailed scrutiny. In business firms job security is not legislated, so bad outcomes for the firms are more likely to be followed by bad outcomes for the responsible managers.

In 1976 John deLorean quit his high-paying job as vice-president of General Motors to start his own automobile company. The costs of the machinery and supplies necessary to compete in the auto industry are enormous. Even though no one had successfully created a major auto company since the 1930s, deLorean managed to obtain the financial backing of the British Government by building his plant in Northern Ireland. Unfortunately, the automobile market collapsed just as deLorean was getting his first cars to dealers. With slow sales, massive amounts of money were required to keep the factory going, and in late 1982 John deLorean was faced with the impending bankruptcy of his company. He was charged with being involved in a major drug deal that, if it had been successful, would have provided the funds to keep his company going. Although there was a videotape of a drug transaction, the jury decided that deLorean was entrapped and he was acquitted. John deLorean clearly fits our image of the entrepreneurial risk taker.

Most business decisions involve tradeoffs that lead to different risks for employees, stockholders, consumers, suppliers, and management. A decision to close an obsolete plant may save the stockholders money that in the long run can be used for creating jobs. In the short run, however, it throws people out of work. The decision to withhold a drug from the market for further testing may minimize the possible hazards of side-effects and prevent future lawsuits, but it denies many others treatment that could help them now.

While many operating decisions made by managers (e.g., which accounting method to use, what inventory level to maintain) seem to have few risks, the strategic decisions are fraught with peril. Consider the Tylenol tragedy in which several bottles of the pain remedy capsules sold in Chicago contained cyanide that caused the death of seven unsuspecting users. Prior to this tragedy Johnson & Johnson, along with many other major pharmaceutical companies, packaged their over-the-counter drugs without any special protective covering to prevent tampering.

There was little time to decide what to do as a nervous public demanded action to stop the mounting death toll and Tylenol sales plummeted. There was little information about what was happening and what was causing it. Was the problem a local Chicago problem or was it more widespread? Were only Tylenol products affected and were only the capsules (but not the solid pills) adulterated? Was the cause unintended and restricted to a malfunction in the production process? Was it the work of a madman, extortionist, or terrorist group that tampered with the bottles randomly in selected retail outlets? Johnson & Johnson had inadequate control of the situation as it examined its options to prevent more deaths, to reassure the public, to better understand the problem, to prevent additional tampering of its products, and to rebuild Tylenol sales.

If Johnson & Johnson did not recall Tylenol capsules in Chicago, more deaths might result. If the recall were not extended to the national market or to other Tylenol products, some other crazed individual or group might try to copy the tragic tampering to capture headlines or to extort financial gain. If recalled capsules were not immediately and systematically tested, management would not know the extent and source of the tampering until other deaths might have occurred.

Facing all these risks simultaneously, the company recalled and tested all Tylenol capsules in Chicago, tested selected lots of capsules from other marketing areas, and thoroughly reviewed their production, testing, and distribution procedures. While these actions were under way, they kept the public informed about the extent of the problem and the steps they had taken to prevent future deaths. Johnson & Johnson assured the public that the tampering had occurred at the retail level and it was restricted to the Chicago area.

Three months after the tragedy had begun Johnson & Johnson announced to the public that Tylenol products were being distributed in a new "tamper-proof" package that had three safety features: a foil seal on the top of the bottle, a plastic ring on the cap, and a cellophane wrap on the box. Despite losing most of its very large 35% share of the capsule pain remedy market due to the tragedy, within a year sales had bounced back to over 25% of the market.

Rolls Royce is synonymous with prestige and success. The image of the luxury car, however, did not carry over to the management of the company in the 1960s. A company that relied on aircraft engine sales to provide over 80% of their revenue, Rolls Royce could foresee that their current aircraft engine sales would dry up within a decade. To assure survival, top management decided that they had to obtain a contract for the engines on one of the new generation of wide-bodied jets. After losing out on the Boeing 747, Rolls Royce made a special effort to make a deal with Lockheed. The engines that they proposed supplying for the Lockheed L1011 required a higher thrust than any aircraft engine that had previously been developed. In addition, the engines were to be extremely quiet and durable. New materials would be used and many other technological advances were promised. The contract involved delivery of engines at a fixed cost three years ahead. Considerable late delivery penalties were accepted. The financial commitment amounted to over 90% of Rolls Royce's total assets. Thus the technological and financial risks were enormous. Management believed they were justified in light of the potential gains and the consequences if the risks were not taken. Unfortunately, these difficulties escalated and Rolls Royce declared bankruptcy three years later in February 1971.

Does this story imply that large risks should not be taken? Not at all. Several years later, Boeing was making aircraft commitments (for the 757 and 767) that involved three times as much as their total assets at the time. Boeing not only survived, they established a position of strong technological leadership. Although the recession of the early 1980s hit them hard, they were in no worse shape than other aircraft companies.

RISKY SITUATIONS

Risk Components: Exposure to a Chance of Loss

The main definition of the verb "risk" in the Oxford English Dictionary is "to expose to the chance of injury or loss." Early references date back to the seventeenth century. The origin is thought to be Italian (risco) but is uncertain. It is worthwhile to reflect on the implications of various aspects of the definition. First, it is necessary that there be a potential *loss* of some amount (we will use "loss" as a general expression to include "injury"). Second, there must be a *chance* of loss. A sure loss is not a risk. Third, the notion "to *expose*" means that the decision maker can take actions that can increase (or decrease) the magnitude or chance of loss. Therefore "to risk" implies the availability of a choice. This exposure may be to the person making the risky decision or to other persons or groups in the environment.

The second definition in the dictionary, "to venture upon," suggests even more of an orientation toward action than the first definition. To the extent that a person has some influence on the state of affairs, he takes risks in order to bring about a more preferred outcome. In 1759 Samuel Johnson was explicit about this aspect when he advocated that we "risk the certainty of little for the chance of much."

NOTE ON THE DEFINITION OF RISK

There is uncertainty about the price of gold at the end of this year but we would not call it a risky situation for you unless there were some consequences to you of the different price levels. Correspondingly, if you knew that a stock that you owned and could not sell was sure to lose half its value over the next month, this situation would not be risky because there was no uncertainty. Hence uncertainty is a necessary condition for riskiness but it is not sufficient. Similarly, potential loss is a necessary condition for riskiness but it is not sufficient. Together, however, uncertainty and potential loss are sufficient for a situation to be risky.

In general "loss" is a relative loss. A particular payoff is a "loss" if it is considered worse than some particular reference level of payoff. The reference level may be a zero payoff, the current status quo, a target or aspiration level, or the best payoff available in a situation. Hence even a payoff distribution consisting entirely of monetary gains is considered risky when each outcome is compared to the best possible outcome. While losses are commonly thought of in monetary terms, they may be anything that is of concern to a particular decision maker.

Two main forms of potential loss should be considered: (1) an outcome that will make us worse off than some reference status quo position, or (2) an outcome that is not as good as some other outcome that might have been obtained. The first case is easily perceived as a real loss; the second case, an opportunity loss, may not be perceived as easily. Opportunity losses can sometimes turn apparently risk-free situations into risky ones when unforeseen events occur. We shall use the terminology *magnitude of loss* to refer to either of these forms of loss.

For simplicity, in the discussion above we did not distinguish between single events and multiple events, or between single types of loss and multiple types of loss. If outcomes depend on only one event, say weather, the situation is less risky than if they depend on many events (e.g., weather, economic conditions, demographic trends, actions of competitors). Similarly, situations in which choices entail possible losses on only a single dimension, say financial, are less risky that those involving losses on many dimensions (e.g., financial, health, social, career).

In summary, then, there are three components of risk—the *magnitude of loss*, the *chance of loss*, and the *exposure to loss*. To reduce riskiness, it is necessary to reduce at least one of these components. Presumably if all of these elements were trivial, then we would hardly call the situation risky. The degree of risk can be thought of as being directly proportional to the chances and size of the loss and to the degree of exposure of the decision maker to the chance of loss.

NOTE ON THE RISK COMPONENTS

In some situations risky alternatives have a formalized assessment of the magnitude and chances of loss. For example, a bet on a single number at an American roulette table has a 97.4% chance (i.e., 37/38) of losing the amount bet. Similarly for other casino games, lottery tickets, and the like, we can calculate the chances of loss directly. The amount of loss is, of course, determined by the size of our bet. We also can calculate the amount of the potential gain.

In other gambling situations, such as the race track, while we know our potential loss, we have no objective estimate of the chances of loss or of the potential gain. Immediately after the betting on a race closes, and before the race is run, we can compute our potential gain, but we still must rely on our subjective estimate of the chances. Presumably the reason we bet is that our assessment of the chances of our horse winning was sufficiently higher than the assessment made by other bettors.

Adopting a Bayesian point of view, we assert that in virtually all situations, a person has some information from which to estimate the chances of the potential gains and losses if they are not given. Hence it does not appear to be a gross oversimplification to consider risky actions that have objectively specified chances of winning and losing. Even when objectively specified chances are given in a risky situation, the decision maker may modify these quantities because he perceives the situation differently from its objective statement.

Basic Risk Paradigm

When research and development offer the possibility of improving an existing product, a manager must decide whether to stick with the existing product or to make the improvements. If the manager stays with the current product, the profits will remain at their current levels. Suppose, for example, that an existing product has a profit level of $20 million. If the product is modified, the profits will depend upon the acceptance by consumers. Suppose market research indicates that there is a 75% chance of strong acceptance, resulting in an increase in profits of $4 million, but there is a 25% chance of weak acceptance resulting in a drop in profits of $12 million. Should the manager go ahead?

This decision illustrates the basic elements in risky situations. There are two actions. One action (called the "sure action") is the status quo while the other action (called the "risky action') has two possible outcomes, a gain or a loss. If we knew that the gain outcome was going to occur, we would select the risky action; if we knew that the loss outcome was going to occur, we would select the sure action. The problem is that we do not know for sure which of these two outcomes will occur. The outcome that occurs depends on an uncertain event for which we have only probabilistic knowledge. This prototypical risky situation will be called the "Basic Risk Paradigm." It provides a foundation for studying risk.

It is helpful to visualize the Basic Risk Paradigm in the form of a *decision tree.* Figure 1.1a shows the decision tree for the decision about modifying the product. The two actions, "modify" and "do not modify" are shown coming out of a square box, which depicts a choice that must be made by the decision maker. The action "do not modify" leads to the current profit of $20 million. The outcome of the action "modify" is dependent on whether consumers like the new product. The event that they do, labeled as "strong consumer acceptance," leads to a rise in profits to $24 million. If they do not, labeled as "weak consumer acceptance," profits will fall to $8 million. Since the outcome depends on an uncertain event (consumer acceptance), the two outcomes are shown coming out of a circle. The chances,

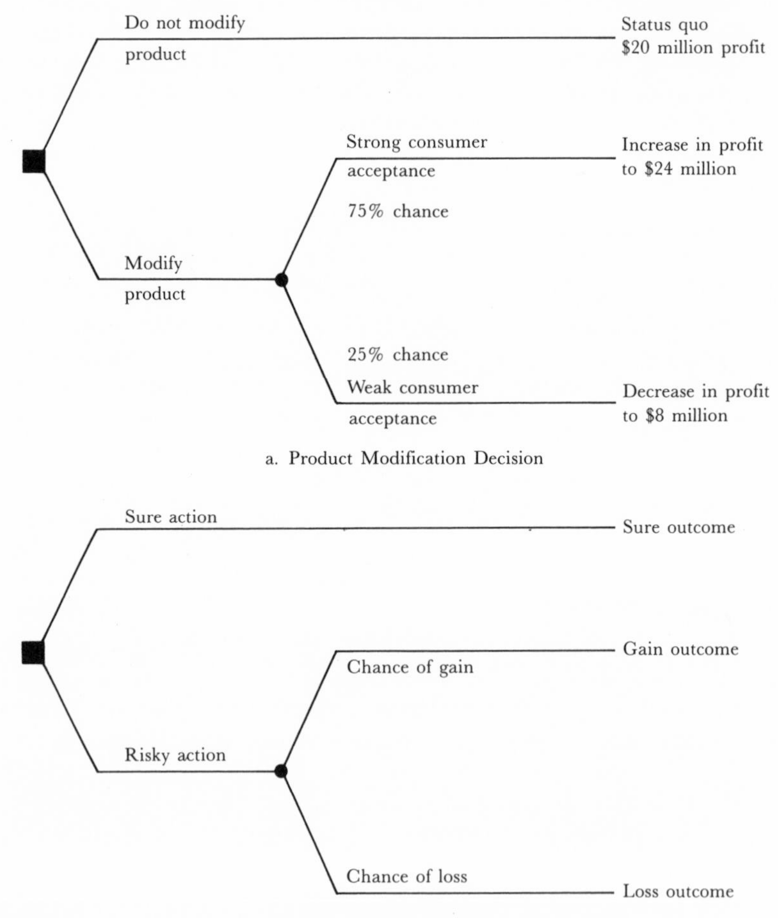

Figure 1.1 Decision Tree Representations of Risky Situations

75% for "strong consumer acceptance" and 25% for "weak consumer acceptance" are noted on the corresponding branches. Thus a square box signifies a choice that the decision maker makes, while the circle signifies an event that is outside the control of the decision maker.

Note that the *expected profit* for the risky action is $20 million. That is, a 75% chance of a $24 million profit and a 25% chance of an $8 million profit would yield an expected profit of $20 million if the uncertain outcome were repeated a large number of times. Since one action yields a sure profit of $20 million, while the other action yields an expected profit of $20 million, this average return cannot be a basis for choosing between the actions. A person's preference or aversion to the "modify" action must therefore depend on his preference for or aversion to the risks that this action entails.

The Basic Risk Paradigm is depicted in an abstract form in Figure 1.1b. For most purposes it will be embellished, but the basic structure will always be present. Although most risky situations will have more alternatives, more uncertain events, and more outcomes, the basic form captures the central elements. The Basic Risk Paradigm will provide the foundation for assessing risk propensity in this book.

NOTE ON THE BASIC RISK PARADIGM

The *expected value* (i.e., arithmetic mean) of a risky action can be calculated as $(1-p) \times G + p \times L$ where G is the gain outcome, L is the loss outcome, p is the chance of loss, and $1-p$ is the chance of gain. We will sometimes refer to the expected value of a risky action as its expected payoff or average payoff.

While the Basic Risk Paradigm is, as the name suggests, the most basic situation for studying risk, in most instances it will be necessary to elaborate upon it. These extensions can take many forms:

1. The sure action does not necessarily have to be the status quo. It can be any action with a sure outcome between the gain and loss outcomes of the risky action.
2. Both actions may be risky, although one of them may be riskier than the other.
3. There may be more than two actions.
4. The risky actions may have more than two possible outcomes.

These extensions, as well as other ones to be discussed, can provide a richer context for studying risk than the Basic Risk Paradigm itself. Even in these cases it is insightful to recognize the basic structure.

When potential loss is higher, the risks are greater. Introducing the modified product if a $60 million loss can occur is riskier than if a

$12 million loss can occur. A $20,000 investment in commodity futures is riskier than a $2,000 investment. Opening a business in a politically unstable foreign country poses a greater magnitude of potential loss than operating the business in North America.

When the chances of loss are higher, the risks are greater. Introducing the modified product when there is a 50% chance of weak market acceptance is riskier than if there is a 25% chance of weak market acceptance. Investing in commodity futures involves a greater chance of loss than investing in government bonds. In stable countries we have few worries about our plant being looted and burned; in unstable countries, the chance of losing our investment is higher.

When the exposure to chance of loss is higher, the risks are greater. Even if the chances and magnitude of loss cannot be restricted, we may be able to affect the risk by reducing our exposure. Exposure to loss for three distinct entities should be considered: (1) the individual who makes the decision, (2) the decision maker's immediate social unit (usually the family or the firm), and (3) society at large. In the modified product example, outcomes to the firm were discussed because we were primarily concerned with the firm's exposure to risk. The uncertain market acceptance of a modified product could also be translated into potential losses for the manager (e.g., loss of reputation, incentive bonus, or job) or consumers (e.g., unavailability of preferred standard product).

In Ford Motor Company's decision on the location of the gas tank in the Ford Pinto, the exposure to risk was very different for the executives who approved the design, Ford which had to pay the lawsuits, and the consumers who were injured or died. Sharing or spreading risk is the most common way to reduce exposure to the individual, family, or firm. This method does not reduce the total loss that is incurred; it just redistributes the exposure to loss among a number of individuals.

Risk Determinants: Lack of Control, Lack of Information, Lack of Time

Inherent in all risky situations are three identifiable determinants: *lack of control, lack of information,* and *lack of time*. If we had complete control over the situation, we could determine the best outcome and there would be no risk. If we had complete information about which event would occur, we could select the best alternative based on this knowledge and again there would be no risk. If we had unlimited time in which to decide which alternative to choose, we could wait until the outcome of the uncertain event was resolved and then choose the best alternative after the fact. This scenario also involves no risk.

Events are uncontrollable for a variety of reasons. The pure uncontrollable events are determined by nature—earthquakes, oil formations, weather, and so forth. Next come events determined by other people, including large aggregates of people, such as the actions of competitors, demand for a firm's product, election results, etc. While there may be a distinction between the controllability of next year's weather versus next year's economic climate, they both seem equally uncontrollable to most of us. When the events are determined by specific people, for example the price of a competing product, we must consider the unpredictability of human behavior.

Another reason for lack of control is lack of suitable resources. You could control the price of silver next month if you had the resources of the Hunt brothers (and lack of control exerted by the SEC and others). You could even affect the weather with suitable amounts of chemicals and airplanes for seeding. Control requires not only potentially controllable events and the appropriate resources, it also requires suitable opportunities to intervene. In order to control a risky situation, we need information on which to base our control actions. In order to know how to control something by pushing the right button, we have to know which button does what. Since control requires the deployment of resources, we have to know the effect of using our resources in one fashion rather than in some other way. To control or influence someone else's behavior, we need to have information about that person's beliefs and preferences. In addition we need time to develop the control options and to gather the required information. Therefore we will have a lack of control whenever we lack information or time.

There are many reasons why there may be a lack of information about the risks in a situation. Since the world never exactly repeats itself, no situation is perfectly identical to what preceded it. No one has any experience with the long-term effects of nuclear energy or genetic technology. On a more mundane level, no one can tell what clothes will be in fashion next year or what the price of gold will be next month. Even if we were prepared to pay to learn more about such risks, there is nowhere to turn.

In many other cases, a particular decision maker may have his uncertainties at least partially resolved by information possessed by others. You may not know whether anyone has died from eating tomatoes, but presumably some medical experts know. If you wanted to acquire more information about the dangers of tomatoes, you probably have a general idea of how to begin to explore the question, but you do not know specifically what you will discover.

In another area, you may not know whether Texas Instruments

has ever failed to pay a dividend, but you know financial information is available that would answer the question. The cost of finding out a sure answer to this question is low.

Some information on virtually any question can be purchased at a price. We can find an "expert" who will advise us on the future price of gold or the ramifications of new technology, but we may have little confidence in the reliability of the information we receive. Some events seem essentially unpredictable, although different people may have different opinions on what is unpredictable. After all, gold experts and futurists thrive.

Even if information is available, and we believe that it is reliable, does this imply that we should obtain it? For many events in which reliable information could be obtained, the cost of acquiring the information is prohibitive. Any gain that we might expect to attain from having the information would be more than offset by the cost. Extensive market research could indicate how a new advertising campaign would be received but it may be cheaper to run the ads and react to the effect than to do the study.

It takes time to gather information, and there may not be sufficient time to gather the needed information for the decision at hand. Many employees have lost their jobs because they delivered an information-filled report to their superiors after the key decision deadline had passed. Therefore situations in which there is a lack of time are necessarily situations in which there is a lack of information as well.

Crisis management situations are inherently risky. Decisions must be made quickly with little knowledge of the options available, the uncertainties involved, or their consequences. Events happen rapidly so crisis managers lose decision options when they do not act quickly. If decisions could be made *after* key uncertain events had occurred, situations would not be risky. It is the requirement of risky situations that decisions must be made before the key uncertainties are resolved that makes time such an important factor.

When the time is insufficient, people cannot understand fully or reduce the magnitude or chances of potential losses to which they are exposed. With insufficient time new control options that could affect exposure to a chance of potential loss cannot be developed.

Even when the degree of control, information, or time is insufficient to eliminate all risk in a situation, these elements can be used to mitigate risk partially. Having partial control over uncertain events allows us to influence which outcomes occur without determining the specific outcome. For example, a firm that has partial control over its labor costs, sources of supply, and the like can shape its production environment to its advantage. Having relevant information on uncertain events allows us to project the likelihood of the possible outcomes and to take steps to reduce our exposure to the events causing the risk. For example, a firm that knows what changes in labor costs, sources of supply, and so on are occurring over the next few years can take steps to expand or contract its operations accordingly. Having additional time allows us to develop new alternatives for handling risky situations even if we cannot wait for the resolution of the key uncertain events.

The relationships among control, information, and time are depicted in Figure 1.2. Gaining control over a risky situation requires both information and time as well as resources. Information is needed to understand the impact of various control options, time is needed to develop them, and resources are needed to implement them. If you do not know that a neighbor is planning to build an addition to his house that will block your view, you will not be able to prevent the construction. If there is insufficient time to act, you also cannot affect the outcome. Even if you know his plans, have sufficient time, and know that you can prevent the building by political pressure or monetary side payments, if you do not have access to the political machinery or sufficient financial resources, those means are

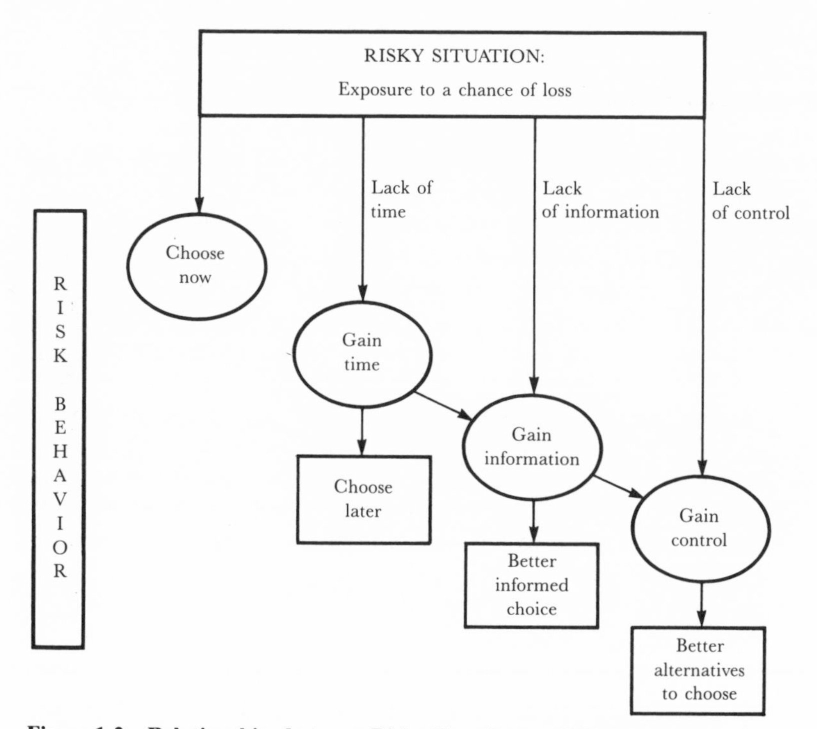

Figure 1.2 Relationships between Risky Situations and Risk Behavior

unavailable to you. In a similar vein, gaining information in a risky situation requires time in order to acquire the information. The reverse relationships are not true. For example, it is possible for information to reduce risk when control is absent (e.g., change chances of loss), and for time to reduce risk when both information and control are absent (e.g., delay decision until uncertain event is resolved.)

In summary, risk as the exposure to a chance of loss is proportional to the lack of control, the lack of information, and the lack of time. Table 1.1 illustrates the relationships between the determinants of risk and the components of risk.

Sources of Risk in Managerial Decisions

Throughout this chapter we have developed the concepts of the *components of risk*, namely the magnitude, chance, and exposure to loss, as well as the *determinants of risk*, namely the lack of control, lack of information, and lack of time. Do managers think of risk in a similar manner? To answer this question, we asked a group of top-level executives the following:

> What do you mean when you describe a business situation as *risky*? What are the important characteristics of a *risky* situation?

About half of the executives responded by identifying specific uncertainties that made their business decisions risky. Frequently mentioned were uncertain events external to the firm concerning product, supplier and financial markets, governmental regulation, and general economic conditions. Factors internal to the firm were also cited including uncertainty regarding labor unrest, technological innovation, management inexperience, and insufficient management resources. The lack of information on these uncertain events or their unpredictability was often mentioned. Most of the remaining responses described situations as risky when there was an unacceptable chance of loss or gain, an imbalance between possible losses and gains, or high stakes involved, or when firm survival was at stake.

Perhaps the best way to communicate the interplay among the components of risk and the determinants of risk is to present several of the managers' responses (italics added).

> "A risky situation is one in which I personally have *little or no effective control*; one in which *outside factors dominate*, e.g., political situations, strikes, foreign exchange fluctuations, etc."
>
> ". . . a situation where there are *unknowns* involved, caused by either *lack of time* to research them or *lack of sources of research*."
>
> "Risky means to proceed based on *limited knowledge*."

Table 1.1 Relationships between Components and Determinants of Risk

	Components of Risk		
Determinants of Risk	*Magnitude of Potential Loss*	*Chances of Potential Loss*	*Exposure to Potential Loss*
Lack of control Natural forces Human forces Insufficient resources Insufficient information Insufficient time	Cannot affect size of potential loss	Cannot affect chances of potential loss	Cannot affect exposure to potential loss
Lack of information Inadequate Unreliable Unfamiliar Unpredictable Insufficient time	Do not know size of potential loss	Do not know chances of potential loss	Do not know exposure to potential loss
Lack of time Must choose before uncertain event occurs	Insufficient time to understand or reduce magnitude of potential loss	Insufficient time to understand or reduce chances of potential loss	Insufficient time to understand or reduce exposure to potential loss

"Situations are risky when there is *lack of experience* by management, lack of funds to proceed properly, . . . *lack of proper planning*, or *lack of market research*."

"There is a *high degree of loss* in undertaking the situation."

". . . a situation where the *probability of success is outweighed by the probability of failure*, with something of value being gambled (*not necessarily money*)."

"*High probability of failure* due to known threats and weaknesses which are *not offset by commensurate rewards*."

Thus the managers tended to view risk in a manner similar to the concepts we have presented. This survey also provided a check on our view of risk in that there were no general aspects of risk mentioned by the managers that could not be readily related to our framework.

Do People Agree on the Riskiness of Situations?

We are all aware of both societal risks and personal risks. The decisions of political leaders in countries as remote as Iran or Libya may plunge the world into a war that could obliterate the ordinary patterns of life. Decisions without aggressive intent, involving energy generation or genetic engineering, could have similar effects. Many other factors can have a potentially devastating effect on a national, regional, or local level. As we decrease the scope of the area affected, we greatly increase the number of risks. In addition to all the macro events, you face risks in what you choose to eat, where you live, when you go to work and so forth.

There are various situations that virtually everyone would agree are risky. Flying in planes with cracks in the wings is riskier than flying in well-maintained planes. Investing in soybean futures is riskier than putting money in a savings account. Living in an urban housing project is riskier than living in a well-policed suburb. Working in an asbestos factory is riskier than working in an office building.

On the other hand, there are many zones of disagreement. There has been a continuing controversy about the risks of nuclear energy plants as contrasted with the alternatives. In fact, one position has been that windmills are more dangerous than nuclear plants.

Most people would agree that a major earthquake along the San Andreas fault could cause tremendous damage and loss of life. Such a situation would be deemed riskier than a major snowstorm in Chicago. However, if we live in Chicago rather than Los Angeles, a snowstorm might pose greater risks to us than an earthquake. Whether a situation is perceived as risky by a person depends on his own exposure, or the exposure of others he cares about. The further one is away from the conceptual "ground zero" of a risk the less personal risk is perceived. One can think of many situations that pose massive risks to other people, but these situations will only elicit action when people perceive things they care about (including abstractions such as human rights) as being threatened. Thus, it makes little sense to talk about one risk being greater than another, without addressing the issue of riskier to whom.

Since the risks we perceive depend on where we stand, we will experience different levels of risk in different parts of our lives. One executive continually may be in the center of business situations that are fraught with tremendous uncertainties and hazards, yet have a peaceful family life. Another executive may operate in a relatively stable business environment, while facing turmoil and upheavals at home.

RISK BEHAVIOR

Choice: The Core of a Risky Situation

Risky situations, as we have discussed, involve two or more alternatives where at least one alternative exposes a person to a chance of loss. The central focus in the traditional "choice" view of risk is on the alternative a person chooses.

The alternatives in such risky situations differ in their riskiness. If we know the riskiness of alternatives, the risk behavior of a person can be assessed by looking at his choices. A person who is risk-averse will select one of the less risky alternatives while a person who is a risk taker will select one of the more risky alternatives.

Clearly we need to ascertain the riskiness of each alternative. If two alternatives are the same except that one has a higher chance of loss, then that one would be riskier. If two alternatives are the same except that one has a higher magnitude of loss, then that one is riskier. If two alternatives are the same except that one has a higher exposure to loss, then that alternative would be riskier.

When alternatives differ in the chances of loss, magnitude of loss, and exposure to loss, we need some way to assess their riskiness. If the alternatives have the same expected value, then some measure of the variation in the outcomes can be used as well as the three principal components of risk.

This focus on choice captures the core of a risky situation—but only the core. At some point a person will make a choice, but a lot of things happen before the choice is made. Knowing these things can often tell us more about risk behavior than the choice itself.

Most risky situations require a person to figure out what the possible alternatives are, instead of having them nicely presented. Most risky situations allow a person to modify the risky situation before having to choose. Both these steps require a *structuring* of the situation rather than a *choosing*. The narrow "choice model" of risk will be broadened to incorporate "structuring" actions as well.

So far we have explored how risky situations involve exposure to a chance of loss. In studying risk, however, we must examine not only risky situations but also the behavior of people confronting risky situations. How do people recognize risks? How do people evaluate the risks they perceive? How do they try to modify the risks they face? Are some people more inclined to take bigger risks?

Recognizing a Risky Situation

Managing risks starts off with an initial *recognition* that a risky situation exists. A person acquires some information about a situation that may result in his losing something of value. Although an omniscient outside observer may be able to make an "objective" appraisal of the risks, the decision maker himself may perceive the situation in a very different way. Clearly, it is the way the decision maker sees the situation that will determine how he acts, whether or not his perceptions accord with reality. Yet it is reality that will determine the outcomes.

The risks in some situations (e.g., speculating in commodity futures or sky diving) are obvious. A person's perceptions depend on what he has learned from others about risks (e.g., in speculating or sky diving) even if he has not engaged in such activities himself. Risk perceptions will also depend on the past experience and the skills of the person himself. If you are an experienced mountain climber, you may not face, or even understand, the risks of a novice.

To assess one's exposure to a chance of loss, we first need to examine how people perceive losses. Most of the examples so far in this chapter have involved monetary losses. In many risky situations these monetary losses could be viewed either from the perspective of actual, out-of-pocket monetary losses or as opportunity losses relative to the best decision that could have been made knowing the event that occurred. Whether you perceive the losses as actual or opportunity losses can influence the choices you make, especially if you are susceptible to regret.

Although losses are usually measured monetarily, there are other types of losses that might be considered in risky situations as well. Executives are frequently concerned with loss of prestige or reputation, loss of management authority, and loss of rapport with superiors, employees, suppliers, and so on. Concern for these nonmonetary losses means that risky situations are not always perceived solely in terms of their monetary losses. The presence of nonmonetary consequences complicates the typical diagram for the Basic Risk Paradigm because in this case each outcome must be described by at least one additional attribute together with the monetary consequence.

How do people perceive uncertain events? Uncertain events that depend upon mechanistic random devices such as roulette tables, playing cards, and dice are usually seen as subject to the laws of probability. The best one can do in these situations is to understand the probabilities of the relevant events and make choices consistent with them. Uncertain events that depend on natural forces such as the weather or large aggregates of people (e.g., claims on insurance policies) may occur often enough so that these observations can form the basis from which frequencies can be derived to predict future occurrence. If the uncertain events have not occurred before, no evidence is available on which to base the probabilities, so only subjective probabilities are possible. Uncertain events that depend upon the actions of specific individuals or groups such as competitors, labor unions, or regulatory agencies may or may not have occurred before, so frequency data may not be available. In addition such events may be subject to control by the decision maker because the other actors may be influenced to change the result of the uncertain events they determine. Thus depending upon the source of the uncertainty, a decision maker might perceive an uncertain event as (l) unpredictable because few, if any, similar events have occurred, (2) predictable and subject to known laws of chance, (3) predictable and subject to estimated laws of chance, or (4) controllable (partially or totally) by the decision maker.

Likewise exposure to loss is perceived quite differently by different individuals or groups. Investing $100,000 in unproved new machinery is a drop in the bucket for General Electric, but may be extremely risky for a local machine shop. Quitting a steady job to undertake an entrepreneurial venture may be relatively easy for a young unmarried MBA with highly marketable skills, but may be fraught with peril for a 50-year-old executive with several dependents and narrow employment opportunities.

Whenever the components of a risky situation are not explicitly stated, a person's perception must be subjective because the components are not well defined. But even when such risk components are explicitly stated (such as the increased chance of dying from lung cancer when one smokes a pack of cigarettes a day), a person's perception is still subjective because of the personal nature of internalizing chances, losses, and exposure.

Data show that the chances of a person being seriously injured in an automobile accident at some time in his life are about 33% (Slovic, Fischhoff, and Lichtenstein, 1978). When presented with this information, you might be tempted to dismiss it. Even after finding out it came from a reliable source, you still might discount the information in various ways. You may discount the one-third chance by transforming it in your mind to "a small chance." You may discount the loss by assuming that if an accident occurs, it will only result in minor injury. You may discount the exposure by thinking that, although the chances and magnitude may apply to other people, you are such a careful driver that your potential exposure is much less than that of other people.

Evaluating a Risky Situation

After initially recognizing and structuring a risky situation, a decision maker makes a preliminary assessment of the acceptability of the risks. If he is already in the situation, does he want to stay in or to get out? If he is outside of the situation, does he want to get in or to stay out?

Most thinking about risk assumes that an individual is already in a risky situation. He may have chosen to enter the risky situation or he may have been thrust into the situation as a result of circumstances beyond his control.

People are in the center of many risky environments and they may encounter many risky situations in these environments. The individual overtly acts to expose himself to some of these risky situations; others he overtly acts to avoid, while others he accepts as they confront him. In each case the individual evaluates the acceptability of the risks.

There is frequently uncertainty about the nature of the risky situation that is being confronted. For example, consider the risky environment of foreign operations in an unstable country. The macro-level decision in this example is whether to get into foreign operations in this country that will involve unknown risks. Until the decision to enter is made, one may not know whether unreliable labor or political instability pose the greater risks to the firm.

If the individual finds the risks unacceptable, he can decide to opt out (stay out) of the risky situation. If he decides to opt into (stay in) the risky situation, he then confronts the risky situation whose risk components become known with time. For example, after beginning foreign operations the firm learns that the lack of reliable labor is the principal source of risk in achieving acceptable profit levels. Once in the risky situation, the individual faces risks with known decision alternatives, uncertain events, magnitudes and chances of loss, and exposure. For example, the individual must choose between importing higher-priced reliable labor or using the unreliable local labor and risking a chance of loss if the local labor is insufficiently productive.

Although a *micro-level* perspective is normally used to observe risk behavior within risky situations, we can also use a *macro-level* perspective to investigate risk behavior. When a person is outside of a risky situation, the macro-level decision is whether to stay outside or enter the situation. When a person is in a risky situation, he must make the macro-level decision whether to stay in or to opt out. Knowles (1976) discusses these two perspectives.

Adjusting the Risks

We will make a distinction between passive and active risk behavior in a risky situation. Active behavior involves trying to adjust the components of the risky situation. For example, one may try to reduce the chance of loss, reduce the magnitude of the loss, or reduce the exposure. Passive behavior simply implies selecting from the alternatives presented. If one is inclined toward risk, one selects a riskier alternative, while if one is inclined away from risk, one selects a less risky or sure alternative.

Many of us treat risk in a passive manner. If a risky situation arises, we consider the alternatives and choose in accordance with our like or dislike of the risk. We neither seek out such situations nor do we shun them. When they occur, we do not try to change them; we simply choose. Other people, though, actively try to change the risky situations that they confront or try to change the components of the alternatives from which they must choose. Let us consider, in some detail, the ways in which such "active" and "passive" types might behave in a business context.

First, in actively seeking or actively shunning risky situations, a manager signals his propensity for risk. In the area of takeovers and acquisitions, the risk-seeking manager will be looking around to see which firms he should acquire and will not be particularly daunted by the prospect of a takeover fight with another firm. The risk-averting manager, on the other hand, will be more concerned with protecting his firm from being acquired by another. By buying back his own firm's stock and other maneuvers, he can try to shelter himself. Note, then, that it is not contradictory to talk about an active approach to risk avoidance. The passive manager will not make any moves to seek or avoid takeover prospects.

Second, when faced with a risky situation (e.g., another firm has made a bid to take over the firm), a manager may exhibit an active stance in handling risks. In this case, the active stance is more likely to be one of lowering the risks rather than raising them, but conceptually it may be either. By various blocking moves (e.g., court injunctions) a manager may try to lower the likelihood of a successful takeover. By working out an agreement with the acquiring firm, he may be able to reduce the magnitude of the loss or the exposure. A more overt risk-seeking response would be to pursue an acquisition oneself (so that it would be too expensive to complete the takeover) or even to take steps to acquire the attacking firm. The truly passive manager, on the other hand, would be considering the choice of whether or not to offer his shares. That is, he would be choosing only from the alternatives explicitly presented.

People who take an active approach to risk are likely to attempt to modify the risky situations they confront by gaining time, information, and control. Time allows information to be gathered and exposure to be assessed within the risky situation. Delaying decision deadlines allows other options to be considered. Delay sometimes allows a cloudy situation to clarify itself before commitments are made. Information can be collected on the likelihood of various events and their outcomes as well as on possible new control options. Control over the exposure can be affected by buying insurance, delegating the decision to others, and so forth.

Risk modifications are not costless. To gain information or acquire control in one area, one must give up something in some other area. Resources allocated to improving product quality are not available for generating more sales. Current levels of resources determine the extent to which information may be gained or control may be exercised. Likewise delaying a decision may reduce choice options if key deadlines are missed.

We can group actions to adjust risks into two categories: (1) those actions that modify the general system outcome (i.e., the chances of the undesired event occurring or the overall loss if the event does occur), and (2) those actions that modify the distribution of consequences among the individual, family, firm, and society (i.e., the exposure), without changing the system outcome. From the point of view of a homeowner, building a dike to prevent a river from causing flood damage falls into the first category, while buying insurance falls into the second category. Moving personal belongings to a location not threatened by flooding could be put in either category depending on how the "event" is defined.

Consider the risk of burglary and the possible actions we might take to reduce the risks. By placing valuables in safety deposit boxes, we can reduce the amount of loss if the burglary occurs. In general the magnitude of loss can be controlled by transfers of resources. Valuable paintings can be moved away from flood threatened areas. Seeding a hurricane may divert it to less populated areas.

By installing a security system, we can decrease the chance of a successful burglary and thus reduce our chance of loss. Ultimate control over the chances of loss is total prevention of the risk-inducing event. In some cases, when the chances are public knowledge such as gambling bets, one might choose the bet with the lower chance of loss. For example, one might bet on the pass line at craps rather than on roulette. Seeding clouds might reduce the chances of a hurricane causing a particular level of damage by reducing the wind velocity.

A common way to reduce personal exposure to loss without reducing either the chances or the magnitude themselves is to share the risk with someone else. Purchasing insurance is a control mechanism that reduces personal exposure in this fashion. Insuring your house, car, or other valuables against theft does not reduce the chances or magnitude of loss if a theft occurs, but it does provide an offsetting effect. The insurance proceeds help to mitigate the loss.

The general mechanism for changing exposure is contracting with others. Insurance contracts cover life, disability, health, property, and a variety of other domains. These insurance contracts guarantee a specified monetary payment if particular events occur. Other forms of contingent contracts guarantee other types of actions when particular events occur. When there are many possible uncertain events and the future is less foreseeable, such contracts become more difficult to write.

Interesting analyses have been done on the effect of contracting on the subsequent behavior of the individuals facing the risk. A reduction in exposure (through purchasing insurance, say) may make the individual less careful (e.g., leaving his house unlocked or not putting his valuables in a safety deposit box) and hence may increase the chances of the event or the magnitude of loss if the event occurs. This is called the "moral hazard" phenomenon.

The most common case in which the magnitude of possible loss is known is when the situation requires an investment or a stake, which can be totally lost. Betting $10 on a horse or investing $10,000 in a mining company limits the amount of possible loss. In other cases the magnitude of loss is not known, so we can adjust the risk by gaining information on the size of the potential loss. Having one's jewelry or art appraised provides information about the size of their monetary loss in a burglary.

Gambling situations are about the only risky situations in which the chances of loss are clearly stated. Even on horse races, however, the chances of winning and losing are not known and must be estimated by the bettors. By collecting information about the rate of burglaries in the neighborhood, a very uncertain situation can be made more certain.

Even after finding out how likely an event is to occur and how much loss it may cause, you still may not know how you are likely to be affected. General information may tell you that the chances are one in a hundred of a house in your neighborhood being burglarized this year and that the average loss is $2,000, but this may not provide specific enough information about your particular exposure. More detailed information on the exposure of your home to burglary might be obtained by a detailed assessment from an expert on home security.

Table 1.2 summarizes how the decision maker can recognize, evaluate, and adjust the risks he faces before having to choose a course of action.

Table 1.2 Relationships between Phases of Risk Assessment Process and Components of Risk

Phases of Risk Assessment Process	Components of Risk		
	Magnitude of Potential Loss	*Chances of Potential Loss*	*Exposure to Potential Loss*
Recognize risks	What losses are possible?	What are the sources of uncertainty?	What is exposed to potential loss and to what extent?
Evaluate risks	Are the possible losses bearable and worth assuming?	Are the chances worth taking?	Is the exposure acceptable?
Adjust risks			
Gain control	How can potential losses be moderated?	How can uncertain events be prevented or made less likely?	How can risks be shared or spread?
Gain information	How much can I lose?	How likely is the potential loss?	Are options available for spreading risk?
Gain time	Can delay reduce loss?	Can delay reduce uncertainty?	Can delay reduce exposure?

Choosing among Risky Alternatives

Choice, as we have observed, is at the core of risk taking. Yet it should be clear that the risk adjustments that are made can often do more to affect the final outcomes than making a choice from the alternatives that initially presented themselves. Some of the adjustments, such as delay or delegation, may be so extreme as to obviate the need for a "final" choice. In most cases, though, some choice is necessary. After arranging for partners to share the costs of an oil drilling program, arranging for insurance to cover disasters, delaying until the weather or political climate is better, and collecting information about the geological and economic prospects, a decision must be made: go or no go.

After making a basic choice in a risky situation, the outcome will be affected by factors outside one's control. Events will occur that make the anticipated outcomes either good or bad. We can exert only so much control, and so some residual uncontrollable forces will partially influence our destiny.

Outcomes are the general results of our choice and of the uncontrollable events. For example, in an oil drilling context the outcome would be the extent of the oil discovery. In the process of adjusting the risks, however, the decision maker likely affected the impact of the general outcome on his personal consequences. A firm that has sold off a large part of its rights may experience very little of either good or bad general outcomes.

Tracking Outcomes

After taking actions in a risky situation, it is usually necessary to monitor the results. In fact, even if one opts out of the situation it may be desirable to track what is happening. Situations do not occur in isolation. One risky situation dissolves into another. There are no one-shot decisions. Even decisions that seem irreversible usually have outcomes and consequences that allow subsequent actions to assure that the longer-run results are closer to what we want.

Since risk is created by the possible occurrence of uncertain events, at some point we will learn which events occurred. The decision maker may have taken actions to prevent, or at least lessen the chances of the events, but the actions may not have had the desired effect. Our house may be burglarized this year even if we have set up a burglar alarm system. The union may go out on strike even if we make a more generous offer. In some cases it may be necessary to expend resources to discover if the events have occurred, but if these events have adverse consequences we are likely to discover them sooner than we would like.

The occurrence of an event will lead to general outcomes that usually affect a number of people in the situation. An event like a strike can have major implications on the striking employees themselves, on employees who do not go out on strike, on customers, on suppliers, and on many others besides the firm we are focusing upon. The general outcomes reflect to some extent whether we have been successful in mitigating the overall impact of the risk-inducing event.

If the decision maker took actions not just to lower the chance of the event and its general impact, but to lower his own exposure, then the personal implications for him may be less than would otherwise be the case. Most common are risk-sharing agreements such as insurance, in which others have been brought in to reduce the personal impact. While burglar alarms did not prevent the burglary and while hiding the jewels did not lessen the overall loss when the burglary occurred, having insured our goods mitigates our loss. Whereas the general outcomes reflected the efficiency aspects of the risk behavior, the specific outcomes reflect its distributional aspects.

When looking at risky decisions there is a danger we may consider a particular decision in isolation from other situations. All the actions taken in a given situation, and all the outcomes that occur, have ramifications for many other situations for the decision maker we are studying as well as for many others. The loss from a burglary, a sour investment, or a strike may affect the way we think and act in the contemporaneous situations we face. The impact of some risky situations may have long-lasting and broad effects.

Thus we can think of the last stage in one risky situation as being the first stage in some other risky situation. In fact, in many cases such as business investments or personnel decisions, it is hard to separate out a single incident from the whole portfolio of risks. How we handle one situation, quite apart from the outcomes that ensue, will affect the way we approach the other decisions in the same portfolio.

REACT Model of Managing Risk

We have described an active way of managing risky situations. Choice is just one part of the management process. How we initially recognize, frame, and structure a risky situation will determine what choices we consider. We cannot make choices that we cannot recognize.

Prior to making choices people invariably evaluate the acceptability of the risks and try to change them to conform to the types of risks they wish to take and to avoid. There are a variety of adjustment actions centered on gaining time, gaining information, or gaining control. Such adjustment processes can be viewed as a restructuring of the risky situation.

These structuring phases (i.e., recognizing, evaluating, and adjusting) are key factors in handling risk. They are, unfortunately, aspects that have tended to get overwhelmed by the heavy emphasis on choice in studies of risk behavior. Even some aspects of choice have received relatively little attention. For example, the decision involving opting in and opting out of risky situations has frequently been taken for granted. However the evaluation on which such decisions are based provides the framework for later adjustments and choices.

Overall, then, we have presented a model of managing risk that has five phases: *recognizing* and structuring the risks, *evaluating* the risks and deciding whether to be in or out, *adjusting* the risks to be more in line with what is desired, *choosing* among the risky actions, and finally, *tracking* the outcomes. The initial letters of the five phases suggest the name REACT for this model of managing risk. This name has the virtue of stressing the active rather than passive nature of handling risk. It should not be taken to imply, though, that one simply sits back waiting for things to react to. A decision maker can recognize an opportunity and initiate a risky situation himself.

Figure 1.3 shows how the various phases of the REACT model fit together. Perhaps it can be reinforced by use of an example. Sup-

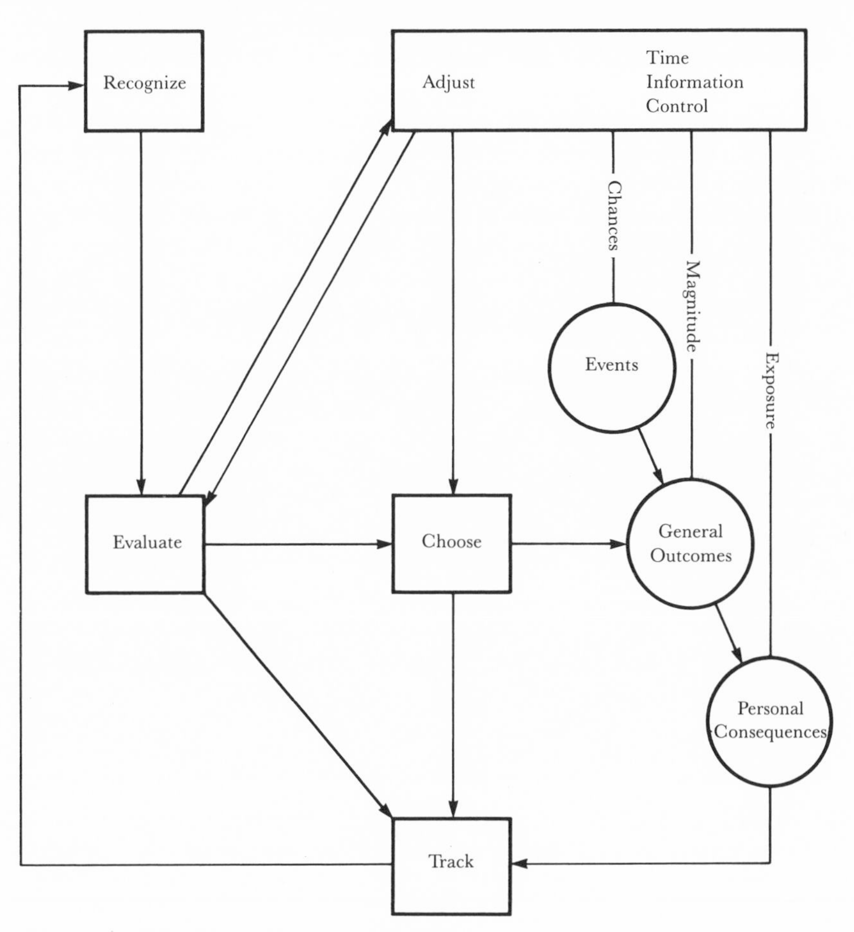

Figure 1.3 REACT Model of Managing Risk

pose you recognize an opportunity to sell some of your firm's products to the government. For example, you may have seen a list of tender proposals. You initially begin to structure the situation: how many products will you sell, at what price, produced in what plants, and so forth.

Based on this initial structuring, you evaluate the risks and decide whether you want to get "in"—that is, to bid on the contract. At this point there are a number of uncertainties that will need to be considered at subsequent stages.

If you decide to get in, you can now try to adjust the situation to your advantage. You can gain time by bidding on contracts with due dates that are further away or by asking for an extension. You can gain information on chances, magnitude, and exposure by finding out under what terms recent contracts have been won. You also can compile further information about your firm's capabilities and costs.

You can gain some control over chances, magnitudes, and exposure in various ways. The chances of loss can be reduced by affecting the uncertain events. For example, the prices charged by your suppliers can be fixed through long-term contracts. This will protect you against possible future price increases. The magnitude of the losses can be reduced by offering to supply fewer units. The exposure can be reduced by forming a joint venture in bidding with another firm.

After making, or attempting to make, the desired modifications, a choice will be necessary. In the case of our example it will involve choosing the explicit terms under which the contract will be handled.

The next step is to track the situation so that if it changes, new structuring and new choices can be made.

Risk Behavior in Managerial Decisions

How managers respond to risky situations is the subject of the rest of the book. Before looking at the responses of managers in our study to situations presented to them, it is useful to examine their answers to the following open-ended question:

> When you have been faced with a *risky* business situation, what specific actions have you taken (or recommended the firm take) to reduce the *risk* to your firm?

In particular we would like to know whether managers handle risky situations in ways similar to those we have described in the previous section.

Two-thirds of the responses specified actions that *adjusted* the risky situation by gaining control, gaining information, or gaining time. Among these risk modifications, control and information were mentioned more frequently than time. Handling risk by gathering more information was the most common response. The most common control action was the sharing of risk by means of insurance, contingent contracts, collateral, performance guarantees, and joint ventures. Attempting to influence the source of uncertainty (by lobbying with government regulatory agencies, dealing with competitors, and using public relations campaigns) and considering more alternatives to the choices at hand were also cited as control mechanisms. Using delay to modify risk was suggested so that information could be gathered and the decision situation could be clarified.

In addition to these risk modifications, about one out of three responses specified actions to control the outcomes of the risky situation as the uncertainties were resolved. These actions were all aimed at achieving the best possible outcome *after* the key risky decision had been made. Specifically mentioned were close management, contingency plans, limiting exposure, and staged implementation.

Several of the managers' answers to this question are presented below (italics added):

> "*Determine all the facts* that can be ascertained with regard to the situation."
> "*Confirm the facts* with at least one outside source."
> "*Demand performance and payment bonds* when dealing with firms of marginal financial stability."
> "*Delay* for more information and more discussion . . . *time clarifies*."
> "*Follow the situation closely* in the early stages . . . be prepared to act when necessary."
> "*Assign best talent possible* to the job to manage it."
> "*Cut losses* as soon as situation seems hopeless."
> "*Go in gradually*."
> "*Use step-by-step approach*."

Thus the methods the executives used to handle risks were consistent with the risk modifications described earlier. It is clear, however, that they continued to take actions to obtain the best possible outcomes in a risky situation, even after a risky alternative had been selected.

While it is hard to predict exactly what effect a particular risky situation will have on us, it clearly can influence whether we opt in or out of other risky situations, try to modify the risks in other situations, or choose a risky alternative in other situations. The results of any one situation can lead to more attention being spent on another. More careful assessment may be made or more detailed plans for implementation or monitoring can be put in place.

RISK TAKERS AND RISK AVERTERS

So far in this chapter we have been discussing the commonalities of risk behavior. Everyone, to some extent, recognizes risks, evaluates risks, tries to adjust risks, and chooses among alternatives that differ in riskiness. Through casual observation, however, we can see major differences in the way people react to risky environments and risky situations. In this section we investigate some of these differences.

In ordinary conversation we talk about risk takers and risk averters. Ironworkers operating at the tops of skyscrapers and heavy investors in penny mining stocks are considered risk takers, while bookkeepers and people who invest all their assets in savings accounts are considered risk averters. We all use such terms to describe people in both their business and personal activities. Yet there is no standard way to assess a person's willingness to take risks. A primary focus of this book is to clarify the meaning of these terms and to develop methods to assess risk propensity. At this point, though, we will take for granted that we can make such a distinction and we will consider differences one would expect between risk takers and risk averters.

Since risk is defined as the exposure to a chance of loss, we can expect risk takers and risk averters to act differently with regard to the components of risk. Table 1.3 summarizes the risk components that risk takers *accept* and risk averters *require*. A risk taker would accept a higher exposure in the sense of taking sole responsibility, acting with less information, and requiring less control than would a risk averter. The risk taker would accept a higher chance of loss, would operate in unfamiliar situations, would tolerate more uncertainty, and would require less information about the chances. Risk takers are willing to play for higher stakes and would tolerate higher maximum possible losses. They would accept higher variability in payoffs and would proceed with less information and less control about the possible payoffs.

We can also trace differences in the way risk takers and risk averters would act in the various phases of our REACT model of risk behavior. Clearly at the *choice* phase a risk-taker would choose riskier alternatives than would a risk averter. Earlier in the process, though, risk takers *recognize* lower risk in the situations they face. While risk averters tend to overrate the risks, risk takers tend to underrate risks. In *evaluating* risk, risk takers tend to accept the information they have on risky situations at face value. They may even adopt optimistic scenarios under the belief that chance is on their side or that they can control the outcomes. Risk averters tend to look

Table 1.3 Characteristics of Risk Averters and Risk Takers

Components of Risk	Risk Averter Requires	Risk Taker Accepts
Magnitude of Potential Loss	Low maximum loss Low stakes, commitment Low variability in payoffs More information on losses More control over losses	Higher maximum loss Higher stakes, commitment Higher variability in payoffs Less information on losses Less control over losses
Chances of Potential Loss	Low chance of loss Familiar environment Few uncertain events More information on chances More control over uncertain events Low uncertainty	Higher chance of loss Unfamiliar environment Many uncertain events Less information on chances Less control over uncertain events Higher uncertainty
Exposure to Potential Loss	Low exposure Shared responsibility More information on exposure More control over exposure	Higher exposure Sole responsibility Less information on exposure Less control over exposure
Other Risk Components	Control by self Contingency plans Consensus Exit from risky situations	Control by others No contingency plans Conflict Participation in risky situations

at worst-case scenarios, bias probabilities of loss upward, and overemphasize the possible losses or their exposure. The differences are particularly prominent at the *adjustment* phase. Risk takers would give only cursory attention to modifying risks, but risk averters could be expected to devote considerable effort to trying to reduce risk. Risk averters would engage in as many of the modification actions described in the preceding section as could be managed. Risk averters would be more concerned about *tracking* how the risky situation develops after their choices so they could take further actions to minimize risks.

In actual situations a person can be a risk taker (or risk averter) without exhibiting all the characteristics we have enumerated. In fact, in many situations we may observe only a single characteristic such as the size of the stake he is willing to risk and on that basis type a person as a risk taker or a risk averter. In the next chapter we will describe some of the bases we use in our empirical study to characterize a person's willingness to take risks.

Different people will respond to seemingly similar risky situations in very different ways. A central focus throughout this book will be whether people can be categorized as risk takers and risk averters on the basis of these responses. Although it is common to talk about people as risk takers or risk averters, we shall emphasize the need to make such characterizations specific to particular situations. There is no a priori reason to believe that a person who takes risks in one situation will necessarily take risks in all situations. Might we not observe financial cautiousness in a trapeze performer and physical cautiousness in a commodity broker? We will use the concepts we have developed about risky situations and risk behavior to help characterize risk propensities that are contingent on situations.

What other factors influence one's risk propensity? Differences in the responses made by individuals to similar risky situations could be partially caused by the individual's personal, financial, or business background. In fact several stereotypical relationships are widely cited. It is claimed that risk takers are younger and have higher wealth and fewer dependents than risk averters. Stereotypically risk takers in business are supposedly found in senior executive positions and in aggressive, sales-oriented firms. Risk averters, on the other hand, are assumed to come from lower executive ranks and are found in banks or insurance companies. We will investigate in this book whether these expectations can be confirmed.

Social factors may also influence one's willingness to take risks. There appears to be a cultural bias in favor of taking risks. Thus some people may take more risks (or say they take more risks) than they are inclined to because they believe it is socially expected of them. If such a bias exists, its origins might be traced back to childhood when games of "I dare you to . . ." and "double dare back" flourished. Another social factor is the risky shift phenomenon that has been observed in some group settings. In the risky shift, when people who are somewhat inclined to take risks are asked to make a group decision, they collectively tend to shift toward an even greater willingness to take risks. Personal exposure to risk is perceived to be lower in the group decision than in the individual decision.

PREVIEW OF THE BOOK

This book is divided into four main parts. Part One consists of Chapters 1 and 2 which introduce the topic of risk. As we have already seen, risk is the exposure to a chance of loss. The degree of risk is determined by the lack of control, lack of information, and lack of time. We developed the REACT model to describe how an individual manages risk. A person initially recognizes and structures the risky situation, and then evaluates whether to be in a situation or to be out. He tries to adjust the risks to make the situation more desirable by gaining time, gaining information, or gaining control. After choosing a course of action, he tracks the outcomes and consequences to recognize new risky situations to consider.

In Chapter 2 we describe some key results from earlier studies of risk taking. We use these results and the conceptual foundation for studying risk developed in Chapter 1 to construct a variety of new methods for assessing risk propensity. We describe a portfolio of questionnaires to provide us with information about risk behavior and risk-related characteristics in four categories: standardized risks, naturally occurring risks, attitudes to risk, and personal, financial, and business characteristics. Overall we consider more than 100 variables related to risk. We also describe our survey of more than 500 top-level business executives and the sampling method we used to contact them. Thus our study examines the risk propensities of people who get paid for handling risk.

In Part Two of the book, Chapters 3 through 7, we present the results of our four main questionnaires for studying standardized risks. In Chapter 3 we embed the Basic Risk Paradigm in an in-basket format, so we can assess risk propensity via three different methods: scale ratings, probability equivalences, and open-ended memos. In Chapter 4 we use the traditional utility function method of assessing risk. We use gain equivalence questions to assess risk propensity in both personal and business investments. In Chapter 5 we present nine personal investment ventures, described in terms of key parameters of a distribution of returns, and infer risk propensity by examining a preference ranking of the ventures. In Chapter 6 we present the executives with three sets of wagers that involve real money payoffs. Within each set a different aspect of the wagers is held fixed and risk propensity is inferred from a preference ranking of the wagers. The implications of the risk behavior in standardized situations are discussed in Chapter 7.

Part Three of the book is comprised of Chapters 8–11. In Chapter 8 we consider eight principal risk measures that emerge from the analysis of the standardized risks in Part Two. We examine the extent to which a person has a consistent risk propensity and whether there are commonalities among a person's risk measures in two particular domains: business versus personal and threats versus opportunities. In Chapter 9 we extend this comparative analysis to two of the other categories: naturally occurring risks and attitudes to risk. Since items from both of these categories have been used in previous studies as measures of risk propensity, we raise questions about the difficulty in interpreting results from such studies. In Chapter 10 we investigate whether the personal, financial, and business characteristics of the managers are related to the risk measures considered in Chapters 8 and 9. We explore the implications of these results for managers in Chapter 11.

Part Four of the book consists of a single chapter, Chapter 12, in which the reader is invited to assess his own willingness to take risks. This chapter also examines the use of Risk Profiles to aid in personnel selection, training, and development of a risk policy for the firm.

An Appendix contains selected items from the questionnaires used in the study.

Chapter 2

Studying Risk

INTRODUCTION

In this chapter we will provide a background to assist in understanding the chapters that follow. We begin by reviewing past studies of risk. This review uses the REACT framework described in Chapter 1 as a guide to the literature. Necessarily this review will be more technical than the text in the rest of the book, so the reader who is not interested in this background can skip it with no loss of continuity.

The latter part of this chapter describes our study. We provide an overview of the individual questionnaires in our Risk Portfolio as well as discussing the design, procedures, and participants in the study. Here too, the reader may wish to skim this material and then refer back to it if questions arise in subsequent chapters.

OTHER STUDIES OF RISK

There have been numerous studies, both theoretical and empirical, directed toward the understanding of risk. Some of this research focuses primarily on the riskiness of situations, while other studies focus on the willingness of people to take risks in such situations. Our review here, which by necessity is brief, will emphasize empirical research over theoretical and emphasize research on people's risk behavior over the riskiness of situations. Guided by the REACT model, we will first look at studies of how people recognize the riskiness of situations and their initial evaluations of the acceptability of such risks. Next we consider studies of risk adjustments, particularly the use of time, information, and degree of control. Then we examine the ultimate evaluations leading to choices among risky alternatives. We will not separately list studies on the post-choice tracking of outcomes because there are so few of them; a notable exception is Barnett and Lofasco (1983). We conclude our examination of the literature with research on risk-related attitudes, comparisons among risk measures, and on the relationship of risk propensity to various characteristics of the decision maker.

Recognition and Evaluation of Risks

Risk taking is relevant only insofar as situations are risky or are at least perceived as being risky. Interesting work has been done on the attributes of situations that lead to their being viewed as more or less risky. Often closely intertwined with this recognition of risks is an evaluation of an acceptable level of risk. Baird and Thomas (1985) present a model of risk taking that focuses on the recognition and evaluation of risks.

Early work on the recognition of risk was concentrated in the area of consumer behavior and is reviewed by Ross (1974) and Jacoby (1976). This research focused on risk perception and sought to identify the risky attributes of consumer products (Bauer, 1960; Cox and Rich, 1964; Cox, 1967a,b; Cunningham, 1967; Popielarz, 1967; Spence, Engel, and Blackwell, 1970; Bettman, 1973; and Peter and Ryan, 1976). Building on the capital asset theory of evaluating investments (Markowitz, 1952, 1959; Sharpe, 1964), research in finance examined investors' perceptions of risk (Cohn et al., 1975; Gooding, 1975; Cooley, 1977). Attention has also been given to assessing political risk in international business (Fitzpatrick, 1983).

Kunreuther and his colleagues (1978, 1979) used large scale field study methods to investigate how individuals perceived the risks of natural hazards such as floods and earthquakes and insured against them. A team led by Kunreuther at the International Institute of Applied Systems Analysis (IIASA) (1981, 1983, 1984) examined the risks of liquefied natural gas facilities and jurisdictional differences in the decision-making processes used in siting decisions.

By far the greatest amount of research on recognizing risks has been done in the area of nuclear energy and other technological hazards. Leaders in this field have been Starr (1969, 1984), Otway (1975, 1976), Slovic, Fischhoff, and Lichtenstein (1976, 1978–1981, 1983), Olson (1976), Kates (1978), Keeney (1980, 1984), Vlek and Stallen (1981), and Kunreuther, Linnerooth, and Vaupel (1984). These studies focused primarily on determining the attributes of technological hazards that make them risky in the eyes of the public. A good summary is given by Slovic, Fischhoff, and Lichtenstein (1980).

A growing field of research deals with analyzing the daily risks we face in such areas as air travel, smoking, and being overweight. Some research has concentrated on objective measures of the riskiness of activities (e.g., Lave, 1971; Cohen and Lee, 1979; Wilson, 1979). Other research focuses on the perceived riskiness of activities (e.g., Slovic, Fischhoff, and Lichtenstein, 1978, 1981). Still other research has generated new methods for trading off survival and consumption decisions (Howard, 1984; Shepard and Zeckhauser, 1984).

Various biases have been observed in the way people perceive risk components. Extremely low probabilities tend to be treated as though they were zero, and similarly, extremely high probabilities tend to be treated as though they were one. When new data concerning an uncertain event become available, people tend to change their assessed probabilities in the direction indicated by the new data, but the change is usually not as large as that required by the normative laws of probability. See Kahneman, Slovic, and Tversky (1982) for a summary of research studies on biases in risk perception. Similarly, how one perceives a situation depends upon how it is presented. More attention is now being given to how people recognize, evaluate, and respond to similar risky situations that have been framed in different ways (Tversky and Kahneman, 1981; Kahneman and Tversky, 1982).

Conceptual thinking on risk perception has also developed. See Arrow (1982) for a review of developments in psychology and economics. Luce (1980) and Fishburn (1982a; 1984b) have developed axioms to represent risk perception as a function of key attributes of risky situations.

Adjustment of Risks

Much more attention has been devoted to the study of how people recognize and evaluate risks and how they make choices in risky situations than to how they attempt to modify the risks they face. However, some interesting work on risk adjustment has been done.

Foster (1984) considered four risk mitigation strategies in the context of natural hazards. He discussed how the hazards can sometimes be eliminated (e.g., melt glaciers). In addition, one can modify the magnitude and intensity of impact (e.g., build dikes), modify the damage susceptibility (e.g., change land use regulations), or modify the loss burden (e.g., implement warning systems).

Janis and Mann (1977) described a variety of ways to adjust risky situations in their conflict theory model of decision making. According to this theory, when the risks of a decision are serious and a better alternative cannot be found, people commonly try three types of adjustments—"procrastinating" (i.e., delaying decision), "buck passing" (i.e., shifting responsibility for decision), and "bolstering" (i.e., psychologically reinforcing the preference for a chosen alternative). Bolstering includes exaggerating favorable outcomes, minimizing unfavorable outcomes, denying aversive feelings regarding unfavorable outcomes, exaggerating the remoteness of the action commitment, minimizing social surveillance of the decision, and minimizing personal responsibility for the decision. Bolstering does not change the objective risks of the decision; it merely changes the individual's perception of the risks.

For the decision maker who believes a better alternative can be found, Janis and Mann cite two additional types of behavior. If there is insufficient time to search for and evaluate a better alternative, the individual frequently panics and indiscriminately searches for information, resulting in an arbitrary final choice. If instead there is sufficient time to search for and evaluate a better alternative, the decision maker searches for new information with an open mind to help him evaluate both the old and new alternatives. Janis and Mann refer to these two types of behavior as "hypervigilance" and "vigilance," respectively.

Cox (1967b) and Roselius (1971) identified several methods used by consumers to reduce the perceived risk of purchases. These adjustments, which aim at decreasing either the chance or magnitude of loss, are relying on the past experience of oneself or others, seeking information, taking precautionary measures, avoiding choices, and delegating purchase responsibility to others who are competent. Similarly, Sheth and Venkatesan (1968) cited active information seeking, predecision deliberation, and brand loyalty as risk-reduction methods for consumer purchases. These results showed that information seeking and prepurchase deliberation declined over time while brand loyalty increased over time.

Although delay can be used as a way to adjust risks, there have been relatively few studies that focused on time per se. Taylor and Dunnette (1974) found that managers with a high willingness to take risks tended to make rapid decisions based on little information. Hunsaker (1975) discovered that people who adapt well to turbulent environments, in which there is little time to decide, perceive them as less risky and incorporate more risk in their decisions than people who do not adapt well.

Studies of information collection have been much more numerous. Acquisition of information by consumers has been examined by Green, Halbert, and Minas (1964), Cunningham (1966), Starbuck and Bass (1967), Bettman and Jacoby (1976), and Bettman and Kakkar (1977). Information handling in gambling situations has been studied by Edwards (1965), Edwards and Slovic (1965), Pitz and Reinhold (1968), Pitz (1969a,b), Fried and Peterson (1969), O'Connor, Peterson, and Palmer (1972), Payne and Braunstein (1978), and Schoemaker (1984). Taylor and Dunnette (1974) discussed information collection in a study of personnel decisions by industrial managers.

Studies of risk adjustment by gaining control have considered a variety of ways to reduce chance, magnitude, and exposure to loss. The most frequently studied way to reduce exposure to loss is through insurance. See, for example, Eisner and Strotz (1961), Greene (1963, 1964), Williams (1966), Hammond, Houston, and Melander (1967), Mantis and Farmer (1968), Kunreuther (1968, 1976, 1978), Neter and Williams (1971, 1973), Friedman (1974), Headen and Lee (1974), Schoemaker and Kunreuther (1979), Schoemaker (1980), Biamonte (1982), Dickson (1982), and Boissonnade and Shah (1984).

McCahill (1971) described the responsibilities of the professional corporate risk manager beyond the identification and insurance of potential property losses. These responsibilities include identifying risks to the firm in its sources of raw materials, machinery, labor, power, and other services as well as suggesting contingency plans should any of these resources be unavailable. In addition, legal liability to employees, consumers, and the general populace for industrial accidents and hazardous working conditions, defective products, and environmental pollution must be measured and planned for.

Anderson (1969) described several risk handling methods used in submitting bids on contracts. These include setting bounds on the maximum amount that could be lost if all major risks were resolved unfavorably, developing alternative design approaches and plans to resolve problems that arise during development or production, and seeking contractual means of reducing exposure to loss concerning the supply of labor and key raw materials or subcontracted components. After winning a contract, Anderson suggested close management control to make sure appropriate actions are taken during the implementation of the contract.

Reum and Steele (1970) analyzed the advantages and disadvantages of using contingent payouts to reduce the risk of corporate acquisitions. This arrangement offers the acquired company's management a greater payment if superior performance is achieved.

Jackson (1980) cited several methods for adjusting risks caused by price fluctuations in raw materials. Some of the risk modifications mentioned were fixed price contracts, purchases of raw materials futures on commodity exchanges, investment in research and development to reduce amount of material needed, and commodity substitution.

Srinivasulu (1981) identified three different types of foreign exchange risk and suggested several methods that are commonly used to modify these risks. The risk adjustment methods include forward market hedging, money market hedging, factoring of accounts receivable, foreign exchange insurance, and strategic management in the choice of products, markets, and sources of supply.

Banker (1983) listed several techniques for managing a firm's international exposure to political and economic risks. These techniques include arranging concession agreements (e.g., tax incentives, tariff protection), purchasing political risk insurance (e.g., against expropriation, war, and blocked currencies), requiring proprietary protection (e.g., patents, trademarks), arranging phased divestitures of risky foreign investments, and reducing foreign currency exposure (e.g., currency swap arrangements, anticipation of currency revaluations). See also Mascarenhas (1982).

Svenson (1984) cited several risk adjustment mechanisms used in the automobile industry. These modifications deal primarily with improving the safety of automobiles.

Choice in Risky Situations

Rules for choice in risky situations have been the prime focus in most of the literature in finance, economics, management, and even psychology. The need for studying risk was made apparent more than two centuries ago by Daniel Bernoulli (1738). He asked how much a person should pay to play a game in which a coin is tossed until a head comes up. If it comes up on the first toss you receive $2, on the second toss $4, on the third toss $8, and so forth. With the payoff doubling each time, and the chance of a very long run of tails before the first head, there is a chance of a very large payoff. It is easy to show that the expected return for this "St. Petersburg Paradox" is infinitely large. Yet most people would only offer to pay a few dollars to play the game. Bernoulli proposed replacing expected value calculations (in which probabilities are multiplied by the monetary outcomes) by calculations of "moral expectation" (in which probabilities are multiplied by the logarithm of the outcomes). The moral expectation calculation reflects the reluctance to put full weight on the low chances of high payoffs. It reflects the natural risk aversion of people to the game.

Since Bernoulli's time, people have used the basic idea of incorporating risk directly as a function of the outcomes, but have considered more general forms than logarithms. The logical foundations of utility functions have been thoroughly investigated by Ramsey (1926), von Neumann and Morgenstern (1947), Savage (1954), and others. Pratt (1964) and Arrow (1971) have independently shown that the only suitable measure of risk propensity for a utility function depends on the ratio of the curvature to the slope (see also Yaari, 1969). Empirical studies of the validity of the underlying axioms are given in MacCrimmon (1968) and MacCrimmon and Larsson (1979). Revised axiomatizations of utility theory have been proposed by Chew and MacCrimmon (1979a,b), Machina (1982), and Fishburn (1982-1984) to increase its descriptive validity. Other researchers have investigated the separation of risk from strength of preference (Bell and Raiffa, 1982; Dyer and Sarin, 1982; Sarin, 1982) and the role of regret and disappointment in decision making under uncertainty (Bell, 1982, 1983, 1985; Loomes and Sugden, 1982; Quiggin, 1982).

Mosteller and Nogee (1951), Davidson, Suppes, and Siegel (1957), Royden, Suppes, and Walsh (1959), Becker, DeGroot, and Marschak (1963a,b; 1964), Meyer and Pratt (1968), Keeney and Raiffa (1976), and others have developed procedures for obtaining utility functions. These methods are reviewed in Farquhar (1984). Sources of bias in these utility functions are discussed in Hershey, Kunreuther, and Schoemaker (1982), McCord and de Neufville (1983), and Hershey and Schoemaker (1984). Reversals in preference have been observed, depending upon whether a person is asked to price alternatives or to choose between them (Lichtenstein and Slovic, 1971, 1973, 1983; Grether and Plott, 1979).

A number of studies have assessed utility functions for managers. Curves have been derived for oil field operators (Grayson, 1960), farm managers (Halter and Beringer, 1960), managers in a chemicals firm (Green, 1963), R&D and production managers (Cramer and Smith, 1964), shipowners (Lorange and Norman, 1971, 1973), and subsistence farmers (Dillon and Scandizzo, 1978). Swalm (1966) obtained risk preference curves for about 100 middle-level managers. Spetzler (1968) studied the development of a corporate risk policy utilizing preference curves of individual managers. Fishburn and Kochenberger (1979) summarized the utility functions found in many of the earlier studies.

The standard assumption in financial models of risk aversion throughout the entire domain of wealth has been challenged ever since Friedman and Savage (1948, 1952) postulated a utility function with both risk-averting and risk-taking segments. Recently, however, there have been new challenges to uniform risk aversion. Risk taking for losses and risk aversion for gains have been hypothesized in the prospect theory developed by Kahneman and Tversky (1979). They have also cited empirical evidence to support their view. Further evidence can be found in the studies of Fishburn and Kochenberger (1979) and other researchers. Hershey and Schoemaker (1980a,b) have examined these claims with results from their own investigations. The importance of a target level of return on evaluating risk is also apparent in the theoretical work of Fishburn (1977) and the empirical studies of Payne, Laughhunn, and Crum (1980, 1981, 1984).

The Basic Risk Paradigm that underlies utility-based studies has been used in a looser way in the choice dilemma approach. Wallach and Kogan (1959, 1961; Stoner, 1961) developed the choice dilemmas questionnaire to obtain a measure of one's risk preference in everyday life situations. In this questionnaire the subject must advise 12 individuals about a choice between a sure and a risky course of action. Choice dilemmas have served as a vehicle for measuring risk propensity in many other studies (e.g., Rim, 1963; Kogan and Wallach, 1964, 1967; Vroom and Pahl, 1971; Taylor and Dunnette, 1974; Reingen, 1976; Ziegler, 1977; Brockhaus, 1980; Hutchison and Lilienthal, 1980; and Hutchison and Clemens, 1980).

Instead of using a utility function to reflect attitude toward risk, one may supplement expected return with some other attribute of an alternative that describes its riskiness. Markowitz (1952, 1959) considered variance in returns along with expected return. Mao (1970) and Hogan and Warren (1974) advocated that investors focus upon expected return and negative semivariance. Telser (1955), Machol and Lerner (1969), Pyle and Turnovsky (1970), and Joy and Barron (1974) suggested placing attention on expected return and the chance of a specific loss. For the foundations of this approach see Fishburn (1979).

Another approach taken in the evaluation and choice of risky alternatives has been the identification of important risk dimensions such as loss amount, chance of loss, and expected loss, as well as the standard moments of expected return and variation. Studies of important risk dimensions have been reported by Edwards (1953, 1954), Slovic and Lichtenstein (1965, 1968, 1972), Alderfer and Bierman (1970), Anderson and Shanteau (1970), Payne (1973), and Schoemaker (1979). This approach is influenced by an information processing perspective of how an individual combines selected pieces of information into an overall evaluation and choice.

An individual's preference for an ideal level of variation in returns has also been the focus of research. See Edwards (1954), Coombs and Pruitt (1960), Pruitt (1962), Slovic and Lichtenstein (1968), Coombs and Huang (1970), and Aschenbrenner (1978). This ideal level can be either no variation so that increasingly lower levels of variation are preferred, extremely high variation, or some intermediate level.

Risk propensity has also been studied in natural situations. In addition to insurance, gambling has been one common focus of such studies (Newman, 1972; Oldman, 1974; Dowie, 1976). An extensive early review of risk and gambling is given by Cohen and Hansel (1956). Other studies of naturally occurring risks have considered the distribution of asset holdings (Watts and Tobin, 1967; Bossons, 1973; Blume and Friend, 1975, 1978; Friend and Blume, 1975; Cohn et al., 1975).

Libby and Fishburn (1977) and Schaefer (1978) provide extensive reviews of models for evaluating risk and risky choice.

Risk-Related Attitudes

Several attitudes have been linked to risk taking in the psychological literature. Two of the most common attitudes are a desire for a stimulating environment and a belief that one can control one's environment. Zuckerman and his colleagues (1964, 1971, 1974, 1978) developed a "sensation-seeking" scale using 34 forced choice questions which has been the principal vehicle for measuring one's optimal stimulation level. Rotter (1966) used 29 forced choice questions to develop an "internal versus external control" scale. This variable has spawned a large number of articles relating it to risk taking (Liverant and Scodel, 1960; Rotter, Seeman, and Liverant, 1962; Baron, 1968; Higbee and Streufert, 1969; Lefcourt and Steffy, 1970; Higbee and Lafferty, 1972; Newman, 1977; Bonoma and Johnston, 1978; Drwal, 1980; McInish, 1982; and Miller, Kets de Vries, and Toulouse, 1982).

Atkinson and his associates developed a theory of the motivational determinants of risk-taking behavior (Atkinson, 1957; Atkinson and Feather, 1966) building on the earlier work on need achievement by McClelland et al. (1953). This theory postulates that people with a high need for achievement tend to approach moderate risks and those with a high need to avoid failure tend to avoid such risks.

Tests of this theory have been carried out by Atkinson and his associates (1960), Meyer, Walker, and Litwin (1961), Hancock and Teevan (1964), Weinstein (1969), Hamilton (1974), and others.

As part of a broader study of attitudes, Shure and Meeker (1967) included a measure of desire for "material-physical risk" that they derived from an earlier study by Guilford and associates (1953). This measure is based on responses to 16 questions such as "Would you like to do stunt flying in an aerial circus?" They characterized people who tended to be unadventuresome and unwilling to expose themselves to hazardous risks as risk averters. Cummings, Harnett, and Stevens (1971) related this measure of risk to characteristics of managers such as nationality and area of functional responsibility.

One last attitude that has been related to risk is the desire for certainty. Brim and Hoff (1957) designed a test to measure this attitude by asking subjects to rate how confident they were in the probability estimates they provided concerning uncertain events for which the subjects had little knowledge. Kogan and Wallach (1964) renamed this test "extremity and confidence in judgment."

The attention given by psychologists to risk-related attitudes led to speculation that risk represents more of a cultural value than conservatism so that people believe themselves to be greater risk takers than they are (Brown, 1965; Teger and Pruitt, 1967). This hypothesis has been supported in the studies of Wallach and Wing (1968), Williams (1969), Levinger and Schneider (1969), and Finney (1978).

Comparison of Risk Measures

Slovic (1962, 1964, 1972) provided evidence on the degree to which a wide variety of risk-related measures were related to one another. Most of these measures were psychologically oriented. They included a dot estimation test, a word meanings test for category width, a test for guessing on multiple choice exams, a life experiences inventory (including recreational activities involving risk, Torrance and Ziller, 1957), a job preference inventory (Williams, 1960), a gambling task, and peer ratings of risk-taking tendencies. The relationships among these measures were either low or not significant.

Kogan and Wallach (1964) did a very extensive study in which they also examined the relationships among a wide variety of risk measures. They included choice dilemmas, actual betting situations, extremity and confidence in judgment, category width, choices among lotteries based on motor skill tasks, number guessing games where information could be purchased, and problem-solving tasks.

They found no evidence of a general risk propensity across situations.

Other studies have found the same lack of agreement on different measures of risk propensity (Greene, 1963, 1964; Maehr and Videbeck, 1968; Brichacek, 1968; Weinstein and Martin, 1969; Weinstein, 1969; Alderfer and Bierman, 1970; Higbee, 1971; and Bassler, 1972).

Slovic (1964) concluded that the lack of agreement among the measures might be due to the multidimensionality of risk and its subjectivity. Kogan and Wallach (1967) reinforced Slovic's claim in their summary of the various determinants of risk taking with special emphasis on the situational influences.

Jackson, Hourany, and Vidmar (1972) studied the multidimensionality of risk using four types of consequences (monetary, physical, social, and ethical) and four types of situations (self-ratings, choice dilemmas, vocational choices, and personality scales). Although they found that willingness to take risks differed for the four types of consequences, they also found a generalized willingness to take risks. The associations between risks involving different types of consequences were generally low.

Characteristics Related to Risk

The relationships between willingness to take risks and the characteristics of the decision maker have also received attention in empirical studies. Personal characteristics that have been considered include age (McClelland, 1958; Wallach and Kogan, 1961; Lampman, 1962; Kogan and Wallach, 1964, 1967; Watts and Tobin, 1967; Vroom and Pahl, 1971; Halter and Dean, 1971; Baker and Haslem, 1974; Cohn et al., 1975; Ziegler, 1977; Martin, 1978; Dillon and Scandizzo, 1978; Blume and Friend, 1978; Hutchison and Clemens, 1980; McInish, 1982), nationality (Cummings, Harnett, and Stevens, 1971; Arnold, White, and Tigert, 1972; Hopkins et al., 1977; Laughhunn, Payne, and Crum, 1980), dependents (Watts and Tobin, 1967; Dillon and Scandizzo, 1978), sex (Wallach and Kogan, 1959; Wallach and Caron, 1959; Slovic, 1966; Baker, 1970; Blum, 1976; Ziegler, 1977; Bonoma and Schlenker, 1978; Coet and McDermott, 1979), race (Lefcourt, 1965; Lefcourt and Ladwig, 1965), and education (Watts and Tobin, 1967; Hammond, Houston, and Melander, 1967; Cohn et al., 1975; Blume and Friend, 1978; Laughhunn, Payne, and Crum, 1980; McInish, 1982).

Financial characteristics that have received attention are wealth

(Lampman, 1962; Hammond, Houston, and Melander, 1967; Halter and Dean, 1971; Lorange and Norman, 1971, 1973; Cohn et al., 1975; Friend and Blume, 1975; Blume and Friend, 1975; Funk, Rapoport, and Jones, 1979; Siegel and Hoban, 1982; Szpiro, 1983) and income (Watts and Tobin, 1967; Hammond, Houston, and Melander, 1967; Ziegler, 1977; Blume and Friend, 1978; Dillon and Scandizzo, 1978; Grey and Gordon, 1978).

Business characteristics that have received attention are executive position (Grey and Gordon, 1978; Laughhunn, Payne, and Crum, 1980; Miller, Kets de Vries, and Toulouse, 1982), functional responsibility (Cramer and Smith, 1964; Cummings, Harnett, and Stevens, 1971; Dickson, 1982), seniority (Laughhunn, Payne, and Crum, 1980), and industry (Laughhunn, Payne, and Crum, 1980).

Comments on Past Risk Studies

Much of the past research on risk has focused on how people perceive risks as well as rules for choice in risky situations. Little of this work has been concerned with the people who must make risky decisions. Instead, most of the studies focus on acceptable risk of technological hazards from a societal point of view. What research has been done on risk taking from an individual viewpoint has tended to use settings that are unrealistic and far removed from the actual risks one faces (e.g., dot estimation, test anxiety, small hypothetical gambles) and those studies have usually been conducted with students as subjects. In the few studies that have been done with practicing managers, the risk measures have been somewhat better, but some are still open to doubt. We are especially skeptical about measures based totally on attitudes, such as the Shure and Meeker (1967) questionnaire, and measures derived from incompletely specified situations that require frequent switching of roles, such as the choice dilemmas of Wallach and Kogan (1959, 1961). Other studies of business risk taking employ measures that are very indirect. For example, Bowman (1982) measured a firm's willingness to take risks by counting the number of instances of the word "new" in its president's letter that accompanied the annual report. Even when a theoretically sound measure of risk propensity has been used, past research has shown that only a small part of the multidimensional nature of risk can be captured. It is no wonder then that Slovic (1962) and others did not find significant relationships among the various risk measures they considered.

What is needed is a study that examines the risk propensities of managers in a wide variety of realistic situations that have solid theoretical foundations. This is the purpose of our study and what makes it distinctive from other studies of risk.

OUR STUDY OF RISK

Any study of how people deal with risk must take into account the riskiness of situations. People must be studied in situations where they are exposed to a chance of loss. Furthermore we need to examine both their behavior and their attitudes. We need to consider not only the riskiness of the alternatives they choose but also how risk-taking they perceive themselves to be and what steps they take to adjust the risks. To guide such an investigation, we need the set of basic concepts formed into the REACT model we described in Chapter 1.

Since there are many kinds of losses, we need to examine a person's behavior in a variety of situations. There is no particular reason to believe that a person who takes risks in one area of life is necessarily willing to take risks in all areas. Such variability suggests that when we are interested in the risk propensity of professional decision makers, we should examine the way they behave in their professional decisions as well as in their personal decisions.

It might seem that the best way to assess a person's risk propensity is to observe that person in a large number of naturally occurring situations and then to make an assessment of how he handles risks. While this approach has the virtue of realism, a major drawback is that making comparisons among different individuals is very difficult. Different people confront different circumstances and have different resources. A person may not engage in hazardous sports or move from a flood plain because he cannot afford to do so. A person may not have risked his life to save a child from a burning building because no burning buildings have been encountered.

The problems caused by a lack of comparability across situations are not to be taken lightly, for after all, the very concept of risk is relative. What would it mean to say someone takes risks in a particular situation unless we had in mind how a variety of other people would respond? We need, then, to have some basis for comparing people. One way to make comparisons is to place people in identical situations and see how they respond. To a limited extent this could be done by observing people in naturally occurring risky situations. For example, we could observe how investors buy and sell stock in a volatile market situation. In such cases, however, the investors would differ in many ways, such as the amount of information they had on individual stocks. To obtain real comparability we are almost forced to create standardized situations that can be offered in the same form to everyone whose risk-taking behavior we wish to study. By carefully designing such situations, we assume that people will respond to them in the same way as they would if they had occurred naturally.

We have highlighted in the REACT model the range of behaviors occurring when a person encounters a risky situation. First he forms an initial impression based on his recognition and perception of risks. This will form the basis for an evaluation of the situation that will serve to guide subsequent actions. The next step will usually be to try to adjust the risks in some way. Common means of adjustment include collecting information, changing the time frame (e.g., delay), and intervening with the source of the uncertainty (e.g., bargaining). These actions will often lead to a revised perception and a re-evaluation of the situation. After sufficient attempts have been made to modify the situation to a more favorable one, the person will be faced with the task of choosing among the alternative courses of action that are available. Lastly, one tracks the uncertain events and their consequences as they unfold, mitigating the unfavorable outcomes wherever possible. In most studies of risk, the sole focus of attention has been on the ultimate choice, but it should be clear that a more thorough focus on all these phases will provide the necessary information about a person's risk propensity.

When we introduced the definition of risk as the exposure to the chance of loss, we emphasized that the loss could be an opportunity loss. That is, even when all the payoffs led to an improvement over the status quo, the person could still face a risky situation by choosing an alternative that failed to yield as good a gain as could have been obtained from some other alternative. Thus even situations that we think of as "pure opportunities" could be risky. Much more common, though, are threats—that is, situations where we can end up worse off than we are now. In "pure threat" situations no matter which action we take we will be worse off, but how much worse depends on how we handle the risks. Most real situations, however, are neither pure opportunities nor pure threats, for they involve both potential gains and losses. There is a chance we will end up worse off but also a chance we will end up better off. A systematic study of risk should consider all three types of situations (i.e., pure opportunity, pure threat, and mixed threat-opportunity).

In addition to the question of what situations to study, we must also determine the type of responses to study. How choices get made is the most common focus in risk studies. As we have indicated, however, it is particularly interesting to look at the other risk modification activities that occur, such as collecting information, attempting to influence sources of uncertainty, mitigating the effects of bad outcomes, and compensating for losses. At the other extreme, that of less action-oriented behavior, it is common to ask people for their attitudes and beliefs. They are often asked to rate themselves and to rate others on various scales. In a thorough study of risk, there is a role for each of these types of responses.

Studying Managerial Risk

While there are some general guidelines for studying risk, such as the ones we have just discussed, putting them into a useful format depends on whose risk behavior we wish to study. We believe the first priority should be to study people whose profession it is to make risky decisions. Prime candidates, then, are managers at the top levels of business firms.

Top-level senior executives in business firms are responsible for making many of the important decisions in our society. Most of these decisions involve risk in one form or another. If we are to understand how these decisions are made, we must learn something about the risk propensities of senior executives. A second important feature of focusing on top-level executives is that, although everyone has some experience with risky situations, executives deal with risk on a daily basis as part of their business lives. Thus executives are likely to view standardized risky situations as similar to previous situations they have faced and bring their experience to bear in their responses. Other individuals, such as college students, who have less experience with risk taking are more likely to respond to standardized risky situations as novel. We will focus, then, on examining the risk propensities of top-level executives in this study.

The Risk Portfolio

In the preceding section we described several attributes of risky situations and risk behavior that are important in any study of risk propensity. These attributes are summarized below:

Phases of risk—recognition, evaluation, adjustment, and tracking of risk as well as choice
Types of risky situations—standardized situations, naturally occurring risks, and attitudes
Types of exposure—personal decisions and business decisions
Range of payoffs—opportunities and threats
Types of responses—choices, rankings, equivalences, ratings, and open-ended replies

We have created a set of questionnaires to assess a person's risk propensity that considers each of these attributes. We will call this set of questionnaires the *Risk Portfolio*. The Risk Portfolio consists of six booklets, of 4 to 16 pages each; selected pages are reproduced in the Appendix.

The usual use of the terms "risk" and "portfolio" together refers to the collection of assets an individual or a company holds and the attempt to have some parts of the collection balance the risks in the other parts. We are using the terms in a somewhat different way. Our "portfolio" consists of a set of questionnaires, each of which is designed to measure some aspect of risk propensity. Because risk is a complex concept, no one questionnaire can satisfactorily assess the inclination to accept or avoid risks. By using multiple questionnaires we can obtain several pictures of a person's risk propensity and the questionnaires can balance or complement each other. Hence the term "Risk Portfolio."

NOTE ON OTHER ATTRIBUTES OF RISKY SITUATIONS

There are many other possible differences between situations that may lead to different risk propensities. Several differences discussed in Chapter 1 are: the *nature of risk* (e.g., financial, health, social, career), *nature of potential loss* (real versus opportunity), *source of uncertainty* (e.g., random devices, nature, other people), *size of risk components* (magnitude, chance, and exposure to loss), and *importance of risk determinants* (time, information, and control).

These and other attributes could play an important part in the design of a risk study. They do not play a major role in our study so that we can focus more attention on the attributes discussed in the text which we believe are especially important.

In describing the Risk Portfolio, we will first discuss the four questionnaires that use standardized situations. Each of these questionnaires is an elaboration of the Basic Risk Paradigm as shown in Figure 2.1. After describing the four standardized questionnaires we will consider the Societal Attitudes Questionnaire. Finally, we will consider the comprehensive General Questionnaire that includes the natural situations along with some self-ratings and risk-related characteristics.

The Risk Portfolio: Standardized Situations

The *Risk In-Basket* questionnaire is important because it allows us to examine an individual's risk propensity in terms of how he tries to

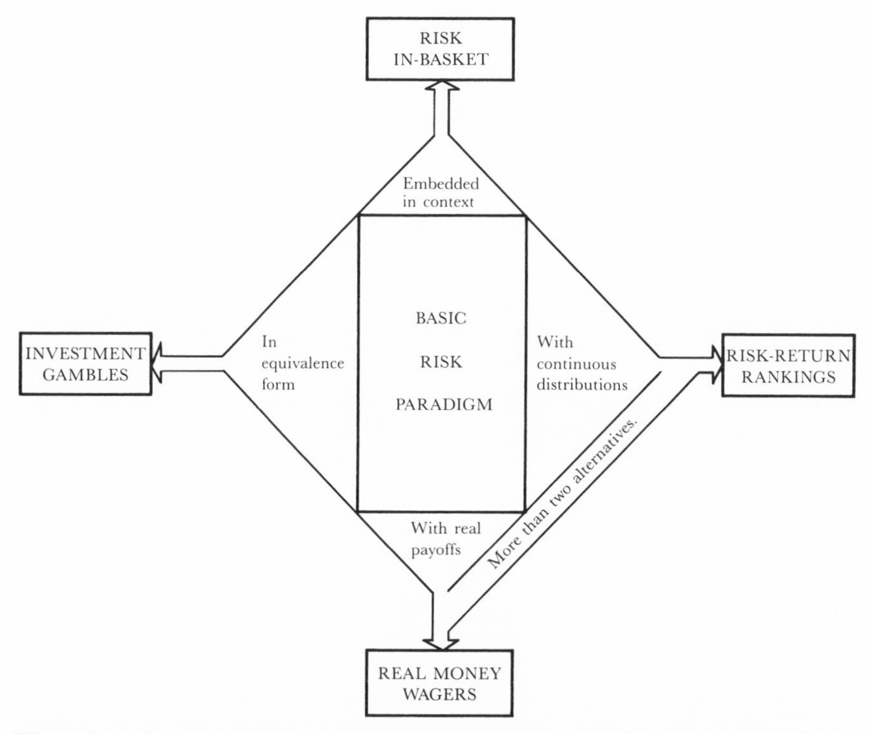

Figure 2.1 Development of Primary Risk Questionnaires from the Basic Risk Paradigm

adjust the risks he faces as well as how he is inclined to choose between risky and sure alternatives. The Risk In-Basket has a high degree of realism. In the Risk In-Basket the person whose risk propensity we are assessing is asked to assume the role of an executive vice-president of a large firm. He is told that he has just taken over the job and that he must deal with a variety of memos in the "in-basket" on his desk before he leaves the office on a long trip. Any actions he wishes to take on the situations he confronts must be specified in writing in the next 45 minutes. The situations are described in a self-contained form in the letters and memos in the in-basket and, although he does not have direct access to his subordinates and secretary, he can leave memos for them. By analyzing the memos he writes, we can assess his risk propensity, as well as observing how he attempts to adjust the risks he faces.

The four situations are:

1. The president of a subsidiary asks whether he should settle a patent violation suit out of court or whether he should fight the case.

2. A major customer of a subsidiary threatens to withdraw his business if a major competitor is supplied.
3. The labor union of a subsidiary threatens to strike if a crucial time-and-motion study is not called off.
4. A competitor offers an opportunity to form a joint venture in entering a new market rather than engaging in separate, competitive entry.

Note that in each situation there are two major choices. One alternative has a sure outcome (e.g., settling out of court). The other alternative is risky (e.g., take the case to court) and has two possible outcomes—a more favorable one and a less favorable one. The description of each situation specifies these outcomes completely as well as giving the chances of each possible outcome.

In addition to writing his memo responses, the executive is asked to specify the lowest chance of the more favorable outcome that he would require before he would switch from the sure to the risky alternative. He also is asked to provide a rating (on an eleven-point scale) of his inclination toward the sure versus the risky alternative.

We can obtain a good indication of a person's risk propensity in each situation because he is providing us with a variety of responses that we can use to check his consistency. To the extent that a person can be expected to exhibit a different risk propensity in dealing, say, with a lawsuit rather than with a joint venture, we are interested in separate measures of risk for each situation.

The *Investment Gambles* questionnaire is even more directly based on the Basic Risk Paradigm. A person is first presented with the prospect of retaining his status quo position (the "sure" alternative) versus risking half his personal net wealth to obtain some substantial gain. The amount of the gain is left unspecified and he is asked to specify the gain he would require in order to take the risky alternative for various levels of the chance of success. In the business version, the outcomes are rates of return on investment of a capital budget rather than personal net wealth. For either case, people who require very high levels of gain to induce them to take the risky alternative are exhibiting less tolerance for risk than people who would accept lower gain amounts.

The *Risk-Return Rankings* questionnaire presents a series of alternatives for investing 10 percent of one's personal net wealth. Each of the nine alternatives is initially described by an expected rate of return and a rate of variation in returns. These two characteristics are then used to generate six other characteristics of each alternative (namely, the chances of losing the whole stake, losing half the stake, losing 10% of the stake, breaking even, making a 50% return, and doubling the investment). A table presenting all these characteristics is given. The order in which a person ranks the nine ventures indicates how he perceives risks (i.e., which attributes he focuses upon) and which risky venture he subsequently prefers most, second most, and so forth. From this ordering we can examine his implicit tradeoffs between expected return and variation.

The *Real Money Wagers* questionnaire asks a person to rank five alternatives (four risky ones and a sure one). Such rankings are requested for three different sets. In one set the maximum loss (with the risky alternative) is held fixed, in another set the maximum gain is held fixed, while in the third set the chances of gain and loss are held fixed. Unlike the other three standardized situations, the payoffs in the Real Money Wagers questionnaire were actually realized; that is, the participants could actually win or lose money. This questionnaire has characteristics similar to both Investment Gambles and Risk-Return Rankings, as well as having some unique features. Like Investment Gambles, it uses alternatives having two possible monetary payoffs and includes a sure alternative. Like Risk-Return Rankings, it obtains preferences in the form of a ranking of a set of alternatives.

These four standardized situations each have a solid theoretical base in the Basic Risk Paradigm. The questionnaires deal with both personal and business situations. Personal decisions are covered by Risk-Return Rankings, Real Money Wagers, and part of Investment Gambles; business decisions are covered by Risk In-Basket and the other part of Investment Gambles. Each questionnaire includes both relative threats and relative opportunities. The choice phase of risk taking receives attention in that choices must be made in each questionnaire. The recognition and evaluation phase of risk behavior is a part of the Risk-Return Rankings and Real Money Wagers questionnaires. Risk In-Basket is the only questionnaire in this set that allows for adjusting the risks. These four questionnaires represent the core of our Risk Portfolio. A summary of the characteristics is given in Table 2.1. Part Two of the book describes these questionnaires in more detail and gives their results (see Chapters 3–7).

NOTE ON USING EQUIVALENCES TO ASSESS RISK PROPENSITY

Using the Basic Risk Paradigm we can create an *equivalence* format for the response mode. Rather than specifying the sure outcome, gain amount, loss amount, and chances of gain and loss and asking for a choice, we can specify all but one of these variables and ask an individual to provide a value for the missing variable so that he is just indifferent between the sure alternative and the risky alternative. If the sure outcome is

Table 2.1 Summary of Questionnaires in Risk Portfolio

Characteristics of Risky Situations	Standardized Risks				Naturally Occurring Risks	Attitudes to Risk		
	Risk In-Basket	*Investment Gambles*	*Risk-Return Rankings*	*Real Money Wagers*	*Past Behavior*	*Sensation Seeking*	*Internal-External Control*	*Self-Ratings*
Context	Respond to risky business situations	Personal and business investment	Invest 10% of personal wealth	Rank wagers involving personal wealth	Asset holdings Debt Life insurance Gambling Resignations	Select more appropriate of two statements concerning personal desire for sensation	Select more appropriate of two statements concerning personal belief in control over one's environment	Self-perception of propensity to take business risks
Format	4 letters	8 questions: 4 personal, 4 business	9 alternatives	3 sets of 5 alternatives each	Varied	10 questions	10 questions	3 scales
Role	Hypothetical vice-president	Own	Own	Own	Own	Own	Own	Own
Type of Responses	•Write memos •Probability equivalence •Rating scale	•Gain equivalences	•Pairwise choices •Overall ranking	•Intra-set rankings •Inter-set ranking	•Provide numerical answers	•Binary choice	•Binary choice	•Rating scale
Phase of Risk	Risk adjustment and choice	Choice	Recognition and evaluation of risk and choice	Recognition and evaluation of risk and choice	Choice	N/A	N/A	N/A

left unspecified, then the individual is required to provide an assessment of the sure amount that would just make him indifferent. This response is called the *certainty equivalence*. Similarly, if the gain outcome is left unspecified, the person's assessment is called his *gain equivalence*. When the loss outcome is left unspecified, the assessment is a *loss equivalence*. One can also leave the probability of gain unspecified, in which case the *probability equivalence* makes the individual indifferent between the two actions.

These different equivalence formats correspond to different forms that a risky choice problem can take. For example, the certainty equivalence format asks what sure amount an individual would require in lieu of a specified risky lottery. The gain equivalence format asks how much gain would be required to enter a risky lottery whose chances and magnitude of loss were specified. The loss and probability equivalence formats have similar interpretations. In the Investment Gambles questionnaire, then, we are using the gain equivalence format and in part of the Risk In-Basket we are using the probability equivalence format.

The difference between the expected value of the risky action and the certainty equivalence that a person specifies is a measure of the *risk premium* that a person requires to undertake the risky action. The larger the risk premium, the more risk-averse the person. If the sign of the risk premium is negative (i.e., the individual requires a sure outcome that is higher than the expected value), then he is risk-taking. Similarly loss, gain, and probability premiums can be calculated and interpreted as measures of risk propensity.

The Risk Portfolio: Attitudes

Attitudes to risks have been used as the sole measure of risk in many previous psychological studies. Attitude questionnaires are less action and choice oriented than any of the questionnaires we have previously described. We will restrict our attention to only two types of attitudes—one's desire to seek or avoid sensation in the environment and one's belief that he can or cannot control his environment.

Among the standard psychological attitudinal measures, the one that seems the closest to risk taking is *sensation seeking*. A person is given a series of choices between two statements. One of the statements reflects a preference for stimulating experiences and uncertainty, while the other statement reflects a desire for the familiar and the stable. A risk-averse person would presumably agree more with the latter statements. We used a subgroup of ten questions from the 34 questions listed in Zuckerman et al. (1964). We eliminated questions that seemed inappropriate for executives.

The other suitable psychological attitudinal measure related to risk taking is *internal-external control*. Here, too, a person is given a pair of statements and is asked to indicate the one that more appropriately reflects his attitude. These questions pertain to the extent that a person perceives his life, and the world in general, to be controllable, rather than being subject to chance. A risk-averse person would presumably believe more in external control than in internal control. Only ten questions that seemed most relevant for executives were chosen from the standard list (Rotter, 1966).

These 20 questions from existing attitude scales were randomly interspersed with ten attitude questions designed especially for this study. These additional questions dealt with tolerance for losing, entrepreneurial beliefs, nationality stereotypes, and so forth. All 30 questions were combined in the same booklet called *Societal Attitude Questionnaire*.

The Risk Portfolio: General Questionnaire

In addition to the specially designed questionnaires described in the preceding sections, it seemed important to obtain risk information of three other kinds: naturally occurring risks, self-ratings, and risk-related characteristics. Each of these types of information were requested in our General Questionnaire.

We requested past behavior for the following *naturally occurring risks*:

1. Insurance holdings (life, disability, travel)
2. Asset distribution (savings, real estate, stocks, commodities, etc.)
3. Debt
4. Gambling activities (frequency, amount)
5. Hazardous recreational activities (scuba diving, skiing, etc.)
6. Resignations (job waiting, no job waiting)
7. Changes in the firm's operations (initiator, participant)

In general, a risk-averse person would tend to hold large amounts of insurance, hold relatively safe assets, hold little debt, engage in no major gambling, avoid hazardous recreational activities, take few career risks, and initiate few changes. Note, then, that we obtained information on risk in both personal and business natural situations.

Rather than simply looking at the outcome of a decision (e.g., the insurance currently held), one may try to get information about the situation that led up to the decision and the process of how the decision was actually made. We obtained such information about business decisions in two forms. First, at the same time as the regular data were collected, we asked the executives to describe what they viewed as risky business situations and how they handled risks in such situations. Some of the executives' answers were given in Chapter 1. Second, we conducted follow-up interviews (to be described later) with a subgroup of the participants. At these interviews, we asked each of them to describe in some detail the process by which a strategic decision, in which he was a major participant, was made. During the interviews we asked specific questions about how risks were perceived and handled.

A very common approach in psychological studies is to ask a person to rate himself on whatever dimensions are being considered. This direct approach is obviously subject to misrepresentation. If nothing else, however, *self-ratings* indicate how people perceive themselves, or at least how they want others to see how they perceive themselves. We obtained self-ratings on three dimensions: tolerance for risk compared to other managers in the firm, propensity to collect more information than others in making decisions, and propensity to take more time than others in making decisions.

Many people believe that age is related to risk propensity. The common view seems to be that as a person gets older, he becomes more risk-averse. Others might argue that older people take more risks because they can afford to, but note that this is mixing together both age and wealth. By obtaining information on characteristics such as age and wealth, we can explore the connections of such aspects with risk propensity, as derived from the questionnaires. Our Risk Portfolio provides data on a large number of *personal*, *financial*, and *business characteristics* of the managers. We will mention here only the primary characteristics in each category. The primary personal characteristics are age, education, number of dependents, and nationality. The primary financial characteristics are wealth and income. The primary business characteristics are industry type, firm size, executive position, authority, and seniority. All the primary characteristics will be related to the risk measures.

In Part Three of the book we shift attention from the individual standardized situations described in Part Two to comparisons of various kinds. We compare risk measures derived from these situations to each other (Chapter 8), to risk measures derived from natural situations and attitudes (Chapter 9), and to the personal, financial, and business characteristics (Chapter 10). A summary of all the key features of the questionnaires is given in Table 2.1.

Table 2.2 summarizes some of the concepts of risk aversion that will be examined in the Risk Portfolio. These concepts are an integral part of the different phases of risk, including recognition of risk, adjustment of risks, evaluation of risk, and choice. Thus the Risk Portfolio includes a wide variety of situations in which a manager's risk propensities can be revealed.

Table 2.2 Coverage of Various Concepts of Risk Aversion in the Risk Portfolio Questionnaires

		Chapter					
		3	4	5	6	9	9,10
Phase	Concepts of Risk Aversion	Risk In-Basket	Investment Gambles	Risk-Return Rankings	Real Money Wagers	Societal Attitudes	General Questionnaire
Recognition	Focus on losses			✓	✓		
	Perceiving things beyond control					✓	
	Rating self as risk-averse						✓
Adjustment	Hedging	✓					
	Delegating	✓					
	Collecting information	✓					✓
	Delaying	✓					✓
Evaluation and Choice	Choosing a sure alternative over risky ones (avoiding losses)	✓	✓		✓		
	Writing in support of sure alternative	✓					

Phase	Concepts of Risk Aversion	*Chapter* 3 Risk In-Basket	4 Investment Gambles	5 Risk-Return Rankings	6 Real Money Wagers	9 Societal Attitudes	9,10 General Questionnaire
Evaluation and Choice	Requiring large chance of gain (i.e., low chance of loss)	✓		✓	✓		
	Requiring high gain amount		✓		✓		
	Preferring lower stakes in investment				✓		✓
	Preferring smaller variation in payoffs	✓	✓	✓	✓		
	Avoiding new experiences					✓	✓
	Holding fewer risky assets						✓
	Holding lower debt						✓
	Holding higher insurance						✓
	Resigning less often						✓
	Gambling less		✓		✓		✓

Development of the Risk Portfolio

The study began in 1972 with a grant from the Department of Industry, Trade, and Commerce of the Canadian Federal Government. The Department was interested in learning why Canadian managers seemed more averse to taking risks than managers in other countries such as the United States. The first phase of the study, lasting approximately six months, involved an extensive study of all the theoretical and empirical investigations of risk taking that we could find. We tried to track down and assess all research questionnaires that had previously been used to measure risk propensity. We made a very thorough assessment of both empirical and theoretical risk-taking studies in a number of disciplines including psychology, economics, decision theory, education, and management. These studies then formed the basis for designing the Risk Portfolio.

The questionnaires chosen for inclusion in the Risk Portfolio had to satisfy a number of goals when viewed both individually and collectively. More specifically, each questionnaire chosen had to

1. Contain some central concept of risk
2. Allow the derivation of one or more risk measures
3. Have relevance for top-level executives
4. Be easy to administer in questionnaire format

Collectively the questionnaires in the Risk Portfolio had to

1. Cover a variety of risky situations in which to assess risk propensity, balanced on several dimensions
    - Standardized versus naturally occurring risks
    - Behavior versus attitudes
    - Personal versus business risks
    - Threats versus opportunities
    - Simple versus complex responses
2. Avoid redundancy and inconsistency
3. Be interesting to do
4. Take a limited amount of the executive's time to complete.

Numerous preliminary questionnaires were tried out in pilot tests. The subjects for the earliest pilot tests were undergraduate and graduate business school students in groups of 24 to 150. After modifying the package of questionnaires in response to student feedback, we conducted another pilot study with 40 top-level business executives from Vancouver, British Columbia and Seattle, Washington. These executives received an extended version of the materials. The results of this pilot study were carefully analyzed to select for inclusion in the Risk Portfolio those questionnaires that seemed most effective and to identify places where further refinement was necessary. The principal changes in the original questionnaires resulting from the pilot studies were:

1. Several questionnaires were dropped because of time restrictions, difficulties experienced by subjects in their responses, and close similarity with other questionnaires in the set.
2. Several questionnaires were clarified and shortened. For example, the original seven-item Risk In-Basket was reduced to four items. A number of questions regarding Investment Gambles that utilized different types of responses and domains were dropped.
3. Realistic expectations were set for the time needed by executives to complete each questionnaire. A total of two hours was set as a practical amount of time for participating executives to respond to the entire Risk Portfolio.

The risk Portfolio that emerged from the pilot tests consisted of the six questionnaires described earlier.

NOTE ON THE USE OF QUESTIONNAIRES

The questionnaire method used in this study differs from the interactive method used by most practicing decision analysts to obtain the risk preferences of managers. The primary advantage of the interactive method is the guidance and feedback that the decision analyst can provide to the manager in assessing his risk propensity. Although the questionnaire method cannot provide these features, it does not expose the manager's risk preferences to the subtle influences of the decision analyst during the assessment process. Moreover, it is not practical to obtain risk propensities from large numbers of executives using the interactive method unless several decision analysts participate in the assessments. Multiple analysts could introduce additional possibilities for bias in the responses. For these reasons we decided in favor of the questionnaire method for this study.

Design of the Main Study

Using the Risk Portfolio we conducted a systematic study of the risk propensities of over 500 senior business executives. The managers were drawn from a wide variety of industries and from both large and small firms. Because of our particular interest in potential differences in the risk propensities of Canadian and American senior executives, we included executives from both countries in our study.

For the Canadian sample a list of 35 industries containing 680 firms was prepared from a number of business publications. These publications included the *Financial Post's Survey of Industrials, Moody's Guides to Industrials, Utilities, Banks and Finance Companies, and Transportation Companies, Standard and Poor's Register,* and annual reports. The industries and firms that we contacted were carefully selected to represent a cross section of the business community. Rather than striving for an even balance, however, we deliberately tried to get a strong representation of financial institutions, resource-based firms, and high technology companies because of the prominence of risk in their activities. Although small firms are represented, we overrepresented larger firms, especially the five largest firms in each industry grouping, because of the importance of the particular firms to the economy of a region or even the country itself.

After selecting the industries and firms, we identified the top three to ten managers in each firm using publications such as the *Directory of Directors*. These executives ranged from the chief executive officer down to vice-presidents in most firms. These executives also represented a broad cross section of functional responsibilities.

The participation of the Canadian executives for our study was solicited either by *direct mail* or through a *personal contact* by one of the principal researchers. The Risk Portfolio together with a covering letter describing the study was mailed directly to the identified executives in 550 of the 680 Canadian firms. This direct mail method solicited the participation of a total of 2720 executives. The Risk Portfolio packet included the questionnaires, a postage-paid return envelope, and two pages of instructions. The instructions offered assistance with interpreting any ambiguities in the questionnaires by giving the addresses and phone numbers of the principal researchers, stressing the importance of providing true responses, and guaranteeing the confidentiality of the executives' responses. The estimated time required was stated as two hours. Completed questionnaires were returned by 192 of the 2720 executives for a direct mail response rate of 7%.

For a subgroup of 130 Canadian firms that were particularly important (and were located in a handful of major geographic centers), we sent only an introductory letter describing the study and not the Risk Portfolio to a key executive in the firm. A week later we phoned this executive to arrange to meet with him. Executives in 90 of the 130 firms contacted in this manner agreed to meet with one of the principal researchers. At each of the appointments we asked the executive to participate and to help to persuade his associates to participate as well. We left a copy of the Risk Portfolio, the instructions, and a postage-paid return envelope for each of the 450 senior executives identified in the 90 firms. Completed questionnaires were returned by 215 of the 450 executives for a personal contact response rate of 48%.

For the American sample a list of firms in 11 key industries was prepared from business publications, as in the Canadian sample. Special attention was given to financial and venture capital institutions, primary resource firms, and chemical/pharmaceutical firms in which risk taking was thought to play a prominent role. Manufacturing firms were excluded from the American sample. From this list 155 firms in three geographic centers—the San Francisco Bay area, metropolitan New York City, and Houston—were identified. The top executives from each firm were identified using a standard business directory.

These executives were invited to participate in the study by means of a personal contact similar to that used in the Canadian sample. A key executive in each firm was sent a letter requesting an interview to discuss the study. For about one-half of the firms, one of the researchers made use of his affiliation with three major universities to identify a top executive in the firm who had previously attended one of these institutions. For about one-third of the firms a "cold contact" was made by mail. Executives in the remaining firms were identified by a process of referral from those contacted earlier. On the basis of the approaches described above, 85 American firms agreed to accept a total of 360 Risk Portfolio packets for distribution to senior executives. Completed questionnaires were returned by 102 of the 360 executives for an American response of 28%.

NOTE ON RESPONSE RATE

Overall 509 executives participated out of the 3530 who received the Risk Portfolio packet for a combined response rate of 14.4% Of course this low response rate was a result of the relatively large number of Risk Portfolio packets sent by direct mail where response rates are usually low. Our 7% mail contact response rate was disappointing but is not unusual, especially given the two-hour time requirement. The higher response rates for the personal contact method were in line with those achieved in similar studies that used this method.

The 509 executives who participated included 375 Canadians from 189 different firms and 96 Americans from 52 firms.[1] The median number of participating executives per firm was three, although this ranges from a low of one executive per firm (for 148 firms) to a high of 14 executives in one firm. Twenty-three firms had five or more participating executives in the sample. Firms with only a single participating executive tended to be represented by a senior executive whereas those with five or more participants tended to have more junior managers included along with top management. Data collection was carried out in 1973.

The only specified inducement to participate in the study was the promise of receiving a personalized Risk Profile. The Risk Profile showed the participant how his risk propensity compared with that of all other executives in the study and with respect to nine specific groups of executives including those from the same industry, those from the same position in the firm, those with the same wealth, and so on.[2] The Risk Profiles were prepared from preliminary analysis of the responses to several questionnaires in the Risk Portfolio and were mailed out several months after the data collection had been completed. In addition, for firms with five or more participants, we prepared a comparative profile of the participants within the firm, and either sent it to the firm or made an oral presentation to them. Risk Profiles will be discussed in more detail in Chapter 12 where readers may assess their own risk propensities.

NOTE ON THE REPRESENTATIVENESS OF THE SAMPLE

We do not know how representative our participants are of the business community in general. Our participants do seem representative of the total group that was contacted in that the response rates were approximately the same across industries, firm sizes, and executive positions. It is possible, however, that the very risk-averse people refused to participate—or maybe the highest risk takers were so busy taking risks that they did not have time to participate.

It is also possible that executives contacted by direct mail differed from those contacted personally. To identify possible differences between these two groups of executives, we compared them on a wide range of variables including personal, financial, and business characteristics as well as the numerous measures of risk propensity derived from the Risk Portfolio as described in later chapters. The only significant difference was the executives' nationality which, of course, was an artifact of the research design which solicited the participation of American executives only by personal contact. Because no important differences were found in either the risk measures or the executives' characteristics, the executives solicited by direct mail and those solicited by personal contact were combined into a single sample. All results reported in this book are based on this combined sample.

Design of the Follow-up Study

Interest in the stability of an executive's responses and a desire to examine risk propensity using a number of different methods led us to undertake a follow-up study of a subsample of the executives one year later. The follow-up study was restricted to Canadian executives who lived in Toronto, Montreal, Vancouver, Winnipeg, Ottawa, Calgary, or Edmonton. Because top-level strategic decisions were to be examined as part of the follow-up, only executives who were vice-presidents and higher were initially solicited. Among the executives in the main study who satisfied these restrictions, 128 agreed to participate in the follow-up.[3]

The Investment Gambles and Risk-Return Rankings questionnaires were administered in the follow-up study in an identical form as given in the main study. A shortened version of the Risk In-Basket was given that asked executives to provide rating and equivalence responses to the four risky situations, but no written memos were requested. The self-ratings that appeared as part of the General Questionnaire in the main study were repeated as a separate questionnaire in the follow-up. Each of these questionnaires was repeated so that the stability of the executives' responses could be assessed.

A number of additional questionnaires were added in the follow-up to gain more information about executive risk taking. Each executive received either a personal or a business supplement to the Investment Gambles questionnaire. This questionnaire asked each executive to provide a sure amount for which he would be just indifferent to a risky situation involving either personal or business wealth. Although the situation was very similar to the Investment Gambles questionnaire, the supplement used a different type of response. Each executive was also given a supplement to the Risk-Return Rankings questionnaire in which he was asked to consider 11 new ventures for investing 10% of his personal net wealth in addition to those considered in the main questionnaire. All 20 ventures were to be ranked in order of preference. Lastly, the Real Money Wagers questionnaire described earlier was given as part of the follow-up study.

After the executives agreed to participate in the follow-up study, they received by mail a follow-up Risk Portfolio that included the repeated questionnaires, extensions of prior questionnaires, and the new Real Money Wagers questionnaire. In a subsequent phone call arrangements were made for one of the researchers to meet with the executive. At this meeting the researcher conducted a structured interview with the executive concerning strategic risky decisions in

Table 2.3 Characteristics of the Executives

	Variable	Median (Range)	Description of Discrete Categories	Number of Executives
Personal Characteristics	Age	47.5 (24–77)	24–43 years	172
			44–50 years	161
			51–77 years	175
	Dependents	3.2 (0–10)	0–2	154
			3	138
			4+	212
	Education		Secondary only	120
			Undergraduate	240
			Postgraduate	138
	Nationality		American	96
			Canadian	375
Financial Characteristics	Wealth	$300,000 ($0–18 million)	Under $240,000	165
			$240,000–$525,000	165
			Over $525,000	162
	Income	$129,000 ($21,000–$1.87 million)	Under $105,000	165
			$105,000–$159,000	161
			Over $159,000	160

	Variable	Median (Range)	Description of Discrete Categories	Number of Executives
Business Characteristics	Position		General manager	174
			Vice-president	188
			Chairman, president, senior VP	147
	Authority	$75,000 ($0–$387,000)	Under $60,000	172
			$60,000–$90,000	133
			Over $90,000	143
	Seniority	60% (0–100%)	Under 36%	167
			36–77%	167
			Over 77%	167
	Firm Size		Under $30 million	128
			$30–$300 million	174
			Over $300 million	207
	Industry		Banking	70
			Venture capital	69
			Primary	61
			Manufacturing	121
			Chemical/pharmaceutical	72
			Other	116

NOTE: Monetary figures are in 1985 dollars.

which he had participated, collected his responses to the follow-up Risk Portfolio, and played out the wager in the Real Money Wagers questionnaire.

The structured interview was designed and pretested during a pilot phase of the study. At the outset of the interview the executive was asked to describe the four most important strategic decisions in his firm over the past two or three years. Each decision was then discussed in terms of its importance to the firm's success or failure, the degree to which the element of risk or uncertainty played an important part in the decision, and the degree of the executive's participation in the decision. The researcher then chose the decision that appeared to be the best vehicle for considering the executive's actual risk-handling activities, and discussed it in more detail with the executive. The researcher systematically elicited from the executive information about the key participants in the decision, the background of the decision, the principal alternative courses of action considered and their origins, the main uncertainties in the decision, the criteria used in evaluating the alternatives, and the risk-handling activities used in the decision. For the questions dealing with sources of uncertainty and the risk-handling activities, checklists were used by the researcher to make sure that no major considerations were omitted during the discussion. The interviews took from one to two hours and averaged about 90 minutes. The follow-up study was conducted during 1974.

Description of Executives in the Main Study

The 509 executives who participated in the main study were a diverse group of individuals. Their personal, financial, and business characteristics are presented in Table 2.3. There was a greater representation of executives in the sample than in the general population from the financial industries (banks, life insurance, venture capital, underwriters: 27%), primary resources industries (oil, gas, forest products, mining: 12%), and the chemical/pharmaceutical industry (14%). This was a consequence of the overrepresentation of these industries in the research design because of the importance of risk taking in these industries. Similarly larger firms were overrepresented in the sample compared with the general population. In the sample 75% of the executives were employed by firms having over $30 million in annual revenues including 41% who came from firms having over $300 million in annual revenues. The preponderance of large firms in industries such as banking, life insurance, primary resources, and chemical/pharmaceuticals is a result of economies of scale in these industries and the concentration of large banks in Canada.

A range of executive positions were represented with heavier emphasis on vice-presidents and above who accounted for two out of every three executives in the sample. Most executives had been with their firms for an extended period with the typical executive having spent 14 years with his current employer. About one out of four executives had been with their firms for 25 years or more and three out of four for at least five years. On a percentage basis, the typical executive in our study had been with his current employer above 60% of his working life.

Only a few (less than 1%) of the senior executives on our lists of top executives were female and none of these female executives returned the Risk Portfolio. As a result, all executives in our sample were male. The typical executive was 47 years old, with only a few executives above 60 years or below 30 years. Most (94%) executives were married and the median number of dependents was three including wife and children. Of every four executives one had only a secondary school education, two had undergraduate degrees, and one had a postgraduate degree (usually an MBA). About three out of four executives in the sample were Canadian citizens, and most of the remainder held United States citizenship. The typical executive had an income of $130,000, assets of $500,000, and wealth of $300,000. The American executives had an average income of $160,000, average assets of $690,000, and average wealth of $450,000. The Canadian executives had an average income of $119,000, average assets of $450,000, and average wealth of $295,000.[4]

These executives, then, make up the sample whose risk propensities we will assess using the Risk Portfolio.

PART TWO

Risk in Standardized Situations

Chapter 3

Risk In-Basket

Adjusting Risky Business Situations

INTRODUCTION

Suppose a subsidiary of your firm faces a threatened lawsuit for patent violation concerning a new product. If the suit goes to court, your legal counsel believes there is a 50% chance the firm will lose $1.6 million (in present value terms) in damages and lost profits from dropping the product line. There is also a 50% chance the firm will win the case and lose nothing. Alternatively, you can settle out of court by dropping the product line and making a cash payment to the litigants (a loss of $800,000 in present value terms). If you faced this situation, what would you do?

We asked the senior vice-president of a large life insurance company to write a memo indicating how he would handle this situation. Here is his answer:

> In my opinion we should fight this case. The potential loss over a period of years is too substantial to back off with a 50% chance of a favorable judgment.

We see that when he faced the choice between a risky alternative (i.e., take the case to court) and a sure alternative (i.e., settle out of court), he simply selected the risky alternative. Thus he viewed the decision on the lawsuit in the framework of the Basic Risk Paradigm presented in Figure 3.1.

We presented the same situation to the president of a medium-size chemical firm. He responded as follows:

> I would be inclined to risk the loss in court. However, I would like the opportunity to meet with [the litigants] and see if we can settle for a more realistic amount, and possibly obtain a license to continue our production. . . . If they refuse to wait for this [meeting], tell them to go ahead and file their case and that we are prepared to defend our side in court, but that I am still prepared to meet with them out of court.

Faced with a choice between a risky alternative and a sure alternative, this executive chose neither. Instead he created a new alternative—to bargain with the litigants either before or after they filed suit. Other managers suggested specific counteroffers for out-of-court settlements as part of a bargaining strategy. While the life insurance executive accepted the risky situation as given and chose between the two alternatives presented to him, the chemical company president *adjusted the risky situation* he faced and thereby widened his decision possibilities.

We explored methods for adjusting risks in the REACT model presented in Chapter 1. There are several ways in which an individual can modify a risky situation in addition to bargaining. Perhaps the most extreme modification is to try to avoid the situation altogether. This might be accomplished in a business decision by delegating the decision to someone else. The chief executive officer of a large manufacturing firm responded to the lawsuit situation by delegating the decision to the president of the subsidiary facing the suit:

> Because of the major impact on your operation, you will have to make the decision based on all the facts you have.

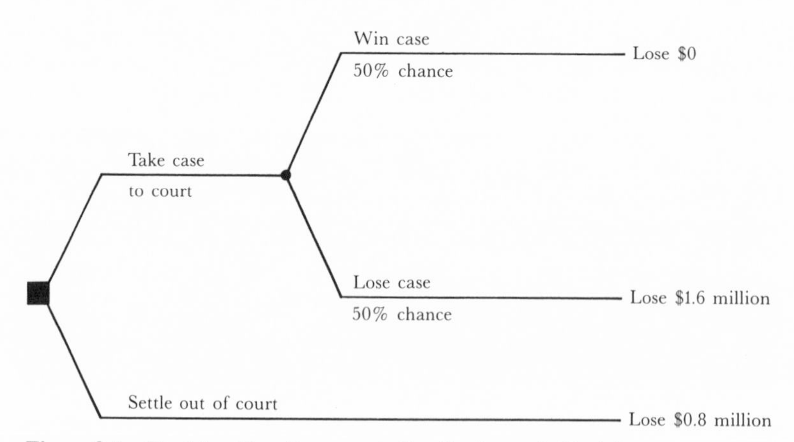

Figure 3.1 Decision Tree Representation for Lawsuit Decision

If complete avoidance is not possible, a risk-averse individual may try to share the risk. In that way, at least, others must take some responsibility if things go wrong. Delegating a decision with a specific recommendation is one way to share risk. For example, the vice-president of finance in a large airline company responded by writing to the president of the subsidiary as follows:

> My tendency would be to go to court and then if the decision appears to be going against us we could settle out of court during the proceedings. It might cost us a bit more, but it appears to be worth the gamble. I know that you have been close to this case for some time, so if you disagree with the above, please follow whatever course you think best and I will give you all the support you need.

Another modification is to delay making a final choice. Delay may not improve a risky situation, but at least the situation can be temporarily avoided while new options are being examined. For example, the president of a medium-size land development firm handled the situation this way:

> If [our counteroffer] does not lead to a settlement or postponement to allow further study, my inclination is to create maximum delay through legal proceedings.

Collecting information requires a special type of delay. By trying to learn more about the possible losses or their chances of occurrence, an individual may be able to reduce his risks. A common reaction among executives to this lawsuit decision is to obtain additional legal opinions regarding the chances of winning the suit in court. A particular kind of information gathering involves exploring whether the uncertainties can be influenced. If the uncertainties concern the behavior of other people (e.g., competitors, government regulators, suppliers, unions), then persuasion, bargaining, and so forth may be tried. This was the approach of the chemical company president. It was also the approach of the senior vice-president of a large bank who responded this way:

> Get someone from headquarters staff to do some digging on [the litigants]. Do we supply them? Do they supply us? Do we cross markets? Who do we know in their organization? How tight for credit are they? Who banks them? Anything headquarters can dig up.

In many of these risk modifications a final choice is not completely avoided, but at least the initial alternatives have been modified or supplemented. When it finally comes down to making a choice, another avoidance attempt might be to give an ambiguous response. Someone may indicate that the risky alternative should be taken with a qualifier such as "however," "but," or "unless" attached. One might fall back on the maxim "when in doubt, mumble."

Clearly, then, we can gain insight into an individual's propensity to take risks by looking at his risk modification behavior as well as which alternative he chooses in a risky situation. To learn about how people modify risky situations, we must allow them to go beyond making a choice when expressing how they would handle the situation. Asking the managers to write a memo indicating how they would handle a risky situation is a natural method for revealing risk modifications that managers use in their own decisions.

OUR STUDY

We used a sixteen-page questionnaire that asked each manager to respond to four hypothetical risky business situations. We will refer to this questionnaire as the *Risk In-Basket*. Segments of this questionnaire are reproduced in the Appendix (pages 307–312).

The executive was asked to assume the fictional role of Bill Bickner, newly appointed vice-president for North American Operations of Multinational Products, Inc. This role is described below:

> Please act as if you are Bill Bickner, Vice-President, North American Operations of Multinational Products, Inc. Formerly the president of the Connecticut subsidiary, you have just replaced James Norton, who died last week of a heart attack. Because you were notified of this new appointment only very recently, you have had little time to become acquainted with the job.
>
> Today is Wednesday, March 14. You have arrived in your new office for the first time. It is 7:45 P.M. and you must leave promptly at 8:20 P.M. to catch the 9:30 plane to Mexico City for an important meeting. You will not be back until Thursday, March 22.
>
> The letters and memos in this booklet were left in the in-basket on your desk by Annabel, your secretary. Read through the set of materials and specify whatever action you deem appropriate on each item. Your assistant will take care of the final drafting of the letters; however, every action you wish to take should be carefully specified in the form of memos and wires. Be sure to indicate in the memos or wires to whom they are addressed.
>
> You are to use your own experience as the basis for your decisions in the role of Bill Bickner.

We used this fictional role because the wide variability in the managers' actual roles makes comparisons across the managers' responses difficult. Asking the managers to use their own experience as the basis for their decisions in this fictional role should reveal their risk propensities in these situations.

Mr. Bickner is asked to respond to four items in his in-basket. The four items are:

1. *Lawsuit.* A letter from Donald Moore, president of a Vancouver subsidiary, about whether his firm should fight a threatened patent violation suit or settle out of court.
2. *Customer threat.* A memo from Bickner's new secretary about a visit from Peter Davis, a major customer of a Montreal subsidiary for the purpose of asking that his major competitor not be supplied—otherwise he will withdraw his business.
3. *Union dispute.* A letter from Stuart White, president of an Atlanta subsidiary, asking that a time-and-motion study be discontinued to avert a union strike.
4. *Joint venture.* A memo from Alfred Kaye, head of a special team to investigate the prospects of an Arizona project, asking whether the project should be pursued individually or as a joint venture.

We have already described the lawsuit situation and the responses of several managers to it.

Each of the four items presented a clear choice between a risky and a safe course of action. Each risky action had two possible outcomes, one favorable and one unfavorable (compared with the sure outcome). The outcomes were clearly specified and so were the probabilities for the possible outcomes. The similar structure of the four situations allowed them to be described using the Basic Risk Paradigm as illustrated for the lawsuit in Figure 3.1. The expected value of the risky alternative was equal to the monetary outcome of the sure alternative in each situation.[1] Thus neither alternative could be preferred because it offered a higher expected payoff. The basis for choice necessarily involved the riskiness of the situation.

Each of the four decisions had characteristics that distinguished it from the others. Some of the more important features are summarized in Table 3.1. The monetary consequences differed markedly across situations ranging from losses only (e.g., customer threat) to gains only (e.g., joint venture). The largest possible monetary loss in the loss situations varied from $7 million annually (customer threat) to a one-time loss of $200,000 (union dispute). Non-monetary consequences also differed across the situations.[2]

The executive was asked to read through the materials and to specify whatever action he deemed appropriate on each item. These actions were to be written on blank memo sheets provided in the questionnaire. The memos could be addressed to whomever the executive chose. The setting for the Risk In-Basket was chosen so as to encourage the manager to respond using only the materials at hand.

Table 3.1 Comparison of Decision Situations in the Risk In-Basket

	Decision Situations			
	Lawsuit	*Customer Threat*	*Union Dispute*	*Joint Venture*
Description	Whether to settle a patent violation lawsuit out of court	Whether to comply with customer request to stop supplying competitor	Whether to comply with union request to discontinue a time-and-motion study	Whether to pursue project individually or as joint venture with competitor
Initiator	Letter from president of subsidiary	Memo from secretary	Letter from president of subsidiary	Memo from project coordinator of special task force
Non-monetary consequences	Possible entanglement in protracted litigation	Impact of action on other customers	Impact of strike on customers, employees, etc.	Implications of cooperating with competitor
Potential controllability of key uncertain events	Bargain with litigant	Reason with customer	Bargain with union	Negotiate with competitor

	Decision Situations			
	Lawsuit	*Customer Threat*	*Union Dispute*	*Joint Venture*
Basic decision tree structure	Basic Risk Paradigm: One sure action and one risky action with two possible outcomes			
Sure action	Settle out of court	Stop supplying competitor	Discontinue time-and-motion study	Pursue project jointly with competitor
Consequence	Lose $800,000	Lose $4 million annually	6.5% return on equity	14% return on investment
Risky action	Fight lawsuit in court	Continue supplying competitor	Continue time-and-motion study	Pursue project individually
Better consequence	Win case Small legal costs	Competitor does not go bankrupt Lose $3 million annually	No union strike 10% return on equity	Capture large market share 22% return on investment
Worse consequence	Lose case Lose $1.6 million	Competitor goes bankrupt Lose $7 million annually	Union strike Lose $200,000	Capture small market share 10% return on investment
Probability of better consequence	0.50	0.75	0.40	0.33
Expected value	Lose $800,000	Lose $4 million annually	Ambiguous	14% return on investment

No outside information was allowed. To discourage delay, the questionnaire stated that Mr. Bickner was scheduled to leave for an important business meeting in 35 minutes and would not return for one week. None of the materials could be taken on the trip.

NOTE ON THE DEVELOPMENT OF THE RISK IN-BASKET

The Risk In-Basket is an outgrowth of using an in-basket format to present several choice dilemma situations. The choice dilemmas have been framed using the Basic Risk Paradigm where each component has been made precise.

An *in-basket exercise* involves having a person play the role of a fictitious manager who must deal with letters, memos, phone calls, etc. that have accumulated in his in-basket. Information about the relationship of the focal person to other individuals in the organization is provided and a limited time is made available for responding to the in-basket items. Although the in-basket has been used for research purposes, it has been used primarily as a personnel selection and training vehicle (Frederiksen, Saunders, and Wand, 1957; Frederiksen, 1962).

Studies of in-basket exercises have demonstrated that participants can identify with the prescribed roles, become very involved in the decisions they face, and generally find the experience enjoyable. The fictitious setting allows some standardization across subjects for comparability, yet still permits individual personal behavior to be reflected. Moreover, the complexity and involvement generated by this technique, as well as the open-ended response, may serve to mask the research objectives of the exercise. An additional advantage of an in-Basket exercise is that its open-ended response mode can reveal the risk modifications used by executives. See Gill (1979) for a review of in-basket research.

In the usual *choice dilemmas*, the subject is asked to advise twelve different individuals in highly dissimilar settings (Kogan and Wallach, 1964, 1967; Stoner, 1961). If the situations imply a range of roles for which a person has no experience (e.g., brain surgery), is it within his capability to evaluate them reasonably? Alternating between roles may also cause confusion and inappropriate transference from one setting to the next. Therefore, it is desirable to create situations associated with a single role that is meaningful to the people whose risk propensity is being assessed. By asking executives to assume the role of a hypothetical manager and use their own experience and attitudes for making decisions in this role, the executives will more likely display their own risk propensities and we can make meaningful comparisons across executives.

Another difficulty with the typical choice dilemma problems is that the consequences are not completely specified. A person is asked the probability of success he would require in order to recommend a career as a concert pianist without being told the consequences of success and failure in that career or the consequences of staying in the current job. Thus differences in responses across individuals or across situations may be due solely to different assumptions about these unknown consequences. By specifying the quantitative aspects of the consequences much of this ambiguity should be removed, and one can also calculate the "break-even" probability that separates risk taking from risk aversion.

In combining the *Basic Risk Paradigm* with a role-playing exercise, however, there is the danger of an executive introducing additional considerations so his interpretation of the situation could be different from the decision structure intended. After anticipating and trying to remove the basis for such difficulties, one must decide whether the possible complications outweigh the additional interest of a richer context than the Basic Risk Paradigm.

We applied the in-basket format to risky situations in a series of pilot studies conducted prior to the main study. These applications involved as many as 13 items, including both business and personal situations. An extensive pilot test of 170 undergraduate students and 30 graduate students provided responses on seven items. In addition to the four items in the current instrument it included a new product introduction, a job offer for the executive, and a letter from the executive's son asking advice on his academic study. The latter item was found to elicit unusable results and was discarded. The remaining six items were further tested in a pilot study of 40 business executives. Although each of the six items was deemed usable, two were dropped to reduce the time requirements for the Risk In-Basket.

After the executive had written his memo responses to each of the four situations, he was asked to respond to each situation in two additional ways. First he was asked to give a rating of his inclination to take the sure or the risky action. Then he was asked to assume that the likelihood of success for the risky action had not been specified and to state the lowest chance for which he would take the risky action. Thus in the lawsuit situation an executive who had taken the sure action (i.e., settling out of court) should have increased the probability of winning the suit from 0.50 up to the point where he would just be indifferent between the two actions. An executive who had selected the risky action (i.e., go to court) presumably would lower the probability below 0.50 to the point at which he was indifferent between the two actions. These numbers are called probability equivalences. The manager was given the opportunity to check a box indicating that he would select the sure alternative no matter what the chances of success of the risky action (i.e., probability of 1.0) or to check a box indicating that he would select the risky action no matter what the chances of success (i.e., a probability of zero). See the Appendix for the specific form used in the lawsuit.

The time for completing the entire Risk In-Basket was specified as 45 minutes. This included 35 minutes for writing the memo responses and 10 minutes for completing the ratings and probability equivalences.

In summary, the principal characteristics of the Risk In-Basket are as follows: (1) it provides a business context in which the executive is asked to play a single hypothetical role; (2) the decision situations are developed around the Basic Risk Paradigm in which all actions, consequences, and probabilities are well-specified; and (3) various types of responses (i.e., written memos, ratings, and probability equivalences) are used to uncover a wide variety of risk modifications and to provide alternative means for the executives to reveal their risk propensities. In our judgment these characteristics are preferable to those offered by the widely used choice dilemma situations, and they provide a richer setting to explore risk modifications than abstract versions of the Basic Risk Paradigm.

To the best of our knowledge, this was the first study that used an in-basket format to measure risk propensity. The use of an in-basket as a context for the Basic Risk Paradigm is one of the unique contributions of this study.

We obtained complete responses—memos, ratings, and probability equivalences—for all four situations from 464 executives. Coding for the ratings and probability equivalences was straightforward.[3] Obviously it is more difficult to code and interpret the memo responses. A representative sample of the written memos revealed that the memos averaged about 75 words for each situation, ranging from a low of three words to a high of about 250 words. The quotes cited in the beginning of this chapter were taken from these memos. Most of the written memos were addressed to the author of the in-basket letter or memo.

We did a content analysis of the written memos to assess the managers' willingness to take risks. An aversion to risk is reflected in

1. An inclination to take the sure action, e.g., settle out of court
2. An inclination to collect more information, e.g., check with another lawyer
3. An inclination to delay, e.g., see if the firm threatening legal action will wait
4. An inclination to delegate, e.g., let the initiator of the memo decide for himself

The content analysis provided us with four separate scores for each written memo. The first score characterized the actions specified in the memo in terms of their *propensity toward riskiness*. The second score described the executive's *propensity to seek information or bargain*. The third score described the executive's *propensity to delay*. The last score indicated the executive's *propensity to delegate*.

Overall, then, we have six scores for each manager in each of the four decision situations—a rating of his inclination to take the sure or risky action, a probability equivalence, and the four scores from the content analysis of the written memo.

NOTE ON CODING THE WRITTEN MEMO RESPONSES AND THEIR INTER-CODER RELIABILITY

The content analysis was performed using two coders. Both coders had business experience, were familiar with the types of situations described, and had handled memos written by executives.[4]

The coders were given coding categories which had been developed by the principal investigators during the pilot phase of the study. Each of the coders and a principal investigator independently coded about 100 written memos (four situations, 25 executives), and the assigned codes were compared. Differences in scoring were discussed to clarify the categories. Finally, the two coders independently scored the remaining written memos.

Three scores were coded for each written memo response. The first score characterized the actions specified in the memo in terms of *propensity toward riskiness*. Each coder assigned either one of eight riskiness codes ranging from strong risk taking to strong risk averting or a separate code indicating no actions were specified. Before using these scores, it is important to examine their inter-coder reliability. When the coding categories under consideration are at least ordinal, the degree of association is an appropriate measure of reliability and Spearman correlation coefficients are suitable.[5] The degree of association between the coders on the eight riskiness codes of the *memo risk score* was moderately high. The correlations ranged from 0.67 to 0.87 in the four situations.[6] We concluded that the inter-coder reliability was sufficiently high to use the eight risk categories as defined. The two coders' scores were averaged to obtain a combined memo risk score.[7]

The second score described the executive's *propensity to seek information*. Five codes were used to describe whether the executive mentioned collecting information and any actions he specified to obtain it. If the executive mentioned bargaining, negotiating, or presenting a new alternative, this was coded in a separate category since it was viewed as an extreme form of information gathering.[8] The inter-coder reliability for the *memo information score* was somewhat lower than for the memo risk score. Including the bargaining responses as an extreme form of information collection yielded acceptable inter-coder correlations of 0.71 and 0.66 for the lawsuit and customer threat situations, respectively. The relatively low degree of association between the coders in the union dispute (0.42) and joint venture (0.58) suggested that some collapsing of response categories would improve the reliability of the data. Subsequently the six-point scale was collapsed into three categories.[9] The two coders' memo information scores were averaged to obtain a combined memo information score.[10]

The third score described the executive's *propensity to delay or delegate* the decision. Delay and delegation were considered on the same scale because we believed executives would not simultaneously delay and delegate the decision. Some actions such as collecting information and bargaining involve delaying the decision. These actions were not coded as delay responses unless they specifically mentioned delaying the decision as well. Three codes each were used for the delay and delegate responses as well as a single code when there was no mention of either delay or delegation.[11] Inter-coder reliability for the *memo delay/delegation score* was generally weak when both the delay and delegation codes were considered simultaneously. When the delegation responses were considered separately, reliability was also low. On the other hand, the inter-coder reliability was acceptably high (0.56 to 0.77) when only the delay responses were considered separately.[12] We concluded that the delay measure was acceptable, but analyses based on the delegation measure must be treated carefully. Codes that combined the two coders' scores were derived separately for delay and delegation. Only simple dichotomous codes that described the presence or absence of an action to delay (delegate) were derived because of the inter-coder reliability problems mentioned above.[13]

RESEARCH FINDINGS

Do Executives Try to Adjust the Risks They Face?

The answer is generally yes. The managers tried to adjust 63 percent of the situations they confronted by either gathering information, bargaining, delaying, or delegating the decision. Only 4 percent of the managers did not modify any of the four situations; 22 percent tried to modify each of the situations they faced. Both of these percentages are more than twice the percentages predicted by chance, indicating managers tend to be consistent in their attempts to modify risky situations.[14] This result may be summarized as follows.

> ***Result:*** Managers commonly attempted to adjust risky alternatives rather than simply choosing among them.

This result can have important implications for management. By studying how a manager modifies the risks he faces, we can better understand how adaptable and imaginative he is in arranging a more favorable situation. The propensity to modify risks reveals as much about a person's willingness to take risks as do his choices among the alternatives themselves.

Now that we know that managers adjust risky situations, we turn our attention to the specific risk modifications and examine how frequently they are used.

Do Executives Attempt to Collect Information or Bargain Before Making a Risky Choice?

The executives specified actions to collect additional (non-bargaining) information in 31% of their memos. In the large majority of these cases they requested specific information (e.g., "try to get an independent estimate of our chances of winning in court") and stated specific actions (e.g., "I want a full briefing on the grounds for the lawsuit on my return from Mexico"). Collecting information was about equally common in all four situations. Executives who collected information in one situation tended to collect it in other situations as well.[15]

The managers tried to bargain in 14% of their memos. Not surprisingly, they recommended bargaining about three times as often in the lawsuit and union dispute decisions where there was an adversarial relationship as in the other two cases.[16] The executives may have felt that it was easier to influence the outcomes in the lawsuit and union dispute situations. For example, they could bargain with the litigant in the lawsuit and with the union in the dispute over the time-and-motion study. The executives may have also considered reasoning with the major customer in the customer threat, but ethical considerations may have precluded it. Bargaining usually took the form of developing new options (e.g., "ask the union leader if he would consider working out a mutually satisfactory agreement"). No manager sought to negotiate in all four situations, although a majority of executives attempted to negotiate in at least one situation.

> ***Result:*** Managers frequently sought additional information before making risky decisions. Attempts at bargaining were common when the uncertainties were due to the actions of other people who might be influenced.

In many risky situations managers cannot control key uncertain events which are determined by such factors as financial markets, consumer markets, and natural forces. This was the case in the joint venture where the market share was unknown. In these cases managers are still likely to seek information about the possible outcomes of risky alternatives and their chances of occurrence. When the uncertain events are determined by identifiable individuals, managers are likely to try to control the events by influencing these people through activities such as bargaining and lobbying. Modifying risky situations by collecting information and bargaining provides a useful means of reducing the risks one faces.

Do Executives Attempt to Delay Risky Decisions?

The managers specified delaying the decision in 28% of their memos. Most of these actions involved a temporary delay until the executive returned from his trip. Only about 2% of the memos suggested a delay of indefinite duration. The propensity to delay was relatively constant over all four decision situations. In another 12% of the memos the managers mentioned delay but rejected it in favor of other risk modifications or choosing between the two alternatives. Executives who delayed their decision in one situation tended to delay decisions in the other situations as well.

Result: Managers frequently delayed their risky decisions.

An effective way for managers to modify the risky situations they face is to control the timing of their decisions. Delaying important risky decisions allows events to evolve, new factors to come to light, and time for new options to be developed. Gathering information and bargaining are other ways a manager can use time to better understand and possibly control his risks. For example, requests for in-depth studies are a common mechanism by which managers can delay difficult decisions under the guise of gathering information. Delay in all of its forms provides a valuable opportunity for reducing the riskiness of a situation.

Do Executives Attempt to Delegate Risky Decisions?

The managers delegated the decision in 30% of the memos. Usually the delegation was to the top executive in the subsidiary who had raised the problem in the first place (e.g., "you are clearly in a better position to handle this than I am"). Delegation was about twice as common in the lawsuit and union dispute cases as in the other situations.[17] This could be expected since the lawsuit and union dispute decisions both involved events at subsidiaries while the other two situations occurred at the head office. Although the executives delegated their decisions, in most cases they made recommendations for the action they would take. Thus they were sharing the risks rather than avoiding them completely (e.g., "although you should decide, I'm inclined to fight it out in court").

Result: Managers frequently delegated their decisions, usually with a recommendation for action. This was more common when a key individual was available to assume responsibility for the decision.

Top-level executives cannot make all the decisions in their firms' operations. Decentralized decision making requires delegation. But delegating a decision also provides a means for sharing or avoiding the risks in a difficult decision. A common form of delegation used to share risks is "decision by committee" where individual accountability for the decision is obscured and personal exposure is limited.

NOTE ON THE RISK MODIFICATIONS

The results on the risk modifications were based on the coders' combined scores as described in the technical note on page 87. Because of the ambiguous way that risk modifications were sometimes expressed in the memos, the classifications made by the coders sometimes differed. By recognizing the modification if either coder scored it, we can obtain an upper bound on its frequency of occurrence; by recognizing the modification only if both coders scored it, we can obtain a lower bound. Generally the coders' combined scores gave results closer to the upper bounds. We presented an analysis of the risk modifications using these upper and lower bounds in MacCrimmon and Wehrung (1984).

The 464 executives who provided complete responses to the Risk In-Basket specified the following risk modifications in the four business decisions. The numbers represent the percentages of executives who requested the specified actions in the particular situations.

ACTIONS SPECIFIED	DECISION SITUATIONS (PERCENTAGES)			
	Lawsuit	*Customer Threat*	*Union Dispute*	*Joint Venture*
Collect (nonbargaining) information	28	26	33	37
Bargain	25	7	22	2
Delay decision	27	26	27	30
Delegate decision	38	23	38	23

Are the Executives Generally Risk-Taking in the In-Basket Situations?

Overall the answer is yes. We found this propensity to take risks in the risk ratings, the probability equivalences, and the written memos. We will examine these results in turn, leaving differences across the four situations to a later section.

Table 3.2 Distributions of Risk Ratings by Decision Situation (Percentages)

RISK RATING		DECISION SITUATION			
Description	*Codes*	*Law-suit*	*Customer Threat*	*Union Dispute*	*Joint Venture*
INCLINED TO TAKE	0.0– 1.0	8	4	16	14
SURE ACTION	1.5– 2.5	11	3	8	18
	3.0– 4.0	10	5	6	11
RISK-NEUTRAL	4.5– 5.5	6	6	5	8
INCLINED TO TAKE	6.0– 7.0	16	7	9	13
RISKY ACTION	7.5– 8.5	28	27	24	15
	9.0–10.0	21	48	32	21
Total		100	100	100	100
Median Risk Rating		7.2	8.7	7.8	5.2
Mean Risk Rating		6.2	7.8	6.2	5.2

The simplest indication of risk propensity is the *risk rating* provided by each executive. This rating gives the executive's inclination to take the sure or the risky alternative on an eleven-point scale. Table 3.2 shows the distributions of these risk ratings for each of the situations. Ignoring the few middle ratings that indicate risk neutrality, we found that more than twice as many executives were inclined to take the risky action over the sure action on average over the four situations. Thus significantly more executives were risk-taking than risk-averting.[18] In fact, half of the risk ratings were at the extreme risk-taking end of the scale.

Executives whose probability equivalence was lower than the break-even chance of success (given in Table 3.1) were willing to give up a *probability premium* to take the risky action.[19] Such negative probability premiums imply risk taking, while positive probability premiums (i.e., probability equivalence higher than break-even probability) imply risk aversion. Table 3.3 shows the distributions of probability premiums for each situation.[20] An average of about 20 percent of the executives over the four situations had probability premiums between −0.10 and 0.10, which we labeled as risk-neutral. Among the remaining executives, twice as many had negative probability premiums as had positive ones, indicating significantly more risk taking than risk aversion. In 27% of the cases the executive indicated he would take the risky action no matter what the chances of the favorable outcome.

The content analysis of the actions specified in the managers' written memos provided a measure of their riskiness on an eight-

Table 3.3 Distributions of Probability Premiums by Decision Situation (Percentages)

Probability Premium		Decision Situation			
Description	*Codes*	*Law-suit*	*Customer Threat*	*Union Dispute*	*Joint Venture*
Risk-Taking	−.90 to −.71		41		
	−.70 to −.51		10		
	−.50 to −.31	8	17	42	18
	−.30 to −.11	27	18	16	11
Risk-Neutral	−.10 to .10	41	9	13	21
Risk-Averting	.11 to .30	20	5	4	29
	.31 to .50	4		7	15
	.51 to .70			18	6
Total		100	100	100	100
Median Probability Premium		−.09	−.55	−.20	.12
Mean Probability Premium		−.04	−.48	−.06	.07

Blank indicates category not possible for decision situation.

point scale. Table 3.4 shows the distribution of *memo risk* scores for the four situations. About 15 percent of the cases were judged to be risk-neutral. The actions specified by the remaining executives indicated risk taking was about twice as frequent as risk aversion, on average over the situations. Here too, then, significantly more executives were risk-taking than risk-averting.

> ***Result:*** Overall, the executives showed a marked willingness to take risks in the in-basket business decisions.

That managers are willing to take business risks is not surprising. Taking risks is an important part of a manager's job.

Note on the risk measures

The risk ratings ranged from 0 (risk-averting) to 10 (risk-taking) and had a risk-neutral value of 5. The probability premiums ranged from $-p$ (risk-taking) to $1-p$ (risk-averting) where p was the break-even probability of a successful outcome in the risky alternative. This value changed in the four in-basket situations ($p = 0.50, 0.75, 0.40$, and 0.33, respectively), so the range changed as well. In each situation the risk-neutral value was zero. The memo risk scores ranged from 1 (risk-averting) to 8 (risk-taking) and had a risk-neutral value of 4.5.

Table 3.4 Distributions of Memo Risk Scores by Decision Situation (Percentages)

Memo Risk Score		Decision Situation			
Description	*Codes*	*Law-suit*	*Customer Threat*	*Union Dispute*	*Joint Venture*
Strong Risk-Averting	1.0–2.0	10	4	13	25
Risk-Averting Inclination	2.5–3.5	12	7	21	20
Risk-Neutral	4.0–5.0	15	14	18	13
Risk-Taking Inclination	5.5–6.5	36	32	15	18
Strong Risk-Taking	7.0–8.0	27	43	33	24
Total		100	100	100	100
Median Memo Risk Score		5.8	6.6	5.1	4.2
Mean Memo Risk Score		5.4	6.0	5.0	4.5

Are the Risk Propensities Derived from an Executive's Written Memos, Probability Equivalences, and Risk Ratings Related?

We found the three different response modes to be interrelated in each of the four situations. The relationships among the memo risk scores, probability premiums, and risk ratings were especially strong in the joint venture and union dispute situations. However, even in the customer threat where these associations were weakest, they were far greater than chance would predict.

> ***Result:*** The executives showed related propensities for risk in their written memos, probability equivalences, and risk ratings.

Just because we find *related* risk propensities using different means to obtain them does not mean that executives show the *same* willingness to take risks. We address this issue next.

Does an Executive Show the Same Willingness to Take Risks in His Written Memos, Probability Equivalences, and Risk Ratings?

We found earlier that there was more risk taking than risk aversion on average over all executives in the four situations. For an individual manager, though, we found somewhat different risk propensities in a situation depending upon which method was used to obtain them. In general the risk ratings (i.e., the inclinations to take the sure or risky alternative) reflected greater risk taking than either the written memos or the probability equivalences, on average over the four situations. The written memos showed somewhat greater risk taking than the probability equivalences, but there was very high variability across the four situations.

> ***Result:*** Managers showed a greater willingness to take risks in their risk ratings than in their written memos or probability equivalences.

That the risk ratings reflected the greatest willingness to take risks should not be surprising. It is easy to indicate on a simple scale that one is more inclined toward the risky alternative than the safe one. Because our culture tends to place a high value on taking risks, attitudinal indications of risk propensity such as the risk ratings are likely to exhibit greater risk taking than behavioral measures derived from written memos and probability equivalences. This result suggests that we should not rely solely on what a manager says is his inclination toward risk. Instead we should augment what he says by observing his behavior in risky situations.

NOTE ON COMPARISONS AMONG RESPONSE MODES

The correlations among the three response modes within a decision situation are given below for the 400 executives for whom all measures were available.

	DECISION SITUATIONS			
RESPONSE MODES	*Lawsuit*	*Customer Threat*	*Union Dispute*	*Joint Venture*
Memo risk vs. risk rating	0.69	0.56	0.72	0.80
Memo risk vs. probability premium	0.58	0.46	0.60	0.70
Risk rating vs. probability premium	0.63	0.42	0.74	0.74

All correlations are significantly positive at far greater than the 0.001 level.

The correlations among the measures derived *within* a situation are moderate to very high. These correlations are highest in the joint venture situation (0.70 to 0.80) and lowest in the customer threat situation (0.42 to 0.56). Thus an executive's responses within a decision situation provide moderately to highly related information regarding his risk propensity.

We also compared the response modes by dividing the executives into three absolute risk categories (risk-taking, risk-neutral, and risk-averting) for each measure. The risk-neutral group for the memo risk score included values 4.0–5.0, for the risk rating included values 4.5–5.5, and for the probability premium included values −0.10 to 0.10. Comparisons involving the memo risk score included 445, 426, 460, and 440 executives, respectively, for the four situations because some written memos specified no actions and were excluded from consideration. The remaining comparisons included 464 executives.

For an average of 75 percent of the executives over the four situations there were no differences in the risk categories for the risk ratings and memo risk scores. In the one out of four cases that differed, the risk rating showed significantly greater risk taking than the memo risk (sign test, 0.01 significance level). More specifically, the table below shows that an average of 64 percent of the executives who were in different categories were more risk-taking in their ratings.

An average of 64 percent of the executives fell into the same risk category for memo risk and probability premium. When the measures differed, the memo risk score on average showed somewhat greater risk taking than the probability premium, but the variation across situations was so high that no firm conclusion could be drawn.

We found no differences in the risk categories for the risk ratings and the probability premiums for an average of 70 percent of the executives. For the cases in which the two measures differed, the risk rating indicated significantly more risk taking than did the probability premium.

Response Modes	Greater Risk Taking	Decision Situations (Percentages)				
		Lawsuit	*Customer Threat*	*Union Dispute*	*Joint Venture*	*Average*
Memo risk vs. risk rating	Risk rating	44	68	77	67	64
Memo risk vs. probability premium	Memo risk	78	21	37	76	53
Risk rating vs. probability premium	Risk rating	75	35	65	84	65

Are the Executives' Risk Propensities in Different Business Situations Related?

We found the relationships across the four business situations to be either weak or nonexistent. This was true even when the same method (i.e., written memo, probability equivalence, or risk rating) was used to assess risk propensity. The probability premiums gave the most consistent relationships across situations. This measure of risk propensity showed weak positive associations across the lawsuit, customer threat, and joint venture situations.

> ***Result:*** A manager's willingness to take risks across different business decisions was at best weakly related.

We tried to make the business decisions in the Risk In-Basket as realistic as possible. Although each decision represented a choice between a sure and a risky course of action, the situations differed on several attributes, as summarized in Table 3.1. These differences in the contexts of the decisions are the likely reason why the risk propensities varied so much across the four situations. We cannot expect managers to show the same risk behavior in situations that differ so greatly, even if they have a common underlying risk propensity influencing their actions.

NOTE ON COMPARISONS AMONG DECISION SITUATIONS

The correlations among the different situations for a *common response mode* are given below. This data is based on 400 executives for whom all measures were available and only correlations significantly different from zero at the 0.01 level are shown.

	COMMON RESPONSE MODE		
DECISION SITUATIONS	*Memo Risk*	*Risk Rating*	*Probability Premium*
Lawsuit vs. customer threat			0.13
Lawsuit vs. union dispute			
Lawsuit vs. joint venture	0.14		0.16
Customer threat vs. union dispute	0.12		
Customer threat vs. joint venture		0.15	0.20
Union dispute vs. joint venture		−0.11	

Ten of the 36 correlations across different situations and *different response modes* were also significantly different from zero. However they were low, ranging from 0.11 to 0.15 in absolute value, and they showed no particular pattern.

The consistency we found among different risk measures *within* a situation (i.e., different response modes) and the lack of consistency *across* situations was confirmed using a factor analysis. Four common factors, each representing a different decision context, explained 80% of the variation in the 12 risk measures (i.e., four situations times three response modes).

This result was also confirmed by comparing each executive's risk propensity to that of the other managers in the study. Among the executives who fell into either the top or bottom third on each of a particular situation's response mode measures, 30% were relative risk takers on each measure and 48% were relative risk averters on each measure, on average over the four situations. A random effect here would find only 12.5% ($1/2^3$) in each of these groups. Among the executives who fell into either the top or bottom third for each situation of a given response mode measure, 10% were relative risk takers in each situation and 9% were relative risk averters in each situation, on average over the three response modes. A random effect here would find 6.25% ($1/2^4$) in each of these groups. These distributions reinforce the observation that the responses within a decision context provide highly related information about an executive's risk propensities, but the responses across decision contexts do not.

Given the considerable variability across contexts, it would be difficult to justify pooling the measures over the four situations to get an aggregate risk score. This variability *across four seemingly related business contexts* reinforces our skepticism about aggregating responses in the standard choice dilemmas in which a person confronts situations as diverse as football, brain surgery, concert performance, and job change.

In Which Decisions Are the Executives Most Risk-Taking and in Which Are They Most Risk-Averse?

The typical executive is extremely risk-taking in the customer threat situation. See Tables 3.2 to 3.4. The customer threat had a higher number of extremely strong risk-taking responses than any other situation.[21] In both the lawsuit and union dispute situations the typical executive is moderately risk-taking. For these three situations we found this same pattern in the written memos, probability equivalences, and risk ratings. In the joint venture the probability premium indicated twice as many risk-averting responses as risk-taking responses. For the risk ratings and memo risk scores, the difference was insignificant.[22] All differences between situations were statistically significant, except for the difference between the lawsuit and union dispute situations.[23]

> ***Result:*** The managers were most risk-taking in the customer threat situation and most risk-averse in the joint venture.

These results mean we can expect managers to show very different willingness to undertake risks in widely different business situations. One noticeable difference between the customer threat and joint venture situations is in the possible outcomes. The customer threat involves only losses, while the joint venture involves only gains. This observation suggests managers might take more risks for losses than for gains. We will address this possibility next.

Are Executives More Risk-Taking in Threat Situations (Involving Only Losses) than in Opportunity Situations (Involving Only Gains)?

The greatest risk taking occurred for the customer threat. This situation involves the possibility of loss (up to $7 million per year), but no chance of gain. The lawsuit and the union dispute both elicited moderate risk taking. The lawsuit involves only losses (with a maximum possible loss of $1.6 million) and status quo, while the union dispute has the possibility of gains and losses. For the joint venture there was a slight inclination toward risk aversion. This situation differs in that there is no chance of loss (the worst that can happen is receiving only a 10% after-tax return). Overall, then, we found the seemingly paradoxical result that executives took risks when there were possibly large negative payoffs, and they avoided risks when there was no chance of an absolute loss (from status quo).[24]

> ***Result:*** The executives were risk-taking for business decisions involving only losses. Risk aversion was more common when only gains were possible.

This result has also been found in studies of Kahneman and Tversky (1979) using monetary gambles. One possible explanation is that if the sure payoff seems quite good (e.g., 14% after-tax return on investment), then people will settle for it in situations in which all payoffs are positive. When no payoffs are positive, people are adverse toward accepting a large sure loss (e.g., settling out of court) and choose the risky action because they either underemphasize the magnitude of the largest possible loss or underestimate the chance of this loss. Another explanation for risk taking over losses but risk aversion over gains is an ecological one. Over a series of major decisions, the person who settles for sure losses is not likely to be promoted, so we would not observe him in our sample of top executives. It is also true that we would not observe the person who takes the risk and loses. Thus, we are most likely to be dealing with people who have experienced relative success in bad situations by taking risks. It would not be surprising that these people are likely to take risks again.

The widespread differences in risk propensity across business decisions indicate that it is inappropriate to generalize a willingness to take risks from one situation to other situations. Generalizations can be particularly misleading if one situation involves only gains and another situation involves only losses. Knowledge of a person's risk propensities in a variety of situations could help to assure that the person's risk propensity corresponded to the attitude toward risk desired by the firm.

Do Executives Who Adjust the Risks They Face Tend to Be Risk-Averse?

If collecting information, bargaining, delaying, and delegating are indicative of an aversion to risk, they should be positively associated with our measures of risk propensity. This was true for a majority of the risk modifications in the four situations.

We related the memo risk score in each situation with the risk modifications.[25] The propensity to use *at least one* of the risk modifications was significantly related to the propensity to avoid risks in each of the four decision situations. Actions to collect information or bargain were significantly related to a desire to avoid risks in three of the four decision situations.[26] The difference was insignificant for the union dispute. Actions taken to delay the decision were significantly associated with the propensity to avoid risks in the customer threat and union dispute situations, but not in the lawsuit and joint venture situations. Actions taken to delegate the decision were significantly associated with risk avoidance in the same two situations.[27]

> ***Result:*** The managers' propensity to modify risks by gathering information, bargaining, delaying, or delegating was positively associated with their propensity to avoid risks by choosing a safe alternative in lieu of a risky one.

Collecting information, bargaining, delaying, and delegating are prudent management practices. We have found, however, that these attempts to adjust risky situations are also related to a propensity to avoid risks. Therefore, if you want to know whether someone will ultimately choose the safer or more risky course of action, you should look to see if he modifies the risks before choosing. An executive who does not like the risky alternatives before him is likely to initiate actions to understand or to influence the underlying uncertain events, to delay, or to shift responsibility for the decision.

CONCLUSIONS

The Risk In-Basket is a very effective way to study risk modifications and to assess risk propensity. We found that the executives frequently preferred to adjust the risky situations they faced rather than to choose *personally, at the present time, with the information given.* We can infer, then, that when an executive does not like the risky alternatives before him, he may initiate actions to shift responsibility for the decision, to delay, to understand, or to influence the underlying uncertain events. Executives who attempted to modify risks in one business decision tended to modify the risks in other situations as well.

The managers did show a marked willingness to take risks in three of the four decision situations. The executives revealed very similar risk propensities in their written memos, their rating of inclination toward the sure or risky alternative, and their probability equivalences. An executive's propensity toward risk varied widely, however, across business situations. Risk taking was common in situations that involved only losses, while risk aversion was more likely when only gains were possible. Modifying risks by collecting information, bargaining, delaying, and delegating was positively associated with a desire to avoid risks. These important relationships highlight the importance of studying an executive's risk modifications to gain better insight into his risk propensity.

By using the Risk In-Basket as a microcosm for risky decision making, we have learned a great deal about the variety of ways in which managers handle realistic risky situations. The Risk In-Basket can also be used as a training device whereby managers in a firm can share their means of dealing with risky decisions in a simulated environment.

RESEARCH CONCLUSIONS

1. The Risk In-Basket provides a unique instrument for studying risk. The coupling of the clear specification of outcomes and probabilities with a common hypothetical role for the subject is a significant improvement over the standard choice dilemmas. The open-ended memo response mode allows the executives to specify how they would handle the risky situation. The congruence of the memo results with those of two additional response modes (i.e., a scale rating and a probability equivalence) provided assurance of the validity of the responses. Few of the findings in this study could have been determined with previous instruments.

2. Our findings have implications for both theoretical and empirical research. The prevalence of attempts to modify risk suggests the desirability of expanding existing theories of risk beyond a narrow focus on choice. We can learn as much, if not more, about risk behavior by studying how decision makers adjust the risks they face through collecting information, bargaining, delaying, and delegating as by examining which alternative they choose. Recent models of risk sharing in an agency context are a step in this direction. The dependence of risk propensity on decision context suggests the need to develop theories of risk behavior con-

ditional on characteristics of contexts such as gains or losses, the presence or absence of adversaries, whether the problem was referred by someone else, and so forth.

3. Our findings also demonstrate the need for more studies focusing on risk modification in a variety of situations. The response modes need to be flexible enough to allow the natural risk modifications to emerge, yet structured enough to allow the empirical results to be related back to theory. The connections we have found between risk modifications and risk avoidance need to be more systematically investigated. Despite the significant relationships we found among different measures of risk propensity, subsequent empirical studies should continue the practice of deriving multiple measures from different response modes. One needs to be particularly cautious about attitudinally-based measures which may tend to provide a bias toward risk taking because of the cultural value attributed to people who take risks.

Chapter 4

Investment Gambles

Choosing in Risky Personal and Business Situations

INTRODUCTION

Suppose you are offered a new venture that requires an investment of half your net wealth. The venture has a 50-50 chance of succeeding. How large would the possible payoff have to be for you to accept the venture? A decision tree representation of this choice is given in Figure 4.1.

Consider various possible answers to the question. First, consider the "actuarially fair" amount: one and one-half times your net wealth.[1] Although people may accept actuarially fair gambles for small stakes (e.g., betting $5 on the toss of a coin), it is extremely unlikely that someone would stake half his net wealth when the possible gain was only half his net wealth. For instance, if an individual had a net wealth of $200,000 we would not expect him to risk losing $100,000 if he could only end up with $300,000 with a 50-50 chance. Most people would require a potential gain much larger than $100,000. Some might engage in the gamble if they could end up with a wealth level of $400,000. Others may require a final wealth of $1 million. Still others may not accept the gamble no matter how much the possible gain.

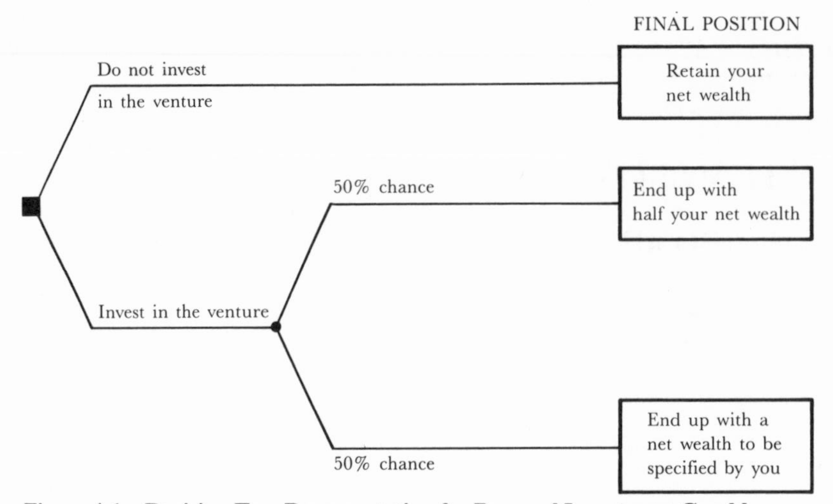

Figure 4.1 Decision Tree Representation for Personal Investment Gamble

---

NOTE ON EXPECTED UTILITY THEORY

The most widely accepted approach to studying risk is expected utility theory. Bernoulli (1738), von Neumann and Morgenstern (1947), and Savage (1954) developed the foundations of the theory. From a set of axioms a representation theorem is developed that requires the choice of the action having the highest expected utility. The expected utility of any action is calculated by multiplying the probability of each uncertain event by the utility of the outcome arising from the event and adding up all these mutually exclusive and exhaustive products. To use expected utility theory as a normative guide to choice, one must have utility functions obtained from preference judgments. There are various techniques for obtaining utility functions, summarized in Keeney and Raiffa (1976) and Farquhar (1984), including the methods of Davidson, Suppes, and Siegel (1957), Becker, DeGroot, and Marschak (1964), and Schlaifer (1971). In terms of the Basic Risk Paradigm we need to specify any three of the four elements of the gamble: certainty amount, gain amount, loss amount, and probability. The element that is left unspecified is supplied by the individual whose utility we are assessing. If we leave the gain amount unspecified, the procedure is called a *gain equivalence* procedure, and similarly for the other elements. Typically a certainty equivalence procedure or a probability equivalence procedure is used. From a theoretical point of view it does not matter which procedure is used because if a person satisfies the axioms and hence maximizes expected utility, we will obtain the same utility function. For reasons to be discussed later, we are using a gain equivalence procedure here.

A person's answer to such questions can be shown on a graph. In Figure 4.2a the horizontal axis depicts multiples of net wealth while the vertical axis is the preference index of the gamble. A dot has been placed at B (i.e., $200,000) which is our example person's current net wealth. Another dot has been placed at A (i.e., $100,000) which represents half of net wealth. These dots represent the specified part of the gamble. The amount required to accept a 50-50 gamble is plotted on the top line. For example, if he would accept a wealth multiple of one and one-half (i.e., $300,000 in our example), then the actuarially fair point C is relevant. More likely the response would be to the right of this point. Point D indicates a multiple of 2 and point E represents a multiple of 5 (i.e., the required ending wealth levels of $400,000 and $1 million discussed above).

The reason for drawing a graph of the response is twofold: (1) when we ask additional questions it is easy to see how the responses fit together into a picture of risk propensity, and (2) it allows us to obtain a visual comparison of the risk propensity of one person versus the risk propensity of others.

Suppose we now change the chances from 50-50 to a 30% chance of losing and a 70% chance of winning. That is, if you had a 30% chance of losing half your net wealth and a 70% chance of ending up with some higher net wealth, how high would this amount have to be for you to accept this gamble rather than rejecting the gamble and keeping your net wealth? The response to this question would be plotted on the second line from the top. The actuarially fair answer is a final wealth position 1.21 times your current one (i.e., a final wealth of $242,000 at point C′ in our example). As before, it seems very unlikely that someone would accept such a gamble. Virtually everyone would require a larger wealth multiple such as $275,000 (point D′) or $440,000 (point E′).

Assume for the moment that we have three people, one of whom gave the answers C and C′, the second gave the answers D and D′, while the third gave the answers E and E′. These answers have been denoted by dots in Figure 4.2a. We have drawn smooth curves through each set of dots, always including the original points A and B in each set. What can we say about the risk propensity of these three people? As we have discussed, person C gives the actuarially fair response. He neither avoids nor accepts risk, so he would be called *risk-neutral*. His *preference curve* is a straight line.

Persons D and E are both *risk-averse* with E being more risk-averse since his answers are further to the right. Their preference curves get flatter as we move to the right. A *risk taker*, who has not been depicted, would have a curve that bends upward.[2]

NOTE ON ASSESSING UTILITY FUNCTIONS

We are assessing a utility function, U, over multiples, k, of net wealth. We can scale the function by arbitrarily assigning a utility value of zero to half of net wealth and a utility value of one to current net wealth, i.e., $U(0.5)=0$ and $U(1)=1$. By the definition of a gain equivalence we must have equal expected utilities for accepting and not accepting the risky investment. Hence, $U(1)=(1-p)U(k)+pU(0.5)$, where p is the chance of loss. After substituting for $U(0.5)=0$ and $U(1)=1$, we obtain $U(k)=1/(1-p)$. For $p=0.5$, we have $U(k)=2$; for $p=0.3$, we have $U(k)=1.43$. These values for U define the heights of the horizontal lines in Figure 4.2. When $k=0.5(2-p)/(1-p)$, we have risk neutrality. The corresponding utility function is $U(k)=-1+2k$, which is an extension of the line between A and B. Risk-averse responses are those for which $k>0.5(2-p)/(1-p)$ and risk-taking responses are those for which $1<k<0.5(2-p)/(1-p)$.

It is possible that someone could be risk-averse in one region of net wealth levels and risk-taking in other regions. This would lead to a preference curve such as the one labeled F in Figure 4.2b. Person F has given responses that indicate he is risk-averse in the region from A to P and is risk-taking in the region from Q to Z.[3]

So far we have only asked two questions. One involved 50-50 chances, while the other involved 70-30 chances. By changing the chances to some other levels and asking more questions we can obtain additional information from which to assess risk propensity.

There is no reason to confine our attention to assessing risk propensity for personal investments. We can just as easily assess risk propensity for business investments. For example, suppose instead of investing your firm's capital expenditure budget in standard projects which provide your usual rate of return, you have an opportunity to invest half your budget in a new project. The new project has a 50% chance of providing no payoff at all, but it has a corresponding 50% chance of yielding a larger than usual payoff. How large would this payoff have to be (in terms of multiples of your usual rate of return) for you to invest?

In the same way that we drew preference curves for your answers to the personal wealth questions, we can draw preference curves for business gambles. Do you think that you would be more risk-averse for personal investments or for business investments? In the remainder of this chapter, we will describe what we found when we used these procedures to assess the personal and business preference curves of the top-level business executives in our study.

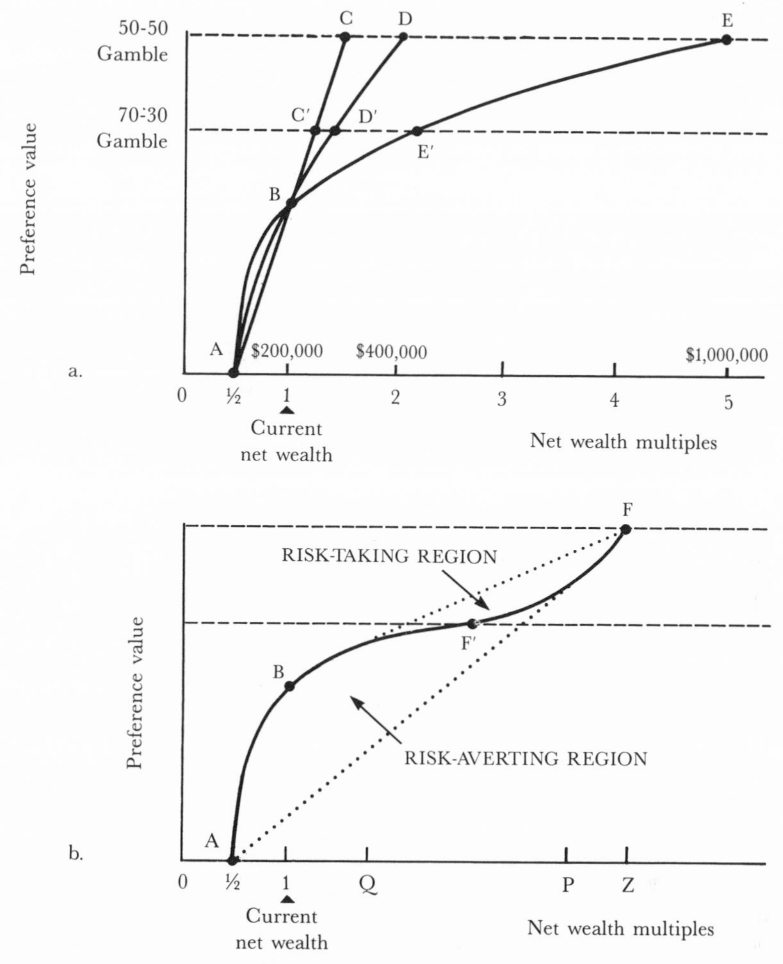

Figure 4.2 Examples of Preference Curves

OUR STUDY

We used an eleven-page questionnaire to obtain the risk preferences of the 509 executives in our study. We will refer to this questionnaire as *Investment Gambles*. Several items from this questionnaire are reproduced in the Appendix (pages 313–316).

An executive was first asked to state his current net wealth. Then he was presented with four hypothetical personal investment gambles. The first involved the possibility of investing half his net wealth in a risky venture with a 50% chance of making an unspecified gain and a corresponding 50% chance of losing his stake. The alternative was not taking the gamble. He was asked to specify the *lowest* final wealth position (after gain) that would induce him to take the gamble.[4] This choice, of course, is the example used at the outset of this chapter. Next he was presented with three more choices which differed only in that the chances of loss were changed to 10%, 30%, and 40%.

The second half of the questionnaire dealt with business investment gambles. Each executive was first asked to state the size of his firm's (or division's) annual capital expenditure budget and the usual rate of return on this budget.[5] Then he was presented with a series of choices between investing all his capital expenditure budget in standard projects (ones that would yield the usual rate of return) or investing half of the budget in standard projects and the other half on a risky venture.

The first choice was between investing all the capital expenditure budget on the usual projects or investing half the budget on the usual projects and the other half on a risky venture having a 50% chance of obtaining a zero rate of return and a corresponding 50% chance of obtaining a substantial rate of return. The executive was asked to specify the *lowest* rate of return on the risky venture (if successful) that would induce him to accept the risky venture. This question was followed by ventures with the chances of loss changed to 10%, 30%, and 40%.

NOTE ON DEVELOPMENT OF INVESTMENT GAMBLES QUESTIONNAIRE

A pilot study was conducted on several groups of students and on 40 business executives from Seattle and Vancouver. In the pilot study a variety of equivalence procedures and domains were used. Certainty equivalences were elicited for personal aspects such as annual employment income and net wealth, as well as for business aspects such as size of operating budget, market share, net profit, rate of return on capital budget, earnings per share, and growth in sales revenue. Probability equivalences were assessed for personal aspects such as net wealth, chance of being fired, and chance of death, as well as for the business aspect of chance of bankruptcy. Gain equivalences were obtained for personal net wealth and for business after-tax net profit.

As we have noted, expected utility theory requires that any of the equivalence procedures provide the same results. At the time the data was collected there were no empirical studies assessing risk propensity using different equivalence procedures or different domains. Our pilot study indicated that there were differences among the procedures. Some of the results are given in Bassler, MacCrimmon, and Stanbury (1973). Subsequently, others have also found differences, see for example Hershey,

Kunreuther, and Schoemaker (1982) and Hershey and Schoemaker (1984).

The results of the pilot test indicated that the gain equivalence questions provided consistent responses, and furthermore they were viewed by the executives as most representative of the way they thought about their actual investment decisions. Hence in the main study we restricted our attention to gain equivalence procedures.

We used personal wealth as the single most appropriate personal domain for utility assessment because of the attention it has received in the literature. Personal wealth was assessed in terms of final levels of wealth rather than increments because final position is implied by the theory. We chose a stake of one-half of personal wealth as our standard to encourage the executives to think carefully about their preferences when a loss could have major effect on their lifestyles. We used probabilities of loss no greater than 50% because the executives were generally unwilling to consider any investment that had worse chances of winning than losing.

We used rate of return on capital budget as the business domain because it provided the best prospects for comparability across different businesses. Here too, 50% was the maximum chance of loss that executives were willing to consider.

To compare risk propensity in personal and business domains, it is necessary to have decisions that are viewed as equivalent in terms of their riskiness. There is no guide in theory as to how to establish such equivalence. How can one tell what stake of capital expenditure budget is equivalent to a stake of one-half of personal net wealth? We used subjective assessments in specifying the stake as the normal rate of return on half of the annual capital expenditure budget. It is possible that some executives will view this situation as less risky and some will view it as more risky than the personal gamble.

We were not able to use the data from all 509 executives in this part of the study. Seventeen executives did not provide information on their net wealth.[6] Reported net wealth ranged from zero ("a stroke of bad luck") to over $15 million with a mean wealth of $700,000 and a median wealth of $300,000 (1985 dollars). Of those who did report their net wealth, 25 did not provide answers to all four personal gambles. Hence we had complete data on personal investment gambles for 467 executives. The multiples of wealth they required for the various questions are shown in Table 4.1. Forty-seven of these responses did not satisfy a consistency requirement and were not analyzed further.[7] Thus the data we consider for the personal investment gambles come from the 420 executives with complete and internally consistent responses.[8]

For the business questions 96 executives did not provide the required information (size and rate of return) on their capital expendi-

Table 4.1 Distributions of Gain Equivalence Multiples for Personal and Business Gambles (Percentages)

Gain Equivalence Multiple	Personal Gamble: Chance of Loss 0.5	0.4	0.3	0.1	Business Gamble: Chance of Loss 0.5	0.4	0.3	0.1
Less than 1.5	1	6	10	37	1	3	6	44
1.5–2.0	11	21	25	34	4	17	23	26
2.0–2.5	15	12	20	11	19	23	29	15
2.5–3.0	10	12	10	4	16	15	15	4
3.0–3.5	13	8	9	3	17	12	7	2
3.5–4.0	3	4	3	1	4	4	2	1
4.0–4.5	5	6	3	1	9	4	3	2
4.5–5.0	9	6	4	1	8	4	3	0
More than 5.0	11	6	3	2	8	7	4	2
Infinite	22	19	13	6	14	11	8	4
Total	100	100	100	100	100	100	100	100
Median	3.33	2.86	2.12	1.50	3.00	2.60	2.20	1.50

ture budgets.[9] Almost 80% of the remaining executives had control over capital expenditure budgets while the other 20% had control over investment, sales, or research budgets. These budgets ranged in size from under $300,000 to over $1.5 billion, with half the reported budgets over $12 million. The usual rate of return on these budgets ranged from under 5% to over 50%, with an average of 15%. Of those who provided this information, an additional 37 did not answer all four business gamble questions. The multiples of their usual rate of return that the remaining 376 executives required for each question are shown in Table 4.1. Fifty-nine of these responses did not satisfy a requirement for internal consistency and so were dropped. Thus we confine our attention here to the 317 executives for whom we have complete and internally consistent data.

RESEARCH FINDINGS

Are the Executives Generally Risk-Averse?

The wealth multiples shown in Table 4.1 indicate that a substantial fraction of executives refused to risk losing half their net wealth *regardless of the amount of the gain*. Twenty-two percent refused to gamble when the chance of loss was 50% and 6% refused to gamble when the chance of loss was only 10%.[10]

To obtain more appropriate numbers for comparison, the wealth multiples of Table 4.1 have been converted to *probability premiums*. Probability premiums represent how much the probability of loss has to be reduced before the person would accept the gamble. Table 4.2 shows that the median probability premiums for the personal investments varied over the four questions from 0.34 to 0.41. Looking at the entire range of responses, more than 90% of the executives were significantly risk-averse. Only about 6% of the executives were risk-neutral. Fewer than 1% of the executives were significantly risk-taking.[11] It is clear, then, that the executives were strongly risk-averse in the personal investment gambles.

For the business investment gambles, there were a substantial number of executives who refused to risk a zero return on half their capital expenditure budget. This fraction ranged from 14% when the chance of loss was 50% to 4% when the chance of loss was 10% (Table 4.1). The median probability premiums ranged from 0.19 to 0.25, indicating considerable risk aversion (Table 4.2). Over 70% of the executives were significantly risk-averse, 25% were risk-neutral, and 1% were significantly risk-taking. Hence on business investment gambles we also found a strong majority of risk-averse responses.

Table 4.2 Distributions of Probability Premiums for Individual Gamble Questions (Percentages)

Absolute Risk Category	Probability Premium Ranges	Personal Gamble Chance of Loss				Business Gamble Chance of Loss			
		0.5	0.4	0.3	0.1	0.5	0.4	0.3	0.1
Risk-Taking	−.50 to −.31	0	0			0	0		
	−.30 to −.11	<1	0	0		1	1	<1	
Risk-Neutral	−.10 to .10	7	7	6	4	31	23	21	21
Risk-Averting	.11 to .30	36	23	24	26	45	42	44	43
	.31 to .50	57	44	40	39	23	19	21	24
	.51 to .70		26	30	19		15	14	5
	.71 to .90				12				7
Total		100	100	100	100	100	100	100	100
Median probability premium all executives		.34	.40	.41	.40	.19	.23	.25	.23
Median probability premium executives accepting the gamble		.30	.35	.37	.40	.17	.20	.22	.23

Blank indicates category not possible for individual question.

> ***Result:*** Overall, the executives were strongly risk-averse for both personal and business investments involving major losses.

This result was not surprising. Managers are likely to be averse to gambles that entail very high possible personal or business losses even when they offer very high gains as well.

Note on measures of risk propensity

Pratt (1964) and Arrow (1971) independently proposed measures of both absolute and relative risk aversion based on the utility function. These measures are local measures of risk propensity because they are based on a ratio of the second derivative to the first derivative of the utility function. To derive such measures one must first fit a utility function to the data and then decide at what level of wealth to measure the risk propensity. Using standard methods we fit a variety of utility functions to our data. However, we ended up using alternative means to measure risk propensity because the Pratt-Arrow measures could not be calculated for the infinite gain equivalence multiples and the ones that could be calculated varied widely for individual executives depending on which wealth level was used.

Gain equivalences are not suitable directly as measure of risk propensity because the personal equivalences depend on the person's net wealth and the business equivalences depend on the person's usual rate of return. In addition, they fail to reflect differences in the probability of loss. Furthermore, they are unbounded when the executives respond that they would not take the gamble no matter what the gain multiple. However, gain equivalences can be transformed into measures that do overcome these difficulties. Three main possibilities are: risk premiums, gain premiums, or probability premiums. The risk premium is the difference between a gamble's expected value and its equivalent sure value. The gain premium is the difference between the gamble's gain outcome and an actuarially fair gain outcome derived by equating the gamble's expected value and its equivalent sure value. The probability premium is the difference between the gamble's probability of gain and an actuarially fair probability of gain derived by equating the gamble's expected value and its equivalent sure value.

All three premiums depend on the probability of loss p. The probability premium has an advantage over the other two premiums in that it does not become infinite when the gain multiples are infinite. The natural boundedness of probabilities forces the probability premium to be bounded when infinite gain equivalences occur. For these reasons we converted the gain multiples for both the personal and business gambles to probability premiums. Specifically, the probability premium for the personal gambles was calculated as $1-p-[1/(2k-1)]$, where k is the gain equivalence multiple. The probability premium for the business gambles was calculated as $1-p-(1/k)$. Thus these premiums can range from $-p$

to $1-p$. Probability premiums equal to zero reflect risk neutrality, positive premiums reflect risk aversion, and negative premiums reflect risk taking. Probability premiums equal to $1-p$ correspond to the infinite gain equivalences, and hence represent the most extreme risk aversion. In reading the results stated in terms of probability premiums, remember that they were obtained by asking gain equivalence questions, not probability equivalence questions.

Are Executives More Risk-Averse When Dealing with Threats or Opportunities?

When the chance of loss is 50%, an investment gamble is quite threatening. In informal discussions with executives in our preliminary study, a number of them indicated that they would automatically reject such a prospect in their actual investment decisions. So we are confident in labeling the gamble with the 50% chance of loss as a *threat*. Compared to a situation in which one has only a 50% chance of succeeding (and a corresponding 50% chance of loss), an investment gamble offering a 90% chance of succeeding is a relative *opportunity*. We will use these two situations, then, as representing a threat and an opportunity.

The executives in our study seemed to be more risk-averse for the threatening situation than for the opportunity in that 22% would refuse the gamble with the 50% chance of loss (of half their net wealth) no matter what the possible gain, whereas only 6% would refuse the gamble when the chance of loss was only 10%. The percentages for the threat versus opportunity in the business gambles were 14% and 4%, respectively.[12] So we see about four times as many people would avoid the threat in comparison to the opportunity. This suggests that people were more risk-averse for threats.

If people are more risk-averse for threats, we would expect that when more money was at stake, the frequency of refusing the gamble would increase. Even though each executive was being asked to consider a stake of half his net wealth, the executives with more wealth had a larger dollar amount at stake and so, in this sense, they faced a greater threat. An analysis of the data, for the personal gamble with a 50% chance of loss, showed that for those executives with under $300,000 at stake, 17% of them refused to invest. For those executives with $300,000 to $1.2 million at stake, 36% refused to invest. For those executives with over $1.2 million at stake, 63% refused to invest. For the gamble with the 10% chance of loss, the figures were 3%, 18%, and 26%, respectively. The data support the conclusion that higher threats resulted in more risk-averse responses.

> ***Result:*** Some executives were extremely risk-averse in that they refused to invest no matter what the possible gains when the chance of loss was too high. These executives were more risk-averse for threats than for opportunities. These results held for both personal and business gambles.

This result illustrates that some executives will not *enter a risky situation* that is perceived as being extremely risky. For these managers it does not seem to matter how much gain is possible to balance the risks. We speculate that such managers would only accept these gambles if they could *adjust* the risks by reducing the magnitude, chance, or their personal exposure to loss. The focus on *choosing between risky and sure gambles* in the Investment Gambles questionnaire did not allow the executives to modify the risky situations they faced.

We can learn more about the effect of increasingly or decreasingly threatening situations by looking at the answers from the majority of executives who did *accept* the gambles. Even if, as we discussed above, the executives were risk-averse overall, they may show less (or more) risk aversion as they move from considering gambles that were more threatening to considering gambles that were less threatening. For an executive who was more risk-averse for threats, we would expect that the probability premium he required would decrease as the chance of loss decreased from 50% to 10%.

Table 4.2 shows that as we move from a 50% chance of loss to a 10% chance of loss, the probability premiums for those accepting the gambles *increased* for both the personal and business decisions. Surprisingly, this suggests that the executives who would accept the gamble required less inducement to take risks when the chance of loss was higher, that is, when the situation was more threatening.

> ***Result:*** The executives who were willing to accept the investment gambles were more risk-taking for threats than they were for opportunities. This result held for both personal and business gambles.

The changes in risk aversion or risk taking for various wealth levels (based on changing the chance of loss) can be seen by drawing a preference curve for each executive. First consider the preference curves for personal wealth. Executives with preference curves similar to persons D or E in Figure 4.2a are risk-averse for all levels of wealth. These curves increasingly flatten out as one moves to the right (that is, as the amounts to be gained increase). On the other hand, in Figure 4.2b, we have seen that even people who are predominantly risk-averse may have some regions in which they would be risk-taking.

NOTE ON HYPOTHESIZED UTILITY FUNCTIONS

The results of other studies that suggest risk taking over losses are contradictory to the usual assumption in economics and finance models of risk aversion for all levels of wealth. Our results are somewhat more supportive in that almost half of the executives were risk-averse for both significant losses and significant gains. Those executives (about 25%) that had a risk-taking segment at intermediate levels were consistent with the hypothesized utility functions of Friedman and Savage (1948, 1952). However, the risk-taking segment occurs for low levels of gains rather than occurring around the status quo point as they suggested.

Analysis of the responses having no tied wealth multiples shows that about 20% of 356 executives were risk-averse throughout all levels of personal wealth. All but one of these managers are in this category because they said, for at least one of the gambles, that they would not invest no matter what the gain amount. An example of this kind of preference curve for the president of a mining company is shown in Figure 4.3a.

Another 25% of the executives had preference curves that generally looked like the preference curve in Figure 4.3a, but had an upturn in the middle. An example is shown in Figure 4.3b for the executive vice-president of a telecommunications company. The segment in the middle suggests that these executives would be willing to take risks in gambles that involved only small positive changes from their current wealth level.

The remaining 55% of the executives had preference curves that were risk-averse for lower levels of investment, but were risk-taking for higher levels. Twenty-five percent of the executives exhibited preference curves having only a single switch in risk propensity. An example of this kind of curve is shown in Figure 4.4a for the president of a life insurance company. The other 30% of the managers had preference curves that started out risk-averse and ended up risk-taking, but in the middle had additional risk-taking and risk-averse segments (in that order). An example is shown in Figure 4.4b for the deputy chairman of a bank.

There are two ways to interpret the risk behavior of the majority of executives who had preference curves of the form shown in Figure 4.4. Since the horizontal scale measures wealth levels, it follows that for gambles involving higher levels of wealth these executives were risk-taking. However, for lower levels of wealth (including losses of up to half their current net wealth), they were risk-averse. The second interpretation is based on the fact that the preference curve was de-

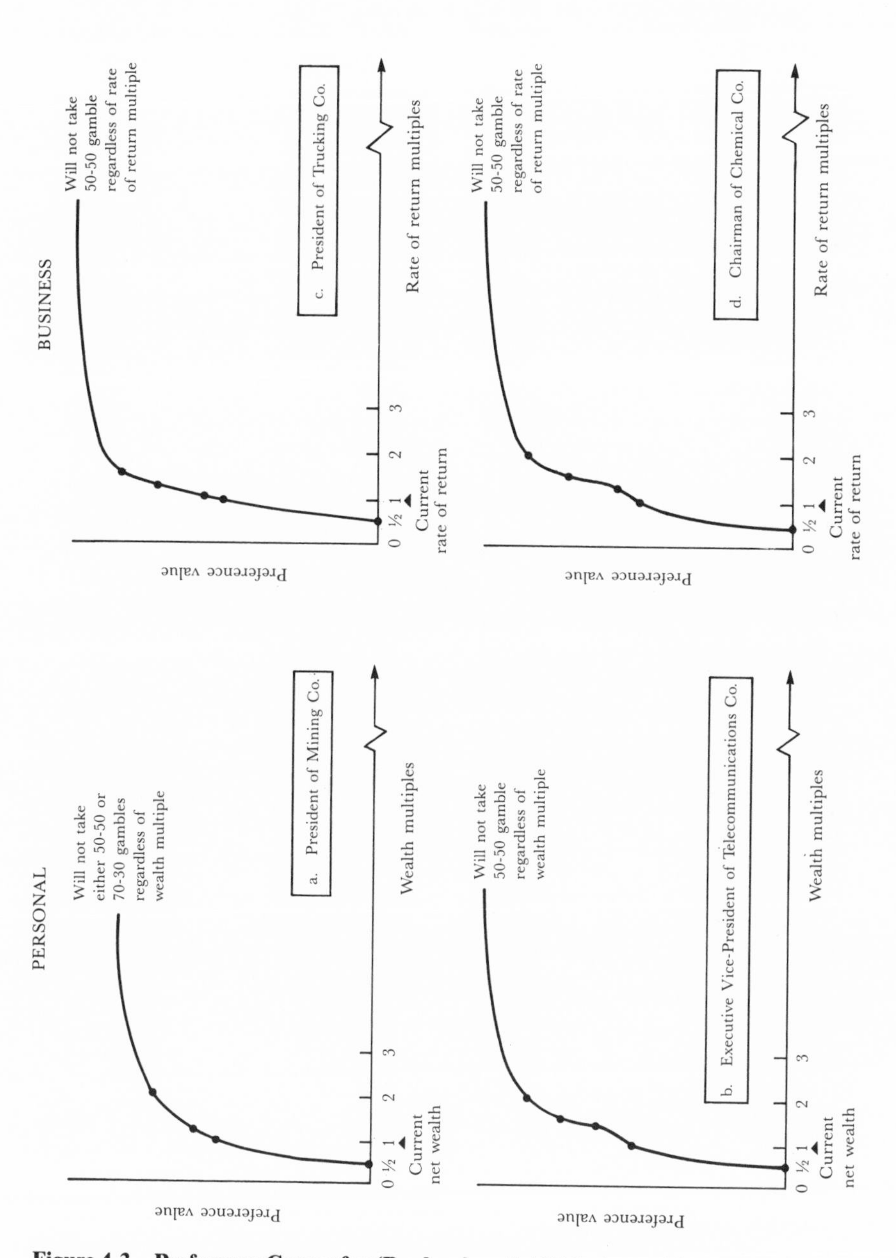

Figure 4.3 Preference Curves for (Predominantly) Risk-Averse Executives

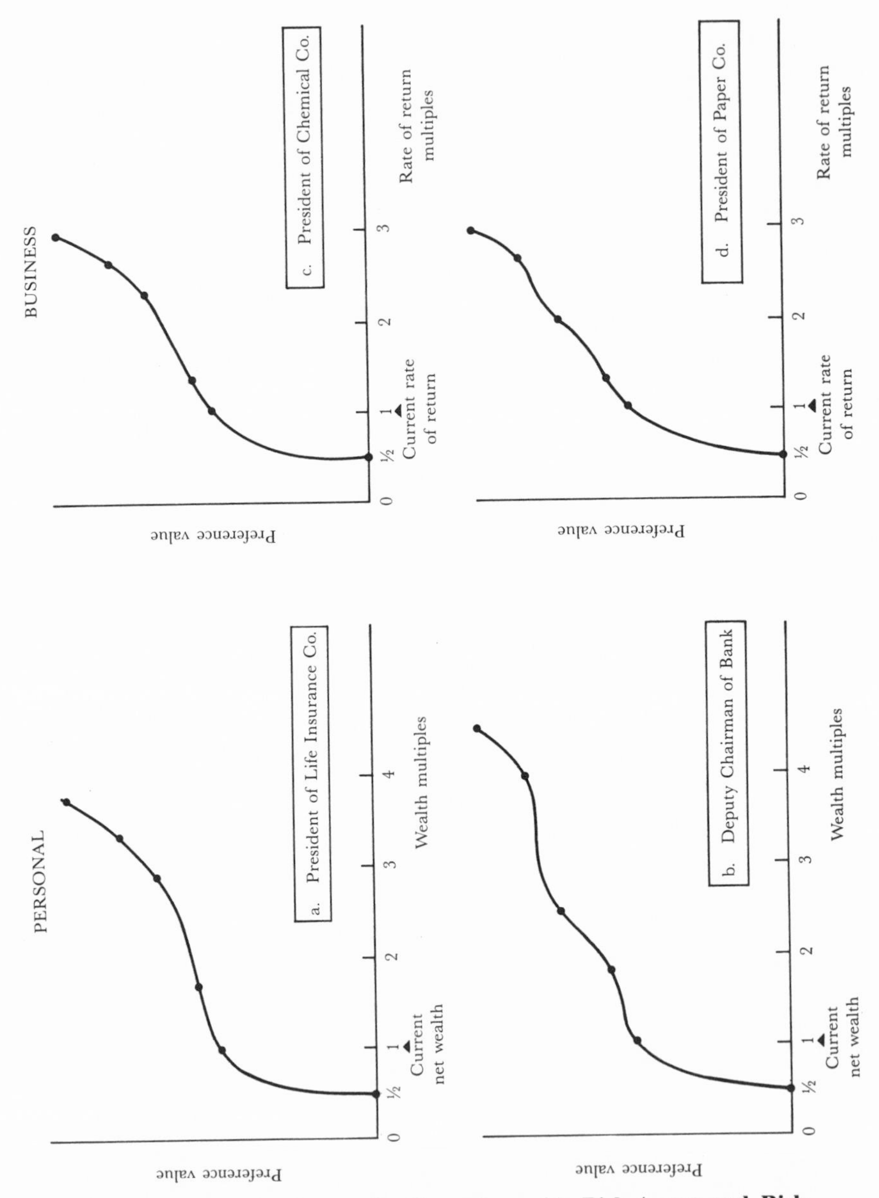

Figure 4.4 Preference Curves for Executives with Risk-Averse and Risk-Taking Segments

termined by changing the chance of loss from 50% to 10% in moving from right to left. Thus the preference curve could be interpreted as indicating risk taking for higher chance of loss and risk aversion for lower chance of loss.

For all executives (see both Figures 4.3 and 4.4), at low levels of possible gain, corresponding to low chances of loss, everyone was risk-averse. At higher possible gain levels, corresponding here to higher chances of loss, roughly half the executives indicated their willingness to take risks when the outcomes involved only large possible gains. If the outcomes also involved the chance of major loss, even these executives were risk-averse.

For the business investments, we observed quite similar results. Among the 256 executives with untied rate of return multiples, 13% were risk-averse for all levels of rate of return.[13] This is exemplified in the preference curve in Figure 4.3c for the president of a trucking company. For the remaining executives we found the same predominant shapes in the preference curves for business gambles as we found for the personal gambles. About 40% of the executives were risk-averse at both lower and upper rate of return levels, including slightly more than 25% having a small risk-taking segment (Figure 4.3d). Close to 60% were risk-averse for losses or low levels of rate of return, yet were risk-taking for high levels of investment. The latter group was about equally split between those who had additional intermediate risk-taking and risk-averting segments and those who did not (Figures 4.4c and d).

> ***Result:*** Despite overall risk aversion, the preferences of a majority of executives suggest risk-taking in gambles in which all outcomes would result in large gains. Correspondingly, these executives did not require a proportionately higher inducement when chances of loss were highest. These results held for both personal and business gambles.

The preference curves we found for our executives show how one's risk preference depends on the possible outcomes of gambles and their chances of occurrence. We should not expect managers to have the same willingness to take risks in gambles that may lead to either gains or losses as in gambles having only gains as possible outcomes.

NOTE ON INTERPRETING OUR RESULTS AND THOSE IN OTHER STUDIES

We are not aware of any other studies which found risk taking for high levels of wealth. Note that this can also be interpreted as risk taking for higher chances of loss because of how the curves were derived. If the executives were actually maximizing expected utility (for if they were not then the utility curves have no meaning), then both interpretations are appropriate—the wealth interpretation since that is how the curve is represented and the probability interpretation because that is how the curve was derived. We can think of various possible reasons for the risk-taking segment at the right end. One possibility is that people really are risk-taking over gambles confined to this interval. For example, an executive with wealth below $1 million may well take a 50-50 gamble resulting in either $2 million or $4 million rather than taking $3 million for sure. For after all, the "loss" outcome of $2 million is not all that aversive.

A second explanation is somewhat related. Since we first presented the 50-50 gamble, a person may have thought carefully and stated some target amount that would satisfy his aspirations. Then he may have used this amount as an anchor in adjusting downward when he was presented with gambles involving smaller probabilities. If he underadjusted, then a derived utility function would have a risk-taking segment for levels based on gambles with the higher probability of loss. The confounding of higher wealth levels with larger probabilities of loss does not allow the separation of these aspects. It has, however, raised some interesting possibilities for future research.

Other studies have found somewhat different results. Laughhunn, Payne, and Crum (1980) found 84% of the executives in their study were risk-taking for below-target levels of personal wealth when gains and losses were small (under $500). Lorange and Norman (1971, 1973) found that 16 of 17 Scandanavian ship owners were risk-neutral or risk-taking when their liquidity position was good, but were evenly split between risk-taking and risk-averting when their liquidity position was poor. Dillon and Scandizzo (1978) studied subsistance farmers in Brazil and found them predominantly risk-averse. Risk aversion was more common in gambles in which there was a possibility of not producing enough to meet subsistence requirements than in gambles that involved only payoffs above household subsistence requirements. Kahneman and Tversky (1979; Tversky and Kahneman, 1981) found that students tended to be risk-taking for pure losses and risk-averting for pure gains when stakes were moderate (under $6000) for personal wealth gambles. Hershey, Kunreuther, and Schoemaker (1982) found that students tended to be risk-taking for pure gains, especially for amounts under $10,000 and for low chances of gain. Hershey and Schoemaker (1980b) showed that by modifying the context of a risky choice the change in risk propensity around a target level could be eliminated.

There have also been several studies of the risk propensities of executives for corporate wealth. Grayson (1960) assessed the preference curves of oil field operators. Green (1963) used questions based on rate of return to assess the preference curves of 16 middle managers in a large chemical company. Swalm (1966) obtained preference curves for business investments from about 100 middle-level managers. Fishburn and Kochenberger (1979) surveyed the preference curves developed in these studies, as well as several other studies, and concluded that the majority of these curves showed risk taking for below-target returns and risk aversion for above-target returns. Cramer and Smith (1964) used an unorthodox method to aggregate preference curves for business investments and concluded that four R&D executives were risk-taking for losses and four production executives were risk-averse for losses. Spetzler (1968) found that six out of seven top executives were risk-averse for business investments and their aversion to risk increased as the stakes increased from $300,000 to $5 million. Laughhunn, Payne, and Crum (1980) found a strong tendency toward risk-taking over business losses except for very large losses. When the probability of bankruptcy was introduced, the executives became risk-averse even though the chance of bankruptcy was low.

Do Executives Take More Risks with Their Own Money or Their Firm's Resources?

Studies that assess preference curves for both personal and business investments have been rare. In one previous study Green (1963) found that middle managers in a chemical company had widely different risk preference functions for personal wealth, but much more similar risk preferences for business investments. Several researchers have speculated on what could be expected. Swalm (1966) asserted that the preference curves he assessed for business investments "appear to be more closely related to the amount with which the executives are accustomed to deal as individuals than to the financial position of the company." Hammond (1967) claimed that a "company's preference curve . . . is usually much less risk-averse than the individual's since the company sees things in the aggregate." One logical reason why there might be greater willingness to take risks in business decisions than in personal decisions is the reduced exposure to loss faced by an executive in business investments where responsibility is diffused and bad financial outcomes are shared with many others.

The results of our study provide evidence on this question. Before looking at the choices our executives actually made, though, let us report what they thought they would do in the two situations. We asked the managers whether they thought they were more likely to take risks in their personal decisions or in their business decisions. A majority (54%) thought they took more risks in their business decisions.

To make comparisons of their actual choices, we have to narrow the sample of 509 executives down to the 285 who gave consistent answers to all four personal gambles and all four business gambles. For the questions involving a 50% chance of loss, 76% of these executives were more risk-averse for personal investments than for business investments, 18% were more risk-averse for business investments, and 6% were equally risk-averse in both areas.[14] The typical executive required a probability premium of 0.34 for the personal investments but only 0.19 for the business gamble.[15] Moreover, an average of 22% of the executives refused to take the personal gamble no matter how large the gain, as contrasted with 16% who refused to gamble in the business investment. The executives who thought they were more risk-averse in their personal decisions than in their business decisions actually were more risk-averse in the personal investment gambles.[16]

Similar comparisons were made for the other chances of loss and the same conclusions resulted. Those executives who were more risk-averse for personal than business wealth at one level of chance of loss also were more risk-averse at other levels.

> ***Result:*** The executives were more risk-averse when their own money was at stake than when their firm's resources were at stake.

This result means that executives do differentiate their personal and business roles when it comes to taking risks. The trend toward greater risk taking in business than personal decisions is consistent with the inherent responsibility of managers to take risks for their firms. We should not automatically assume, therefore, that an executive who takes few chances with his personal resources will also refuse to take risks in his business role.

NOTE ON COMPARABILITY OF PERSONAL AND BUSINESS GAMBLES

As noted earlier, the conclusion that executives were more risk-averse for personal gambles than for business gambles relies on the assumption that the situations are roughly equal in their riskiness across the two domains.

In an earlier technical note, we gave reasons supporting this comparability. To bias the results against our conclusions, we also compared the business probability premium for the 50% chance of loss gamble with the personal probability premium for the 10% chance of loss gamble. Even for this comparison, the executives were more risk-averse for personal than business investments.[17]

What Dimensions Underlie Risk Propensity?

The Investment Gambles questionnaire required the executives to answer eight questions about the possible gain they would require to invest in various situations. So far in this chapter we have used these answers to examine risk propensity. At this point we need to step back and ask: "Are an executive's eight answers related to each other?" "What does the set of all eight answers suggest about the underlying dimensions of risk propensity?" "Do the executives show similar risk propensities in situations having common attributes?"

We found that all eight answers (in terms of their probability premiums) were significantly related to each other. The answers were more closely associated for two questions that both dealt with personal decisions or both dealt with business decisions than for two questions that both had a particular chance of loss (say, 50%) but one dealt with personal investment and the other with business investment.[18]

We used statistical procedures to obtain a spatial representation of the relationships among the responses (see Figure 4.5). In this diagram risk measures that have the strongest relationships appear closest together and those with weak relationships appear further apart.[19] Note that the four probability premiums for the personal gambles (denoted as P10, P30, P40, and P50) cluster together on the extreme left, while the four probability premiums for the business gambles (denoted as B10, B30, B40, and B50) cluster together on the extreme right. This confirms the importance of the personal versus

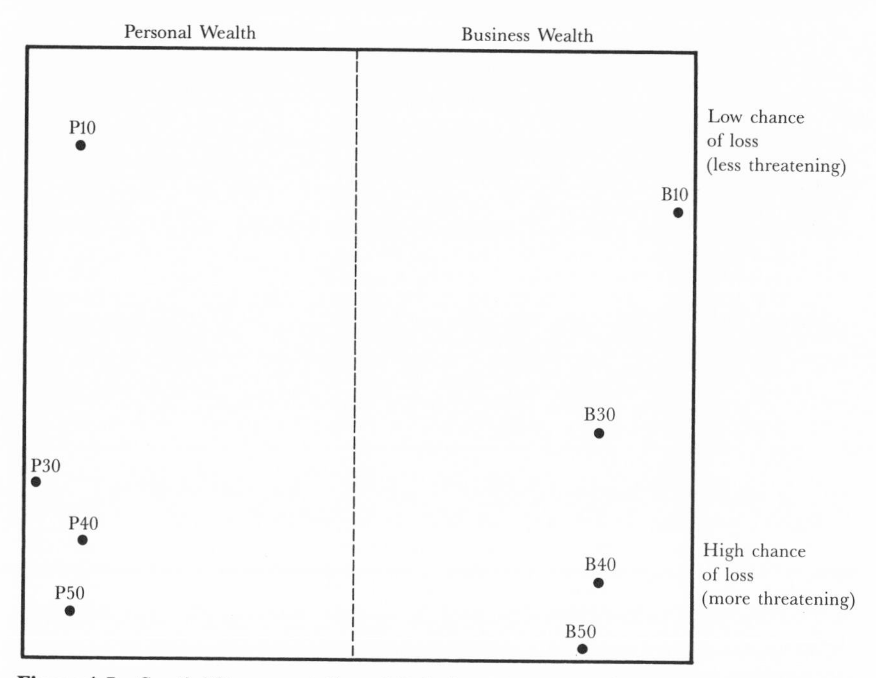

Figure 4.5 Spatial Representation of Relationships among Responses to Investment Gambles

business distinction that emerged when we looked at the relationships among the responses.

Figure 4.5 shows us that the chance of loss is also an important dimension of risk propensity. Note that for personal and for business investments, the responses corresponding to various chances of loss increase consecutively in moving from the top of the diagram to the bottom. Since the higher chances of loss (i.e., 50%) represent threats and the lower chances of loss (i.e., 10%) represent opportunities, the bottom of the diagram corresponds to threats and the top of the diagram corresponds to opportunities.

> ***Result:*** Two dimensions underlie the executives' risk propensities: (1) personal versus business decisions, and (2) threats versus opportunities.

Managers do not show the same willingness to take risks in all situations. Finding different risk propensities in personal and business decisions reinforces our earlier conclusion that managers do differentiate their personal and business roles when taking risks. Risk propensity also differs in situations with different risk components, such as the chance of loss, that influence how threatening the situation is.

CONCLUSIONS

Virtually all executives were strongly averse to the risk of losing half their personal wealth and to the risk of losing their usual rate of return on half their capital expenditure budget. About 5% of the executives would not take the risky investment no matter how high the possible gain even when there was a 90% chance of success. Not one executive emerged overall as a risk taker on both his personal and his business investments.

There were, however, some indications of local risk taking. Although the question was not directly asked, we can infer that about half the executives would take a risky alternative (that is, a "fair gamble") if all the outcomes were confined to large gains. Looking at this result more directly, these executives were not as risk-averse as the other executives when faced with a threat (of a 50% chance of losing half their wealth) compared to their risk aversion for a relative opportunity (a reduction in the chance of loss to 10%).

Two clear dimensions seem to underlie the risk propensity exhibited by the executives. First, there is a strong distinction between personal and business decisions, with a greater willingness to take risks in business investments. Second, there is a difference between investments at various chances of loss. The executives who were willing to accept all eight gambles were more risk-averse at the lower chances of loss. This can be interpreted as a greater willingness to take risks when faced with threats than when faced with opportunities.

Research conclusions

From a research point of view, there are five major conclusions:

1. The assumption of risk aversion made in most theoretical models was supported empirically. Fewer than 2% of the more than 3000 responses were risk-taking.

2. There seems to be a local region of risk taking for high levels of wealth. However, our design does not permit us to separate this effect from a possible effect of risk taking for higher chances of loss. We have found two main types of utility functions, each occurring about equally often. The existence of utility functions that are convex for higher wealth levels is not consistent with the models mentioned in item 1. Other studies have not found a convex segment for higher wealth. In some cases it may be because these studies did not ask questions covering this part of the domain. More attention needs to be devoted to uncovering and explaining the risk propensities at different levels of outcomes and probabilities.

3. Two dimensions of risk emerged: personal versus business and chance of loss. These dimensions should have been apparent to the executives by the design of the Investment Gambles instrument. It would be useful to see if these dimensions emerge when the instrument makes them less obvious.

4. A solid foundation for the comparability of personal and business risks needs to be developed. We found a greater willingness to take risks in business gambles than in personal gambles based on our assessment of their comparability. However, the observed differences in risk propensity may be due to differences in the perceived riskiness of these investments rather than differences in attitudes regarding personal and business responses.

5. Gain equivalences deserve more attention. While any equivalence procedure will yield the same utility function for an expected utility maximizer, biases may occur in any of the procedures. It may be that a number of our executives were anchoring on their first response. When the probability of loss was decreased, they may have adjusted their earlier response downward, and in the process given a different (higher) equivalence than they would have given otherwise. If such a bias exists, there will be difficulties in interpolating to local intervals in utility functions derived from gain equivalences with different loss probabilities (as in item 2 above). Correspondingly, our results suggest caution in interpreting utility functions developed from certainty equivalence procedures when extrapolating beyond the intervals specifically asked. For a discussion of the differences between gain and certainty equivalences, see Wehrung, MacCrimmon, and Brothers (1984). This article also considers the stability of risk preferences over a one-year period as does MacCrimmon and Wehrung (1985a).

Chapter 5

Risk-Return Rankings

Evaluating Risky Attributes of Personal Investments

INTRODUCTION

Suppose you have to choose between two risky personal investments, each requiring a stake of 10% of your net wealth. One alternative offers an expected return of 15% while the other has an expected return of 25%. For a person whose net wealth is $300,000, the stake would be $30,000. The 15% investment would, on the average, yield a gain of $4500 (i.e., 15% of $30,000), while the 25% investment would yield an average gain of $7500 (i.e., 25% of $30,000). What choices would you expect?

If the investment alternatives were equally risky, the choice would be clear-cut. You would choose the alternative with the higher expected return. However, if the alternative with the higher return was riskier, then you might want to weigh the higher risk against the higher return. A common way to think about risk propensity is in terms of the tradeoff made between risk and return. A risk-averse person would require a higher return to compensate for a given level of risk than would a risk-taking person.

Consider risk as exposure to a chance of loss in this personal investment decision. For example, we might define risk as the chance of losing half one's investment (i.e., in our example, losing $15,000). Suppose the alternative with the 15% expected return has no chance of losing half that investment, while the alternative with the 25% expected return has a 17% chance of losing half the investment. Some people may decide that the extra risk of the latter alternative is more than offset by the greater return. Others may decide that the extra risk is not adequately compensated by the higher return. Choices that people make in such circumstances can be used to assess their risk propensity.

There is no reason why risk needs to be measured in terms of "chance of losing half the investment." For example, we could consider more serious outcomes such as the "chance of losing your total investment." On the other hand, we could even consider the chance of not gaining more than some target amount, such as the "chance of not making at least 50%."

Consider the following more elaborate description of the two alternatives discussed above:

Expected Return	15%	25%
Chance of losing the total investment	0%	6%
Chance of losing at least half of the investment	0%	17%
Chance of losing at least 10% of the investment	11%	33%
Chance of not breaking even	23%	38%
Chance of not making at least 50% return	96%	62%
Chance of not doubling your investment	100%	83%

Note that the alternative with the 15% return has a lower chance of losing at all four levels of loss. That is, the 25% alternative has a higher chance of losing the total investment, losing at least half the investment, losing at least 10% of the investment, and losing anything (i.e., not breaking even). In this sense, the 25% alternative is clearly riskier. It has a higher *downside* loss potential.

On the other hand, the alternative with the 25% return has a higher *upside* potential. While there is certainty (i.e., a 100% chance) that the 15% alternative will not yield a doubling of the investment, the 25% alternative has only an 83% chance of not doubling in value. Stating this in other terms, there is a 17% chance that the 25% alternative will yield at least a 100% return, but there is no chance that the 15% alternative will pay off that well. So if risk is defined in terms of failure to meet some upside target, the 15% alternative is riskier.

NOTE ON USING PROBABILITIES TO DESCRIBE RISKY INVESTMENTS

The basis for the particular probabilities used in the text and given in the graph is the assumption that the alternatives are described by a Gaussian (i.e., normal) distribution with a standard deviation of 20% for the 15% alternative and a standard deviation of 80% for the 25% alternative. The graph below gives the cumulative distribution functions for these two alternatives showing the probability of not receiving more than the payoff amount on the abscissa.

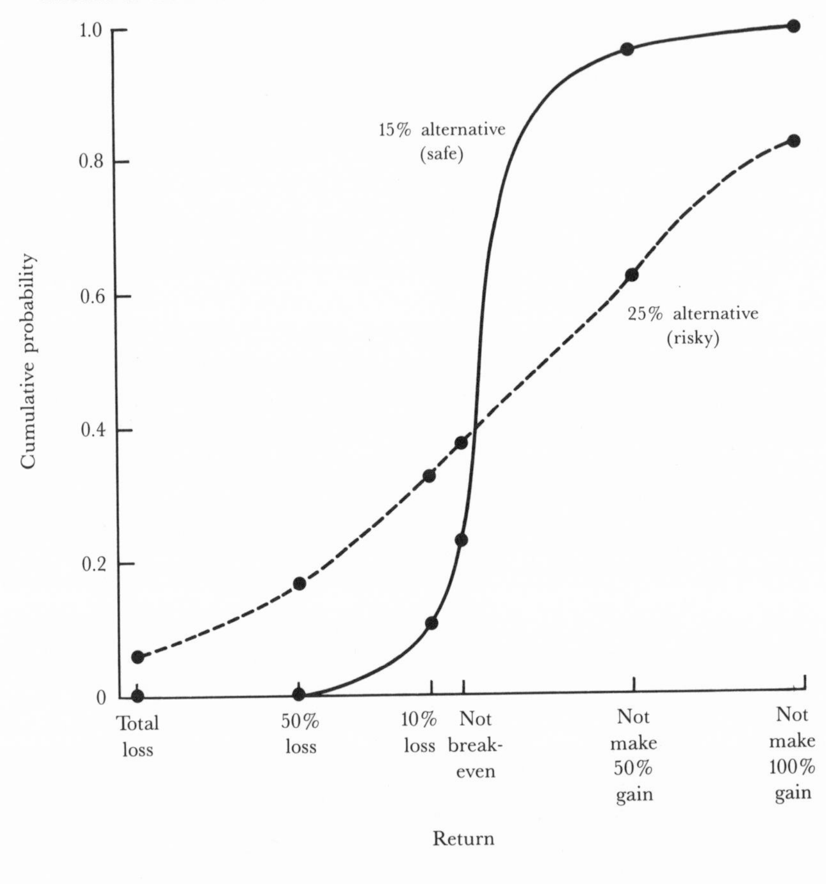

The reason that the 25% alternative has both a higher downside risk and a higher upside potential is that it has a higher overall variability in possible returns. A common index of variability is called "standard deviation." The standard deviation for the 25% alternative is 80%, while for the 15% alternative the standard deviation is only 20%. Variability, in terms of standard deviation, is sometimes used as an index of riskiness of alternatives.

Of the two investment alternatives we have been discussing, which would you choose? Although the 25% alternative has a higher chance of doing badly (e.g., losing the total investment), it also has a higher chance of doing really well (e.g., doubling your money). Your choice, then, provides information about the extent to which you focus on gains versus losses. Since in choosing you are balancing the return and the risk, your choice provides information about your risk propensity.

When a person is presented with a number of alternatives described by several attributes, we can infer the attributes of interest to him from how he ranks the alternatives. We can tell which people focus on losses and which people focus on gains. We can tell which loss or gain amounts are most important to the person. From his ranking of such alternatives, we can make inferences about his risk propensity.

NOTE ON LITERATURE ON INVESTMENT DECISION MAKING

The available literature on risk taking in investment decision making is very large and has many contributors. The early work of von Neumann and Morgenstern (1947), Savage (1954), and Marschak (1950) established the expected utility model as the predominant normative model for decision making under uncertainty, including decisions regarding personal investments. This model uses the entire distribution of possible investment returns.

Other researchers summarized the distribution of investment returns in terms of its moments—the mean, variance, and sometimes skewness. Most notable among these contributors was Markowitz (1952, 1959) who was influential in establishing variance as a standard measure of riskiness in investment decision making. Using mean and variance to summarize investment opportunities, Markowitz introduced the efficient frontier as the appropriate reduced set of choice by assuming investors preferred investments with higher means and smaller variances. Although Markowitz and others (e.g., Mao, 1970) have suggested replacing variance with negative semivariance below some target level, mean absolute deviation, or a weighted combination of mean and standard deviation (Baumol, 1963), variance has persisted as the predominant measure of riskiness.

Some researchers have based their studies of investment decision making on indifference curves in the "mean versus variance" context. In this context reference levels of expected return and variance are specified and then different combinations of these variables are sought that are equally preferred to this reference point.

Borch (1963) has investigated the relationships between the "mean vs. variance" paradigm and the form of utility curves and subjective probability distributions that would be consistent with choosing according to this paradigm. See Fishburn (1979) for a review of the foundations of the "mean vs. variance" model.

Quirk and Saposnick (1962) and Hadar and Russell (1969) introduced the concept of stochastic dominance as a means of comparing entire distributions of returns. The relationship between stochastic dominance and the form of utility functions also has been examined (Fishburn, 1977).

Coombs and his associates (Coombs and Huang, 1970); Combs and Pruitt, 1960) have suggested that some people may seek an ideal level of risk that is other than the minimal possible level. Defining riskiness as variance in returns, Coombs and Pruitt demonstrated that the majority of subjects rank uncertain prospects in a way that is contrary to minimizing variance when expected return is held fixed.

Several others have proposed models that first eliminate some investment opportunities by means of an investment constraint before selecting the most preferred venture based upon an investment objective. See Roy (1952), Telser (1955), Kataoka (1963), Machol and Lerner (1969), Pyle and Turnovsky (1970), Joy and Barron (1974), and Ranyard (1976) for illustrative models.

Other researchers have focused on characterizing the riskiness of alternative investment ventures. Stone (1973) and Fishburn (1977) have postulated models in which risk is measured by a probability-weighted function of deviations below a target level specified by the investor. Pollatsek and Tversky (1970) developed an axiom system that requires the riskiness of an alternative to be measured as a weighted combination of its mean and variance.

Investment decision making has also been studied from an information processing point of view. Clarkson (1962) and Slovic (1969) examined the investment behavior of individual investors to understand what investment attributes they focused on and how they processed these attributes. Slovic and Lichtenstein (1968) investigated the relative important of probabilities and payoffs in risk taking. Gooding (1975) provided some insights regarding investors' perceptions of common stock. See Slovic (1972) and Libby and Fishburn (1977) for reviews of behavioral models of risk taking in investment and other business decisions.

Instead of the two alternatives we have been discussing, suppose you were offered the nine alternatives shown in Table 5.1. How would you rank them from best to worst? Note that the two alternatives we have been considering are listed in the table. The alternative with the 15% expected return is labeled as "S" while the alternative with the 25% expected return is labeled as "R."[1] Alternative "S" has the lowest variability (and lowest chance of losing half the investment), while alternative "R" has the highest standard deviation (and highest chance of losing half the investment). Thus the "S" stands for "safe" and the "R" stands for "risky." If you dislike risk you will presumably rank alternative S high and alternative R low. Correspondingly, if you are a risk taker you will rank S low and R high.

Table 5.1 Attributes of the Nine Investment Alternatives

		Investment Alternatives								
		Safest *S*	*A*	*B*	*C*	*D*	*E*	*F*	*G*	*Riskiest* *R*
Primary Attributes	Expected return (%)	15	25	10	35	20	5	30	15	25
	Variation in returns (%)	20	40	30	60	50	40	70	60	80
Supplementary Attributes	*Chances of:* 100% gain	0	.03	0	.13	.05	.01	.16	.08	.17
	50% gain	.04	.26	.09	.40	.27	.13	.38	.28	.38
	Break-even	.77	.74	.63	.72	.66	.55	.66	.60	.62
	10% loss	.11	.18	.24	.23	.27	.35	.28	.34	.33
	50% loss	0	.03	.02	.08	.08	.08	.13	.14	.17
	Total loss	0	0	0	.01	.01	0	.03	.03	.06

The alternatives presented in Table 5.1 are presented in the form of a decision tree in Figure 5.1. This tree format allows us to note that the decision problem presented here is an extension, in several ways, of the Basic Risk Paradigm discussed in Chapter 1. First, even in considering two alternatives, we have allowed both alternatives to have uncertain outcomes, rather than one alternative having uncertain outcomes and one alternative being a sure thing. Second, we have described each risky alternative by a set of outcomes with associated probabilities rather than having only two outcomes.[2] Finally, we have moved from a choice between two alternatives to a choice among nine alternatives.

Each of these three extensions helps to capture some important aspects of real-world personal investment situations. When people choose between two investment alternatives, generally both alternatives are perceived as risky. Seldom, if ever, do investors confront an investment alternative that offers a completely sure outcome. While some people prefer the safety of federally insured savings accounts,

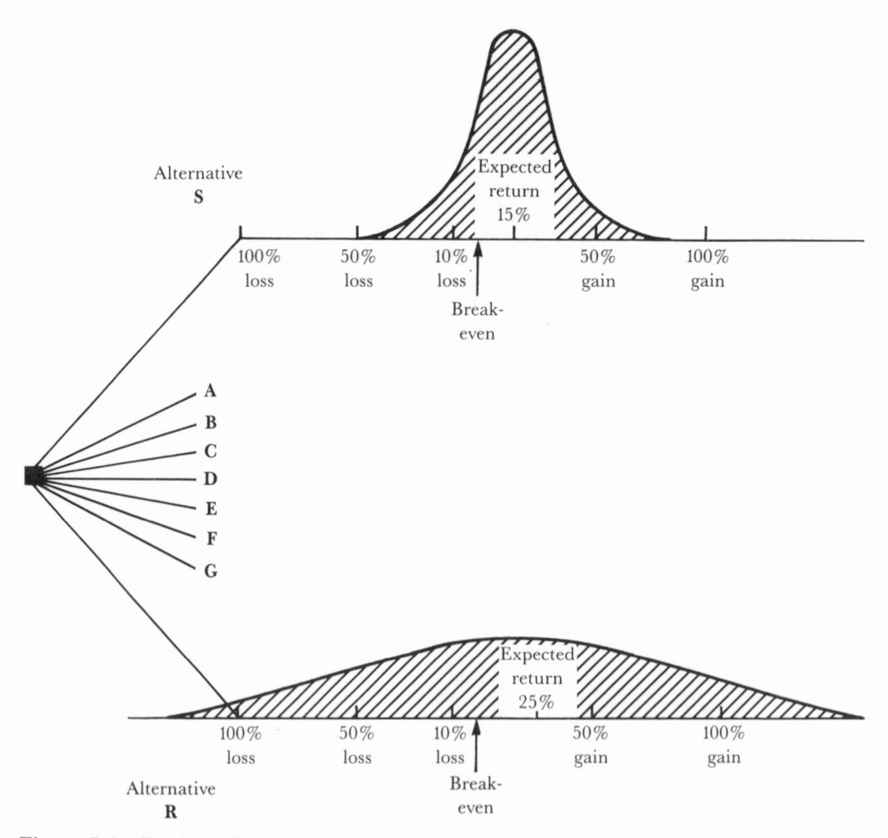

Figure 5.1 Decision Tree Representation of the Nine Investment Alternatives

others risk total or partial loss of their investment in exchange for a chance at substantial returns. Common stocks vary in their riskiness from the highly speculative gold mine stocks to the well-known blue chip stocks and the diversified mutual funds. Similarly some non-stock investment options such as business ventures offer moderate to high risk while investments in bonds and personal real estate have been relatively safe.

Personal investments require staking a portion of one's net wealth to obtain an unknown rate of return that depends on how uncertain events turn out. A number of focal attributes of an investment may be considered, such as the chance of losing the whole investment or the chance of doubling your money. While being presented with a whole distribution of possible rates of return is the exception rather than the rule, careful investors tend to obtain considerable information before putting up their money.

Finally, while investors may often think in terms of a choice between two alternatives, the two alternatives are usually part of a larger set of possibilities. In making a decision, the investor may make a number of pairwise choices while deciding on his preferences over the set of alternative investments.

NOTE ON THE DEVELOPMENT OF THE RISK-RETURN RANKINGS QUESTIONNAIRE

Various forms of the Risk-Return Rankings questionnaire were administered in a series of pilot tests. Subjects included undergraduate and graduate business students as well as a sample of 40 top-level executives. The pilot tests were useful in resolving several design issues described below.

The questionnaire was developed to examine personal investment decisions in a context that provided greater motivation and a wider set of investment attributes than in previous research designs. Increased motivation was provided by asking the executive to consider investing 10% of his personal net wealth in an investment venture rather than the usual small amounts. This percentage was selected to represent a significant amount of the individual's wealth and yet remain within the realm of a single investment decision. The wider set of investment attributes was provided by including six important cumulative probabilities along with expected return and standard deviation to characterize each investment opportunity. This inclusion of probabilities as well as moments of the return distribution allows much stronger tests of the descriptive validity of decision-making models such as the "mean vs. variance" paradigm. The focus on probabilities as well as moments is also consistent with the more recently developed information processing models of decision making (Payne, 1973).

The six cumulative probability levels were chosen to correspond to six important target levels which investors may focus upon. Although investors may choose different target levels in their decision making, the six chosen levels were judged to span the relevant targets and include the most commonly mentioned ones.

The presentation of eight explicit attributes for each of the nine investment ventures could make the preference rankings somewhat burdensome because of the excessive amount of information to be considered. Based on feedback during our pilot sessions, we decided to ease this cognitive burden by eliciting the overall preference ranking in several steps. First, the executive was asked to give his pairwise preferences between a reference venture D and each of the remaining ventures. Subsequently, he was instructed to list the ventures he preferred to D in one box and those ventures not preferred to D in a second box. Lastly, the executive was asked to rank the ventures preferred to D, to rank the ventures not preferred to D, and then to combine all nine ventures into a single ranking.

By characterizing the investment opportunities with a wide range of attributes, we have a rich decision situation in which to compare the actual investment preferences of executives against those prescribed by normative theories. We can also derive from the data other attributes such as expected loss and expected gain to examine the descriptive validity of normative theories based on these attributes. Using these attributes we can characterize an executive's propensity to take risks by examining his relative preference for investments with low variation in returns, low probability of loss, and other objective indicators of riskiness. In addition, we can infer from the preference rankings what attributes the managers focus on when evaluating alternative risky personal investments.

OUR STUDY

The executives in our study were given a seven-page questionnaire (see pages 317–323 in the Appendix) containing the set of nine alternatives presented in Table 5.1. The investment alternatives were summarized in a table where their expected return and variation in returns were prominently displayed. The probabilities of attaining key target levels for each alternative could be found by noting the expected return and the variation. The executives were asked to make a series of pairwise choices among the alternatives and finally to give a complete ranking of the nine alternatives in terms of their preference for investing 10% of their net wealth. The anticipated time for completing this *Risk-Return Rankings* questionnaire was 20 minutes.

Complete preference rankings over all nine investment alternatives were given by 464 of the executives. The other 45 executives either failed to include each of the ventures or they listed ventures more than once.

With nine alternatives there are 362,880 possible rankings, so we expect to see a wide variety of preference orderings.[3] The most frequent ranking (CFRADGSBE) was given by only 24 of the executives. Three other rankings occurred 12 or more times, while 25 other rankings appeared at least three times. An additional 31 rankings occurred twice. Hence we see that there was no strong agreement on the most preferred orderings. In fact 218 executives gave a ranking that no other executive gave.

We will examine the investment rankings with the following questions in mind. First, how do executives evaluate personal investments described in terms of attributes of the distribution of returns? Second, which investment attributes do executives focus on when making these evaluations?

In analyzing the rankings provided by the executives, we made the assumption that a person preferred higher values of expected return, chance of breaking even, chance of gaining at least 50%, and chance of gaining at least 100%. Correspondingly, we assumed that they preferred lower values of chance of losing at least 10%, chance of losing at least 50%, chance of losing the total investment, and standard deviation.

NOTE ON RELIABILITY OF RANKINGS

Before analyzing the rankings, we need to ascertain whether they seem reliable. To check on reliability, we had each executive make eight pairwise choices prior to making the overall ranking. They were asked to choose whether they preferred the reference alternative D versus each of the other eight alternatives. A test of the reliability of the rankings, then, can be obtained by comparing the pairwise choices to the relative position of each alternative in the ranking vis-à-vis the position of the reference alternative D.

A reliable ranking would be one in which the position of each alternative in the ranking was the same as the pairwise choice. Since having to rank nine alternatives is no easy matter, to find perfect consistency is a good test of reliability. We found that 429 of the 464 executives were perfectly consistent. Of the 35 executives who did not have perfect consistency between the ranking and the pairwise choices, all but nine had only a single inconsistency. Thus the independence of irrelevant alternatives axiom (Arrow, 1951) seems to hold for the investment rankings. We have some evidence then that the choices were thought out and are worth analyzing.

Another check on reliability is to see how many times a stochastically dominated alternative was chosen. One alternative stochastically dominates a second if the first has at least as high a cumulative probability of receiving a payoff as good as or better than a specified level for each of the specified levels. Of the 464 executives, 422 (i.e., 91%) satisfied stochastic dominance for the six key probability levels. This high percentage gives extra assurance of the reliability of the preference rankings.

RESEARCH FINDINGS

Are the Executives Risk Averters or Risk Takers?

Earlier we argued that investment alternatives S and R could be considered the safest and the riskiest ventures, respectively. A simple way to examine the riskiness of a person's investment ranking is to look at where these two alternatives are placed in the ranking.[4]

The distributions of preference ranks for ventures S and R are shown in Figure 5.2 for the 464 complete rankings. We see that almost 70% of the executives put the safest venture in one of the three least preferred ranks. More than one out of three executives ranked it dead last! These bottom three ranks were less preferred than the rank a risk-neutral person would give (i.e., an ordering of the alternatives solely on the basis of expected return). Less than 10% of the executives put the safest venture in the three most preferred ranks. The ranks for the riskiest venture were more widely distributed than the ranks for the safest venture. About two out of five executives put the riskiest venture in the three most preferred ranks compared with one

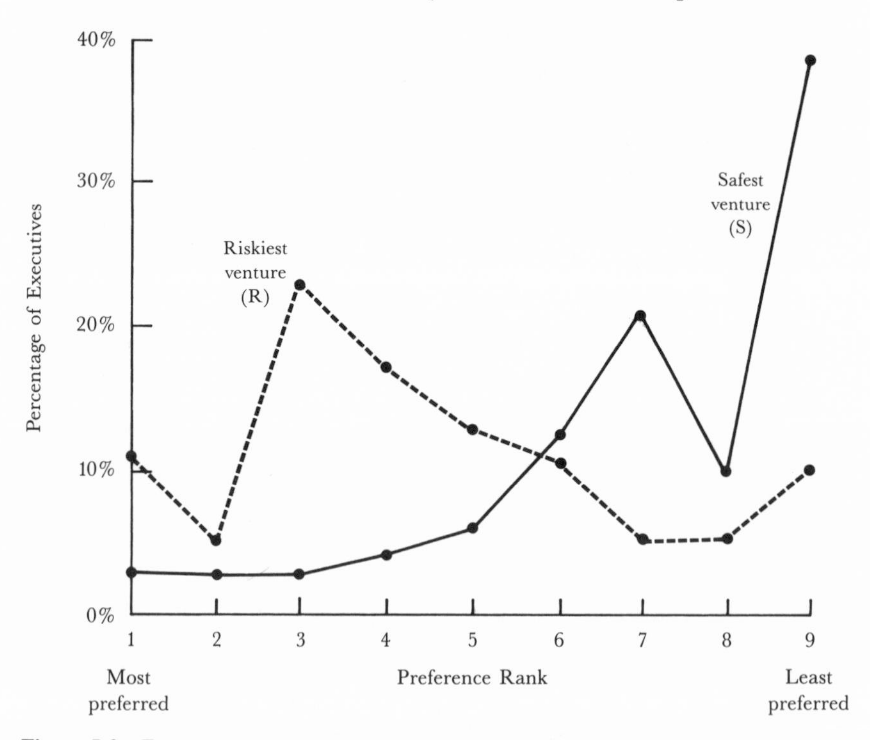

Figure 5.2 Percentage of Executives at Each Preference Rank for the Safest and the Riskiest Ventures

out of five executives who put it in the three least preferred ranks. The most common positions for the riskiest venture were third and fourth most preferred among the nine ventures, which is what a risk-neutral person would answer. More than three out of every four executives preferred the riskiest venture over the safest venture.

The extremely undesirable preference rankings for the safest venture and the moderately desirable rankings for the riskiest venture suggest that overall the executives' investment rankings were relatively risk-taking.

Result: Risk taking was more prevalent than risk averting.

When investing 10% of net wealth, clearly the executives wanted a run for their money. The relatively safe alternative was just too safe. While it did not threaten much chance of losing a major portion of the investment, neither did it offer the chance to do really well.

It might be thought that an investment of 10% of net wealth would not be treated seriously. Remember, though, that 10% of net wealth amounts to $30,000 for the average executive in our study. Few of them are likely to view $30,000 as play money. In addition, we have data on asset holdings so we know that most of the managers did not have $30,000 of highly liquid assets. (For example, more than 30% of them held no wealth in savings accounts.) The majority of the managers would have to liquidate some asset holdings to cover a 10% loss in net wealth.

Since we have information on an executive's holdings of risky assets (see Chapter 9), we can look at the portfolio implications of their choices. Those executives who held a high proportion of their assets in safe categories tended to be more risk-taking in investing the marginal 10% of their net wealth. Those executives who held a low proportion of their assets in safe categories tended to be more conservative in their marginal 10% investment.[5]

Thus, investment alternatives should not be considered in isolation. Any investment of significance (and 10% of net wealth on a single venture is quite significant) should be treated as a change in portfolio holdings. To attain the desired risk position, it may be necessary to act somewhat conservatively in a particular setting to balance an overemphasis on risk in other situations.

Are Executives Consistent in Their Risk Propensity?

We can learn more about a person's risk preference by examining where he ranks the safest venture, S, and where he ranks the riskiest venture, R, relative to all the participants in the study. Consistent risk-averse executives would be expected to be in the top third in their ranking of S but in the bottom third in their ranking of R. Eighty-eight executives can be called consistent risk averters in this sense. On the other hand, consistent risk takers would be in the bottom third in their ranking of S and in the top third in their ranking of R. One hundred executives were consistent risk takers in this sense.[6]

> ***Result:*** Managers who preferred the riskiest venture showed consistent risk propensity by disliking the safest venture, and vice versa.

Thus slightly over 20% of the managers were consistent in their preference for risk (and their aversion to safety), while slightly under 20% of the managers were consistent in their aversion to risk (and their preference for safety). Not all managers can be expected to show clear-cut risk propensities but those who are consistent are easier to predict.

Evaluating Risky Attributes

Cognitive psychologists and artificial intelligence experts have determined that people have very limited capabilities for processing information. While few of these studies have involved business executives, we know that when anyone is faced with choosing among a number of alternatives described in terms of several attributes, only a few attributes are considered. In investment decisions, it would be useful to know *how many* attributes are taken into account. Furthermore we would like to know *which* investment attributes receive the most attention and how they are combined to reach an overall choice. When only a single attribute is considered, does expected return or some chance of loss predominate? How much attention does expected return receive compared to variation in returns? Do gains or losses serve as focal points?

In answering these questions we will first consider the extent to which a focus on a *single* attribute of an investment can explain the preference ranking of the alternatives. Then we will consider the possibility that the executives focused on *two* attributes. Finally, we will see if the results are more consistent with a focus on *more than two* attributes.

NOTE ON ANALYSIS OF PREFERENCE RANKINGS

Three major approaches were taken in the analysis of the rankings provided by the executives. First we assumed that the ranking had to be a "perfect fit" with a given focal ranking in order for it to be classified as consistent with that ranking. No allowance was made for error. Since some focal rankings involved ties (because some alternatives had the same values of particular attributes) we considered a ranking given by an executive to be an exact fit if it was identical to any of the tied rankings.

In the second approach, called "close fit," we allowed the possibility that executives might make slight errors. We determined which observed rankings were significantly correlated with selected focal rankings using Spearman rank correlations ($\rho > 0.783$, $\alpha = 0.01$, one-tailed test).

In the last approach we determined which of several focal rankings best matched each observed ranking. This approach was called "closest fit." The best match was found by determining the maximum positive Spearman correlation between an executive's ranking and each of the selected focal rankings. This maximum correlation had to be significantly positive at a 1% level in order for the match to be made.

Do Executives Focus on Only One Investment Attribute?

Remember that the nine investment alternatives were each explicitly defined by two attributes (expected return and variation). These two attributes in turn allowed the executives to look up six additional attributes (involving chances of gains, losses, and break-even) in a table. Keeping in mind that using multiple attributes is complicated, we would expect only a few attributes to be the basis of a person's ranking. But which attributes? It seems likely that only a single attribute may be used. Let us start out with that view, then later look at whether a second or third attribute helps to explain an executive's ranking.

Many of the 362,880 possible rankings of the nine investment alternatives would not seem to make much sense. However, some rationale can probably be given for most of the rankings no matter how bizarre. Very few of these rankings, however, are perfectly consistent with a focus on a single attribute. For example, only four of the possible rankings are a perfect fit with a focus on maximizing *expected return*.[7] So the chance that an executive would provide one of these four rankings by choosing randomly is very small (i.e., about one chance in 100,000). As it happens, all four of these rankings actually occurred. In fact, 11% of the 464 executives provided one of these four rankings. Thus, a significant number of executives seemed to be choosing solely on the basis of expected return.

A slightly different analysis would recognize that although a manager may use an expected return criterion, he may deviate from it slightly, due to a mistake or a slight shift in focus. Thus we need to look at those rankings that are very close to the expected return criterion even if they do not match it perfectly. Almost two-thirds of the 464 rankings were a close fit to the expected return criterion. Hence the managers in our study did seem to focus strongly on expected return.

The next most common single focus was the criterion of maximizing major *gain* (either 50% gain or 100% gain). There are four possible rankings that are consistent with such a focus on major gains. These rankings actually occurred in 4% of the cases. (Remember that random choice would lead to the miniscule 0.001%, i.e., 4/362,880.) When we allowed for slight deviations, we found that 49% of the executives had a ranking close to the 50% gain criterion, while 36% had a ranking close to the 100% gain criterion. It is apparent, then, that a focus on gain was very common.

Breaking even was not as common a focus. Only one executive had a ranking that perfectly matched one of the two possible break-even rankings. Allowing for slight mistakes, we found that 11% of the rankings were closely related to the break-even criterion.

Surprisingly, a focus on *loss* was even less prominent. Only one executive had a ranking perfectly consistent with minimizing loss, although there were 103 possible rankings that were a perfect match with minimizing loss. Fewer than 1% of the rankings were close to a total loss criterion and only 2% were close to a 50% loss criterion. Seven percent were close to a 10% loss criterion. Clearly minimizing loss was not a prominent focus of the executives in their investment decisions.

Even less attention was given to the criterion of minimizing *variation*. While four possible rankings reflected this criterion, none of them actually occurred. Obviously minimizing variation was not a criterion used by these managers. Even when we allowed for slight errors, we found fewer than 1% of the rankings were closely related to the criterion of minimizing variation.

> ***Result:*** Most rankings were consistent with a focus on a single investment attribute. Executives focused most strongly on the criterion of expected return. Many executives also focused on the prospect of major gains. Few executives focused on major losses. Virtually no executives were concerned about variation in payoffs per se.

These results are clear-cut. The managers did select investment alternatives as if they were trying to maximize some single criterion. By far the most popular criterion was maximizing *expected return*. Almost half (49%) of the rankings were best explained by a criterion of expected return in the sense that expected return gave the closest fit among the individual investment criteria. Those managers who did not try to maximize expected return tended to focus on maximizing the chance of significant *gain* (24%). A focus on breaking even best explained about 6% of the rankings, while a focus on minor losses (10% loss) best explained 4% of the rankings. Very few (i.e., less than 1%) of the rankings could be best explained by minimizing significant loss (50% or 100% loss). Variation was even less of a focus than major losses. Only a single manager gave a ranking that could best be explained by minimizing variation. Fifteen percent of the rankings could not be explained by any of these single criteria.

NOTE ON SINGLE-ATTRIBUTE MODELS

When we required a "perfect fit" to assign an executive's ranking to a focal criterion, we found that only 70 of the 464 rankings could be assigned. In the text we made some allowance for mistakes or slight deviations by looking at how many rankings were close to a focal criterion in the sense that they had significant Spearman correlations at the 0.01 level. In addition to simply assigning an actual ranking to any focal ranking which it was close to, we also ascertained which focal ranking it was *closest* to (i.e., its maximum positive correlation). The table below shows the complete picture for "perfect fit," "close fit," and "closest fit." Note that the criterion of expected return comes through even more strongly in the "closest" analysis. Of the 464 rankings, 227 were closest to expected return. The next highest assignment was 62 executives to the criterion of 50% gain. For 71 rankings the best correlation was not good enough so they could not be assigned to any criterion. Thus the criterion of expected return had more cases assigned to it than all the other criteria put together.

Number of Executives Whose Preference Rankings Can Be Explained By a Single Investment Attribute

Investment Attribute	Number of Rankings Explained: *Perfect Fit*	*Close Fit*	*Closest Fit*
Expected return	49	302	227
Major gain			
100% gain	13	165	51
50% gain	6	225	62
Middle level			
Break-even	1	49	29
10% loss	1	33	19
Major loss			
50% loss	0	9	4
Total loss	0	3	0
Variation	0	4	1
Inadequate fit	394	N/A	71
Total	464	N/A	464

We did not explicitly consider the investment attribute coefficient of variation (i.e., standard deviation divided by expected return) in the analyses. Ordering the alternatives from lowest to highest on coefficient of variation gave the same focal ranking (except for ties) as maximizing the chance of breaking even. Thus this attribute was considered implicitly although it was confounded with the break-even criterion.

These results are not surprising. Maximizing expected return on investment is often a stated management goal. In addition, each alternative was directly characterized by the expected return that it offered. The expected return criterion embodies the overall effect of an alternative. A change in any of the other attributes would affect the expected return.

The strong consideration given to the chance of significant gain could also be expected. Since the executives were considering an investment of 10% of their total wealth, the amount was significant enough to matter but not a disaster if it was all lost. With such "discretionary" funds, the investor might be particularly concerned about making some major gains.

However, what is surprising is the almost complete lack of attention given to the chances of major loss and to minimizing variation. When there is a chance that an investment prospect could result in losing the entire stake, one might expect that a manager might try to minimize the chance of large losses. Such a focus was almost nonexistent here.

We also would have expected that minimizing variation might have received some attention. After all, it was featured as a descriptor of each investment alternative just as prominently as was expected return. In addition, in portfolio analyses of risk-return, risk is usually characterized by variation. On the other hand, variation is a much more subtle concept than the others, and thus is harder to grasp and interpret.

Do Executives Use Investment Attributes as Goals and Constraints in Their Decisions?

So far we have looked at whether a single attribute, such as expected return, can explain the rankings of the investment alternatives given by each executive. Although 85% of the 464 rankings were significantly related to one of the single attributes, only 70 of the rankings were a perfect match. Hence we need to check whether the observed rankings can be better explained by assuming that the managers focused on two attributes.

Note on noncompensatory models for combining two attributes

In analyzing two attributes, we applied the "perfect fit" approach by looking at dominance relations. For some of the pairwise combinations in an executive's ranking, one alternative is better than a second alternative on each of two attributes (or at least better on one and not worse on the other). A "dominance test" then requires that the ranking given by an executive cannot be inconsistent with any of the dominance relations implied by particular pairs of attributes. This is a "noncompensatory" procedure in that high values on one attribute cannot compensate for low values on a second attribute. Each attribute of an alternative has to be as good as or better than the corresponding attribute of the second alternative in order for the first alternative to be deemed better. We give the results for the mean-variance dominance model later in the chapter. The results for dominance models based on other pairs of attributes are given in Bassler et al. (1978).

A second noncompensatory model assumes that people use one attribute as a constraint to eliminate alternatives that are unsatisfactory on that attribute and then they order the remaining alternatives using a different attribute as a goal. We will describe this method more fully in the text. For the general class of such methods see the discussion of sequential elimination procedures in MacCrimmon (1973). In analyzing two attributes using the closest fit approach, we first derived 305 focal rankings involving one goal and one constraint from among the eight explicit attributes and different numbers of alternatives in the constraint set. We then found the maximum positive Spearman correlation between each observed ranking and these focal rankings to determine the closest fit.

Libby and Fishburn (1977) reviewed several empirical studies of investment decision making and concluded that both compensatory and noncompensatory features should be included in investment models. They suggested a model in which risk first plays a role as a ruin constraint and then interacts with expected return as a tradeoff parameter.

A common way of dealing with two attributes involves a two-stage process. First, one attribute is used as a constraint (i.e., a cutoff). All alternatives not meeting this constraint are eliminated. Then, and only then, is attention turned to the second attribute. This attribute is used as a goal to order the remaining alternatives. For example, a manager may first rule out particular ventures because they threaten a high chance of significant loss. Then the remaining investment ventures are ordered from highest to lowest on expected return. Note that the manager may not obtain the alternative with the highest expected return by using this procedure since he may have eliminated it earlier if its chance of significant loss was too high. By using such a procedure, a manager can take advantage of the investments that offer the highest average payoffs without having to worry about exposing himself to large possible losses.

While the particular two-stage process involving significant loss and expected return seems reasonable, it was used by fewer than 5% of the managers in our study. Table 5.2 shows the two-way tabulation of the investment rankings viewed in terms of constraints and goals. The right margin of this table shows that only 38 managers out of 464 used significant loss as a constraint. Almost six times as many managers (209) used significant gain as a constraint. That is, they first eliminated those alternatives not promising significant gains before ordering the remaining alternatives in terms of a goal. The next most common constraint was expected return (153 managers), followed by break-even (49 managers). Only 15 managers used variation as a constraint.

The totals in the bottom margin of Table 5.2 tell us which attributes were used most frequently as goals. Forty percent of the managers (187 managers) used the goal of maximizing expected return in the second stage of the process. Almost 30% of the managers (129 managers) used significant gain as the goal, while 89 managers used break-even probability. Very few managers used either significant loss (46 managers) or variation (13 managers) as a goal.

NOTE ON MEAN-VARIANCE DOMINANCE MODELS

In the academic literature, the most frequently used pair of investment attributes is the expected return and the variance or standard deviation in returns. Markowitz (1952, 1959) laid the groundwork for this focus with the mean-variance dominance model. This model requires a particular preference ranking for 13 of the 36 pairs of investment alternatives (i.e., nine alternatives taken two at a time).

We found considerable differences in the extent to which the executives satisfied an expected return-standard deviation focus over these 13 pairs. When two alternatives with the same standard deviation but different expected returns were considered (i.e., C versus G and A versus E), 98% of the executives in both cases preferred the higher expected return. When two alternatives with the same expected return but different standard deviations were considered, in one case (A versus R) the alternative with the lower standard deviation was preferred (by 61% of the executives), but in the other case (S versus G) the alternative with the higher standard deviation was preferred (by 69% of the executives). Cases with different expected returns and standard deviations ranged between these extremes. The expected return–standard deviation dominance model worked best when both attributes were high rather than when both were low. When we looked at each executive's preference ranking as a whole, we found that only 91 (20%) of the 464 executives satisfied all 13 dominance relations for the expected return–standard deviation model.

Table 5.2 Frequency of Observed Rankings Explained by Constraints and Goals

Focal Constraints	Focal Goals					
	Expected Return	*Significant Gain*	*Break-Even*	*Significant Loss*	*Variation*	*Total*
Expected return	36	45	42	22	8	153
Significant gain	112	39	33	21	4	209
Break-even	18	27	1	2	1	49
Significant loss	16	12	10	0	0	38
Variation	5	6	3	1	0	15
Total	187	129	89	46	13	464

We know now which investment attributes are most likely to be used as constraints and which as goals, but we have not yet considered which particular combinations are most common. For the information about constraint and goal combinations we need to look at the numbers in the table itself. We are not surprised to see that 112 managers (i.e., 24% of the total) appear first to have eliminated alternatives if the alternatives did not promise a high enough chance of significant gain and then to have ordered the remaining alternatives from highest to lowest on expected return.

Next most common were other combinations in the top left-hand side of the table. Forty-five managers used expected return as a constraint and significant gain as a goal, 42 managers used expected return as a constraint and break-even as a goal, 39 managers used only significant gain (as both a goal and as a constraint), 36 managers used only expected return (as both a goal and as a constraint), and finally 33 managers used significant gain as a constraint and break-even as a goal.

> ***Result:*** The managers' rankings were generally consistent with using one investment attribute as a constraint and another attribute as a goal. Most attention was focused on expected return and significant gain. Least attention was paid to significant loss and variation. The most common two-stage process was to eliminate alternatives that offered too low a chance of significant gain and then to order the remaining alternatives in terms of expected return.

It is somewhat surprising that the downside risks received relatively little attention. While we would not expect that significant loss would be a prominent goal, it did seem likely that it would be a prominent constraint. This was not the case.

There are a number of implications of these results for managers. First, two-stage decision thinking seems to be very common. Managers do use one attribute as a constraint or a cutoff and then assess the remaining alternatives using some other attribute. Using two attributes in this sequential fashion is easier than trying to make tradeoffs between the two criteria. Managers who do not commonly think in terms of constraints and goals should consider it.

Second, while much of the academic literature on investment appraisal focuses on the downside risks in investment decisions, our top-level managers seem to have focused strongly on the upside potential of investments. Although a number of managers used the chance of significant gain to order the (remaining) alternatives, significant gain was used more frequently as a constraint. Thus each alternative was compared in terms of the chances of getting a major return (such as 50% or 100%). Any alternative that offered too low a chance, say less than 10% of doubling the investment, was eliminated.

Most specifically, the managers in our study eliminated an alternative if the chance of significant gain was not high enough and then they ordered the remaining alternatives in terms of expected return. This appears to be a useful combination of investment attributes for considering the upside potential.

Perhaps as the investment stake increased, the attention devoted to the downside risk might increase. In our study, the stake was 10%. While 10% of the typical executive's net wealth of $300,000 is a lot of money, 50% is a lot more. With a 50% stake, there could well be more concern about the downside risk.

NOTE ON EXPECTED GAIN AND EXPECTED LOSS

Since expected return seems to be such a prominent focus, it seems worthwhile to determine whether two conditional notions of expected return explain the rankings—namely, expected return calculated only over the gains, called "expected gain," and expected return calculated only over the losses, called "expected loss." The dominance model based on expected gain and expected loss was satisfied by almost 40% of the executives. (This was very closely related to the dominance model involving the chance of 50% gain and the chance of 50% loss.)[11]

For each of the 464 executives we fit the best linear model of expected gain and expected loss to the preference ranks. This allowed us to examine the relative weight given to expected gain and expected loss in tradeoffs between them. For 86% of the executives (397) we could fit a significant ($\alpha = 0.05$) model. Almost 40% of the executives (171) had rankings in which only expected gain had a significant coefficient. In 99% of these cases, the coefficient was positive indicating a criterion of maximizing expected gain. In less than 5% of the cases expected loss was significant and expected gain was not. In 95% of these cases, the criterion was minimizing expected loss. Fifty-two percent of the significant regression models had both coefficients significantly different from zero. In every one of these models higher expected gain was preferred and in 90% of them (191 versus 19) lower expected loss was preferred.

Overall the rankings of almost half the executives were consistent with a focus on either expected gain or expected loss in isolation. The rankings of the remaining executives were consistent with tradeoffs between expected gain and expected loss.

When all 464 rankings were included in the same regression analysis, expected gain and expected loss explained 58% of the variation in preference ranks. The coefficients indicated the executives preferred higher expected gain and lower expected loss. The beta weight for expected gain was more than twice as high as for expected loss.

The conclusion from considering expected gain and expected loss, then, is that the rankings of the executives were consistent with these attributes even though the attributes themselves were not presented to the executives. The much stronger focus on expected gain, over expected loss, is consistent with our earlier analysis of the focal attributes that were presented. The executives in our study paid much more attention to gains than they did to losses. See Wehrung and MacCrimmon (1985) for a more complete discussion of the model of expected gain and expected loss.

Do Executives Trade Off Expected Return and Variation in Returns?

Another way of dealing with two attributes involves trading off one attribute against the second. For example, a manager may decide that he would be willing to accept a 15% increase in the chance of total loss for every extra 10% improvement in expected return. Unlike the two-stage method described above, a worsening on one attribute can be compensated by an improvement on the second attribute.

To study this compensatory method, we first considered the rankings collectively in a single model in which preference rank was regressed against all pairs of explicit attributes.[8] The best overall two-variable model was: 0.69 + 22.34 [expected return] − 9.93 [chance of total loss]. Adding chance of total loss to the model did not significantly increase the ability of expected return by itself to explain the rankings.[9] So, from a compensatory view, no second investment attribute significantly improved the explanatory power of expected return.

We next regressed preference rank against expected return and standard deviation for each executive considered separately. We chose these two attributes because of their prominence in portfolio analysis of risk-return. Eighty-three percent (385) of the complete rankings were significantly explained by one or both of these attributes.[10] Forty percent of these executives (153) gave rankings in which only expected return was a significant explanatory variable. In each case the ranking was consistent with maximizing expected return. Fewer executives had rankings in which only standard deviation was a significant explanatory variable. In most of these rankings (13 versus 2) the ranking was consistent with maximizing variation in returns rather than with minimizing it! Fifty-six percent of the rankings had two significant explanatory variables. In every one of these rankings executives preferred higher values of expected return. *Higher* standard deviation was preferred in about two of three such rankings. Thus it appears that most executives who make tradeoffs between expected return and standard deviation prefer higher rather than lower values of variation.

> ***Result:*** A substantial number of executives did not make tradeoffs between expected return and variation in returns. Most of these executives restricted their attention to maximizing expected return. The managers who did trade off these two attributes all preferred higher expected return, but more preferred *higher* variation in returns to lower.

This result shows that managers do not always prefer smaller variation in returns. Thus one is likely to find a preference for higher variation in other risky situations as long as the stake is not too large. Whenever a reasonable chance for significant gain is desired, it usually requires a corresponding high variability in returns as well.

Do Executives Use More Than Two Investment Attributes?

Various analyses were done to see whether the rankings given by the executives indicated a focus on more than two attributes. Although we found evidence that most executives did *consider* more than two investment attributes, such incremental attributes did not appear to add much to *explaining* the executives' rankings. There is no reason to believe that someone would use three (or more) attributes when one or two attributes were sufficient.

NOTE ON THREE OR MORE ATTRIBUTES

It was not possible to use a dominance analysis because the pairwise preferences predicted by the three-attribute models were identical to the pairwise preferences predicted by one of the dominance models involving only two of the attributes. Hence the rankings could be consistent with using three attributes but cannot be distinguished from using only two attributes.

The vast majority of rankings satisfied stochastic dominance on the six probability levels as described in an earlier technical note on reliability (see page 135). This suggests that the managers considered more than two attributes in their rankings.

Another analysis of multiple attributes used a stepwise linear regression on all rankings considered collectively. Variables were added to the model as long as they provided a significant improvement in explanatory power. The best explanatory model involving three attributes added only 2.5% improvement in explanatory power over the two-attribute model involving expected return and chance of total loss. The model 0.52 + 15.07 [expected return] − 30.63 [chance of total loss] + 7.48 [chance of 50% gain] explained 61% of the variation. Here too, there seemed to be little rationale for moving to a three-attribute model when it offered so little improvement over the two-attribute model. Note though that the best three-attribute model includes both major gain and major loss along with expected return.

CONCLUSIONS

In choosing an investment on which to stake 10% of their net wealth, more than three out of four of the executives in our study preferred the riskier alternatives. Even though data was provided on a variety of investment attributes, the large majority of the choices were consistent with focusing on maximizing the expected return. To the extent a second attribute was considered, it was used as a cutoff to eliminate alternatives that were not good enough on this attribute. The attribute that was most frequently used as a cutoff was the chance of significant gain. After eliminating alternatives that did not offer a high enough significant gain, the executives preferred the remaining alternatives based on expected return. Neither variation in returns nor chance of various levels of loss seemed to receive much attention.

Tradeoffs between investment attributes were common, but not universal. Overall the two-stage cutoff procedure seemed more consistent with the rankings of most managers than the use of tradeoffs. That only one or two attributes were needed to explain the executives' rankings supports the view that, when offered a wide variety of information on investments, managers use only limited information for their decisions.

Overall, gain was more important than loss and expected return was more important than variation in returns in explaining the rankings. In addition, there was evidence that many investors preferred higher rather than lower variation. Thus, our results suggest that the executives focused more on the upside possibilities (i.e., expected return and chance of gain) than the downside risks (i.e., variation and chance of loss).

RESEARCH CONCLUSIONS

There are five major research conclusions:

1. When we examined each executive's ranking separately, there was a great deal of variability in the best explanatory models across individuals. This was true for both single-attribute and two-attribute models. This finding reinforces the notion that there are important individual differences among the executives in the determination of their investment rankings.

2. A two-stage model in which investors first use one attribute to eliminate unfavorable alternatives and then select a second attribute to compare the remaining alternatives performed well in explaining the rankings. Such a model makes managerial sense and deserves more attention from researchers.

3. Because the mean-variation model has played such an influential role in the normative theory of portfolio selection, we would expect more than 20% of the executives to satisfy this form of dominance. This is true whether one's goal is to validate the normative model with the data presented or to measure the impact that this model has had on actual investor preference. For a given variation, executives did seem to maximize expected return, but for a given mean, the preference was more commonly for higher variation than for lower variation. Likewise very few executives seem to maximize expected return subject to a constraint on variation or to minimize variation subject to a constraint on expected return.

4. The rankings of almost half of the executives were not consistent with a tradeoff between mean and variation. Most of these rankings could be explained by maximizing expected return and some by *maximizing* variation. The rankings for the other half of the executives were consistent with tradeoffs, but our analyses gave conflicting results regarding whether higher variation was compensated with higher or lower expected return. These results suggest that a majority of executives found other attributes or evaluation methods sufficiently important to forego the mean versus variation model in their rankings. However, because of the high salience of expected return and standard deviation in the description of the ventures in the Risk-Return Rankings instrument, it is unlikely that the executives did not compare the ventures on these two attributes. It is possible that some executives preferred an intermediate level of variation

rather than successively lower or higher amounts. We will explore this concept in Chapter 6.

5. Although they were not presented as investment attributes, expected gain and expected loss provided considerable power in explaining the rankings. Twice as many rankings satisfied the two-attribute dominance model based on these attributes compared with the mean-variation dominance model. In addition the vast majority of rankings were consistent with a significant linear model involving one of these attributes or a tradeoff between the two attributes. The relative importance of expected gain over expected loss is consistent with the earlier conclusion that chance of gain was more important than chance of loss in determining rankings. Therefore, combining gain and loss amounts with their chances of occurring did not change the results.

Chapter 6

Real Money Wagers

Evaluating Gambles with Common Risk Components

INTRODUCTION

We can learn about a person's risk propensity by observing the relative emphasis he gives to losses versus gains. A risk-averse person is more likely to be concerned about losses.

A concern for losses has two components: the amount of loss and the chance of loss. Of course anyone would want to reduce both the chance and amount of loss. What we are talking about here, however, are situations in which if the chance of loss or amount of loss is decreased, then the amount to be gained is correspondingly decreased so that the expected payoff is the same in both circumstances. Because a risk-averse person pays differential attention to gains and losses, the change in loss will have a more significant impact on his perception of the wager than the change in gain.[1]

To take a specific example, consider alternatives I and II.

I: 62% chance of gaining	$20.00
38% chance of losing	$ 6.20

or

II: 62% chance of gaining	$40.00
38% chance of losing	$38.60

Even though both of these alternatives offer an expected payoff of about $10, a risk-averse person will prefer alternative I to avoid the higher loss of $38.60. Note that in the above example the chance of loss is fixed at 38% and only the amounts of gain and loss vary. We may summarize this risk concept as follows:

> In choices among two-outcome wagers having equal expected payoffs and the same chance of loss, a risk-averse person will prefer wagers with lower loss amounts.

We may also consider situations in which the expected payoff and the amount of loss are fixed and the chance of loss varies.

III: 90% chance of gaining	$13.20
10% chance of losing	$20.00

or

IV: 62% chance of gaining	$28.50
38% chance of losing	$20.00

Here the risk-averse person will prefer alternative III. Although alternative IV offers the chance of a larger gain, the increased chance of losing $20 more than offsets the positive side. This risk concept is summarized below:

> In choices among two-outcome wagers having equal expected payoffs and the same loss amount, a risk-averse person will prefer wagers with lower chances of loss.

The above risk concepts look at the chance and amount of loss separately. One way of combining them is to compute the expected loss by multiplying together the amount of loss and the chance of loss. This method of combining loss components helps us to make predictions when the loss amount changes in one direction while the chance of loss changes in the other direction. Consider, for example, the following alternatives:

V: 28% chance of gaining	$40.00
72% chance of losing	$ 1.40

or

VI: 62% chance of gaining	$40.00
38% chance of losing	$38.60

Note that in alternative VI, while the amount of loss is significantly higher than in alternative V, the chance of loss is lower. On balance, however, the expected loss is larger for alternative VI ($14.67 vs.

$1.00). Hence a risk averter would prefer alternative V. We may summarize this notion of risk as:

> In choices among two-outcome wagers having equal expected payoffs and the same gain amount, a risk-averse person will prefer wagers with lower expected losses.

An alternative notion of riskiness is also present in these situations. Note that for the second alternative in each of the examples above, the variation in payoffs is larger. This suggests that a risk-averse person will want to avoid situations in which variation is high. We may summarize this concept as follows:

> In choices among two-outcome wagers having equal expected payoffs, a risk-averse person will prefer wagers with lower variation in payoffs.

We will consider one last pair of alternatives:

VII: 100% chance of winning $10.00

or

VIII: 62% chance of winning	$28.50
38% chance of losing	$20.00

As with the other risky options, alternative VIII has an expected payoff of $10.00. So we have here a sure $10.00 versus a gamble having an expected return of $10.00. The sure alternative of winning $10.00 has four important properties: the chance of loss is zero, the loss amount is zero, the expected loss is zero, and the variation in payoffs is zero. This view of the sure alternative leads us to the following special form of risk aversion inherent in the previous concepts of risk:

> A risk-averse person will prefer the certainty of getting the expected payoff of a wager to the wager itself.

The riskiness of the wagers presented above has been characterized in terms of the wagers' components. Our concepts of risk have implicitly assumed that wagers increase in riskiness with increases in loss amounts, chances of loss, expected losses, and variation in payoffs. A preference for wagers low in these attributes will be interpreted as an indication of risk aversion.

OUR STUDY

We used a seven-page questionnaire to obtain the executives' rankings over two-outcome wagers such as those described above. We will refer to this questionnaire as *Real Money Wagers* because real money was at stake in the wagers. An example from this questionnaire is reproduced in the Appendix (page 325).

The questionnaire consisted of three sets of five alternatives each. Within each set there was one alternative that offered $10 for sure, while the other four alternatives involved simple two-outcome wagers with specified probabilities. All of the alternatives had the same expected payoff of $10.[2] See Table 6.1 for a summary of the actual alternatives used in this study.[3] The variation in payoffs was measured using the concept of "standard deviation." A decision tree representation of the choice among alternatives in set A using the Basic Risk Paradigm is given in Figure 6.1.

In set A the loss amount was held fixed, while the chance of loss and the gain amount varied. In set C the chance of loss was held fixed, while the loss amount and the gain amount varied. In set B the gain amount was the constant while the loss amount and the chance of loss changed (in opposite directions).

In sets A and C the wagers increased (or stayed the same) in riskiness from alternative 1 to alternative 5 as measured by chance of loss, loss amount, expected loss, and variation in payoffs. In set B riskiness increased (or stayed the same) from alternative B1 to alternative B5 as measured by loss amount, expected loss, and variation. However, if we measure riskiness by chance of loss, we see that riskiness increased in the order B5, B4, B3, and B2 with the lowest riskiness for the sure wager B1.[4] Therefore in set B the riskiness of the wagers depends upon which risk component is considered.

Because wagers A5, B5, and C5 had the highest variation in payoffs, expected loss, and either loss amount or chance of loss within their respective sets, they were chosen as the "riskiest" alternatives. For obvious reasons the sure wagers A1, B1, and C1 were chosen as the "lowest risk" alternatives within their sets.

Each executive was asked to give several rankings among the wagers. First he was asked to rank the five wagers in set A. Next he was asked to rank the five wagers in set B. Lastly he was asked to rank the five wagers in set C. After the three sets had each been ranked separately, the executive was asked to consider the most preferred wager from each of the sets and to rank these three wagers. In order to encourage the executives to think carefully about their rankings they were told that they could not change them later if they were chosen to play out a wager. The anticipated time for completing the questionnaire was 15 minutes.

The instructions in the questionnaire emphasized that the wagers involved real money. Each executive was told that he had a one-third chance of being selected to play out his most preferred wager from one of the sets (to be chosen by the experimenter). Whether he was

Table 6.1 Summary of the Wager Alternatives

	Wager Number	Best Outcome	Worst Outcome	Chance of Worst Outcome*	Expected Loss*	Standard Deviation*
Set A	A1	10.00	10.00	—	0.00	0
	A2	13.20	− 20.00	0.10	− 2.00	10.0
	A3	28.50	− 20.00	0.38	− 7.60	23.5
	A4	89.00	− 20.00	0.72	−14.40	48.9
	A5	414.00	− 20.00	0.93	−18.60	110.7
Set B	B1	10.00	10.00	—	0.00	0
	B2	40.00	7.80	0.93	0.00	8.3
	B3	40.00	− 1.40	0.72	− 1.01	18.6
	B4	40.00	− 38.60	0.38	−14.67	38.2
	B5	40.00	−274.00	0.10	−27.40	94.2
Set C	C1	10.00	10.00	—	0.00	0
	C2	20.00	− 6.20	0.38	− 2.36	12.7
	C3	30.00	− 22.40	0.38	− 8.51	25.4
	C4	40.00	− 38.60	0.38	−14.67	38.2
	C5	50.00	− 54.80	0.38	−20.82	50.9

*Based on chances of best and worst outcomes as summarized in the questionnaire.

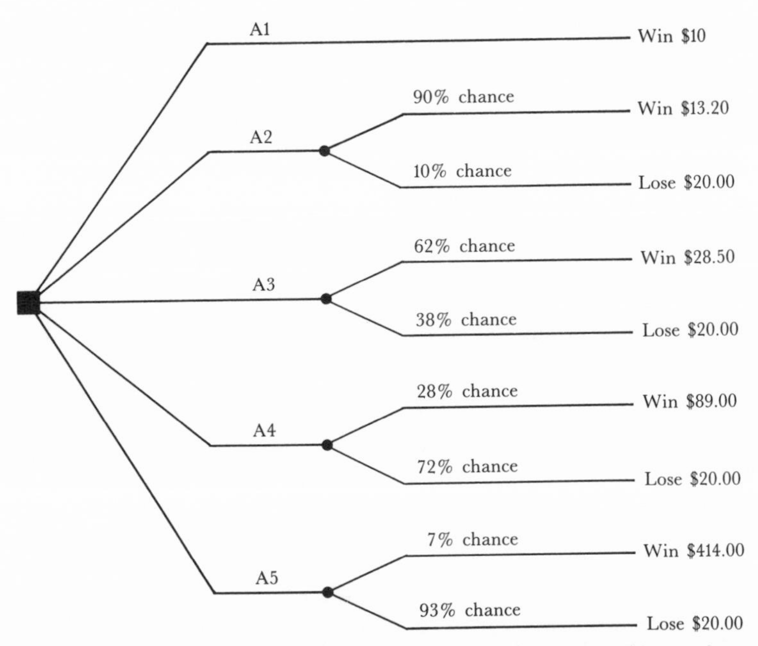

Figure 6.1 Decision Tree Representation of Choice among Alternatives in Set A

selected to play out a wager would be determined by rolling a die after the questionnaire had been completely answered. To make the payoff more immediate, we showed our checkbook and asked the executives to indicate how they would pay us if they lost.

A mechanism based on stock prices and their fractional parts was used to determine the outcome of a chosen wager. This mechanism was thoroughly explained to the executives and the resulting chances for obtaining each outcome were summarized with each wager.[5]

Note, then, some of the distinctive features of the Real Money Wagers questionnaire. First, real money payoffs were used. We could lose over $400 on a single wager and the executive could lose almost $300, depending on the choices he made. Second, within each set, five alternatives had to be ranked in order of preference. Since all these alternatives had an identical expected return, the ranking was determined by preference or aversion to risk. In each set, one alternative offered a certain payoff (which was the same as the expected payoffs of the four risky alternatives). Third, in each of the three sets of wagers, one element of risk was held fixed, so that the risk focus of the executive could be ascertained. In addition, some less important features, such as the stock price mechanism for generating the outcomes, added to the distinctiveness of this questionnaire.

NOTE ON DEVELOPMENT OF THE REAL MONEY WAGERS QUESTIONNAIRE

The Real Money Wagers questionnaire was designed with several important considerations in mind. For example, when using professionals as subjects, it is desirable for motivational reasons to use a context related to their special knowledge and interest. Since we were dealing with executives, we developed a probability mechanism based on stock prices and their fractional parts, with which executives may have had prior experience, to generate the uncertain outcomes for our wagers rather than using urns, dice, or cards.

Even more important than using this investment context for determining uncertain outcomes is the use of real, rather than hypothetical, payoffs. The subject's realization that his stated preferences will determine an immediate, real money outcome to himself provides a powerful incentive for him to give careful thought to his preferences and to reveal them truthfully and accurately. In the few previous cases in which the wager preferences of business executives have been studied, the payoffs were hypothetical.

In the usual studies with college students, the payoffs are either hypothetical or involve only pennies (Mosteller and Nogee, 1951; Edwards, 1953, 1954; Coombs and Pruitt, 1960; Kogan and Wallach, 1964). On the few occasions where more significant sums of money had been involved, the subjects were usually given a prior stake, or had an expectation of not losing money. In our study, on the other hand, we used wagers involving possible losses up to $274 and possible wins up to $414! Wagers were played out with a subset of the executives chosen randomly and real money actually changed hands.

Slovic, Lichtenstein, and Edwards (1965) have provided evidence that subjects tend to become bored when asked to make a large number of hypothetical choices in a short period of time. As a result they use simple strategies induced by the boredom effect. In order to circumvent this boredom effect it is important to keep the number of responses requested relatively low. With our instrument there were only a relatively small number (33) of paired comparisons required to determine the preference rankings within each of the three sets of wagers and across the three most preferred wagers from these sets. We believe that the relatively small number of required judgments together with the use of real money wagers of moderate size and a familiar context serve to eliminate effects due to boredom.

In determining whether an individual focuses upon some particular risk component as a basis for rankings, it is desirable to ascertain the conditions under which one focus is found versus another. Do individuals focus on chance of loss when loss amount is held constant but on loss amount when gain amount is held constant? If they focus on chance of loss each time it varies, what do they focus upon when it is held constant? Researchers have been paying increasing attention to risk components and context effects (Slovic and Lichtenstein, 1968; Payne and Braunstein, 1971; Payne, 1973). In each of the three sets of wagers either chance of loss, loss amount, or gain amount was held constant. This design permits us to address these questions and related context-oriented issues.

Various theoretical and empirical studies of risk have raised concerns about the presence of a risk-free alternative. Some of the experimental results in decision studies have shown that individuals tend to treat certain alternatives quite differently from risky alternatives. The inclusion of a sure alternative in each of the three sets of our instrument allows us to examine risk behavior both when this alternative is included in the analysis and when it is not.

A version of the Real Money Wagers instrument was included in pilot tests with undergraduate and graduate business students. In these sessions the use of actual monetary payoffs was not employed. Subsequently, the instrument was given to our sample of 40 senior business executives for further testing. Actual monetary consequences were used in this study, although the expected value of each alternative was $5 rather than $10. These pilot tests helped to refine the instrument and improve its administration.

Because of constraints on the amount of time that each executive had to participate in the study, the Real Money Wagers questionnaire was not administered to all executives in the main study. One hundred twenty-eight Canadian executives who were being followed up in conjunction with other questionnaires were asked to complete the Real Money Wagers questionnaire.

Eighty-eight executives answered the questionnaire. Complete rankings (that included each alternative once and only once) were given by 88, 87, and 86 executives, respectively, in sets A, B, and C.

Of the 88 executives 19 were given a chance to play out a wager.[6] In each case the most preferred wager across all three sets was played out. The six winning executives won an average of $81.60 (much increased by the *payment* to one executive of $414 from wager A5). The 13 losing executives lost an average of $10.72, including four who lost $20 each on wager A5.

NOTE ON RELIABILITY OF THE RANKINGS

Wagers B1 and B4 are identical to wagers C1 and C4, respectively. This observation provided a simple test of the reliability of the executives' rankings across sets. For consistency to hold, the executive must either prefer B1 to B4 and C1 to C4 or he must prefer B4 to B1 and C4 to C1. Reversals of preference between these two wagers in sets B and C demonstrate inconsistency.

Of the 85 executives who provided complete rankings for wagers in both sets B and C, 76 (89%) were consistent. Although this result suggests the data satisfy an acceptable level of reliability, the inconsistent responses deserve careful attention. These responses will be examined more fully in a later technical note (see page 163).

RESEARCH FINDINGS

Some executives may be strongly predisposed to evaluating the alternatives in a risky situation in terms of a specific risk component such as the chance of loss. How do they react, then, when that risk component is held constant or when it varies in a situation where other risk components of concern are held constant? The Real Money Wagers questionnaire was designed to gain insight into these questions by holding constant a different risk component in each set of wagers.

Are the Executives Risk-Averse in Wagers Where the Chance of Loss Is Held Fixed?

We will see that the answer is overwhelmingly yes. First recall that the risky alternatives in set C all had the same 38% chance of loss. The sure alternative, C1, of winning $10 was clearly the least risky alternative. Earlier we showed that wager C5 was the riskiest wager in set C because it had the highest loss amount, expected loss, and variation in payoffs.

Table 6.2 shows the executives' preference ranks for the sure alternative and the riskiest wager in each set. We see in set C that two out of three executives placed the sure alternative first or second in their rankings and fewer than 10% placed it last. Almost 90% of executives indicated that the riskiest wager C5 was lowest in preference. Thus a large majority of the executives were highly risk-averse in ranking the wagers in set C.

> ***Result:*** The executives were highly risk-averse in ranking wagers that had a common chance of loss.

Fixing the chance of loss at a relatively high level (38%) may have increased the perceived riskiness of the wagers in set C. A common way to deal with situations that are viewed as highly risky is to choose a low risk alternative as the large majority of our managers did in this set of wagers. If the chance of loss had been fixed at a much lower level, say 10%, the situation may have been perceived as not very risky and the executives may have shown more risk taking in their rankings.

Table 6.2 Distributions of Preference Ranks for Sure Alternatives and Riskiest Wagers (Percentages)

Preference Rank		Sure Alternatives			Riskiest Wagers		
		A1	*B1*	*C1*	*A5*	*B5*	*C5*
Most preferred	1	30	14	25	15	3	6
	2	16	21	42	11	4	1
	3	20	44	16	8	5	0
	4	17	16	8	10	4	4
Least preferred	5	17	5	9	56	84	89
Total		100	100	100	100	100	100
Median preference rank		2.7	2.8	2.1	3.6	3.9	3.9

Are the Executives Risk-Averse in Wagers Where the Loss Amount Is Held Fixed?

All the risky alternatives in set A required the executives to stake $20, so they all had the same loss amount. Wager A5 was the riskiest wager in this set because it had the highest chance of loss, expected loss, and variation in payoffs. How did the executives rank the sure alternative (A1) and the riskiest alternative (A5) in this set?

Slightly more executives (46%) ranked the sure alternative high than ranked it low (34%), indicating a slight trend toward risk aversion. A greater indication of the overall risk aversion is apparent when we note that the riskiest wager was least preferred by 56% of the executives. However, some executives showed extreme risk taking by ranking the riskiest wager first (15%) or ranking the sure alternative last (17%). Thus risk aversion was predominant in the rankings of most, but not all, executives, although it was not as pronounced as it was in set C.

> ***Result:*** The executives were generally risk-averse in ranking wagers that had a common loss amount, but some managers were risk-taking.

Holding the amount of the stake fixed at a relatively low level ($20) may have decreased the perceived riskiness of the wagers in set A because it limited the downside risk. Perceiving the wagers in set A as less risky than those in set C may have led most executives to be less risk-averse in their rankings in set A and some even became risk-taking.

NOTE ON MOST PREFERRED WAGERS IN SETS A AND C

We have concluded that the most risk-averse responses were given in set C and the least risk-averse responses were given in set A. We based this conclusion on the results in Table 6.2 that involve rankings *within* individual sets. The relative risk propensity of executives *across* sets can also be examined by comparing the most preferred wagers from these two sets.

Forty-eight percent of the executives had lower wager numbers (i.e., less risky) for their most preferred wager in set C than in set A, 17% had lower wager numbers in set A than in set C, and 35% had tied wager numbers. For example, wager C2 was most preferred in set C by about two out of three executives. The wager most preferred in set A by these executives had a higher (more risky) wager number (i.e., A3, A4, or A5) much more frequently than a lower (less risky) wager number (i.e., A1). This analysis reinforces the conclusion that substantially more risk-averse responses were given in set C than in set A.

Are the Executives Risk-Averse in Wagers Where the Gain Amount Is Held Fixed?

The risky alternatives in set B all had the same gain amount of $40. Although the gain amount is not a "risk component" of a risky alternative as defined in Chapter 1, it is still an important attribute because it describes the upside potential of the wager. The importance of potential gains as a focal point comes through strongly in the results of Chapter 5. The riskiest wager in set B was B5 because it had the highest loss amount, expected loss, and variation in payoffs. As in the other sets, alternative 1 was the sure payoff.

More executives (35%) ranked the sure alternative high than ranked it low (21%), and an overwhelming number of executives (84%) ranked the riskiest wager as their least preferred. The degree of risk aversion shown by the rankings in this set was, therefore, intermediate between that shown in the other two sets.

> ***Result:*** The executives were risk-averse in ranking wagers that had a common gain amount.

The common gain amount allowed the executives to focus solely on the downside risks. The very high loss amount in wager B5 ($274) apparently made this wager highly undesirable. The low actual (or opportunity) losses in wagers B2 and B3 apparently made them preferable to the sure alternative for many executives.

NOTE ON INTERPRETING THE EFFECTS OF HOLDING RISK COMPONENTS FIXED

Differences in the riskiness of the wager rankings could be due to either (1) differences in the individual wager attributes or (2) the context effect of holding one attribute fixed at some specified level. Let's first consider the wagers in sets A and C. The wagers in both these sets have very comparable expected losses ranging from zero to about $20. Their standard deviations are also somewhat comparable, although there is a trend toward higher standard deviations in set A. Neither of these attributes could explain why more executives gave risk-averse responses in set C than in set A, although the other wager attributes might.

On the other hand, the loss amount is held fixed at $20 in set A and the chance of loss is held fixed at 38% in set C. When faced with the wagers in set A, the executive might perceive the fixed $20 loss amount as a highly visible indication of the limit on his downside risk. Consequently, he may view all the alternatives in set A as somewhat less risky than if they did not have a common (low) loss amount. In set C the fixed 38% chance of loss might be perceived as a noticeable reminder of the riskiness of the wagers in that set. As a result, the executive may have evaluated all the wagers in set C as somewhat more risky than if they did not have a common (relatively high) chance of loss. Such context effects could explain the greater preponderance of risk-averse responses in set C than in set A.

Next compare the wagers in set B with those in set A. Wager A5 is less risky than wager B5 in terms of their loss amount and expected loss, and they are similar in variation. This observation by itself can explain why 15% of the executives most preferred wager A5, while only 3% preferred B5. The common limit on the loss amount together with the high gain amounts makes wager A5 relatively desirable. In set B the common gain amount of $40.00 makes the uncertain wagers desirable, but not enough to cancel out the negative effects of the high loss amount in B5. In the comparison between sets A and B the individual wager attributes seem to have played a more important role than the context effect of holding an attribute fixed.

Lastly, we compare the wagers in sets B and C. The data show that substantially more executives gave risk-averse responses in set C than in set B. This result could be explained by the context effects in support of risk-averse responses in set C (i.e., a relatively high chance of loss) and in support of risk-taking responses in set B (i.e, high gain amount). However, the fact that the wagers in set C are more risky than those in set B on expected loss and standard deviation could also explain this result.[7] In this situation we cannot clearly distinguish whether the difference in responses across sets is due to the context effect of holding an attribute fixed or to the individual wager attributes.

Earlier we found several preference reversals involving wagers B1 and B4 which are identical to wagers C1 and C4. These reversals violate Arrow's (1951) axiom regarding the independence of irrelevant alternatives. Because these wagers have identical attributes, a preponderance of reversals in one direction can be directly linked to the context effects of holding attributes fixed within sets. Among the nine executives who exhibited this inconsistency, eight executives preferred both B4 to B1 and C1 to C4, and only one executive preferred B1 to B4 and C4 to C1. Thus in all but one of these cases, when the chance of loss was fixed at 38%, the executive preferred the sure alternative to the risky wager, but when the gain amount was fixed at $40, he preferred the risky wager to the sure alternative. These data add support for the view that fixing the chance of loss at a relatively high amount in set C may influence executives to give more risk-averse responses and fixing the gain amount at a relatively high level in set B may do the opposite.

Are the Risk Propensities Derived from an Executive's Preferences for a Sure Alternative and the Riskiest Alternative Related?

A relationship was found when either the chance or magnitude of loss was held fixed. In these two sets (C and A) the degree of association between the preference for the sure alternative and preference for the riskiest wager was significant. It was not true when the gain amount was constant; in this case no significant association was found.

> ***Result:*** The executives preferences for the sure alternative and the riskiest wager were related when the chance or magnitude of loss was held constant.

This result reinforces our earlier assumption that we can learn about an individual's willingness to take risks by examining his preference for either sure or risky alternatives. Both approaches generally provide consistent information about the individual's risk propensity. However, as we have noted in the preceding chapters, such information is not always consistent across all risky situations as we found here for wagers with a constant gain amount. This might be due to the fact that chance and magnitude of loss are true risk components whereas gain amount represents upside potential rather than a risk component per se.

Are the Executives' Risk Propensities Related for Wagers with Different Risk Attributes Held Constant?

A high preference for the sure alternative in one set was significantly related to a high preference for this alternative in another set, regardless of which risk attribute was held constant. A low preference for the riskiest wager when the chance of loss was constant was significantly associated with a low preference for the riskiest wager when the magnitude of loss was constant. Low preference for the riskiest wager when the gain amount was fixed was not significantly associated with either of these. Preference for the sure alternative therefore provided more related information about risk propensity when different risk attributes were constant than did preference for the riskiest wager.

> ***Result:*** The executives' preferences for the sure alternative were related regardless of which risk attribute was constant. Preferences for the riskiest wagers were only related when chance and magnitude of loss were constant.

This result may be partly due to the fact that the sure alternatives were identical in each set, and the riskiest wagers were different in each set. Nonetheless our results demonstrate that one's propensity for taking risks generally does transfer across risky situations where different risk attributes are held constant.

Note on relationships among risk measures in wager rankings

The Pearson correlations among the risk measures both within and across sets are given below for the 85 executives having all six measures. Only correlations significantly different from zero at a 1% level are shown. All measures were scaled so that higher values corresponded to risk taking.

Measures of Risk Propensity		Set A: Sure alternative	Set A: Riskiest wager	Set C: Sure alternative	Set C: Riskiest wager	Set B: Sure alternative	Set B: Riskiest wager
Set A	Sure alternative		.37	.54	.30	.56	
	Riskiest wager				.31	.33	
Set C	Sure alternative				.55	.56	
	Riskiest wager					.25	
Set B	Sure alternative						
	Riskiest wager						

These correlations clearly show that preference for the riskiest wager B5 in set B is not significantly related to any of the other five risk measures.

We further examined these correlations with principal component and smallest space analyses. In both analyses we confirmed that preference for wager B5 was highly distinct from the preferences for the five other alternatives both within and across sets. This result is likely due to the very high loss amount ($274) in wager B5 which differs markedly from the other "riskiest" wagers and the sure alternatives.

Do Executives Prefer Wagers with Increasingly Lower or Increasingly Higher Variation in Payoffs?

According to the theory of preference for financial investments (Markowitz, 1952, 1959), investors faced with uncertain ventures having equal expected payoffs will prefer them in the order of decreasing variation. The five alternatives within a set can be ranked in 120 ways. Only one of these rankings is consistent with preference for decreasing variation. Do the observed cases of these rankings constitute significantly more than the expected number, 0.8% (i.e., $= 1/120 \times 100\%$), of cases?

On this undemanding comparison, the 17%, 5%, and 23% of observed rankings for sets A, B, and C, respectively, were all highly significant.[8] Only in set A was the preference for decreasing variation the most common one. Although it occurred significantly more than by chance, there were more than five times as many other rankings as there were rankings for decreasing variation over all three sets.

Because executives may not treat a sure alternative in the same way they treat a risky alternative, we removed the sure alternative and repeated our comparison. With just four alternatives, there are 24 possible rankings, and the one ranking consistent with a preference for decreasing variation represented 34%, 28%, and 84% of the executive rankings in the three sets. These were also significantly different from a chance occurrence. The 84% of actual wager rankings that preferred decreasing variation in set C was striking. Overall, though, we see that an assumption of preference for decreasing variation would fail to explain half the cases even when the sure alternative was removed.

Instead of preferring increasingly lower variation in payoffs, do some executives prefer increasingly higher variation? Only one ranking is consistent with this preference. Considering all five alternatives, there were 7%, 0%, and 6%, respectively. This is significantly different from chance in sets A and C. Without the sure alternative, these figures changed to 16%, 1%, and 7%. Thus the presence of the sure alternative did not make a difference in sets B and C, but did in set A. Overall, increasingly lower variation in payoffs was preferred by about four times as many executives as increasingly higher variation.

> ***Result:*** Fewer than half of the executives preferred increasingly lower variation in payoffs. Preference for increasingly higher variation was much less common. Higher variation was preferred most noticeably when the loss amount was held fixed and lower variation was preferred when the chance of loss was fixed.

A majority of executives preferred neither increasing nor decreasing variation in payoffs in their wager rankings. Do most executives prefer an intermediate level of variation or do they use other risk components in their evaluation and ranking of the wagers? We will address these issues next.

NOTE ON UNFOLDING PREFERENCE RANKINGS
WITH RESPECT TO AN IDEAL LEVEL OF A RISK ATTRIBUTE

Determining whether preference rankings are consistent with an ideal level of a risk attribute is due to Coombs (1964). He referred to this concept as unfolding the preference ranking with respect to the attribute. In the previous sections we examined whether the executives' rankings were consistent with an ideal level of variation. Although we could extend this analysis to other risk attributes, including chance of loss, loss amount, expected loss, and gain amount, we have not done so because of space limitations. A more thorough analysis of preference rankings using unfolding theory, based on a pilot study of the Real Money Wagers questionnaire with 40 business executives, is presented in MacCrimmon, Stanbury, and Wehrung (1980).

Do Executives Prefer Wagers with Intermediate Variation in Payoffs?

We will say that an executive has an ideal level of variation in payoffs if he prefers wagers that are closer to the ideal level to wagers that are further away. Thus, the common assumption of preference for increasingly lower variation is simply a special case in which the ideal level is zero variation. Similarly, preference for increasingly higher variation is a special case where the ideal level is at (or above) the highest variation in the risky alternatives being considered. What we wish to know, then, is whether the executives choose as if they have an ideal level of variation that is intermediate between these two extremes.

In sets A, B, and C the percentages of executives whose rankings showed an intermediate ideal level of variation were 45%, 62%, and 66%, respectively. This compares with 24%, 5%, and 29%, respectively, that showed an ideal level at one extreme or the other. Although only 14 possible rankings were consistent with an ideal intermediate level of variation, representing 12% of the total possible rankings, they accounted for an average of 58% of the executives' rankings over the three sets. Assuming random order as a benchmark, the observed rankings were highly significant.

> ***Result:*** More than half of the executives preferred an intermediate level of variation in payoffs. This was much more common than a preference for either increasingly lower or increasingly higher variation.

Advice is routinely given to managers on how to choose in order to minimize variation for a given rate of return. However, our research indicates that managers may not always want to minimize variation. While a lower variation reduces the downside potential losses, it also cuts out the upside potential gains. Rather than assuming that everyone wants to minimize variation in returns, a better understanding should be obtained of the decision maker's preferences for or against variation.

NOTE ON THE EFFECT OF THE SURE ALTERNATIVE

The sure alternative is noticeably different from the risky alternatives in that uncertainty plays no part in the outcome. Do the executives handle the sure alternative in the same way as the risky wagers? We examined this question in a variety of ways and found that at least in some contexts the presence of a sure alternative tended to decrease an individual's ability to focus on a single wager attribute. Therefore some executives may have found the sure alternative difficult to rank among the uncertain wagers using a single attribute, so some additional wager attributes may have been considered as well. When the chance of loss was held fixed, as in set C, the sure alternative seems to have been treated like the uncertain wagers. This issue is examined in more detail in MacCrimmon, Stanbury, and Wehrung (1980) in connection with a pilot test of the Real Money Wagers questionnaire.

Also discussed in this earlier study is an analysis of whether the executives differentially attended to part of their wager ranking. Some executives may have been motivated to concentrate hard on determining their most preferred wager in each set because their real money outcome would depend on it. Yet they might give little thought to the remainder of their rankings. In the main study, as in the pilot, we found no evidence that the executives attended differentially to part of their rankings.

CONCLUSIONS

The wager rankings were more risk-averse than risk-taking. However, the executives did not automatically prefer the sure gain of $10. Even though they did not improve their expected payoff by selecting a wager with higher risk (measured in terms of variation), they preferred a moderate level of risk to either a high level of risk or a low level of risk. A preference for increasingly higher variation in payoffs was considerably less common than a preference for increasingly lower variation. These findings reinforce the notion that executives are cautious when gambling with their own money, but many are willing to accept a moderately risky wager.

We found the greatest number of risk-averse rankings in set C where the chance of loss was held fixed. The greatest number of risk-taking rankings was found in set A where the loss amount was held fixed. When the gain amount was held fixed in set B, the rankings were not as risk-averse as those in set C or as risk-taking as those in set A. We hypothesize that fixing the chance of loss at a relatively high level (38%) may have increased the perceived riskiness of all the wagers in set C, thus leading to the highly risk-averse responses. Similarly, holding the loss amount fixed at a relatively low level ($20) limited the downside risk and may have decreased the perceived riskiness of the wagers in set A, leading to the high number of risk-taking responses. Fixing the gain amount at a relatively high level ($40) may have increased the perceived desirability of the wagers in set B, but its influence on the riskiness of the wager rankings seems less clear.

The executives' preferences for the sure gain of $10 were related across all three sets. This was not the case for the preferences for the riskiest wagers in a set. A high preference for the sure alternative was significantly associated with a low preference for the riskiest alternative in two of the three sets. These results are consistent with our finding in the preceding chapters that risk propensity is associated across many, but not all, situations in which we have measured it.

RESEARCH CONCLUSIONS

Four main conclusions can be drawn:

1. Holding wager attributes such as chance of loss, loss amount, and gain amount fixed within a set of alternatives can influence the perceived riskiness of all wagers in the set. As a result, the riskiness of the responses is influenced as well. Researchers must be careful not to induce a particular risk behavior by inadvertently framing risky situations to increase or decrease their perceived riskiness.

2. One out of ten executives reversed his preference ranking between a sure alternative and a risky alternative when the alternatives were

presented in two different contexts. In all but one of the reversals, when the chance of loss was fixed for the wagers in set C, the executive preferred the sure alternative to the risky alternative, but when the gain amount was fixed in set B, he preferred the risky alternative to the sure alternative. This finding is consistent with the interpretations of the context effects given in the main conclusions, and it reinforces the significant influence that context effects can have on perceptions or riskiness and risk propensity.

3. The sure alternative of winning $10 was not popular. In fact, the presence of the sure alternative seemed to lead to less coherent rankings among the uncertain wagers in some contexts than was the case when it was removed. Some executives may have found the sure alternative difficult to rank among the uncertain wagers. These problems did not occur when the chances of each wager in a set were held fixed. We hypothesize that the presence of the sure alternative among the risky wagers decreases an individual's ability to focus on a single wager attribute. Perhaps the unique characteristics of the sure alternative cause it to be compared with uncertain wagers on the basis of the holistic alternative rather than individual wager attributes.

4. The possibility of real losses seemed to lead to more risk-averse responses. Few, if any, studies have used real payoffs of the magnitude used here (i.e., potential gains of over $400 and potential losses of almost $300). More attention needs to be directed to creating appropriate payoff structures in empirical studies.

Chapter 7

Managerial Summary and Implications

Studying Risk in Standardized Situations

INTRODUCTION

In Chapter 1 we discussed the pervasiveness of risk. Risk is unavoidable; no actions are free of risk. Even doing nothing is risky. We defined risk as exposure to a chance of loss. Risk is brought about by a lack of time, a lack of information, or a lack of control. Thus we can mitigate risk by gaining time for uncertainties to be resolved, by gaining information, or by gaining control over possible losses, key uncertain events, their chances of occurrence, and our exposure. Our REACT model identified five important phases: recognizing the risks, evaluating the risks, adjusting the risks, choosing among the available alternatives, and tracking the outcomes of the uncertain events.

Chapter 2 showed how our study is distinctive from the past studies of risk. We assessed the willingness to take risks of top-level managers who have experience confronting important risky situations as part of their work. The sample size is very large, with over 500 executives in the main study as well as hundreds of students and managers in pilot studies. Our measures of risk propensity have strong foundations based on the theories of risk found in mathematics, economics, psychology, and management. We used a wide variety of risky situations to assess a manager's willingness to take risks. Our

Risk Portfolio includes risks in standardized situations, naturally occurring risks, and attitudes toward risk. The risky situations are relevant for managers and they incorporate highly realistic settings for the managers to reveal their willingness to take risks. The Risk Portfolio examined risk disposition in the recognition and adjustment phases of risk as well as in the more commonly studied choice phase. Risks in both personal and business decisions were considered as well as risks in both threat and opportunity situations.

In each of the Chapters 3 through 6, we presented our results from various standardized risky situations. Standardized situations allow us to make comparisons across managers because they all confront the same situation. Each standardized situation had at its core the Basic Risk Paradigm in which a person must decide between two or more alternatives each of which has clearly specified outcomes and their corresponding chances of occurrence. This feature allows us to tell whether a person is risk-taking or risk-averse and to make comparisons with other people.

The Risk In-Basket was presented in Chapter 3. This questionnaire had a manager assume the role of a hypothetical vice-president who must deal with various risky situations described in memos in his in-basket. Chapter 4 had the manager specify the gains he would require if 50% of his personal wealth or 50% of the usual return on his capital investment budget were at stake. Personal investments described by various attributes (including expected return, variation, chances of gain, and chances of loss) were the central elements of Chapter 5. In Chapter 6 the manager had to specify his preference for wagers in which he could actually win or lose hundreds of dollars.

The rest of this chapter will summarize the results we found in studying risk in these four standardized situations and will develop several important implications for business and government. We will focus on the general conclusions that arise from Chapters 3 to 6. For specific conclusions on each questionnaire see the conclusion section in the individual chapters.

RISK RECOGNITION AND EVALUATION

When presented with several important attributes of risky investments, managers focused on only one or two attributes. Everyone's ability to deal with a broad range of information on investment attributes is limited. Busy managers must identify the most salient information. Thus decisions can be facilitated by highlighting the attributes that are most important to the manager. Decisions can also be made more easily when the information on each attribute is shown in a way that makes similarities and differences most apparent.

The most prominent focus was on the expected return of an investment. Even when considerable information is available on variation in returns, chances of gains, and chances of loss, expected return receives the most attention.

When we note that expected return consolidates all the possible gains and losses and their chances of occurrence, it is not surprising that managers should focus most strongly on the average payoff. Most targets are stated in terms of a particular rate of return which, when uncertainty is present, is considered to be the expected return.

The second most important attribute, in investments involving 10% of personal wealth, was the upside potential gain. The two investment attributes that have been the primary focus of financial theories, expected return and variation, did not explain the choices of our executives. After focusing attention on expected return, they looked at the chances of making major gains. Little attention was paid to variation or the chances of loss.

In many investment situations the "upside possibilities" can be more important than the "downside risks." This seems to have been the case for managers investing 10% of their net wealth. Even when the risks of investment are great, investors should carefully consider the upside potential gain to determine whether the possible gains justify the risks.

With information available on numerous attributes of investments, managers used two-stage decision thinking; they first used one attribute as a constraint (i.e., cutoff level) and then used a second attribute as a goal. The mangers first eliminated all the investment alternatives that did not meet the constraint level on the first attribute. From the remaining set of acceptable alternatives they then chose that alternative that provided the best level on the second attribute. Using this two-stage decision thinking is easier than trying to make tradeoffs between the two attributes.

The most common two-stage decision thinking used the attributes "chance of major gain" as the constraint and "expected return" as the goal. First, alternatives not offering a high enough chance of a 50% or a 100% gain were eliminated. Then the remaining alternatives were ordered in terms of expected return.

Although some managers used "chances of major loss" or "variation" as the cutoffs, they were definitely in the minority. The finance literature emphasizes the downside losses and, in particular, the use of expected return and variance (a measure of variation) as investment criteria. Perhaps more attention should be devoted in theory and practice to the upside potential of investments when that is what managers are most concerned about.

When managers did focus on variation in returns, they did not necessarily prefer investments that had lower variation. Instead they preferred intermediate levels of variation when gambling for up to hundreds of dollars of real money, and they preferred higher variation when investing 10% of their personal net wealth.

Even when the expected returns of investments are equal, managers may not want to minimize risks. To select an investment with a lower variation means to pass up a better chance at higher potential gains.

When investments share a common value for an important attribute, this value and the attribute itself can affect the choice. When there is a high chance of loss common to all investments, all of the alternatives may be viewed as risky. Thus risk-averse choices are made. When there is a relatively low amount of loss common to all investments, all the alternatives are viewed as relatively safe. In this case, risk-taking choices are made. These tendencies should be kept in mind when evaluating alternatives with common chances of loss or common stakes.

RISK ADJUSTMENT

Rather than taking the chances of potential loss, magnitude of loss, and exposure as fixed, the managers tended to adjust the risky situations to make them more attractive. Choices tend to be made only when further adjustment cannot be made. Most attention in the risk literature is concentrated on choices rather than on adjustments. Why focus on choosing among the best of a set of risky alternatives when they can be changed into something more desirable? Managers do, and should, try to adjust risky situations. In every situation they should ask, "What changes can I make here?"

The managers used a variety of means to try to adjust the risky situations. Among the most common adjustments were the collection of more information, the attempt to have some control over the uncertain events, delay, and spreading responsibility for losses.

Executives should be aware of the variety of risk adjustments that can be used to gain time, information, and control in risky situations. More specifically, they should think about how they can reduce the downside risks without sacrificing too much of the upside potential. By observing how a manager adjusts the risks he faces, we can better understand how adaptable and imaginative he is in arranging a more favorable situation.

The managers used risk adjustments to avoid risks in some situations. Collecting information, bargaining, delaying, and delegating are prudent management practices. However, these and other adjustments can be used to avoid risks. Managers should be aware of such adjustments when they wish to avoid risks in appropriate circumstances. Moreover, it is important to know when other people are using risk adjustments to avoid risks. In order to know whether someone will ultimately choose the safer or more risky course of action, one should look to see if he modifies the risks before choosing.

Managers frequently sought additional information before making risky decisions. Collecting information about the possible outcomes of risky alternatives and their chances of occurrence is a useful and widely known means of adjusting risks. Managers should also consider whether they can influence uncertain events determined by other people such as competitors, government policy makers and regulators, opinion trend-setters, and the like. Information exchanges in the form of bargaining and lobbying can often change the chances of these uncertain events even if they cannot dictate the actual outcomes. Excessive requests for information and in-depth studies of risky decisions may be a sign of risk avoidance.

Managers frequently delayed their risky decisions. Delaying important risky decisions allows events to evolve, allows new factors to come to light, and allows time for new options to be developed. Gathering information and bargaining are other ways a manager can use time to better understand and possibly control his risks. For example, requests for in-depth studies are a common mechanism by which managers can delay difficult decisions under the guise of gathering information. Delay in all of its forms provides a valuable opportunity for reducing the riskiness of a situation. Excessive delay, however, is likely a sign of risk avoidance.

Managers frequently delegated their risky decisions. Top-level executives cannot make all the decisions in their firms' operations. Decentralized decision making requires delegation. But delegating a decision also provides a means for sharing or avoiding completely the risks in a difficult decision. Delegation is most common when a key individual is available to assume responsibility for the decision. A common form of delegation used to share risks is "decision by committee" where individual accountability for the decision is obscured and personal exposure is limited.

The Risk In-Basket is a very effective way to study risk adjustments in standardized situations. By using this questionnaire as a microcosm for risky decision making, we have learned a great deal about the variety of ways managers modify risks in realistic business situations. The Risk In-Basket can be used as a personnel selection device to identify individuals who handle risks in a way that is desired by the firm. It can also be used as a training device whereby managers in a firm can share their means of dealing with risky decisions in a simulated environment.

Government can facilitate risk adjustment by business in a variety of ways. It can provide business with adequate information on key uncertainties (such as governmental regulations) over which it has partial or total control. It can allow flexible timing in the implementation of its new policies to allow for smooth transitions by business. Government can also assist by helping to develop selected control options (such as risk-sharing schemes) for business to reduce exposure to potential loss.

RISKY CHOICE

The managers showed a very different willingness to take risks across the standardized situations. Managers choose the time and place to take calculated risks rather than accepting all risks confronting them. When investing 10% of their net wealth, they wanted a run for their money. The relatively safe alternative was just too safe. When the stake increased to half their net wealth, some managers refused to invest and the remainder held out for a chance at exceptionally large gains before accepting the gamble. With only a small amount at stake in the real money wagers, many managers were willing to take a moderately risky gamble and few managers preferred the sure outcome. In their business decisions the managers tended to take risks in the lawsuit, customer threat, and union dispute situations. However, they were much more cautious in the joint venture and the capital expenditure budget investment. Knowing when to take and when to avoid risks is a valuable asset for any manager.

Managers were more risk-averse when their own money was at stake than when their firms' resources were at stake. Executives do differentiate their personal and business roles when it comes to taking risks. We should not automatically assume, therefore, that an executive who takes few chances with his personal resources will also refuse to take risks in his business role. Greater risk taking in business decisions than in personal decisions is consistent with the inherent responsibility of managers to take risks for their firms. People who are self-employed and therefore represent themselves in their "business" role should be aware of this tendency when combining their common roles.

Risk taking was more common in the recognition and adjustment phases of risk than in the choice phase. We found the greatest risk taking in those situations which focused more on the recognition and adjustment of risks than on the choice among risky alternatives. The greatest risk aversion was found in the situtions in which choices had to be made without any possibility for adjustment.

This finding shows how firms or governments can influence the degree of risk taking at various phases in the risk management process. At the risk recognition phase, intervention can be used to alter the perceived risk of the situation to make it less (or more) risky. During the adjustment phase, intervention can take the form of introducing new options to increase time, information, and control. An organization that wishes to promote risk-taking behavior should intervene in whatever phases of risk show consistent risk aversion. Correspondingly, a desire to discourage risk taking requires intervention wherever risk taking is predominant.

Managers were more willing to take risks once in a risky situation than in entering a risky situation. The biggest step in taking risks seems to be putting oneself in risky situations. If a firm or individual stays away from risky situations, it can avoid risks. Organizations, and in particular governments, can foster risk-taking behavior by encouraging firms to enter risky situations via a variety of incentive schemes and publicity concerning opportunities in new industries, markets, and so forth.

A manager's willingness to take risks in one standardized situation was only weakly related to his willingness to take risks in seemingly similar situations. Taking risks was generally unrelated across the four in-basket business decisions. Weak associations were found between a manager's inclination to risk 50% of his personal net wealth and his willingness to risk 50% of the usual return on his capital investment budget. Somewhat stronger associations were found when managers assessed alternatives for investing 10% of their personal net wealth in that those who preferred the riskiest venture disliked the safest venture (and vice versa). Correspondingly, the managers' preferences for the sure alternative were related across the three sets of real money wagers.

This finding reinforces our conclusion that managers pick selected situations in which to take risks. Although a risk taker in one situation is *more likely* to be a risk taker than a risk averter in other situations, he will usually avoid risks in some circumstances. Therefore we must be careful when assuming someone who takes a risk in one decision will naturally take a chance in his next decision. We have already pointed out how factors such as personal versus business decisions can influence one's willingness to take risks in different situations.

In the next three chapters we will examine the relationships among various measures of risk as well as the relationship between willingness to take risks and personal, financial, and business characteristics. A summary of these chapters is given in Chapter 11.

PART THREE

Relationships Among Risk Measures

Chapter 8

Comparison of Risk Measures in Standardized Situations

INTRODUCTION

People have different risk propensities in different situations. One manager might be averse to taking risks in both his personal and his business decisions. Another manager might be risk-taking in business decisions and risk-averting in personal decisions.

What differences would you expect in willingness to take risks in personal and business situations? There are good reasons to believe a person will be more risk-averse in his personal decisions. All the consequences of personal decisions fall on the individual and his immediate family. In business decisions the possible losses are spread over many more people. Responsibility for a poor outcome is difficult to attribute to any single individual when many people are involved in a business decision. Highly mobile managers may not be around when the bad consequences of earlier decisions occur.

The distinction between threat situations and opportunity situations is also important. Situations are viewed as *threats* when most of the possible outcomes leave you worse off than your present state. For example, a lawsuit or a new entrant in your market is usually seen as a threat. Other situations are *opportunities* in that any alternative improves your situation. Opportunities, as well as threats, can be risky. An investment in one stock may yield a 20% return, which

---

Note on threats versus opportunities

The magnitudes of potential loss and gain amounts, their chances of occurrence, and the exposure to potential loss contribute to the degree of threat (versus opportunity) in a risky situation. As the chance, size, or exposure to potential losses (including opportunity losses) increases, the degree of threat increases. Increases in the magnitude, chance, or exposure to potential gain increase the "opportunity" aspect.

Recent evidence casts doubt on this usual hypothesis of greater risk taking for opportunities than for threats. Studies by Kahneman and Tversky (1979) and others suggest that when facing a gamble such as a 50-50 chance of gaining \$5000 or nothing a person might settle for a sure gain of \$2000 in lieu of the gamble, hence displaying risk aversion for this opportunity. When the amounts are made negative, however, people are willing to take the 50% chance of losing \$5000 or nothing rather than having to pay \$2000 for sure. Thus one finds risk taking for threats. The evidence to date is not particularly strong because of the difficulty in observing comparable opportunities and threats in realistic settings.

One of the best studies of threat situations examined the decisions of people confronting natural disasters. Kunreuther and his associates (1978) conducted a field study of homeowners residing in high-risk flood and earthquake areas. They found that relatively few homeowners had personally protected themselves against potential losses from these hazards. In parallel laboratory experiments on insurance the authors found that people refused to consider events whose chance of occurring was below some threshold even when high losses might occur. This study provides striking evidence that people prefer to insure against high-probability, low-loss events rather than the low-probability, high-loss events that characterize most natural hazards. These findings are contrary to most theories of risk that postulate risk aversion for losses.

---

sounds good until you learn that another investment would have yielded 50%.

Most people would expect greater risk taking in opportunities than in threats. Opportunities present a favorable climate for taking chances as long as the fall-back position is acceptable. Threats always involve the chance of downside losses.

The questionnaires that make up our Risk Portfolio include personal and business situations as well as threats and opportunities. We will use the executives' answers to the questionnaires described in Chapters 3 through 5 to see how their willingness to take risks changes in different standardized situations. Business risks occur in the Risk In-Basket and the Business Investment Gambles. Personal risks occur in the Risk-Return Rankings and the Personal Investment Gambles. Both threats and opportunities are explored in each questionnaire. The Real Money Wagers questionnaire (Chapter 6) will not be used in this comparison of standardized situations because it was used only in the follow-up study, not the main study.

MEASURES OF RISK PROPENSITY

A common feature of the questionnaires described in Part Two of this book is that standardized risky situations were used. This standardization allows the answers given by the executives to be meaningfully compared. These risky situations have strong theoretical foundations, so the measures of risk propensity derived from them have extra meaning. In Chapter 9 we will consider secondary risk measures from natural situations and from attitudes. Risk-related characteristics of the executives will be discussed and compared with the risk measures in Chapter 10. Figure 8.1 gives an overview of these chapters.

The standardized risky situations and the risk measures derived from them are summarized in Table 8.1. A schematic picture of the risky choices facing the executives is shown.

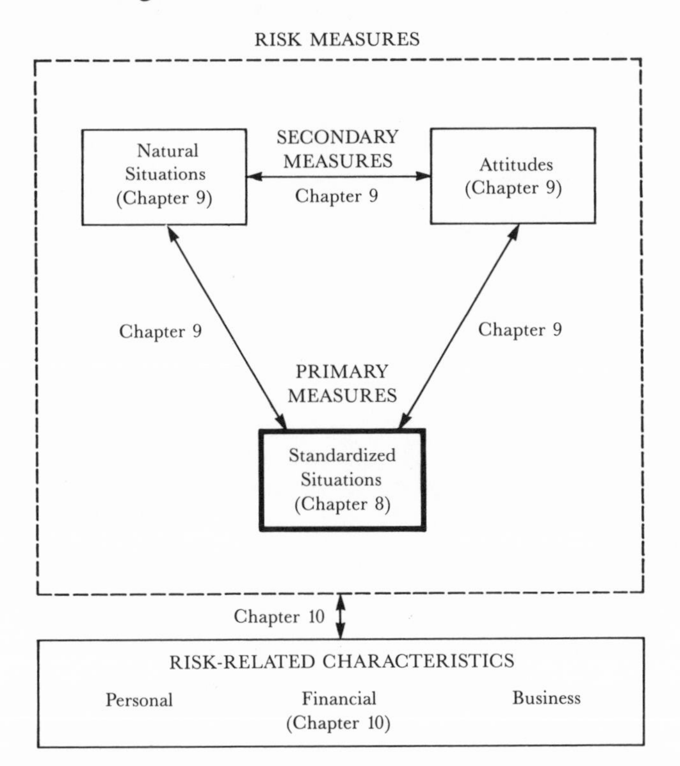

Figure 8.1 Overview of Chapters 8–10

Table 8.1 Summary of Questionnaires Used to Measure Risks in Standardized Situations

INSTRUMENT	RESPONSE MODE	RISK MEASURES	RISK PARADIGM
RISK IN-BASKET Assume role of hypothetical executive vice-president. Presented with four risky decisions: (1) lawsuit (2) customer threat (3) union dispute (4) joint venture	-write memo for each situation -rate inclination toward risk on 11-point scale for each situation -specify probability of preferred outcome required to be indifferent between risky and sure actions in each situation	Probability premium in *In-Basket lawsuit* situation (IB:LAWSUIT)	Take case to court: p Win case — $0; 1-p Lose case — -$1.6 million Settle out of court — -$0.8 million
		Probability premium in *In-Basket* joint *venture* situation (IB:VENTURE)	Pursue venture alone: p Win large market share — 22% ROI; 1-p Win small market share — 10% ROI Pursue as joint venture — 14% ROI
INVESTMENT GAMBLES *Personal*: Assumed to stake 50% of personal net wealth on gamble in which could lose stake or gain amount to be specified versus status quo. Four situations presented each with a different chance p of losing stake.	Specify gain required to be indifferent between risky personal gamble and status quo in each situation	Probability premium in *personal gamble* with p = *50%* chance of losing stake (PGAMBLE50%) Probability premium in *personal gamble* with p = *10%* chance of losing stake (PGAMBLE10%)	Take gamble: 1-p — G; p — Half of current net wealth Do not take gamble — Current net wealth

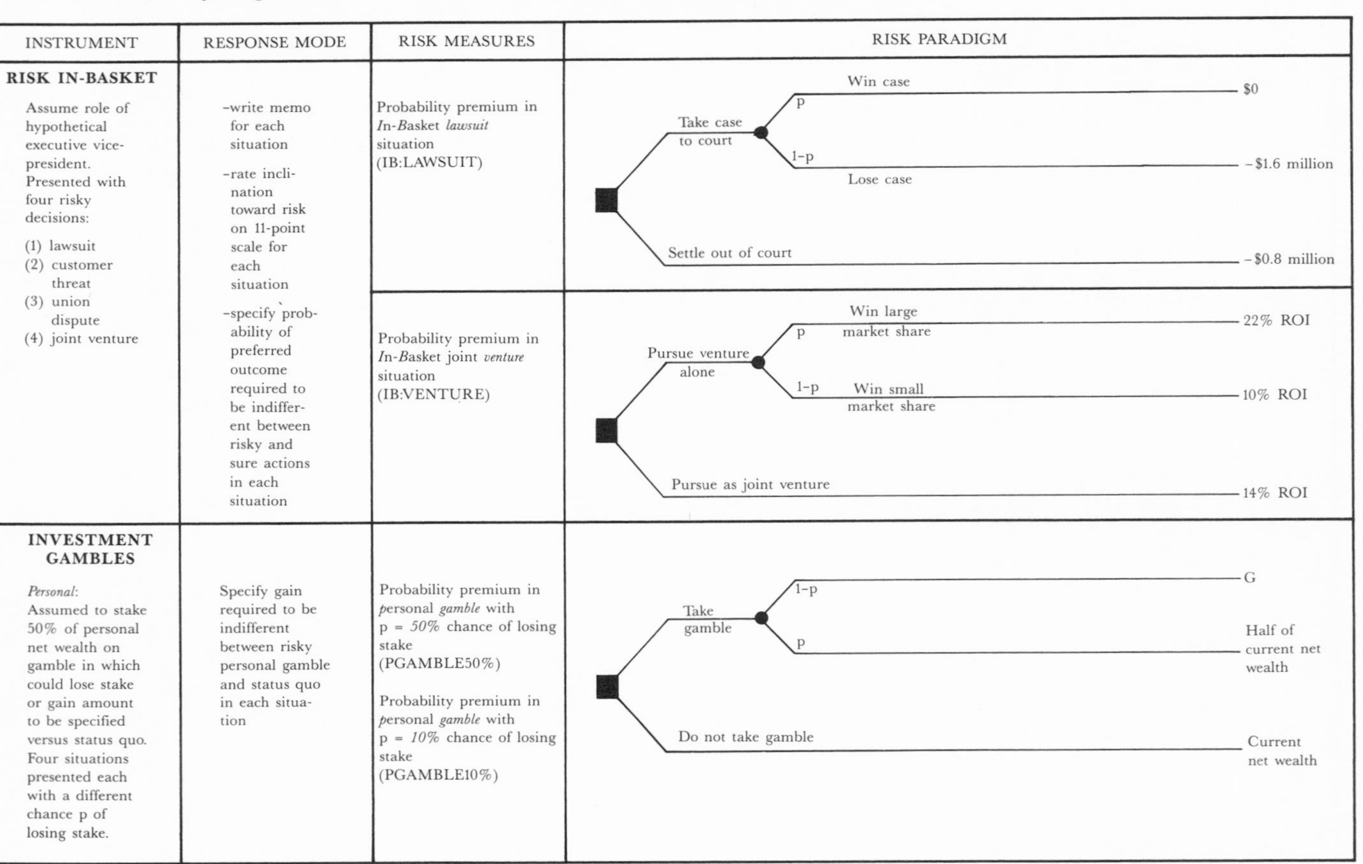

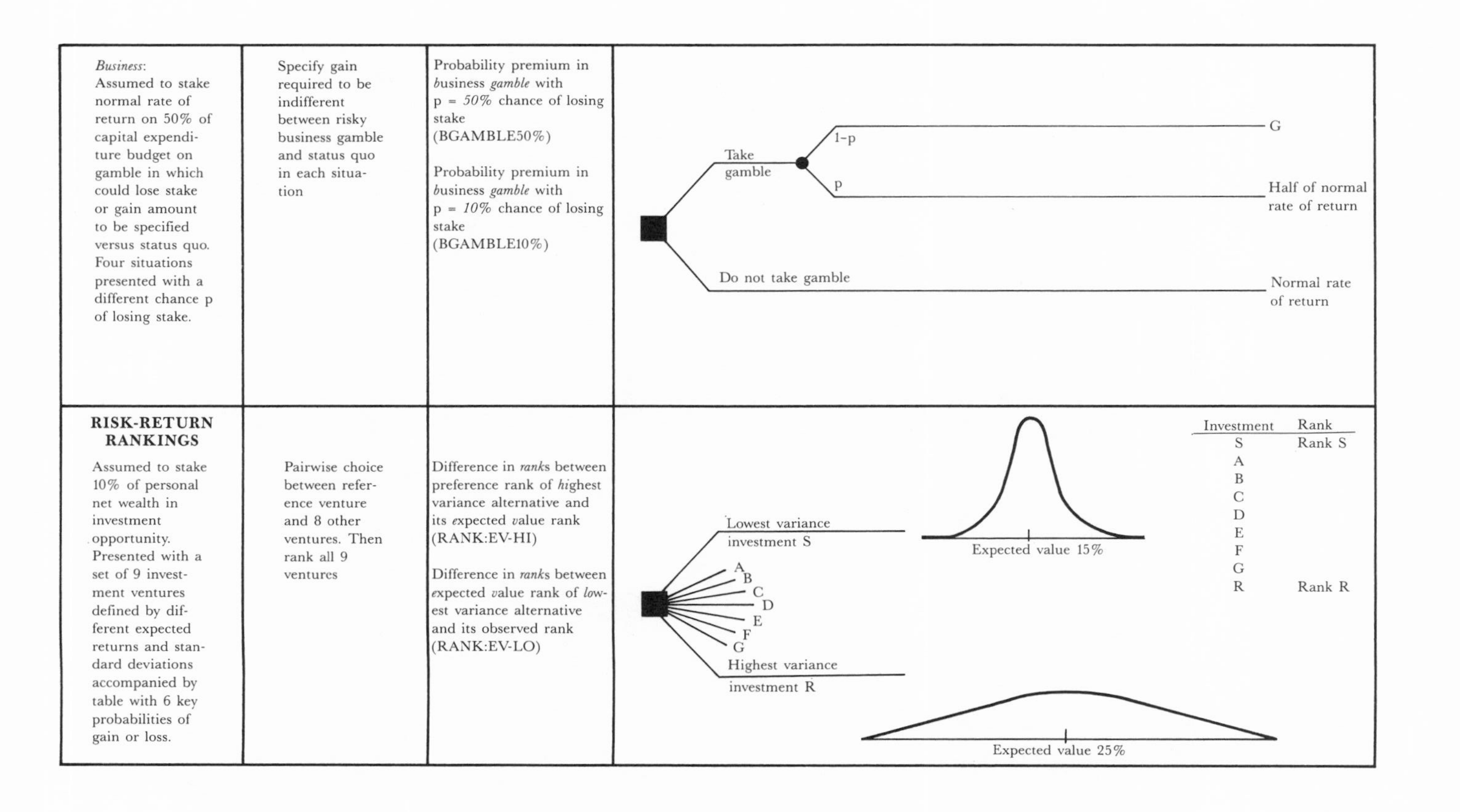

Business: Assumed to stake normal rate of return on 50% of capital expenditure budget on gamble in which could lose stake or gain amount to be specified versus status quo. Four situations presented with a different chance p of losing stake.	Specify gain required to be indifferent between risky business gamble and status quo in each situation	Probability premium in *business gamble* with p = *50%* chance of losing stake (BGAMBLE50%) Probability premium in *business gamble* with p = *10%* chance of losing stake (BGAMBLE10%)	
RISK-RETURN RANKINGS Assumed to stake 10% of personal net wealth in investment opportunity. Presented with a set of 9 investment ventures defined by different expected returns and standard deviations accompanied by table with 6 key probabilities of gain or loss.	Pairwise choice between reference venture and 8 other ventures. Then rank all 9 ventures	Difference in *ranks* between preference rank of *hi*ghest variance alternative and its *e*xpected *v*alue rank (RANK:EV-HI) Difference in *ranks* between *e*xpected *v*alue rank of *lo*west variance alternative and its observed rank (RANK:EV-LO)	

The *Risk In-Basket* decisions involved a business context. The executive was asked to assume the role of a hypothetical vice-president who confronts four situations: a lawsuit, a customer threat, a union dispute, and a joint venture. We will restrict our attention to the lawsuit, which consists only of losses (i.e., a threat) and the joint venture, which consists only of gains (i.e., an opportunity). The manager was asked to state the smallest chance of winning the lawsuit that he would require to take the case to court in lieu of the riskless out-of-court settlement. Similarly, he was asked to give the smallest chance of capturing a large market share that he would require to "go it alone" in lieu of the riskless joint venture. These answers provided the basis for deriving risk measures for these two situations.

The *Personal Investment Gambles* involved a choice between no investment and risking half of one's personal wealth in return for a chance of substantial gain. We asked the manager to specify the ending wealth position he would require from a successful investment to be indifferent between investing and not investing. The *Business Investment Gambles* offered a choice between two alternatives for investing the manager's capital expenditure budget. The first alternative consisted solely of standard projects which would yield the usual rate of return. The second alternative involved putting half of the budget in standard projects and risking the other half on a special project that would yield either zero rate of return or a substantial rate of return. The manager was asked to specify the rate of return he would require from the special project so that he would be indifferent between the two alternatives.

Four different questions were asked in both the personal and business gambles. These questions corresponded to different chances of loss (on half of personal wealth or on rate of return for half of capital budget) ranging from 50% to 10%. We will consider only the situations involving 50% and 10% chance of loss. The first situation represents a threat because of its high chance of loss and the second represents an opportunity because a 10% chance of loss corresponds to a 90% chance of gain. The answers provided by the managers to the threat and the opportunity in both the personal and business situations allowed us to derive four risk measures.

Nine personal investment alternatives were presented in the *Risk-Return Rankings*. Each investment was described by its expected return and variation in returns. The chances of attaining six key levels of return were also provided to make the investment more understandable. We asked the executive to consider investing 10% of his wealth and to rank all nine alternatives in order of preference.

The "most threatening" alternative in terms of having the highest chance of losing half or all of the investment had an expected return of 25% and the highest variation in returns. The "least threatening" alternative (and hence a relative opportunity) had an expected return of 15% and the lowest variation in returns with very small chance of major losses. The ranks given to these two alternatives provided the basis for two additional risk measures.

In summary, then, we have drawn a total of eight risk measures from the questionnaires. The four personal measures are drawn from situations that involve investing either 10% or 50% of personal wealth. The four measures of business risk deal with either the investment of a capital expenditure budget in business projects or business decisions made by the executive in an assumed role of a hypothetical vice-president.

We have used chance of loss, magnitude of loss, and variation in returns to define *relative* threats and opportunities within each questionnaire. We have categorized threats as having higher chances of loss (e.g., 50% versus 10%), higher monetary losses (e.g., actual loss versus opportunity loss), or higher variation in returns than do opportunities. In each questionnaire we selected the situations or questions that gave the greatest spread on these components, so as to accentuate differences between threats and opportunities.

Note on risk measures

In Chapter 1 we presented the basic paradigm for studying risk. This paradigm allows us to assess differences in risk propensity in a theoretically valid manner. We used this paradigm in different forms in Chapters 3–5. Each form incorporated the concept of expected value and the components of risk (magnitude, chance, and exposure to potential loss). Table 8.1 provides the correspondence between the standardized risky situations and the theoretical paradigm for studying risk.

In the Risk In-Basket the executives were asked to write a memo indicating what actions they would take and to indicate on an eleven-point scale their inclination to take the risky action, in addition to providing their probability equivalences. The probability premium derived from the probability equivalence was chosen as our risk measure because it had a firm theoretical foundation as a measure of risk propensity and it did not have the arbitrariness inherent in rating scales nor the coding problems inherent in content analysis of written memos. The probability premiums will be denoted IB:LAWSUIT and IB:VENTURE to indicate they were derived from the Risk *In-B*asket and involved a *lawsuit* and a joint *venture*.

Probability premiums were also chosen as the risk measures for the Investment Gambles. They were derived from the gain equivalences provided by the executives in order to circumvent difficulties in the analysis of infinite gain equivalences. See Chapter 4 for a more detailed discussion of the choice of risk measures. The personal risk measures will be denoted PGAMBLE50% and PGAMBLE10% to indicate they were derived from a *p*ersonal *gamble* with either a *50%* or a *10%* chance of loss. The business risk measures will be denoted BGAMBLE50% and BGAMBLE10% for similar reasons.

The Risk-Return Rankings involved an extended form of the Basic Risk Paradigm with nine rather than two alternatives and with continuous rather than discrete outcomes. A risk-neutral person would base his ranking of the investments on their expected returns. In comparison, a risk taker would rank the highest variance alternative more favorably and the lowest variance alternative less favorably. Therefore we chose as our risk measures for the "most threatening" and "least threatening" alternatives the difference between their observed ranks and their ranks based on expected returns. These risk measures will be denoted RANK:EV-HI and RANK:EV-LO to indicate they were the difference between the observed *rank*s and the ranks based on the *e*xpected *v*alue of the *hi*ghest and *lo*west variance alternatives, respectively. More specifically, RANK: EV-HI is the observed rank for the highest variance alternative minus 3.5 (i.e., its rank based on expected return) and RANK:EV-LO is 6.5 (i.e., the rank for the lowest variance alternative based on expected return) minus its observed rank. With these definitions, positive values for all eight risk measures correspond to risk aversion and negative values correspond to risk taking.

In previous chapters we have mentioned some of the measures that have been developed and used in other studies to assess risk propensity. In general they range from weak to possibly acceptable. The tasks that underlie these measures are often trivial (e.g., dot estimation) and student-specific (e.g., test anxiety). This should not be surprising because most studies of risk, as well as most other behavioral topics, have used students as subjects.

The measures have been somewhat better in the few studies of risk done with actual managers. For example, Laughhunn, Payne, and Crum (1980) based their measures on risky choices made in a theoretically sound, expected utility framework similar to the one presented in Chapter 4. Other measures are still open to some doubt. For example, Cummings and associates (1971) used the Shure and Meeker questionnaire (1967) to assess the risk propensities of managers from different countries. This questionnaire derived a risk measure from the managers' responses to questions about whether they would like to race cars or jump off high diving boards. The validity of such responses with actual managerial risk taking is dubious at best.

We will illustrate our main results with the answers given by two typical executives, Alan Abbot and Bill Baxter, to the eight standardized situations. Table 8.2 summarizes their responses.

Alan Abbot would take the lawsuit to court if there was at least a 35% chance to win the case. We can compare this answer with a risk-

Table 8.2 Absolute Risk Propensity of Two Typical Executives in Standardized Situations

Situation	Risk-Neutral Response	Alan Abbot		Bill Baxter	
		Actual Response	*Absolute Risk Propensity*	*Actual Response*	*Absolute Risk Propensity*
Risk In-Basket: Lawsuit	Requires 50% chance of winning case	35%	Risk taker	80%	Risk averter
Risk In-Basket: Joint Venture	Requires 33% chance of large market share	25%	Risk taker	60%	Risk averter
Personal Investment Gambles: 50% chance of loss	Requires 1.5 times net wealth	2.2	Risk averter	Will not gamble	Risk averter
Personal Investment Gambles: 10% chance of loss	Requires 1.05 times net wealth	1.33	Risk averter	10.0	Risk averter
Business Investment Gambles: 50% chance of loss	Requires 2.0 times usual rate of return on special project	2.0	Risk neutral	2.5	Risk averter
Business Investment Gambles: 10% chance of loss	Requires 1.11 times usual rate of return on special project	1.2	Risk averter	1.75	Risk averter
Risk-Return Rankings: Highest variation in returns	Rank 3.5	3	Risk taker	7	Risk averter
Risk-Return Rankings: Lowest variation in returns	Rank 6.5	9	Risk taker	6	Risk averter

neutral response to obtain a measure of Abbot's *absolute risk propensity*. A risk-neutral manager would not take the suit to court unless there was at least a 50% chance of winning. Because Abbot will take the case to court when there is a lower chance of winning, we say he is a risk taker in the lawsuit situation.

How did Alan Abbot respond to the other seven standardized situations? In lieu of the joint venture he would take the riskier option of "going it alone" if there was at least a 25% chance of capturing a large market share. Abbot would risk losing half his personal wealth (of $1.8 million) for a 50% chance to end up with 2.2 times his wealth (i.e., $4.0 million) or a 90% chance to end up with 1.33 times his wealth (i.e., $2.4 million). He would risk a zero rate of return on half his capital expenditure budget by investing in a special project if it had a 50% chance of at least 2.0 times the usual rate of return or a 90% chance of at least 1.2 times the usual rate of return. Among the alternatives for investing 10% of his personal wealth Abbot ranks the alternative with the highest variation third in his preference and the one with the lowest variation ninth.

When we compare these answers with the risk-neutral values summarized in Table 8.2, we see that Alan Abbot is a risk taker in both situations from the Risk In-Basket and Risk-Return Rankings questionnaires. He is a risk averter in the Personal and Business Investment Gambles with the exception of the business gamble having a 50% chance of loss where he is risk-neutral. Hence we see that Abbot is not very consistent in his risk propensity in different situations.

Bill Baxter requires at least an 80% chance of winning the lawsuit to take it to court. Baxter requires a 60% chance of success in "going it alone" if he is to forego the joint venture. He will risk a 10% chance of losing half his personal wealth (of $350,000) if there is a 90% chance of ending up with at least 10.0 times his wealth (i.e., $3.5 million). However, he would not risk a 50% chance of such a loss regardless of the amount to be gained. Baxter requires at least 2.5 times the usual rate of return to invest half his capital budget in a special project which has a 50% chance of a zero rate of return. When there is only a 10% chance of no return, he still requires at least 1.75 times the usual rate of return to invest in the special project. Baxter ranks the personal investment alternatives with the highest and lowest variation in returns seventh and sixth, respectively. The summary in Table 8.2 shows that Bill Baxter is a risk averter in all eight situations.

In the next section we will compare the answers given by the executives to draw several important conclusions about risk propensity measured in different standardized situations.

NOTE ON RELIABILITY OF THE RISK MEASURES

We can examine the reliability of the risk measures from several viewpoints. The simplest test of reliability is whether the responses underlying the measures make sense. In Chapters 3–5 we found that the vast majority of executives answered each questionnaire and their responses were both reasonable and the right order of magnitude. Relatively few executives gave answers that could not be translated into usable risk measures.[1]

We looked at other types of reliability on a questionnaire-by-questionnaire basis. These tests examined the reliability of our eight selected risk measures against responses from the various questionnaires that were not themselves risk measures. All Pearson correlations cited below are based on the 224 executives for whom all eight primary measures were available as well as the auxiliary responses.

In the Risk In-Basket we checked whether the multiple responses provided by the executive in a single situation agreed in their assessment of risk propensity. In addition to the probability equivalence, the executive also gave a scale rating of his inclination toward the risky action and wrote a memo outlining how he wished to handle the situation. For the lawsuit the probability premium had a correlation of 0.66 with the scale rating and 0.59 with the memo riskiness score. For the joint venture these correlations were 0.75 and 0.70, respectively. These correlations indicate that our measures IB:LAWSUIT and IB:VENTURE are reliable.

In the Investment Gambles we investigated whether the gain equivalences were monotonically increasing as the chance of loss increased. If this were true, then there should be high correlations among the measures based on different chances of loss. We derived probability premiums from the gain equivalences for the situations involving 30% and 40% chances of loss just as we did for 50% and 10%. In the personal gambles the correlations between our two chosen risk measures and the two auxiliary measures ranged from 0.69 to 0.92. In the business gambles these correlations ranged from 0.71 to 0.94. These high correlations lead us to conclude that our measures PGAMBLE50%, PGAMBLE10%, BGAMBLE50%, and BGAMBLE10% are reliable.

In the Risk-Return Rankings we checked whether the ranking of the highest and lowest variance alternatives agreed with a risk measure that indicated how much the executives focused on minimizing variation in returns in their ranking of the seven remaining alternatives. First we constructed a focal ranking of the seven alternatives based jointly on minimizing variation in returns and the chance of losing half or more of the stake. Our auxiliary risk measure was the rank order correlation between the executive's actual ranking and this focal ranking. This auxiliary measure had correlations of 0.59 and 0.54 with RANK:EV-HI and RANK:EV-LO, respectively, demonstrating that those measures are reliable.

RESEARCH FINDINGS

Are the Executives Generally Risk-Taking or Risk-Averse?

Alan Abbot was a risk taker in four standardized situations and not a risk taker in four others. Bill Baxter was a risk averter in all eight situations. Does this difference in one's willingness to take risks in different situations extend to the larger sample of managers?

The percentage of executives who were risk takers in each standardized situation is shown in Table 8.3. The situations are arranged by whether they involve personal or business decisions and threats or opportunities. There is a very wide difference in risk taking across situations ranging from under 1% of executives in the Personal Investment Gambles to over half the executives in two other situations.

As a group, the executives displayed the full range of risk-taking and risk-averting responses in the Risk In-Basket and the Risk-Return Rankings questionnaires. Several executives required very high chances of success (e.g., as high as 100%) before they would take the lawsuit to court or "go it alone" in lieu of the joint venture. The ranks given by Abbot and Baxter in the Risk-Return Rankings were typical of most executives. The ranks for the highest variance alternative differed widely across executives, but the lowest variance alternative tended to receive the four least preferred ranks.

In the Investment Gambles questionnaire risk taking was almost nonexistent and extreme risk avoidance was common. This was true for both the personal and business decisions. No more than 4% of the executives were risk-taking in situations where either half their personal wealth or the usual rate of return on half their capital budget was at stake. For example, neither Abbot nor Baxter were risk-taking in any of the Investment Gambles. In fact Baxter refused to

Table 8.3 Percentage of Executives Who Were Absolute Risk Takers in Standardized Situations

	THREATS	OPPORTUNITIES
Personal		
Investment Gambles	Under 1	0
Risk-Return Rankings	39	68
Business		
Investment Gambles	4	2
Risk In-Basket	53	44

risk a 50% chance of losing half his personal wealth regardless of the possible gain. Risk taking occurred much more frequently (39–68%) in the Risk In-Basket and Risk-Return Rankings situations.

> ***Result:*** The executives gave the full range of risk-averting and risk-taking responses in the Risk In-Basket and the Risk-Return Rankings. They were overwhelmingly risk-averse in both the Personal and Business Investment Gambles.

Some situations appear to inhibit risk-taking behavior. Even people who are willing to take risks on occasion will be risk-averse when the conditions are not conducive to risk taking. In the following sections we will consider what some of these conditions are.

NOTE ON DISTRIBUTIONS OF RISK MEASURES

We provide a more detailed description of the executives' responses and derived risk measures in the table below:

		Median		Percentage Extreme*	
Situation	Number of Executives	*Actual Response*	*Risk Measure*	*Absolute Risk Taker*	*Absolute Risk Averter*
IB:LAWSUIT	464	40.5%	−.095	5	2
IB:VENTURE	464	45.3%	.119	18	4
PGAMBLE50%	420	3.71	.344	0	23
PGAMBLE10%	420	1.50	.400	0	6
BGAMBLE50%	317	3.26	.193	0	16
BGAMBLE10%	317	1.50	.234	0	4
RANK:EV-HI	464	4.16	.66	11	10
RANK:EV-LO	464	7.38	−.88	37	3

*Executives who gave most risk-taking (averse) response possible

The numbers of executives for whom a risk measure could be derived correspond to those described in Chapters 3–5. The positive median values for six of the eight risk measures indicate an overall tendency toward risk aversion. The high median probability premiums for the four Investment Gambles show the predominance of risk aversion in these situations. This finding is strongly reinforced by the substantial fraction of executives who would not accept the gambles regardless of the possible gains (i.e., the extreme absolute risk averters). Many executives were extreme risk takers in the joint venture (IB:VENTURE) and their ranking of the lowest variance investment alternative (RANK:EV-LO).

Are the Executives More Risk-Taking in Business Decisions than in Personal Decisions?

We found greater risk taking in business decisions than in personal decisions when we restricted attention to the Investment Gambles where the situations are comparable. This result was supported by a significantly lower average risk measure in the business gambles than in the personal gambles.[2] Bill Baxter illustrates this trend. When there is a 10% chance of loss, he requires substantially larger possible gains to risk his personal wealth than he would require for his business resources. When there is a 50% chance of loss, he will not risk his personal wealth at all, but will still risk his firm's resources. See Chapter 4 for a more detailed discussion of this finding.

> ***Result:*** The executives were more willing to take risks in business situations than in comparable personal situations.

Managers who will not risk their personal resources may still take risks in their business roles. These differences in risk propensity likely depend on how much personal exposure to loss the manager faces in his business decisions.

Are Executives More Risk-Averse When Facing Threats than When Facing Opportunities?

We found greater risk taking in the threat situation three times out of four when comparing threats and opportunities within the *same* questionnaire (see Table 8.3). Risk taking was more frequent in situations involving only losses (i.e., the lawsuit) than in those involving only gains (i.e., the joint venture). It was also more frequent in gambles having higher (50%) rather than lower (10%) chances of major losses. This finding was supported by significantly lower average risk measures for threats than opportunities within the Risk In-Basket and Investment Gambles.[3]

However, we found greater risk aversion in the more threatening situation when comparing situations from *different* questionnaires. The two *personal threat* situations are comparable because both involve investments of personal wealth. Putting 50% of one's wealth at risk is much more threatening than putting 10% at risk. Here a greater percentage of executives were risk takers in the less threatening situation as shown in Table 8.3. Similarly within the *personal opportunities* a greater percentage of managers were risk takers when a smaller percentage of personal wealth was at stake.

The comparability between situations is not as great within the *business threats* or within the *business opportunities* as in the personal situations. Nonetheless the business gambles seem much more threatening than the lawsuit or joint venture in that greater resources are at stake,[4] and they evoked less risk taking as shown in Table 8.3. For the comparisons of situations from different questionnaires, then, we have found greater risk taking when lower stakes were at risk.

Our conflicting results on whether there is greater risk aversion or risk taking in threats versus opportunities highlight the different aspects that influence a situation's degree of threat. We will summarize our conclusions using these aspects.

> ***Result:*** The executives were more willing to take risks when there were losses only (versus gains only), higher (versus lower) chances of loss, and lower (versus higher) stakes.

When already in a situation that offers little or no chance of gain, people take risks. They gamble on a chance of breaking even although if things go wrong they may incur very large losses. To settle for a medium-size sure loss is an admission of defeat.

When deciding on how much to stake on a risky situation, one is not yet committed to the situation. If the prospects are threatening, one tends to stake less than if the prospects are brighter. Hence when later faced with choices within these situations one takes more risks in the lower-stake situations.

NOTE ON RISK PROPENSITY IN THREATS: PHASES OF RISK

Our observation of greater risk taking in situations involving only losses than in situations involving only gains supports the recent findings of Kahneman and Tversky (1979) and others. Finding greater risk taking when chances of loss are higher suggests an extension of prospect theory that incorporates probability along with the value dimension. However, greater risk taking in situations involving *lower* stakes seems contrary to prospect theory. This latter finding may be explained by variables other than the amount at stake, namely the phase of risk being considered.

We described in Chapter 1 the REACT model of risk that consisted of five phases (i.e., recognition, evaluation, adjustment, choice, and tracking). Can the differences in risk propensities be explained by the phase where the risk is measured?

In Chapter 2 we classified the standardized risky situations by the phase of the risk model with which they were most closely associated. In both the Risk In-Basket and the Risk-Return Rankings the manager had to *evaluate* the risks *within a risky situation*. The *adjustment* of risk was central in the Risk In-Basket and the *recognition* of risk was paramount in the Risk-Return Rankings. In the Investment Gambles the executives had to decide whether to *enter a risky situation*. The central focus of the Investment Gambles was the *choice* between a risky and sure alternative.

The substantially greater risk taking in the Risk-Return Rankings (39–68%) and the Risk In-Basket (44–53%) than in the Investment Gambles (0–4%) could be attributed to differences in the phase of risk being examined. The executives were greater risk takers within a risky situation than when entering a risky situation. Alternatively, they were greater risk takers when recognizing or adjusting risks than when choosing within risky situations.

The phase of risk is confounded in our research design with the amount at stake across different questionnaires. This confounding prevents us from understanding its relative effects on the greater risk taking in the Risk In-Basket and Risk-Return Rankings than in the Investment Gambles. Our finding of greater risk taking in situations with lower stakes must remain tentative until further research clarifies the influence of these individual phase effects.

Is an Executive's Willingness to Take Risks in One Situation Related to His Risk Propensity in Other Situations?

We have already seen that one's risk propensity depends on the situation he confronts. For example, Alan Abbot is a risk taker in the lawsuit and the joint venture, but a risk averter in the personal gambles. Even though a manager might not show the *same* willingness to take risks in every situation, his risk propensity might still be *associated* across situations. We can see whether such an association exists by examining the relationships among the risk measures.

The strongest relationships occurred between situations drawn from the same questionnaire. The associations were especially high between the two Business Investment Gambles and between the two Personal Investment Gambles where only the chance of loss differs. The ranks given for the alternatives with the highest and lowest variation in returns in the Risk-Return Rankings had a slightly lower degree of association. A much weaker relationship occurred between the executive's answers to the lawsuit and the joint venture which differ in many respects.

We found the next highest relationships between Personal and Business Investment Gambles that had the same chance of loss. These associations were moderate and somewhat higher when the chance of loss was 50% than when it was 10%. Slightly weaker relationships occurred for the remaining comparisons of Investment Gambles when both the "personal versus business" and the "chance of loss" dimensions differed. Weak or nonsignificant relationships were found for the remaining pairs of situations.

Result: In general we cannot call a manager a risk taker or a risk averter without knowing the type of risky situation facing him. One's willingness to take risks does not transfer across all situations, but there are some relationships.

Common wisdom suggests that people have a fixed propensity to take or avoid risks. Managers, academics, and lay people all seem to use risk propensity to characterize people. A John deLorean is called a risk taker while a Paul Volcker may be called risk-averse.[5] People making such characterizations would probably admit that the terms "risk taker" and "risk averter" are intended to apply only within particular situations and not to everything the individual does. Most people would concede that differences in willingness to take risks could be expected in the same individual making decisions in different circumstances.

Note on relationships among risk measures in standardized situations

We investigated the associations among the risk measures by examining their pairwise correlations. To facilitate this analysis, and others made in this and subsequent chapters, we rescaled all the risk measures between − 1 and + 1 so that higher values correspond to risk taking and lower values correspond to risk aversion.

The Pearson correlation coefficients among the measures are presented below:

Risk Measures	IB:LAWSUIT	IB:VENTURE	PGAMBLE50%	PGAMBLE10%	BGAMBLE50%	BGAMBLE10%	RANK:EV-HI	RANK:EV-LO
IB:LAWSUIT		.16						
IB:VENTURE								
PGAMBLE50%				.67	.42	.26		
PGAMBLE10%					.24	.33	.15	.17
BGAMBLE50%						.68		
BGAMBLE10%							.19	
RANK:EV-HI								.54
RANK:EV-LO								

Only correlations significantly different from zero at a 0.001 level are shown. Sample sizes ranged from 285 to 464 because all measures could not be derived for all managers.

We see that 11 of the 28 possible correlation coefficients show significant associations between pairs of measures. All of these coefficients are positive as would be expected by our scaling of the risk measures.[6]

We performed a factor analysis on the relationships among the eight measures to see whether they could be explained by a smaller number of factors. This analysis was based on 249 executives for whom all the risk measures were available.[7] The first factor in a rotated two-factor model loaded heavily on the four measures from the Investment Gambles. The second factor loaded heavily on the measures from the Risk-Return Rankings. Thus the factor analysis was dominated by an *instrument effect* and no clear domain effect emerged.[8] A principal components analysis of the measures also showed a strong instrument effect.[9]

Obviously no single study (or even a series of studies) can rule out the existence of a concept of a "uniform risk propensity" for a particular individual. On the other hand, remember that each of our measures was based on a standardized situation that had a strong underlying theory of risk. If the measures based on a cohesive, well-developed theory do not show strong uniformity, then measures derived from a weaker theoretical basis (see Chapter 9) can be expected to show even less congruence.

On the positive side, the various measures of risk obtained from a single individual do seem more related than the responses across individuals. The significant correlations, by themselves, do not prove that a concept of risk propensity is responsible for linking these responses. If the result is not due to chance (and the high level of significance suggests that it is not), then perhaps it is due to a design artifact of the study such as an instrument effect. Although the instrument effect explains some of the associations among the measures, we show later in this chapter that significant relationships continue to exist even when we account for the instrument effect. More plausible is the possibility that some trait such as "desire for control" or some characteristic of the individual such as age is a better explanation for the results than is risk propensity. We consider this possibility in the next two chapters. However, because the questions were designed to assess risk propensity, it seems more likely that we are indeed observing a reflection of a risk-taking trait.

What Dimensions Underlie the Executives' Risk Propensities?

Do the executives show similar risk propensities in situations having common attributes? For example, do the managers have similar risk propensities in all their personal decisions? In all their business decisions? Is their willingness to take risks the same in all threat situations? When they face opportunities?

We have already seen that the managers tend to show similar risk propensities in situations taken from the same questionnaire. One useful way to look beyond this result in search of common risk dimensions is to examine a *spatial representation* of the relationships among the measures. Using standard analyses, we constructed Figure 8.2. In this diagram risk measures that have the strongest relationships appear closest together and those with weak or insignificant relationships appear further apart.

This diagram confirms the strong connection between measures derived from the same questionnaire. The four measures from the Investment Gambles cluster together as do the Risk-Return Rankings measures and the Risk In-Basket measures. The spatial representation, however, allows us to see beyond this questionnaire effect to search for important dimensions underlying risk propensity.

Note that all four business measures lie to the right of the four personal measures. Therefore we may view the *horizontal dimension* of Figure 8.2 as a *personal versus business* dimension. The Risk In-Basket situations were created to simulate very realistic business decisions and their measures are at the far right. The business gambles are closer to the personal side, possibly because they are similar in form to the personal gambles. The positioning of the personal and business measures is clear evidence for a personal versus business dimension.

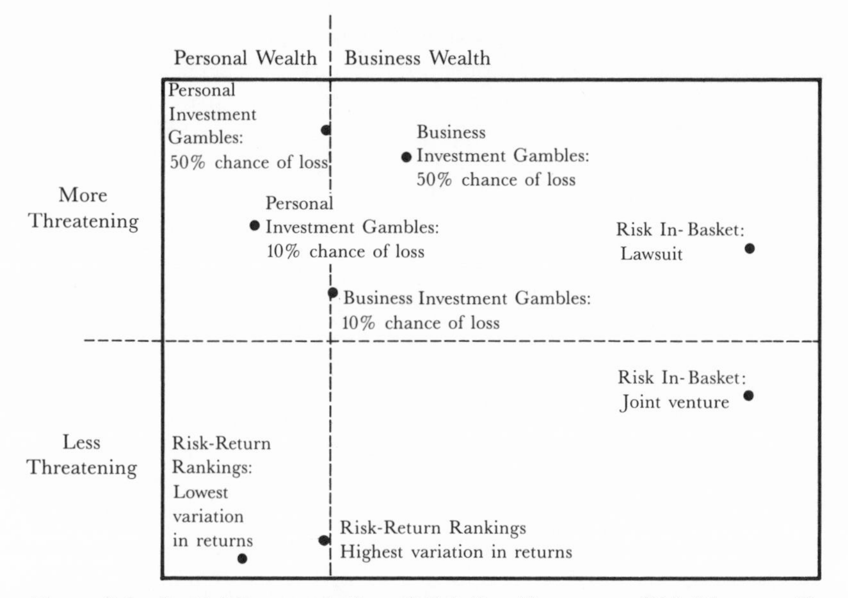

Figure 8.2 Spatial Representation of Relationships among Risk Measures Derived from Standardized Situations

The executives show stronger similarities in their willingness to take personal risks than in their willingness to take business risks as can be seen in the diagram by the smaller average distances between the personal measures than between the business measures.[10]

> ***Result:*** The executives showed different propensities for personal and business risks. They showed stronger similarities in their personal risks than in their business risks.

In personal decisions an executive has more control. In business decisions other people are involved and so his response to these situations, even when he is considering the decisions separately, may tend to show less similarity from situation to situation. However, even with differences among business situations, there is a clear difference between the risks taken in business situations and the risks taken in personal situations.

The vertical dimension can be interpreted as the *degree of threat* in the risky situation with greater threats nearer the top of the diagram. We base this interpretation on several comparisons of the standardized situations using the different aspects of threats discussed earlier. Our definitions of relative "threats" and "opportunities" *within* questionnaires used chance of loss, variation in returns, or predominance of gains or losses as the determinant of threat. Within each questionnaire we see that the threat measure lies above the opportunity measure. Therefore in these comparisons the more threatening situations have greater chances of loss, higher variation in returns, and only losses (versus only gains).

The situations also differ *across* questionnaires on another threat aspect, the amount at stake. Half of one's personal wealth is at stake in the Personal Investment Gambles compared with only 10% of wealth in the Risk-Return Rankings. The positioning of the former measures above the latter measures in the diagram is consistent with interpreting situations with higher stakes as more threatening. On the business side the joint venture clearly involves lower stakes than either of the business gambles because only gains are possible. The comparison between the lawsuit in which $1.6 million is at stake and the business gambles is more problematic because the stake in the business gambles differs across executives depending on the size of the capital budget and the usual rate of return. The placement of the four business measures is consistent, then, with our interpretations of degree of threat with the possible exception of the lawsuit measure.[11]

> ***Result:*** The executives showed different risk propensities in situations that differed in their degree of threat (i.e., chance of loss, variation in returns, predominance of gains or losses, amount at stake).

In addition to the distinction in risk propensity between personal and business situations, a secondary distinction is due to the degree of threat in a situation. This suggests that serious attempts should be made to establish the degree (and sources) of threats and to recognize that people's risk propensities in future situations may be predictable from past situations in which the degree of threat was similar.

NOTE ON THE SPATIAL REPRESENTATION OF THE RISK MEASURES

We derived Figure 8.2 using a Guttman-Lingoes smallest space analysis for two dimensions assuming weak monotonicity. The data for this analysis were the pairwise correlations among the risk measures for the 249 managers who had all eight measures.[12] The axes have been rotated orthogonally and the origin has been moved to permit maximum interpretability. The coefficient of alienation was 0.14 and Kruskal's stress statistic was 0.08. A three-dimensional representation gave results similar to Figure 8.2 on its first two dimensions, but the third dimension was not easily interpretable.

The results of this analysis can help us to identify situations in which people can be expected to have similar risk propensities. We have seen that an individual's willingness to take risks in personal decisions differs systematically from his risk propensity in business decisions. The stronger correspondence among personal risks than business risks may be due to the fact that the four personal situations all involved investing personal wealth, while the four business situations involved two very different settings. The dependence of one's risk propensity on the degree of threat in a risky situation also became apparent once the strong instrument effect was lessened.

Slovic, Fischhoff, and Lichtenstein (1980) identified three dimensions of perceived risk in their study of 18 risk characteristics for 90 hazards. They labeled these dimensions dread, familiarity, and number of people exposed. Their study investigated risk perception rather than risk propensity and its dimensions are not directly comparable to the ones we have identified. However, the Slovic et al. study provides evidence for the existence of systematic, underlying relationships among risk characteristics similar to what we have found. Subtle influences among the characteristics that affect risk perception will likely play a similar role in domain differences underlying risk propensity through its recognition phase.

Do the Executives Show the Same Risk Propensity in Different Situations Relative to Other Managers?

Up to now we have compared each manager's answers with risk-neutral values to get an indication of his *absolute* risk propensities.

Instead we might compare these answers with the answers given by all other executives in the study. Such comparisons provide an indication of the manager's *relative* risk propensities.

For each of the eight standardized situations we divided the managers into three groups of approximately equal size.[13] We will call the most risk-taking third *relatively risk-taking*, those in the middle third *relatively risk-neutral*, and those in the most risk-averting third *relatively risk-averting*. For example, in the lawsuit if you required between a 0% and 37% chance of winning to take the case to court, you were a relative risk taker. If you required a 38%–50% chance of winning, you were relatively risk-neutral, and if you required a 51%–100% chance of winning, you were a relative risk averter.

Our comparison of an individual's answers with those of other managers in the study means that someone who is risk-averse in an absolute sense may be a relative risk taker. For example, Alan Abbot is an absolute risk averter in the personal gamble because he would only risk a 50% chance of losing half his wealth if there was a chance he could end up with at least 2.2 times his wealth. This amount is greater than the 1.5 times wealth a risk-neutral person would require. However, he is a relative risk taker because more than two-thirds of the managers in the study required an even higher gain to risk losing half their wealth.

The question we ask in this section is whether managers tend to show the same *relative* risk propensity in different situations. We found that more managers than predicted by chance did have a common relative risk propensity. For example, even though Alan Abbot was not consistent in his absolute risk propensities across situations, he was a relative risk taker in all eight situations.

However, the number of managers with a common relative risk propensity was not very large. Among 249 executives for whom all the measures were available only *two* were relative risk takers on all eight measures and *two* were relative risk averters on all eight measures. Even when we included managers who had a common relative risk propensity on five or more of the measures (and were relatively risk-neutral on the remainder), these numbers increased to only 12 and 14, respectively. We will call these managers *consistent risk takers* and *consistent risk averters*.

> ***Result:*** More managers were consistent in their willingness to take risks across situations than chance would predict. However, their numbers were not high.

Knowing a person is risk-averse (risk-taking) in one situation makes it more likely that he will be risk-averse (risk-taking) in another situation. A small group of managers was found to be much more risk-averse (risk-taking) across all eight situations than would have been expected by chance.

NOTE ON RELATIVE RISK PROPENSITY

If a manager's responses to the risky situations were unrelated, we would expect him to fall into the relative risk groups for each measure in proportion to their sizes. We will use this random model to derive an expected number of executives who fall into the same relative risk group on all measures for comparison with the actual number of executives.

If the three relative risk groups had equal sizes, then the chance of someone being a relative risk taker (averter) on all eight measures under the random model is one chance in 6561 (= 3^8). Because these groups were not exactly of equal size, the chance of consistent relative risk taking was one chance in 3846 and of consistent relative risk averting was one chance in 10,000. With a sample size of 249 executives who had all eight measures, the expected numbers of people in these categories were each less than one-tenth of a person. We found two managers in each category. This difference between expected and observed frequencies was significant far beyond the 0.0001 level using a chi-squared test.

To have a larger number of people to compare, we considered managers who were relative risk takers (averters) in five or more situations and relatively risk-neutral in the remaining situations to be "consistent" risk takers (averters). Our rationale was that consistent managers might deviate slightly from their common risk propensity, but they would not deviate so far as to be classified in the other extreme group. This "deviation" might occur either through mistakes or because other, less consistent people give extreme responses from time to time. Since our groups were relative ones, these responses could displace some of the confirmed risk takers (averters).

Five managers were relative risk takers in seven situations, three were relative risk takers in six situations, and two were relative risk takers in five situations. Coupled with the two relative risk takers in all eight situations, we found a total of 12 consistent risk takers. The expected number of consistent risk takers under the random model was only 4.8.

In addition to the two managers who were relative risk averters in all eight situations, we found one who was a relative risk averter in seven situations, four who were relative risk averters in six situations, and seven who were relative risk averters in five situations. This total of 14 consistent risk averters contrasts with 2.6 managers expected under a random model. These differences were significant beyond a 0.0001 level using a chi-squared test for both the consistent risk takers and the consistent risk averters.

These analyses show that when we compare an individual's risk propensity to other managers in the study and focus on the relative risk takers and relative risk averters, we find a stronger indication of a uniform risk propensity across situations than we obtained from the analysis of absolute risk propensity. The results of this section provide strong evidence for commonalities among the primary risk measures for the same individual. Coupled with the significant (although low) correlations among the measures, a stronger basis begins to emerge for a construct of risk propensity.

Are Risk Averters More Consistent than Risk Takers?

We found more than five times as many consistent risk averters as would be predicted by chance.[14] However, there were fewer than three times as many consistent risk takers as predicted by chance.[15]

We examined this question further by considering the consistency of the manager's risk propensity within both personal and business situations and within both threats and opportunities.[16] We found there were more consistent risk averters than chance would predict in all four types of situations, considered individually and in combinations.[17] The relative risk takers were consistent in their personal decisions and threats, less so in their business decisions, and showed no significant consistency for opportunities or for any combinations of these types of situations.[18]

> ***Result:*** Risk averters were generally more consistent in their risk propensity than risk takers. This difference occurred in opportunities and situations that differed on several dimensions and was not apparent in personal decisions or threats.

The greater consistency for risk averters than for risk takers suggests interesting possibilities. There may be a basic asymmetry. Managers who are at the risk-averse end of the spectrum tend to be relatively risk-averse in most of the situations they face. Perhaps the most risk-taking managers are not as set in their ways and are willing to take risks in some situations but avoid risk in other situations.

CONCLUSIONS

The managers showed the full range of risk-taking and risk-averting answers in some situations, but were overwhelmingly risk-averse in other situations. In no situation did we find overwhelming risk taking. Consistency in risk propensity across situations was the exception rather than the rule. This was true whether we measured one's willingness to take risks against risk-neutral values or against the responses of all managers in the study. It is clear that we cannot label someone as a risk taker or risk averter by observing his behavior in only a single situation. We found the strongest consistency in risk propensity for situations where personal wealth was at stake.

Two dimensions emerged along which risk propensities tended to differ. The more important dimension is "personal versus business" where we found that managers take more risks with their firm's resources than with their personal wealth. The second dimension is the "degree of threat" in the situation as indicated by such aspects as chance of loss, amount at stake, predominance of losses (versus gains), and variation in returns. On this dimension we found managers more willing to take risks in situations involving losses only (versus gains only), higher (versus lower) chances of loss, and lower (versus higher) stakes.

It would be desirable to have a standardized way to assess risk propensity. The dependence of risk propensity on the type of situation in which it is assessed suggests a caution. Using a single measure to assess risk propensity will be inadequate, no matter how strongly it is based in theory. Developing a portfolio of risk measures that assesses risk propensity in a variety of situations is imperative. Alternatively, if we wish to predict a person's behavior in a particular risky situation, then we should examine the individual's risk propensity in a similar situation. For example, if we are interested in predicting behavior in a business situation, then business decisions should be studied.

We also found that risk averters were more consistent in their risk propensity than risk takers, especially in particular situations, such as opportunities. This intriguing result leads us to conclude that risk takers may not be as set in their ways as risk averters.

RESEARCH CONCLUSIONS

Four main conclusions can be drawn from the comparison of risk measures:

1. The data provide support for a concept of risk propensity. Although there were differences in the various risk measures for a single individual, the differences among individuals were even stronger. Moreover the correlations between pairs of measures were significantly different from zero and there were more consistent relative risk averters and risk takers far beyond what chance alone would predict. Although factors other than risk propensity might explain these results; our focus on this construct, with its theoretical foundation in the Basic Risk Paradigm, makes other explanations less likely. The absence of a risk propensity that is uniform across all contexts seems attributable to a strong domain effect which we confirmed in the smallest space analysis with its "personal versus business" and "degree of threat" dimensions. For a more

detailed discussion of these issues see MacCrimmon and Wehrung (1985c).

2. The "degree of threat" dimension is especially interesting because it seems to have several related aspects. Our findings partly support and partly challenge Kahneman and Tversky's (1979) prospect theory. Greater risk taking when only losses are involved than when only gains are possible is consistent with this theory. The relationship between greater risk taking and higher chances of loss suggests an extension of the theory. A trend toward greater risk taking when lower stakes are at risk is contrary to prospect theory.

3. The confounding of various domains in our research design limits our ability to reach firm conclusions regarding specific domain effects on risk propensity. A strong instrument effect is confounded with the personal versus business domains. Similarly the instrument effect is confounded with the phase of risk. We were able to circumvent the former confounding with the smallest space analysis and demonstrate a strong personal versus business dimension to risk propensity that transcends the instrument effect. However, we have no effective means to overcome the latter confounding. Thus our conclusions that executives seem more willing to take risks once in a risky situation than in entering a risky situation and that risk taking seems more common in the recognition and adjustment phases of risk than in the choice phase must remain tentative.

4. In studies that purport to show differences in risk propensity among people in different careers, cultures, and so on, the following questions should be asked: In which domain? Using which instruments? With which measures? Realizing that different ways to assess risk can lead to widely different results, it becomes difficult to see how the existing studies, with their single measures of risk propensity (and often dubious measures at that) can reach the confident conclusions they do about cultural or other influences on risk. Moderating this pessimistic conclusion, we would suggest that future studies should not only use theoretically sound measures, but should use several measures. Then the question of whether there are significant enough differences in the factors being studied to overcome differences in the measures would be more compelling evidence for the results.

In this chapter, we have investigated the relationships among our primary measures of risk in standardized situations. We have studied the effect of domain of choice. In the next two chapters, we will look at other risk factors. In Chapter 9 we look at attitudes toward risk and see whether they are closely associated with any of the primary measures of risk. As we will discuss there, these attitudes have often themselves been used as risk measures, although they have little theoretical justification. We will also look at naturally occurring risks (such as the holding of personal assets, life insurance, etc.) to see if responses to these risks either tell us more about which are the best risk measures to use, or can serve as risk measures themselves. In Chapter 10 we will study the correspondence between the primary and secondary risk measures and a variety of risk-related characteristics of the decision maker.

Chapter 9

Measuring Risk in Natural Situations and Attitudes

INTRODUCTION

We used standardized situations in Chapters 3–8 to derive our primary measures of risk propensity. Using standardized situations facilitates comparisons across individuals because they confront the same set of alternatives in the same decision environment. A potential disadvantage is that people may not act in the standardized situation as they would if they actually faced that situation.

To overcome this limitation, we examined the actual choices the executives made in naturally occurring situations. We then inferred a risk propensity from these choices. For example, if a person held a high proportion of his assets in risky assets (such as commodity futures or speculative stocks), one would likely conclude that he was a risk taker. It should be remembered, though, that in natural situations different people have different choice opportunities. Thus choices made in standardized situations facilitate comparisons but may be unrepresentative, while choices made in natural situations are representative but comparison is difficult.

Another way to measure risk propensity is to ask about attitudes toward risk. For example, if you express a liking for racing high-speed cars or sky diving (whether you actually participate in these activities or not), you are reflecting a positive attitude toward risk. One may infer from these attitudes that you would also make risky decisions. While attitudes provide some information, we believe that the best guide to what a person will do in a risky situation is what he actually does in similar situations rather than an attitude he expresses. Nonetheless we include risk attitudes along with natural situations and standardized situations as part of our comprehensive Risk Portfolio. The boldface lines in Figure 9.1 show the comparisons that will form our focal point in this chapter.

NATURAL SITUATIONS

Description of Natural Situations

People confront a great many natural situations from which a risk propensity might be derived. If we examine a person's status at any time, we should remember that it is the result of both the decisions he has taken and uncontrollable events that have occurred. Hence we must be careful in inferring risk propensity from actual situations be-

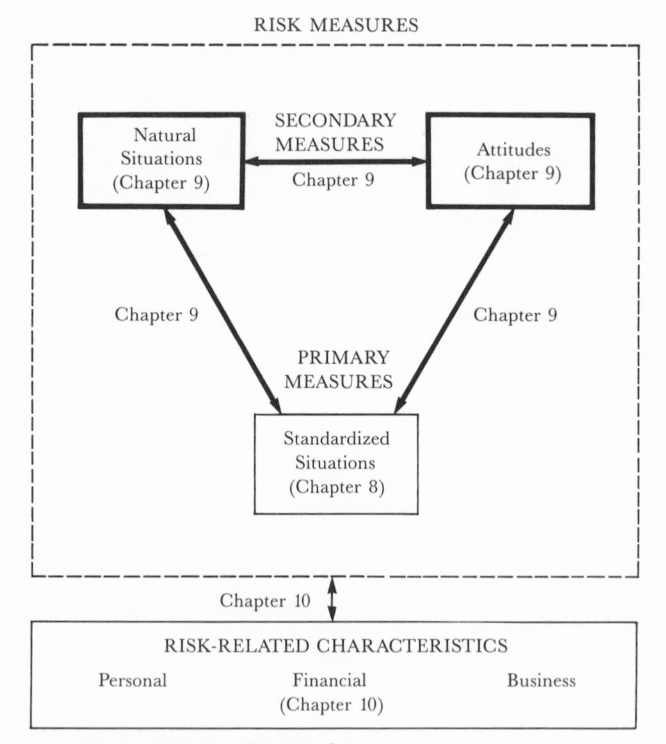

Figure 9.1 Focus in Chapter 9

cause what happened may not be what a person intended. For example, an individual's large debt may have resulted from a very unlucky break rather than from a conscious decision to incur a high debt in order to take advantage of some risky investment opportunities.

We chose natural situations that people widely encounter so that we have benchmarks for comparison. Thus, we studied financial situations involving risky assets, debt, life insurance, and gambling. We included one question about a person's career that dealt with resignations. All of this data was obtained from the General Questionnaire reproduced in the Appendix (pages 299–306).

We expect a risk-averse person to hold most of his personal assets in relatively safe categories and to shun the more volatile assets. Eight asset categories were listed to help the executives record their personal asset holdings. We asked each executive to give the percentage of his assets held in each category.

The overall distribution of asset holdings for the 501 executives who provided the necessary information is presented in Table 9.1. The typical manager held $500,000 in assets including about 40% in real estate, 20% in common stock, and no more than 10% in each of any of the other well-defined categories. The category "other" averaged 20% of personal assets and consisted of a variety of assets including bonds, pension funds, cash value of life insurance policies, bank deposits, and personal property.

We used commonly held views to classify the five riskiest categories as commodity futures, business ventures, long/short stock positions, common stock, and mutual funds. Savings accounts and the assets included in the "other" category were clearly the lowest risk assets. Real estate was somewhat problematic, but because the predominance of values in this category consisted of homes and cottages, it seemed to belong in the "safe" category.

The risk measure we will use is:

> The percentage of gross personal assets held in the five riskiest categories.

Overall, 30% of the executives held 10% or less of their assets in the riskiest categories. In fact, 8% of the executives held no assets in these five categories. Twenty-six percent of the executives held more than half their assets in the riskiest categories, including 2% who held more than 90%.[1] The typical executive held 25% of his gross assets in the risky categories.

A risk-averse person can be expected to shun debt. For a given net wealth, of say $200,000, the risk-averse person will have $200,000 in assets and no debt. The risk taker is more likely to have $1 million in assets and $800,000 in liabilities. Therefore the proportion of as-

Table 9.1 Distribution of Asset Holdings (Percentages)

Percentage of Gross Assets Held in Category	"Risky" Categories					"Safe" Categories		
	Commodity Futures	*Business Ventures*	*Long/Short Stock*	*Common Stock*	*Mutual Funds*	*Real Estate*	*Savings Accounts*	*Other Assets*
0	99	76	95	14	72	8	30	25
1–20	1	12	5	49	25	21	67	40
21–40	0	4	0	18	3	24	2	17
41–60	0	5	0	9	0	23	1	11
61–80	0	2	0	7	0	18	0	5
81–100	0	1	0	3	0	6	0	2
Total	100	100	100	100	100	100	100	100
Median	0.0	0.2	0.0	15.0	0.2	40.0	2.5	12.2
Mean	0.2	7.1	0.5	23.3	2.5	41.1	5.1	20.2

sets held as debt is a measure of risk propensity. Specifically, we define our risk measure as:

> The percentage of total assets held as liabilities.

The median value for this measure was 16% over the 489 executives who provided the necessary information.[2] Nineteen percent of the executives held no liabilities, and 57% had a debt ratio of 20% or less. Eight percent of the executives had a debt ratio of more than 50%.

We expect a risk-averse person to hold more life insurance than a risk-taking individual. Life insurance by itself is inappropriate as a measure of risk propensity because higher values may reflect higher salary and more dependents rather than risk aversion per se. For a given salary level we can expect increased life insurance holdings to reflect risk aversion. We will use as our risk measure:

> The ratio of total life insurance to annual salary.

Among 466 managers who responded, the typical executive carried life insurance worth $380,000 or about 3.3 times his salary.[3] Seventeen percent of the executives had a ratio of 2 or less, 37% had a ratio of more than 4, while 2% of the executives held life insurance worth more than ten times their salary.

A risk-averse person can be expected to avoid gambling. We asked the executives how often, in the past year, they had gambled in established casinos, bet on their own recreational activities (e.g., golf), and bet on professional sports. We also asked the average wager per occasion. The 472 executives who answered the gambling questions reported a low level of gambling activity. Forty-one percent of the managers had not gambled at all in the past year. Even for those who had gambled, the average amount was only $45. Only 9% of the managers reached an annual gambling level of $1000 and only 2% exceeded $3000.[4]

Because gambling level may be directly affected by wealth (i.e., those with higher wealth can "afford" to gamble more), we normalized the gambling level by net wealth. The measure used was:

> Total amount wagered in the past year on recreational wagers as a proportion of net wealth.

The typical executive in the study wagered only 0.01% of his net wealth during the year, and only 3% of the executives wagered more than 1% of their net wealth.[5]

The financial decisions described above are some of the most prominent decisions in one's personal life. For business executives, career decisions are also extremely important. A risk-averse person will change jobs infrequently and, even if he changes jobs, he will not be inclined to do so without another job lined up. We can define a measure of career risk as:

> The number of times in the past 15 years that a person has voluntarily resigned.

Overall, 60% of the 435 managers who answered this question had not resigned voluntarily in the last 15 years. Sixteen percent had resigned once, 13% had resigned twice, 6% had resigned three times, and only 5% of the executives had resigned more than three times.

NOTE ON NATURAL SITUATIONS

Only one of the 509 executives failed to complete the General Questionnaire, but several executives did not respond to some questions. Most of the data were numerical or frequencies, so coding was straightforward. We will label the five risk measures derived from the natural situations as follows:

RISKYASSETS
DEBTRATIO
SELFINSURED
GAMBLING
RESIGNATIONS

To derive a risk measure from the data on asset holdings, it was necessary to classify the assets according to their riskiness. Ideally, we would like to base this classification on the executive's own perceptions. Lacking this information, we based the classification on commonly held views of risky assets. Several measures of the riskiness of behavior were derived using this characterization of asset riskiness. Measures were also based on the percentage of gross assets held in the four riskiest categories (the five mentioned in the text excluding mutual funds) and on the percentage of gross assets held in the six riskiest categories (the five mentioned in the text plus real estate). The different measures did not give noticeably different results. A measure in which the category "other" was excluded gave no significant difference in results.

Total life insurance holdings were used rather than life insurance purchased by the executive because the latter amount depends critically on how much life insurance is purchased by the executive's firm. This measure was rescaled by subtracting it from a fixed constant so that higher values correspond to risk taking, making it consistent with all the natural situation measures. We have used the label SELFINSURED rather than INSURANCE to indicate this rescaling.

It would have been desirable to restrict the RESIGNATIONS measure to resignations without jobs waiting. We obtained that information but there were so few cases that we used the measure defined above. The extent to which executives had careers shorter than 15 years when this study was conducted would potentially reduce this measure of voluntary resignations for younger executives. Of particular concern would be managers under 35 years of age who would in most cases have career lengths of less than 15 years. Since only 10% of the executives were under 35 years of age, this potential bias should not be a problem.

While many more risk measures from natural situations could be derived from our data, we will confine our attention to the five measures described above.

Are the Managers Generally Risk-Averse in Natural Situations?

We suspected that they would be for two reasons. First, we chose measures of personal financial status for most of our natural situations and we have already seen a strong tendency toward risk aversion in personal decisions in Chapters 4 and 8. Second, if the managers show different propensities toward risk in natural and standardized situations, it seems likely that they will be more risk-averse in actual situations than in the hypothetical standardized situations.

The answers of the executives support this view. We could not compare these answers with "risk-neutral" values because the natural situations did not have an underlying theory of risk as the stand ardized situations did. Instead, we chose reasonable values to serve as "risk-neutral" benchmarks:

Half of personal assets in common stock, mutual funds, long/short stock positions, business ventures, and commodity futures
Half of personal assets financed with debt
Life insurance worth twice annual salary
Annual recreational gambles worth 0.1% of personal wealth
Three or more voluntary resignations within the past 15 years

Therefore we considered the managers to be risk takers if they held more than half their personal assets in the risky categories, financed more than half their assets with debt, and so on.

Table 9.2 shows the percentage of risk takers in each of the natural situations, the standardized situations, and the attitude questionnaires. We see that no more than about one out of four managers were risk takers in any of the natural situations. This predominance of risk aversion continued to hold even when we chose other values to serve as risk-neutral values.[6] Comparisons among the different types of situations will be made after we examine the attitudes of the executives.

Table 9.2 Risk Taking in Standardized Situations, Natural Situations, and Attitudes

Type of Situation		Risk Taker	Percentage of Executives Who Are Risk Takers
Standardized Situations	*Risk In-Basket*	Requires less than 50% chance of winning lawsuit	53
		Requires less than 33% chance of large market share to forego joint venture	44
	Personal Investment Gambles	Requires less than 1.5 times personal wealth when chance of loss is 50%	Under 1
		Requires less than 1.05 times personal wealth when chance of loss is 10%	0
	Business Investment Gambles	Requires less than 2.0 times usual rate of return on special project when chance of loss is 50%	4
		Requires less than 1.11 times usual rate of return on special project when chance of loss is 10%	2
	Risk-Return Rankings	Ranks investment alternative with highest variation in returns in top three	39
		Ranks investment alternative with lowest variation in returns in bottom three	68

Type of Situation	Risk Taker	Percentage of Executives Who Are Risk Takers
Natural Situations	Holds more than half of personal assets in common stock, mutual funds, long/short stock positions, business ventures, and commodity futures	26
	Finances more than half of personal assets with debt	8
	Carries life insurance worth twice annual salary or less	17
	Wagers more than 0.1% of personal wealth annually on recreational gambles	22
	Has resigned voluntarily three or more times during the past 15 years	11
Attitudes	Rates himself as more willing to take risks than other managers	56
	Makes four or more sensation-seeking choices out of seven items	50
	Makes four or more internal control choices out of seven items	94

> ***Result:*** The managers were generally risk-averse in the natural situations that dealt primarily with their personal financial status.

This observation means we can expect managers to be cautious in their decisions concerning personal finances. Although a manager's role often requires him to be a risk taker with corporate resources, he usually does not hold a high-risk personal portfolio, is not highly levered with debt, does not gamble excessively, and does carry high life insurance.

Are the Managers' Risk Propensities Related in Different Natural Situations?

If a manager reveals his risk propensities in different natural situations, then we would expect significant relationships among the natural situation risk measures. Is this true in the data?

The manager's debt ratio was significantly associated with each of the other measures. A higher debt ratio was significantly related to both a higher level of recreational gambling and more resignations. However, the reasons for these relationships may not be primarily due to risk propensity. For example, heavy gambling or more frequent job changes might require debt financing.

One would expect that increased holdings of risky assets would also require debt financing. Strangely enough higher debt ratio was associated with a lower proportion of personal risky assets. We also unexpectedly found that higher debt ratio was associated with higher life insurance holdings. This seems to contradict our interpretations of higher debt ratio and lower life insurance as indications of greater risk taking. Perhaps these results are due to the effect of another factor, age. Younger executives have most of their assets in their homes (categorized as "safe" assets) but have large mortgages. They also carry greater life insurance to protect younger dependents.[7]

The only other significant relationship was between life insurance holdings and resignations. The more times a manager voluntarily resigned his position, the more life insurance he carried. The use of insurance to offset job instability makes some sense when one takes a portfolio perspective on handling risk. Age may also play a part in explaining this result in that younger executives who carry more life insurance also tend to change jobs more frequently during the early stages of their careers.

> ***Result:*** The managers' willingness to take risks was associated across some natural situations, especially debt ratio.

However, the relationships were not all consistent with our interpretations of the natural situations in terms of risk propensity.

The negative relationships highlight the limitation of treating variables such as debt ratio, proportion of risky assets, and life insurance holdings as measures of risk propensity. Using risky asset holdings to characterize a manager's risk propensity will give very different results from using his debt ratio. We must be careful then in deciding which one, if any, of the natural situations best reveals one's willingness to take risks. Characteristics of the executives such as age can have an important effect on how they behave in natural situations. One must not overlook these factors in a study of risk propensity.

Note on relationships among the risk measures

To the extent that there is a single construct of risk propensity, then all the measures in the Risk Portfolio should be significantly related. If this demanding standard is not met, we still might expect that we would find significant relationships among measures within the same category. In particular, the natural situation measures—if indeed they can serve as measures of risk propensity—should be interrelated.

We present the Pearson correlations below for the 16 measures in the Risk Portfolio, including the eight primary measures, five natural situation measures, and three attitude measures. The attitude measures are discussed more fully later in this chapter. Briefly, SELFRATING measures one's self-perception of willingness to take business risks, SENSATION indicates one's desire for a stimulating environment, and I/E:CONTROL measures one's belief that he can control his environment. Recall that all 16 measures have been scaled so that higher values correspond to risk taking.

Only correlations that were significantly different from zero at the 0.001 level are shown. Sample sizes ranged from 270 to 495 because all measures could not be derived for all managers.

We will first consider correlations between measures derived from the same type of situation (i.e., standardized situations, natural situations, and attitudes). The correlations among the primary measures from the standardized situations were the highest we found in the study. Eleven out of the 28 possible correlations were significantly positive.

Five of the ten possible correlations among pairs of natural situation measures were significantly different from zero. This result is encouraging, but the fact that three of these correlations were negative casts doubt on at least some of these measures as indicators of risk propensity.

Among the attitude measures only one pair had a significant positive correlation. However, we will not dwell on the relationships among the attitude measures because they were only included in the study so they could be contrasted with the other measures.

Measures of Risk Propensity		IB:LAWSUIT	IB:VENTURE	PGAMBLE50%	PGAMBLE10%	BGAMBLE50%	BGAMBLE10%	RANK:EV-HI	RANK:EV-LO	RISKYASSETS	DEBTRATIO	SELFINSURED	GAMBLING	RESIGNATIONS	SELFRATING	SENSATION	I/E:CONTROL
		Standardized Situations								Natural Situations					Attitude		
Standardized Situations	IB:LAWSUIT		.16														
	IB:VENTURE																
	PGAMBLE50%				.67	.42	.26										
	PGAMBLE10%					.24	.33	.15	.17								
	BGAMBLE50%						.68								.21		
	BGAMBLE10%							.19							.22		
	RANK:EV-HI								.54								
	RANK:EV-LO																
Natural Situations	RISKYASSETS										−.14						
	DEBTRATIO											−.18	.17	.21			
	SELFINSURED													−.20			
	GAMBLING																
	RESIGNATIONS																
Attitude	SELFRATING															.22	
	SENSATION																
	I/E:CONTROL																

Intra Standardized Situation Comparisons

Intra Natural Situation Comparisons

Intra Attitude Comparisons

Overall 41% (17/41) of the correlations within categories were significant at the 0.001 level. This is much greater than expected by chance, reinforcing our belief in an underlying risk propensity.

Across categories, however, we found little evidence of strong relationships, but weaker associations were apparent. Only 3% (2/79) of the correlations across categories exceeded 0.20 (significantly different from zero at the 0.001 level). Using less stringent significance levels, we found many more significant correlations in the 0.10 to 0.20 range than predicted by chance. For example, using a 1% level, less than one significant correlation was expected, yet we found eight positive and two negative correlations, and even the negative associations gave a coherent picture once age was considered. These significant associations across standardized situations, natural situations, and attitudes, although weak, provide support for a unified construct of risk propensity that can be uncovered by different measures.

Are the Managers' Risk Propensities Related in the Natural Situations and the Standardized Situations?

In Chapters 3–5 we presented the standardized situations from which the eight primary measures discussed in Chapter 8 were derived. In Chapter 8 we analyzed the relationships among these standardized measures. Let us now consider the possible relationships between the standardized measures and five natural situation measures.

Although we found no strong relationships, the weaker associations did reveal some interesting patterns.[8] Managers who held higher proportions of personal risky assets were *less* willing to risk losing half their wealth in the Personal Investment Gambles. This is understandable if one considers the effect of wealth. Greater wealth means there are greater possible losses in the personal gambles making one less willing to gamble. Having extra wealth also allows one to hold a greater percentage of assets in risky categories without jeopardizing a fixed amount in safer assets. These effects of wealth will be discussed in more detail in Chapter 10.

Managers who risked more of their wealth on recreational gambles were more risk-taking in all of the Personal and Business Investment Gambles. In addition, they were more willing to gamble with the Risk In-Basket lawsuit by taking it to court. Thus gambling behavior seems to be related across both natural and standardized situations.

Lastly, executives who carried greater life insurance holdings were greater risk takers in the Business Investment Gambles and the Risk-Return Rankings. We have no explanation for this finding contrary to our risk interpretation.

Result: The managers' risk propensities were related in the natural situtions and the standardized situations, but the associations were weak.

Finding some coherence between the managers' answers in the natural and standardized situations reinforces our belief in an underlying risk propensity. However, we had expected to find much stronger relationships among the managers' behavior in these different types of situations. The absence of such relationships means that we cannot predict very accurately a person's risk status in natural situations if we know only his response to standardized risks.

NOTE ON OTHER NATURALLY OCCURRING RISKS: INITIATING CHANGES IN A FIRM'S OPERATIONS

We looked at several other natural situations that could be used to measure risk propensity. One such situation that we considered was whether the executive personally initiated significant changes in his firm's operations. A risk-taking manager can be expected personally to initiate such changes, while an executive who avoids initiating changes or who initiates them only as a member of a decision-making group may be thought of as more risk-averse. In this situation the executive's risk varies greatly because of his different exposure to possible failure.

We dropped this situation from our list of the five principal natural situations considered in this chapter because it was highly dependent on the manager's perceptions of which changes were "significant" and whether they were "personally" initiated, and managers could be expected to overrepresent their roles in making changes. Even with these problems, this natural situation can provide useful information on the executive's own view of his role as an innovator and a change-agent in his firm.

We developed a measure called CHANGES by calculating the percentage of the total significant changes in the firm's operations that were personally initiated by the executive.[9] Twenty-seven percent of the executives said they personally initiated no significant changes, while 28% claimed that they initiated at least half of all significant changes in the firm's operations over the last five years. This latter group included 4% who said they personally initiated all significant changes during this period. The typical executive initiated 25% of the significant changes in his firm's operations.

To compare CHANGES with the primary and secondary risk measures we first separated the executives into those who had initiated no significant changes in their firms and those who had initiated at least half of the significant changes. Personally initiating significant changes was related to risk taking on five of the 16 risk measures, including all three attitude measures (*t*-test, 0.01 significance level). More specifically, initiating significant changes was related to a greater willingness to invest in a business gamble (BGAMBLE10%), investing more of personal assets in risky categories (RISKYASSETS), rating oneself as a risk taker (SELFRATING), belief in internal control (I/E:CONTROL), and a desire for a stimulating environment (SENSATION). Observing the role an executive takes in initiating changes in his firm provides a useful natural situation in which to measure one's propensity for business risks.

ATTITUDES

Description of Attitudes

In this section we will examine three risk-related attitudes and their relationships to risk propensity measured in standardized and natural situations. These attitudes include two measures derived from widely used personality questionnaires. These questionnaires record a person's reaction to the state of the world rather than his responses to actual choices with real outcomes. First, though, we will consider the executives' self-appraisal of their attitude toward risk.

We asked for a *self-rating* of risk propensity using the following question as part of the General Questionnaire:

> How would you rate your own willingness to undertake risky business propositions as compared to other executives at or near your level in your firm?

We provided a seven-point scale with endpoints "much less willing to accept risks" and "much more willing to accept risks." The answers given by the managers provided a direct measure of their risk propensity:

> A person's comparative self-assessment of risk propensity on a seven-point scale.

Twenty-four percent of the 502 executives who responded rated themselves near the risk-taking end of the scale (i.e., values 5.5–7.0), while 10% were near the risk-averse end (1.0–2.5). The remaining managers rated themselves about equally willing to take risks as other executives (3.0–5.0).

A risk taker is presumably someone who *seeks sensation*. When under stress, a sensation seeker would take a break by doing something new and different while a sensation averter would want something relaxing. There is a standard psychological questionnaire that purports to measure one's desire for sensation. This questionnaire was developed by Zuckerman, Kolin, Price, and Zoob (1964) and it uses 34 items. Each item represents a pairwise choice, such as:

(a) I prefer a guide when I am in a place I don't know well.

(b) I like to explore a strange city or section of town by myself, even if it means getting lost.

A sensation seeker would choose (b), while a sensation averter would choose (a). In addition to very specific questions about what the reader himself would do, the scale also contains generalized questions of the following kind:

(a) A good painting should shock or jolt the senses.
(b) A good painting should give one a feeling of peace and security.

Here sensation seeking seems less clear-cut, but it is asserted that a sensation seeker would choose answer (a), while a sensation averter would choose (b). Many of the 34 items were not appropriate for business executives, so we dropped them. The remaining ten items were given to the executives as part of our Societal Attitude Questionnaire.[10] During the analysis, we further pruned the ten items to seven items for which the executives' responses were highly related. The seven items included the two described above. We chose as our measure of sensation seeking:

The number of sensation-seeking choices out of seven items.

The values on this scale ranged from zero to seven. To the extent that sensation seeking is associated with risk taking, higher values correspond to greater risk taking.

Overall 31% of the 488 managers who answered all items could be categorized as high sensation seekers (values 5–7), with 3% of these making the sensation-seeking choice on all seven items. Twenty-seven percent were classified as low sensation seekers (0–2) including 3% who made no sensation-seeking choices. The remaining 42% of the managers made moderate numbers (3–4) of sensation-seeking choices.

Another psychological variable that relates to risk propensity is one's belief in his ability to control the environment. If you believe you can control the outcomes of risky decisions, you can afford to take chances. If events are beyond your control, the safe way may be best. Rotter (1966) developed a 29-item questionnaire to assess a person's attitude toward *internal versus external control*. This questionnaire included items such as:

(a) When I make plans, I am almost certain that I can make them work.
(b) It is not always wise to plan too far ahead because many things turn out to be a matter of good or bad fortune anyhow.

A person who believes he can internally control events, and hence is more inclined to take risks, would presumably select (a). The person who believes events are externally controlled (i.e., inclined toward risk aversion) would select (b). As with the sensation-seeking questionnaire, the internal-external control questionnaire also used generalized questions. One such item is:

(a) By taking an active part in political and social affairs, people can control world events.
(b) As far as world affairs are concerned, most of us are the victims of forces we can neither understand nor control.

Here the internally controlled person would select (a).

We also pruned this questionnaire down to ten items by dropping items that seemed inappropriate for business executives and eliminating redundant questions. The ten items we used, including the two above, were presented to the managers as part of the Societal Attitude Questionnaire. Again the managers' responses were highly related for only seven of these items, so we dropped the other three. Our measure of belief in internal control was:

The number of internal control choices out of seven items.

The values on this scale ranged from zero to seven with higher values corresponding to greater risk taking.

Thirty-four percent of the 501 executives who answered all items made the internal control choice all seven times. A total of 86% were at the internal control end of the scale (i.e., values 5–7). Only 2% were at the external control end of the scale (0–2) with the remaining 12% in the middle (3–4).

NOTE ON ATTITUDES

Previous studies of risk have often used measures of a person's attitudes as indicative of his risk propensity. We believe that inferences about choice behavior are best made from choices and not from attitudes. However, because attitudes have frequently formed the basis of risk assessments, we included them in our study so that we could compare them with choice-oriented measures—in both standardized situations and in natural situations.

Many possible objections can be raised to using self-appraisal as a method for measuring risk propensity. For example, there is no incentive for someone to tell the truth, even if he knew what the "truth" was. In addition, the self-rating question is so general that it cannot possibly reflect different risk propensities in different situations—even if they were known. These are only a few of the possible objections. On the other hand, because little has been known about how to assess risk propensity, the possibility that a person can provide a meaningful self-assessment could not be completely dismissed. To cover the possibility that such a response could yield useful information, we included it in our portfolio of risk measures.

The ten sensation-seeking items and the ten internal-external control items were combined with ten other pairwise choices, pertaining to risk, that the researchers developed. The thirty items were randomly dispersed in an instrument called the "Societal Attitude Questionnaire." The risk-taking response and the risk-averting response of each pair were randomly put in the (a) or (b) position.

In analyzing the executives' responses, we first checked the inter-item reliability. For each of the ten sensation-seeking questions, the item score[11] was correlated with the total of the other nine items. The Cronbach standardized alpha score[12] was 0.52. The reported item reliability scores in previous studies have been 0.68 to 0.74 for the set of 34 questions. Another check on reliability can be obtained by computing separate scores for odd-numbered and even-numbered items. Using the Guttman split-half coefficient[13] we got a reliability of 0.56. We concluded that our ten-item sensation-seeking instrument was adequately reliable.

The same analyses were conducted for the internal-external control questions. The Cronbach alpha score for item correlation was 0.50. Previous studies have reported reliabilities of 0.65 to 0.79. The Guttman split-half coefficient was 0.45. We concluded that our ten-item control instrument was adequately reliable.

Careful reading of the example questions for each instrument might have suggested that there is an apparent overlap between some of the items on the sensation-seeking and internal-external control scales. Note that the question on exploring a new city could equally well pertain to internal-external control and the question about planning could pertain to sensation-seeking. To uncover possible relationships, we conducted a smallest space analysis of the 20 sensation-seeking and internal-external control questions considered jointly. If they were separate concepts, we would expect the ten questions on each scale to cluster together.

We found that seven sensation-seeking and seven control questions clustered separately. The other three control questions and two of the sensation questions were located between these two clusters and were as close to each other as they were to the major cluster to which they were supposed to belong. The remaining item was the only item that, when omitted, led to an increase in the average item correlation (from 0.52 to 0.57) and was the only variable of the ten that had negative correlations with any other item. The seven control questions used were Rotter's (1966) numbers 2, 4, 6, 9, 13, 16, and 28. The seven sensation questions used were Zuckerman et al.'s (1964) numbers 1, 7, 10, 22, 31, 32, and 33.

From these results we concluded that more distinct scales could be constructed for both sensation seeking and for internal-external control by including only the seven items in each scale which formed a distinct cluster. These reduced scales formed the basis for our attitude measures.

We will call the three attitude measures:

SELFRATING
SENSATION
I/E:CONTROL

Note that higher values correspond to risk taking for all three attitude measures. This scaling is consistent with the natural situation measures and the (rescaled) primary measures. These labels will be used throughout the rest of the book.

Do the Managers Generally Rate Themselves as Risk Takers or Risk Averters Compared with Other Managers?

Rating oneself as a risk taker was significantly more common. Fifty-six percent of the managers thought they were more willing to take business risks than other managers at similar levels in their firms. Only 30% believed they were less willing to take business risks. An average response of 4.4 on the seven-point scale was significantly above the value of 4.0 where the manager rated himself equally risk-taking as his peers, confirming this result.[14] This tendency for the *average* executive to rate himself as more willing to take risks than his peers is consistent with a cultural bias in favor of taking risks.

> ***Result:*** The managers generally rated themselves as more willing to take business risks than other managers at similar levels in their firms.

This result says that we cannot rely on what someone says about his risk propensity. Because managers generally preferred to be seen as risk takers, we must discount these self-appraisals and augment them with other measures of risk propensity.

NOTE ON RATINGS OF THE FIRM'S RISK PROPENSITY

Do managers perceive their firm's willingness to take risks to be the same as they see their own attitude toward risk? To address this question, we asked each executive, "How would you rate your firm's willingness to undertake risky business propositions as compared to other firms in the industry?"

A seven-point scale was provided with endpoints labeled as "much less willing to accept risks" and "much more willing to accept risks." Of the 499 executives who answered this question, 17% indicated that their firm was much less willing to take risks than other firms (scale positions 1 to 2.5), while 20% indicated that their firm was much more willing to take risks (scale positions 5.5 to 7). The remaining 63% saw no major difference. This distribution of responses had a mean of 4.1 near the risk-neutral level of 4.0.

We conjecture that there will be a match between the firm and the manager. Managers are likely to be attracted to firms that they perceive as having similar attitudes toward risk taking. Once in the firm executives whose risk propensity is different from their firm's will tend either to conform in their behavior (or perception) to match that of the firm or to leave the firm.

The results showed that managers who perceived their firms as very risk-averting (1–2.5) rated themselves as significantly less willing to take risks than managers who perceived their firms as very risk-taking (5.5–7). In addition the ratings of self and firm risk propensity fell within one scale position for 65% of the managers. Thus for the majority of the executives there was strong evidence that a match existed between the executives' perceptions of their own willingness to take risks and their firm's willingness to take risks. This match increased the longer the executive had been with the same firm.

When a manager's self-rating of risk propensity is different from his firm's, we conjecture he will rate himself as more willing to take risks than his firm. We based this conjecture on a cultural bias toward taking risks in our society, especially among top executives. We found that the two ratings differed by more than one scale position for 176 executives. Of these managers 62% rated themselves as more risk-taking than their firm, while 38% showed the reverse. We conclude that, when there is a difference, there is a tendency to rate oneself more willing to take risks than one's firm.

Do the Managers Seek a High Degree of Sensation in Their Environments?

The typical manager made as many sensation-seeking choices as sensation-avoiding choices. Overall, 50% of the managers chose four or more sensation-seeking responses. Thus we saw no preference for a high degree of sensation. If desire for sensation is an indication of one's risk propensity, we found that the executives were risk-neutral on average.

Result: The managers sought an average amount of sensation from their environment.

It would be difficult to reach specific conclusions about a person's preference for sensation without knowing more about how "sensation-filled" his life already was. A person who leads a very active life, as most top-level managers do, may indicate a preference for more relaxation. Such a "portfolio" choice would not reflect the degree of stimulation he could tolerate and may be a very inadequate guide to the risks he was prepared to assume.

Do the Managers Believe They Can Control Their Environments?

The answer is overwhelmingly yes. Ninety-four percent of the executives made four or more internal control choices, including 34% who gave internal control responses to all seven items. We should expect that "being in control" would be highly valued among executives. When confronted with rather obvious internal versus external control questions such as whether one can make plans work out or whether outcomes are determined by chance or by others, any self-respecting executive is pushed toward the internal response. After all, why is he in his job if he cannot make plans work out?

> ***Result:*** The managers believed strongly that they could control their environments.

This widely held belief in internal control among executives could be used as a partial check on whether a prospective employee had "management potential." Similar beliefs commonly held by managers concerning an orientation toward action, willingness to assume responsibility, and so forth might be examined in an extended attitudinal questionnaire.

NOTE ON THE LITERATURE REGARDING ATTITUDES

A number of studies have seemed to show that the risks taken by a group are more extreme than would be taken by the members individually. Early research on this group-induced "risky shift" suggested that this effect might be a result of a cultural bias in favor of risk taking. According to this interpretation (Brown, 1965; Teger and Pruitt, 1967), taking risks is more culturally valued than not doing so. The result is that people believe themselves to be greater risk takers than their peers. Several studies (e.g., Wallach and Wing, 1968; Willems, 1969; Levinger and Schneider, 1969) examined this hypothesis by asking subjects to respond to several risky situations first acting on their own behalf and then predicting the responses given by the majority of their peers. The risky situations consisted of choice dilemmas developed by Kogan and Wallach (1964; Wallach and Kogan, 1959, 1961) and discussed in more detail in Chapter 3. These studies supported the cultural bias in favor of risk taking as do the responses of our executives to the self-appraisal of risk.

The median number of sensation-seeking responses was 3.5 out of 7. Zuckerman and associates (1964) presented data on the use of their scale with male and female college undergraduates. Converting their scale to one ranging between +1.0 (for all sensation-seeking responses) to −1.0 (for all sensation-averting responses), we find average scores ranging from 0.10 to 0.18. Our business executives had an average score of zero on this scale, so they rated sightly lower in sensation seeking than did the students. With questions such as the desire to travel (see Zuckerman question 1), it is not surprising that college students would express a higher preference for travel than would executives who are most likely doing more traveling already than they would prefer.

The median number of internal control responses in our study was 6.0. Rotter's (1966) study showed a lower proportion of "internals." Converting the scales to +1.0 (for all "internal" responses) to −1.0 (for all "external" responses), over a series of studies Rotter's scores ranged from an average of 0.31 (for 18-year-old Boston males) to 0.58 (for male Peace Corp trainees). The average score for our executives on this scale was 0.66. Clearly the executives strongly preferred the response indicating internal control. The standard deviation of responses of our executives was about the same as those found by Rotter. Thus our executives were more internally controlled, but equally homogeneous in their beliefs as the other groups. Miller, Kets deVries, and Toulouse (1982) confirm this result in their study of top-level managers.

Are the Managers' Risk-Related Attitudes Associated?

Rating oneself a risk taker, a desire for a stimulating environment, and a belief in internal control all seem to be indications of a willingness to take risks. Therefore we expect to find significant relationships among our three attitude measures.

The self-rating and desire for sensation were significantly related. Managers who rated themselves as more willing to take business risks than other managers in their firms also made more sensation-seeking choices. Managers who believed they could control their environment also tended to rate themselves as risk takers and to seek greater sensation, but the associations were weaker.[15]

> ***Result:*** The managers showed similar risk propensities in three diverse risk-related attitudes.

The associations among these three attitudes reinforce our belief that people do have an underlying attitude toward risk that influences their behavior. Whether this attitude reflects the managers' behavior is the next topic.

NOTE ON OTHER ATTITUDINAL MEASURES OF RISK: TOLERANCE FOR LOSS

We considered several other attitudes related to risk. One question was designed to uncover the attitude of our managers toward losing. The question was worded as a selection between:

(a) I don't mind losing when there is little at stake.
(b) I hate to lose at anything.

We compared the responses of this attitude toward losing with the 16 risk measures. We found no significant differences in the standardized situations between the executives who could tolerate losing and those who could not. There was a significant difference only for RISKYASSETS among the natural situation measures. Managers who hated to lose at anything tended to hold less of their assets in risky categories than managers who indicated they could tolerate losing if there wasn't much at stake. Such managers apparently preferred always winning with safe assets to sometimes losing with risky ones. Among the attitude measures only SENSATION showed a significant difference. In this case, the desire for a stimulating environment was associated with "I hate to lose at anything." Overall, we conclude that there are no major relationships between tolerance for losing and our risk measures. Tolerance for losing may be a very interesting attitude for further study, but its lack of association with other risk measures reduces its potential as a risk-related factor itself.

Are the Managers' Attitudes Toward Risk Related to Their Behavior in Standardized Situations?

We found some moderately strong relationships here. Managers who rated themselves as more willing to take business risks than their peers were significantly more willing to invest in the uncertain project in the Business Investment Gambles.

Generally, however, the associations were weak.[16] Executives who were high on sensation seeking tended to take greater risks in the Personal and Business Investment Gambles and in the Risk-Return Rankings. Managers who believed they had greater control over their environment tended to take greater risks in the Business Investment Gambles and the Risk-Return Rankings.

> ***Result:*** The managers' attitudes toward risk were related to their behavior in the standardized situations. The strongest association was between self-rating of business risk propensity and willingness to take risks in the Business Investment Gambles.

This finding partially offsets our earlier conclusion about measuring risks using attitudes and behavior in natural situations. There is a connection between a manager's attitude toward taking generalized business risks (i.e., his self-rating) and his willingness to take some specific business risks (i.e., the standardized situation concerning investment of a capital expenditure budget). We must still be cautious, however, because the self-rating was not associated with other business risks such as the lawsuit and the joint venture in the Risk In-Basket. Although it would be nice to have a single measure of business risk propensity, we are unlikely to find one because there are too many types of business risks.

NOTE ON PROPENSITY TO GATHER INFORMATION AND PROPENSITY TO TAKE TIME MAKING DECISIONS

We also considered the following two self-ratings concerning the executive's propensity to gather information and to take time deliberating when making decisions:

> When making decisions, do you gather more or less information than other managers?
>
> When making decisions, do you take more or less time deliberating than other managers?

For each question a seven-point scale was provided with endpoints labeled as "more" (scale position 7) and "less" (scale position 1). The typical executive reported that he gathered *more information* (median scale position, 4.9) and spent *less time* deliberating decisions (median scale position 3.5) than other managers. These results are statistically different from the neutral scale positions (4). Excluding the middle responses reinforced these conclusions.

These responses suggest there may be cultural biases toward gathering information and making quick decisions. To the extent that making quick decisions is related to risk taking, a cultural bias toward making quick decisions is consistent with the hypothesized cultural bias toward risk taking. A propensity to gather more information, however, is not consistent with either of these biases if risk taking is related to gathering *less* information. A possible explanation is that extra information tends to be sought only if it does not prevent making quick decisions.

A secondary effect of collecting information is that it generally implies a delay in making a decision. Thus we might expect a positive relationship between these two self-ratings. A significant correlation of 0.25 between these variables for 497 executives confirmed this expectation.

To determine whether risk-averse managers collected more information in making decisions, we compared executives who gathered substantially more information than other managers with those who gathered substantially less information to see if they differed on any of the risk measures (t-test, 0.01 significance level). The results showed that gathering more information was significantly associated with settling the lawsuit out of court (IB:LAWSUIT), holding a smaller percentage of personal assets in risky categories (RISKYASSETS), rating oneself as a risk averter (SELFRATING), and seeking few sensations in one's environment (SENSATION).

A similar test was used to see if risk-averse managers took more time deliberating decisions. Taking more time deliberating decisions was significantly associated with rating oneself as a risk averter, seeking few sensations in the environment, and "I don't mind losing when little is at stake." Each of these relationships is consistent with interpreting the gathering of more information or taking time deliberating decisions as indications of risk aversion.

Overall, these additional risk-related attitudes reconfirm our earlier results that diverse risk-related attitudes are significantly related among themselves, but are only weakly related with risk propensity measured in standardized or natural situations.

NATURAL SITUATIONS AND ATTITUDES

Do Managers Show More Risk Taking in Their Attitudes or Their Behavior?

At least half the executives showed a willingness to take risks in each of the three attitude measures. The self-appraisal provided a direct measure of risk propensity, whereas desire for sensation and belief in internal control of the environment had only indirect relationships with attitude toward risk. In comparison, no more than 26% of the executives were risk takers in any of the five natural situations (see Table 9.2 on pages 214–215).

We can also compare the attitudes toward risk with the executives' willingness to take risks in the standardized situations from Chapter 8. Only two of the eight standardized situations had a majority of risk takers and four situations had fewer than 5%. Thus the executives were substantially more risk-taking in their attitudes than in either the natural situations or a majority of the standardized situations, both of which required behavioral responses.

> ***Result:*** The managers were more risk-taking in their attitudes than in their behavior.

This result rules out using attitudes as the sole basis for measuring risk propensity. Managers have a tendency to say they are risk takers, but in their actions they are more likely to be risk averters.

Are the Managers' Attitudes Toward Risk Related to Their Behavior in Natural Situations?

The answer is generally no. None of the attitude measures showed a strong relationship with any of the natural situation measures. However, we did find some weak associations. Managers who rated themselves as risk takers had higher debt ratios and resigned more frequently, consistent with our interpretations in terms of risk. They also carried more life insurance which is contrary to our interpretations. Executives who sought greater sensation also resigned more frequently, possibly to take more stimulating jobs.[17]

> ***Result:*** Generally the managers' attitudes toward risk did not reflect their behavior in natural situations.

We see from this result that actual behavior can be very different from one's attitudes. This discrepancy might be due to a desire to be seen as a risk taker whether or not it is true. Putting a self-avowed risk taker in charge of an important new venture may not result in his taking the risky actions desired by the firm.

Alternatively, there is no reason to believe that a self-rating of one's willingness to take *business* risks should be strongly related to measures of one's *personal* financial status such as debt ratio. But even if we know someone's attitude about a particular risky decision, there is no guarantee that he will choose actions that will be consistent with that attitude. For example, the staunchly anti-communist Richard Nixon made bold overtures to China and the Soviet Union as part of his detente strategy while President.

What Dimensions Underlie the Executives' Risk Propensities?

Our examination of the standardized situations in Chapter 8 revealed two dimensions to the managers' risk propensities. The first dimension was whether the risky situation involved personal or business decisions. The second dimension was the degree of threat posed by the risky situation. We found these dimensions by examining a spatial representation of the relationships among the eight primary measures.

Do the managers show different risk propensities in personal and business decisions with differing degrees of threat when we consider risk measures from the five natural situations and the three attitudes along with the eight standardized measures? The answer is yes. We developed a new spatial representation using the relationships among all 16 measures. See Figure 9.2. Recall that risk measures that have strong relationships appear close together in this diagram and those with weak or insignificant relationships appear further apart.

We can interpret the horizontal dimension of Figure 9.2 as a personal versus business dimension just as we did in Figure 8.2. The four personal measures from standardized situations, debt ratio, and resignations all lie to the left of the dotted line. The recreational gambling measure also lies close to this line, perhaps because part of this gambling is done on the golf course as part of one's business role.

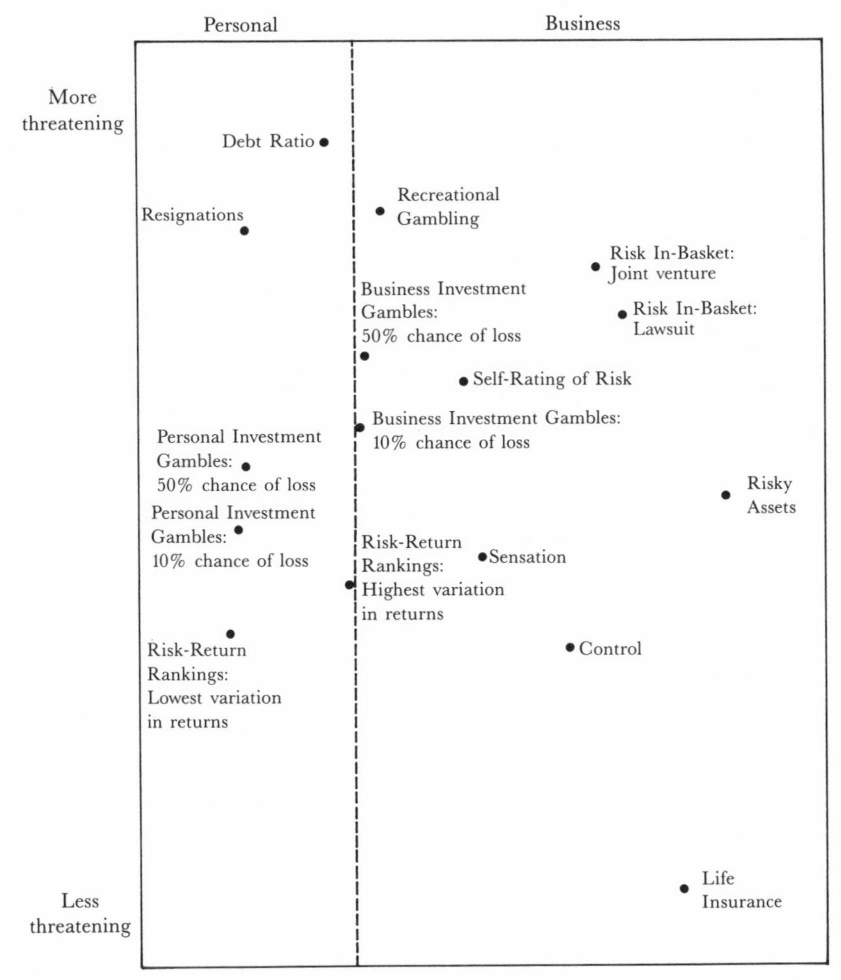

Figure 9.2 Spatial Representation of Relationships among Risk Measures Derived from Standardized Situations, Natural Situations, and Attitudes

The only measures of personal risk propensity that lie far to the right of the line are life insurance holdings and proportion of risky assets.

The four business measures from standardized situations and the self-rating of business risk propensity all lie to the right of the line. The position of the self-rating close to, and at the center of, the four business measures gives some credibility to its use as a measure of business risk propensity in generalized situations.

> ***Result:*** The managers showed different propensities for personal and business risks. This was especially true for the standardized situations and for some of the natural situations.

This finding means that we cannot predict someone's behavior in risky business situations based on his behavior in his personal life. For example, managers who are mortgaged to the hilt or who gamble on the golf course will not necessarily take risks at work. Similarly, executives who hold all their personal wealth in secure assets or who purchase excessive life insurance may be their firms' greatest risk takers.

We interpret the vertical dimension of Figure 9.2 as degree of threat. We find debt ratio, recreational gambling, and resignations at the top of the diagram representing extremely threatening natural situations. This positioning is consistent with the focus on losses of these three situations. At the other extreme is life insurance which is intrinsically nonthreatening because it protects against losses. In between these extremes are the measures from the standardized situations. The managers may view these situations as less extreme on this dimension because they require hypothetical rather than actual behavior.

> ***Result:*** The managers showed different risk propensities in situations that differed in their degree of threat.

We learn from this result that someone who takes chances in a low-threat situation need not be a risk taker in high-threat situations. For example, an executive who invests 10% of his capital expenditure budget on new machinery in hopes of achieving significant productivity gains will not necessarily risk a major change in his firm's product line away from a steady revenue producer to capture a potentially large, but undeveloped market segment.

NOTE ON DIMENSIONS OF RISK PROPENSITY

The lack of strong relationships among the measures suggests that risk propensity is a multifaceted characteristic and that there is no way to assess it with a single measure or even a small set of measures. In this case one would like a better understanding of the underlying dimensions of risk so a representative portfolio of risk measures could be established.

We first performed a principal components analysis on the correlations among the 16 measures. Eight components had characteristic roots greater than one. Four of the first five components loaded heavily on individual instruments: Business Investment Gambles, Personal Investment Gambles, Risk-Return Rankings, and Risk In-Basket. Thus there was a strong instrument effect for risk measured in standardized situations as we found in Chapter 8 when the secondary measures were included.

The natural situation measures formed two separate components—one loaded heavily on DEBTRATIO and GAMBLING and the other loaded heavily on RESIGNATIONS and SELFINSURED (negative loading). The affinity between DEBTRATIO and GAMBLING may be due to their intrinsic nature as threats because of their focus on losses. RISKYASSETS also loaded heavily along with IB:LAWSUIT and IB:VENTURE on the Risk In-Basket component.

The attitude measures formed two separate components. One loaded heavily on SENSATION and SELFRATING and the other principally on I/E:CONTROL with a minor loading on IB:VENTURE. SELFRATING also loaded on the Business Investment Gambles component.

Overall the components were made up principally of measures derived from the same category of instrument. We did find, however, some loadings across categories.

We next developed a spatial representation of the relationships among the risk measures using a Guttman-Lingoes smallest space analysis for two dimensions assuming weak monotonicity. The data for this analysis were the pairwise correlations described in the "Note on Relationships Among the Risk Measures" (see page 218). The coefficient of alienation is 0.25 and Kruskal's stress statistic is 0.22. We rotated the axes orthogonally to permit maximum interpretability. A three-dimensional representation gives similar results to Figure 9.2 on its first two dimensions. The third dimension is not easily interpretable. However, it might be interpreted as the controllability of the risky situation.

The relative positions of the eight measures from the standardized situations are similar to what they were in Figure 8.2. Measures from the same questionnaire are very close together indicating the strong instrument effect. The personal versus business dimension is again apparent with the Risk In-Basket measures far to one side of the figure. Within each questionnaire the measure with the higher degree of threat lies above the measure with the lower degree of threat except for the Risk In-Basket measures. Across questionnaires we still find the Personal Investment Gambles with their potential loss of half of personal wealth more threatening than the Risk-Return Rankings with their lower potential loss of 10% of wealth. The positioning of the joint venture above the Business Investment Gambles which themselves lie above the Personal Investment Gambles is not consistent with our interpretations of their relative degree of threat discussed in Chapter 8. Such discrepancies are due of course to the influences of the secondary measures on the primary measures.

We chose our dotted line in Figure 9.2 to get the best separation between personal and business risk measures. We can choose another line to increase interpretability on the degree of threat dimension with a resulting loss in separation between personal and business measures. Such a line would go through BGAMBLE10%, SENSATION, and I/E:CONTROL. DEBTRATIO now shifts to the business side, but SELFINSURED shifts to the personal side. RESIGNATIONS which is partly a personal measure and partly a business measure also moves to the business side. This line corresponds better to the degree of threat in the Personal Investment Gambles, Business Investment Gambles, and Risk-Return Rankings that we found in Figure 8.2.

Do the Managers Show the Same Risk Propensity in Different Situations Relative to Other Managers?

We found in Chapter 8 that more managers were consistent in their risk propensities for standardized situations than chance would predict. Risk averters were also found to be more consistent than risk takers. These results were based on comparing each manager's answers with the responses given by all other managers in the study rather than against risk-neutral values. That is, for each of the standardized situations we divided the executives into thirds depending upon whether they were *relatively risk-taking*, *relatively risk-neutral*, or *relatively risk-averting*. We then looked for managers who were in the same group for several standardized situations.

We now ask the same question for natural situations and attitudes toward risk. Again the answer is that there were many more consistent relative risk averters than chance would predict. This was true for the natural situations and attitudes considered separately or together. It was also true when we considered the standardized situations, natural situations, and attitudes jointly. However, we did not find more consistent relative risk takers than predicted by chance for any of these groups of measures.

> ***Result:*** Many more managers were consistent risk averters across standardized situations, natural situations, and attitudes than chance would predict. There was no such group of consistent risk takers across these situations.

This finding means that firms that prefer more conservative management should have an easy time finding managers with a consistent propensity toward risk aversion that matches the needs of the firm. Firms that prefer managers who are consistent in their risk-taking will have a harder time finding suitable managers. Training programs using simulation or other types of exercises might be developed to foster consistent risk taking.

Note on the Consistent Relative Risk Averters and Risk Takers

We first considered the *five natural situation measures*. With five measures and three relative risk categories, there are 3^5 (=243) possible overall configurations for a given executive. To make the analysis manageable, we focused on those cases in which an executive was classified as risk-averse on a majority of the measures. Thus we call a person a consistent (relative) risk averter if he was classified as risk-averse on three or more of the five measures. Correspondingly, a person will be called a consistent (relative) risk taker if he was classified as risk-taking on three or more of the five measures.

The question we ask then is whether there are more consistent risk averters (takers) than would be expected by chance if there were no consistent risk propensity. The number to be expected by chance can be calculated by assuming that the five measures were independently distributed and using the probabilities of being placed in any category on a given measure (which are roughly equal to one-third[18]) derived from a binomial model. We considered only the 187 executives for whom all 16 measures could be calculated (i.e., the eight standardized measures, the five natural situation measures, and the three attitude measures).

For these 187 executives, 125 were classified as consistent risk averters and 17 were classified as consistent risk takers on the basis of the natural situation measures. Under the random effects model we would expect 39 executives in each category. Hence there is strong evidence for a category of consistent risk averters (chi-squared test at the 0.001 level), but not for a category of consistent risk takers.

Next we considered the *three attitude measures*. Here we classified an executive as a consistent risk averter (taker) if he was classified as risk-averting (taking) on a majority of the three measures. In this case we expected 48 of the 187 executives in each category, but we observed 101 consistent risk averters and 51 consistent risk takers. Once again strong evidence emerges for a category of consistent risk averters (chi-squared test, 0.001 level), but not for consistent risk takers.

When we considered simultaneously the natural situation measures and attitude measures, a similar picture emerged. Here we say an executive is a consistent risk averter (taker) if both a majority of the five natural situation measures and a majority of the three attitude measures classified him as a risk averter (taker). Of the 187 executives we expected 10 in such category, but observed 73 consistent risk averters and only 6 consistent risk takers.[19]

Thus the secondary measures, considered together or separately as natural situation measures and attitude measures, indicate there is a group of consistent risk averters far in excess of a chance effect. There is no statistical support for a group of consistent risk takers based on the secondary measures.

Lastly we examined whether this group of consistent risk averters extended to include the primary measures as well as the secondary measures. We found a group of consistent risk averters in the measures from the standardized situations in Chapter 8, but the low correlations between the primary and secondary measures have raised doubts about how closely associated these measures were.

In this analysis we say an executive is a consistent risk averter (taker) if he was classified as risk-averting (taking) on a majority of each of the eight standardized measures (i.e., at least five of the eight), the natural situation measures (i.e., at least three of the five), and the attitude measures (i.e., at least two of the three). Thirty-six executives were classified as consistent risk averters and two were classified as consistent risk takers. This compares with less than one executive expected by chance.[20] We see that while the group of consistent risk averters extends to the secondary measures the group of consistent risk takers does not.

CONCLUSIONS

The managers were cautious in the personal financial decisions that we used to examine naturally occurring risks. We found significant associations between risks taken in different natural situations, especially those involving debt ratio. These associations were not, however, always consistent with our interpretations of the managers' answers as indications of risk propensity. These results highlight the limitation of using natural situations as indications or risk propensity and the influence of personal characteristics such as age and wealth.

The vast majority of managers believed they could control their environments. Because a primary role of managers is to control their environments through their actions, a belief in internal control might be used as a screening device for potential managers. Attitudes toward risk were significantly related. However, we should not use attitudes alone to measure one's risk propensity because managers are generally more risk-taking in their attitudes than in their behavior, perhaps due to a cultural bias toward taking risks. In particular managers tended to rate themselves as more willing to take risks than other managers in their firm. Attitudes toward risk did not reflect the managers' behavior in the natural situations, but they were significantly related to risk propensity in some standardized situations. One noteworthy finding was a strong association between the manager's self-rating of his willingness to take risks in generalized business situations and his willingness to take business risks involving his capital expenditure budget.

The managers' risk propensities in the natural situations were significantly associated with their willingness to take risks in the standardized situations. This result provides evidence for a concept of risk propensity underlying the managers' actions. Because these associations were weak, other characteristics of the risky situations (e.g., personal versus business) and of the managers (e.g., age, wealth) must be influencing the responses. Our findings on the dimensions of risky situations and the characteristics of managers (see Chapter 10) that affect risk propensity confirmed this belief. The results reinforce our belief that we must assess risk propensity using a portfolio of risk measures that are carefully chosen to cover a variety of settings that complement one another.

We found that managers took different risks in their personal and business decisions and in situations that differ in their degree of threat. This confirms our findings in Chapter 8. Therefore we cannot predict a manager's response to a business risk from his behavior in personal risky situations, and we cannot be sure that a manager who takes small business risks will take chances when greater risks are involved.

A large number of managers were consistent in their risk aversion (relative to other managers) across the standardized situations, the natural situations, and their attitudes. We found few managers who were consistent risk takers across these settings. This finding shows that the consistent risk taking over standardized situations that we observed in Chapter 8 does not extend to natural situations and attitudes. It does, however, reinforce our earlier finding of differences between consistent risk averters and consistent risk takers. We conclude that risk-averting managers are more concerned about avoiding risks than risk-taking managers are concerned about taking risks.

Using natural situations and attitudes to assess risk propensity has added useful extensions and insights to our earlier focus on standardized situations. Together this variety of settings provides a complementary portfolio in which to observe managerial risk taking.

Research conclusions

There are four main research conclusions:

1. With a cultural bias toward risk taking, the more transparent a question, the more likely the risk-taking response will be given. When it could be expressed by a simple self-rating the executives preferred to be seen as risk takers. Similarly, by simply selecting an (a) or (b) response the executives preferred to be perceived as controlling their environment. Thus one must be careful about inferring a risk propensity from only attitude measures. Rather than a real risk propensity (if such a construct exists), one is more likely to obtain an indication of what people think is expected of them and how they would like to be perceived. However, the self-rating of risk propensity, despite its lack of a theoretical justification

and its bias, was not noticeably weaker than the other risk measures. It seems to correlate reasonably well with other attitude measures and some of the measures derived from the standardized and natural situations.

2. Overall the relationships were stronger between measures in the same category (i.e., standardized situations, natural situations, attitudes) than between measures across categories. For example, at a 1% level of significance, 51% (21/41) of the correlations between measures within categories were significantly different from zero, compared with 13% (10/79) of the correlations across categories. This result provides useful support for the categories we have developed. Moreover the significant relationships across categories, at a rate far greater than chance would predict, support our hypothesis that a risk propensity underlies the managers' responses.

The relationships, however, tend to be neither strong nor robust. Other factors influence the managers' responses. We have explored in some detail in this chapter and the preceding one what dimensions of a risky situation might influence risky behavior. Significant research remains to be done to identify these dimensions. In particular, what factors determine a situation's degree of threat? Amount of the stake? Chance of loss? Controllability of the outcome of the risky situation? These are only some of the factors we have identified in this study as potential aspects of the degree of threat. In the next chapter we will examine characteristics of the managers and their business roles that may interact with their generalized risk propensity to determine behavior.

3. The lack of strong relationships among the risk measures means that studies using one measure may have very different results than studies using seemingly related measures. For example, studies that used a natural situation measure such as RISKYASSETS are likely to have very different findings from studies that use other natural situations (e.g., DEBTRATIO), attitudes (SELFRATING), or standardized situations (PGAMBLE50%). This observation casts grave doubts on the robustness of the conclusions from previous studies of risk in which only one or two measures were used.

4. Which risk measure is the most representative of the managers' portfolio of risk measures? Using a 5% significance level, the measures with the greatest number of significant correlations with the other measures were PGAMBLE50%, BGAMBLE50%, and BGAMBLE10%. Each of these measures was significantly related to eight of the 15 other measures. Close behind were PGAMBLE10%, RANK:EV-HI, SELFRATING, and GAMBLING (seven significant correlations), and DEBTRATIO (six significant correlations). Thus no clear representative emerges.

The three measures that best seem to indicate the managers' risk propensities in standardized situations, natural situations, and attitudes were BGAMBLE50%, DEBTRATIO, and SELFRATING, respectively. Not only are these measures correlated highly with other measures in the same category, but they have significant positive correlations among themselves (i.e., 0.21, 0.16, and 0.10).

Chapter 10

Characteristics Related to Risk

INTRODUCTION

Carl Chapman is a 38-year-old chief executive officer of a small United States oil exploration firm. He has been with the firm for three years. He has an MBA and is married with no children. His income is $300,000 and his net wealth is $2 million.

David Drew is a 63-year-old vice-president of a large Canadian bank. He has been with the bank for 35 years. He has a high school education and is married with three children. His income is $125,000 and his net wealth is $500,000.

Who do you think will be the greater risk taker, Carl Chapman or David Drew?[1] Most people say Chapman. On almost every dimension he comes closer to the picture of a stereotypical risk taker than does Drew. Chapman is an aggressive, young MBA who, at the age of 38, has already attained a high position. He is mobile and is in a position to take business risks. His personal financial position allows him to take personal risks. Drew, on the other hand, has been with the bank for almost his whole career. He is close to retirement and does not want to jeopardize the position he has attained. With his responsibilities at home, he cannot afford to take high personal risks.

Most of us hold stereotyped views such as these about who does, and who does not, take risks. Sometimes these views are based on careful observation of those around us. Sometimes they are based on "logic." However, we need to be careful about generalizing from the particular people we come in contact with every day, and a "logical" argument can often be built to support either side. We do know though that these views have not been based on sound empirical evidence, since such evidence has not been available to date.

In this chapter we will take a careful look at the relationship between risk and a number of personal, financial, and business characteristics. We will study the Carl Chapmans and the David Drews, as well as less extreme cases, to ascertain which of the stereotypes hold up.

Figure 10.1 shows how the focus of this chapter relates to that of the preceding two chapters. In Chapters 8 and 9 we found that different risk measures often gave different results. In those chapters we considered 16 different measures of risk propensity. When we focus on the relationship between risk and other characteristics, it would be overwhelmingly complex to continue to consider all 16 risk measures.

To focus attention on the characteristics that may be related to risk, rather than on risk measures themselves, we will simplify the discussion in this chapter. Even though we will do the analysis on all

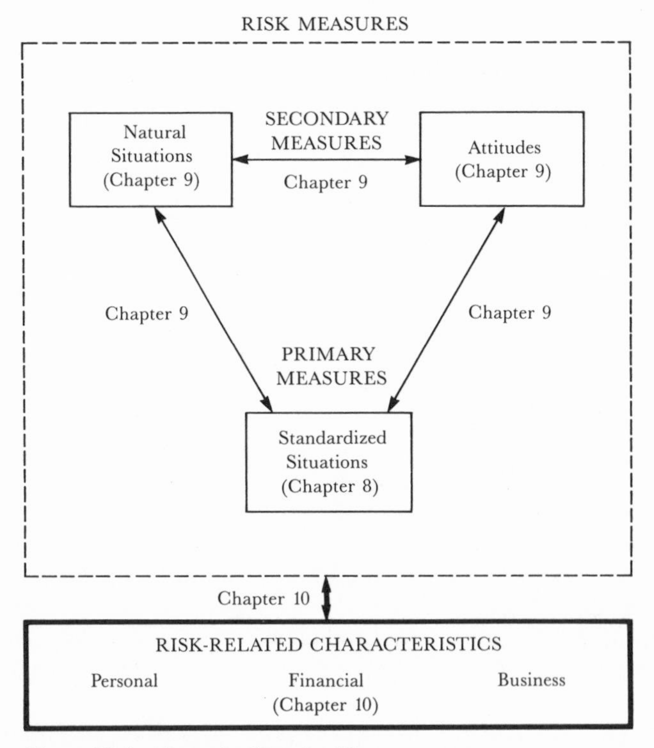

Figure 10.1 Focus in Chapter 10

NOTE ON UNIVARIATE ANALYSES

The effects of personal, financial, and business characteristics were first analysed using univariate procedures. We confined our attention to the managers who were in the top third on risk taking and those in the bottom third. Thus we are focusing on relative risk propensity in this chapter.[3] Taking one characteristic at a time, we ascertained whether a characteristic was significantly different between the risk-taking and the risk-averting groups using a one-tailed *t*-test at the 0.05 level for each of the risk measures. For a continuous variable such as income, we found that average income is $225,000 for the risk-taking group and $114,000 for the risk-averse group (using the measure RISKYASSETS). Not surprisingly this turned out to be significantly different. For a categorical variable such as firm size, we found that managers from small firms make up 36% of the risk-taking group but only 18% of the risk-averse group (for the measure RISKYASSETS). This was also a significant difference.

---

16 measures, we will select a single representative measure as a focus of our attention. This measure is the percentage of personal assets held in risky categories. Thus in discussing the relationship between risk propensity and a characteristic such as managerial position, we will be describing the relationship between a manager's position and his holding of risky assets. See Chapter 9 (page 209) for details of this measure. We will be careful, though, to indicate the extent to which the other 15 measures support or contradict this particular result.[2]

One problem with a simple analysis is that an apparent relationship between a particular characteristic and risk propensity may be due to the effect of some other characteristic. For example, an analysis might show a significant relationship between nationality and risk propensity. Canadian managers may seem more risk-averse than American managers. However, since Canadian managers generally have a lower education level, if we confine our attention to managers with a high education level we may not find a relationship between nationality and risk. Similarly, if we then consider managers with other levels of education, we may not find a relationship between nationality and risk. Hence the apparent relationship between nationality and risk was due to the connection between nationality and education and in turn to the real relationship between education and risk. So in studying the relationship between risk and any particular characteristic we need to consider the possible effect of other characteristics. We need to determine the relative importance of the various characteristics.

NOTE ON THE TYPE OF MULTIVARIATE ANALYSES USED

If we observe a significant univariate relationship between nationality and risk propensity and between education and risk propensity, as well as a high correlation between nationality and education, we need to sort out the relative strength of the effects. For this reason, we use a multivariate procedure in which we look for a relationship between nationality and risk propensity, with education held constant, as well as a relationship between education and risk propensity, with nationality held constant.

We used two forms of multivariate analyses: multiple regression and discriminant analysis. Both gave similar results. The conclusions we report here are those based on the discriminant analysis. The focus of a discriminant analysis is a search for the best linear relationship among the explanatory variables (the characteristics) that best separates the risk measure into the two categories of interest: risk takers and risk averters.[4] The test of explanatory power is the percentage of risk averters correctly classified as risk averters and the percentage of risk takers correctly classified as risk takers based on the linear relationship of the characteristics. The discriminant analysis was performed using both forward and backward methods. In the forward method variables were added stepwise if their coefficient was significant at the 0.05 level. In the backward procedure variables were dropped if their incremental contribution was not significant at the 0.05 level. Even if a discriminant function can be obtained, it may turn out that it cannot predict better than various "base-case" procedures. We applied stringent tests for the base-case, in that we required the discriminant analysis to predict better than one could do by assigning everyone to the most populous category.

We obtained significant discriminant functions for 14 of the 16 risk measures. The percentage of executives correctly classified ranged from 55% to 91%. See MacCrimmon and Wehrung (1985b) for the complete results from the discriminant analysis.

We will also focus on how people with different personal, financial, and business characteristics view themselves as risk takers. Each manager was asked to rate his own willingness to undertake risky business propositions as compared to other managers at or near his level in his firm. See Chapter 9 (page 221) for a further description of this measure. We are especially interested in whether such self-perceptions correspond to actual differences for the various characteristics.

There are many personal, financial, and business characteristics that could be related to risk. We will focus on the characteristics that were used in describing Carl Chapman and David Drew. First, we will consider four personal characteristics: age, dependents, education, and nationality. Next, we highlight two financial characteristics: wealth and income. Then we will look at five business characteristics: position, authority, seniority, firm size, and industry.

We will also address two additional questions in this chapter. First, is there any relationship between risk propensity and success? Success is clearly related to a number of the characteristics such as wealth, income, position, and firm size. However, success is more complex than any single characteristic. We will use two means of identifying the most successful managers who participated in our study and then we will determine whether they are greater risk takers than the (relatively) less successful managers. Second, do the consistent risk takers and the consistent risk averters whom we identified in Chapter 8 differ on any of the characteristics? If there are differences, we may learn not only which types of managers seek or avoid risks, but which ones are consistent in their risk propensity from one situation to the next.

NOTE ON THE RELATIONSHIPS AMONG THE CHARACTERISTICS

Multivariate procedures require that the correlations between characteristics should not be too high. The collinearity difficulties if there are strong relationships can distort the interpretation of the results. Hence, we need to check for such relationships. If we find high correlations between characteristics we need either to remove or modify at least one of the variables. Many potentially high correlations, such as would result from use of variants of the same variable, were omitted from the outset. Initially, we considered a variable called "assets" but it had a correlation of 0.96 with "wealth" so assets was dropped from consideration. "Income" had a correlation of 0.54 with "authority" and a correlation of 0.30 with "wealth," so when income was used in multivariate analyses, authority and wealth were both removed.

The only other correlations over 0.33 were 0.37 between authority and position (CEO level) and 0.35 between nationality and industry (chemical/pharmaceutical). The authority-position relationship was circumvented by dropping authority in particular analyses. The nationality-industry relationship was due to a design artifact in that chemical-pharmaceutical companies were much more prominent in the American sample than in the Canadian sample.

As a check on the distinctiveness of the remaining personal, financial, and business characteristics, we conducted a principal components analysis. The results indicated separate factors for all the variables. Even with 10 factors only 36% of the variance was explained. Thus we have some assurance that our basic set of risk-related characteristics comprises distinct characteristics and they can safely be used in multivariate analyses.

RISK AND PERSONAL CHARACTERISTICS

Are Older Managers More Risk-Averse?

Most people believe that as a person gets older he becomes more conservative. This belief carries over to managers. The common stereotype is that the young are somewhat rash compared to more risk-averse older people.[5] One basis for this belief is that if a person takes risks which turn out badly, the older person has less opportunity to start over, while the young person has plenty of time to try again.

When we looked at the effect of age by itself, older managers were not more risk-averse in terms of our focal measure of risk (i.e., the holding of risky assets). When we took other factors in account, however, we did find a negative relationship between age and risk. This means that when we controlled for factors related to age, such as dependents or position, older managers did have a tendency to be more risk-averse.

NOTE ON PREVIOUS STUDIES OF RISK-RELATED PERSONAL CHARACTERISTICS

A number of studies have found that willingness to take risks decreases with age. See, for example, Wallach and Kogan (1961), Lampman (1962), Kogan and Wallach (1964), Watts and Tobin (1967), Vroom and Pahl (1971), Dillon and Scandizzo (1978), Martin (1978), Blume and Friend (1978), Hutchison and Clemens (1980), and McInish (1982). One noticeable exception is the study by Cohn and colleagues (1975) that found older people invested a greater fraction of their total assets in risky assets than did younger people.

Dillon and Scandizzo (1978) found that willingness to take risks decreased as the number of dependents increased for small farm owners in Brazil. In their study of consumer expenditures Watts and Tobin (1967) found that as family size increased mortgage and installment debt increased as did life insurance premiums, but cash balances in banks decreased.

Laughhunn, Payne, and Crum (1980), Cohn and colleagues (1975), and McInish (1982) examined the relationship between risk propensity and education, but found no significant associations. Watts and Tobin (1967) found that mortgage debt and life insurance premiums increased as education increased. Hammond, Houston, and Melander (1967) also found that life insurance premiums increased with more education. Blume and Friend (1978) found education was positively associated with risk-taking behavior in their study of individual investment portfolios.

Nationality differences in risk propensity have been found in several previous studies. Cummings, Harnett, and Stevens (1971) found that American managers were the most risk-taking of five regional groups. Hopkins and associates (1977) found that Japanese managers were more risk-taking than American managers, but the differences were not statistically significant. Both of these studies used Shure and Meeker's (1967) Personality Attitude Schedule to assess risk propensity. Arnold, White, and Tigert (1972) found that Canadians were more financially conservative than Americans. Laughhunn, Payne, and Crum (1980) also found differences in risk propensity between Dutch and German managers.

A number of other measures very strongly supported this finding that age was negatively related to risk taking. More than half a dozen of our 16 measures showed that older managers were more risk-averse. Only one measure seemed to contradict the negative relationship. We can assert with confidence, then, than younger managers take more risks and that older managers take fewer risks.

We asked managers at each of the age levels how they saw their own risk propensity relative to other managers they had regular contact with in their firm. The results were very strong. Older managers saw themselves as significantly less willing to take risks than younger managers saw themselves. This relationship was true looking just at age by itself as well as looking at age holding other factors constant.

Overall we obtain a clear-cut result.

Result: Older managers were more averse to risk. Younger managers were more risk-taking.

Although other factors (such as career status) can tend to obscure the relationship between risk propensity and age, when these other factors are taken into account, we find that people become more risk-averse as they get older. This change is apparently recognized since older managers rate themselves as more risk-averse. Firms desiring an aggressive posture toward risk should place more control in the hands of the young, while firms desiring a more cautious position should shift power to older managers.

NOTE ON THE DEFINITION OF PERSONAL CHARACTERISTICS

Most of the personal characteristics are self-explanatory. Age was obtained by asking year of birth. Age was usually treated continuously but when it was separated into categories, the categories were: youngest 24–43, middle 44–50, and oldest 51–77. This categorization divided the executives into approximately equal sized groups. Dependents was usually treated continuously. For categorical purposes groups (0–2 dependents, 3 dependents, and more than 3 dependents) were approximately of equal size.

Education was obtained by asking "Secondary (highest grade completed)," "Higher education (degrees, specialization)," and "Professional/technical qualifications (e.g., CPA, CA, P.Eng., etc.)." For analyses we used the categories: secondary education only, some university/college undergraduate work, and some post-university study or training. The nationality characteristic was based on both citizenship and current residence. We excluded the few cases in which the answers were different, so to be labeled "American" (Canadian) required both American (Canadian) citizenship and residence. There were very few managers who were neither American nor Canadian, so they were dropped from the analysis.

Table 2.3 in Chapter 2 summarizes the numbers of executives in each category used for the personal characteristics as well as for the financial and business characteristics.

Do Managers with More Dependents Avoid Risk?

People commonly believe that the more dependents a person has, the less willing he is to take risks. In making either personal or business decisions he has to take into account the potential negative effect on others if things turn out badly. The family man with four children is viewed as acting much more cautiously than the carefree bachelor.

In our study we did find that managers with fewer dependents took more risk; people with more dependents took less risk. As may be expected, managers with more dependents put a higher proportion of assets in relatively safe categories such as housing. When we held other characteristics constant, the negative relationship between risk and dependents became even stronger. This confirms that what we are observing is really the effect of differences in dependents rather than some other factor.

The other measures of risk provided mixed support. The relationship with dependents was negative for some measures but positive for others.

The self-perception did not support the relationship we found between risk and dependents. In fact, managers with more dependents were more likely to view themselves as higher risk takers than did managers with fewer dependents.

Our conclusion, then, is that there is some basis for assuming a weak negative relationship between risk and number of dependents.

> ***Result:*** Managers with more dependents seem to be more averse to risk than managers with fewer dependents.

Until the effect of the number of dependents is more clear-cut, implications should be made with some caution. If subsequent studies do confirm that managers with more dependents tend to be more risk-averse, then one would not want to place such managers in situations that required major risks to be taken.

NOTE ON THE RELATIONSHIPS BETWEEN AGE, DEPENDENTS, AND EDUCATION AND THE 16 RISK MEASURES

In the multivariate analysis, age entered negatively into the discriminant functions for the risk measures RISKYASSETS and SELFRATING (as highlighted in the text) as well as IB:VENTURE, PGAMBLE50%, BGAMBLE10%, DEBTRATIO, RESIGNATIONS, and SENSATION. The only discriminant function in which age entered positively was SELFINSURED. There is thus strong evidence that older managers were more risk-averse.[6]

The number of dependents does not enter as strongly as age in the multivariate analyses. The relationship between dependents and risk as measured by RISKYASSETS and SELFINSURED was negative, but the relationship between dependents and risk as measured by IB:VENTURE and DEBTRATIO was positive. The results overall were somewhat mixed and depend on the relative weight one places on particular measures.

The relationship between risk and education (post-college level) was positive for RISKYASSETS, IB:LAWSUIT, and SELFRATING in the multivariate analyses, but it was negative for PGAMBLE10% and PGAMBLE50%. In the univariate analyses, however, both BGAMBLE10% and RESIGNATIONS were positively related.[7] The only difference between college level and high school level was in SELFRATING. Managers who had gone to college viewed themselves as more risk-taking than their associates. On balance, then, more education is related to a higher risk-taking propensity.

Do Managers with Higher Levels of Education Take More Risks?

The relationship expected between risk and education has been argued in both directions. Some people think that higher levels of education inhibit risk taking. Everyone knows of high school drop-outs who work diligently to get enough money to sink into some invention they believe in. The self-made man takes risks and triumphs, while the risk-averse types waste their time in school and contract "analysis paralysis" (Peters and Waterman, 1982). Conversely, others believe that this picture is mostly myth. They assert that education allows one to assess risk and benefits carefully. People learn to recognize the good risk and shun the bad. So beliefs about the relationship between risk and education run in both directions. What are the facts?

Among our managers there was a significant positive relationship between education and risk. Managers who had postgraduate training were higher risk takers than managers with less education. Looking at the group of managers with postgraduate training, we found that they constituted 33% of the risk takers but only 19% of the risk averters. Managers with a bachelor's degree, though, were not more risk-taking than high school graduates.

When we took into account all the personal characteristics (i.e., not simply looking at education versus risk), the positive relationship between education and risk was confirmed. Even holding constant other factors such as age, those managers with postgraduate training took more risk than did people with less education. Other measures of risk provided only mixed support for this result.

The relationship between education and risk agreed with the self-perception of risk. Managers with a higher level of education viewed themselves as bigger risk takers compared to other executives in the firm than did managers with less education.

> ***Result:*** Managers with postgraduate training were greater risk takers than were managers with a bachelor's degree or managers with only a high school degree.

Higher education seems to promote risk taking rather than deterring it. While higher education may not be responsible for providing the spark for taking risks, it does not seem to extinguish the flame. To the extent that companies want to encourage managers to take greater risks, they should not be reluctant to bring in those with MBAs and other postgraduate training.

Are Canadian Managers More Risk-Averse than Americans?

American managers are generally considered more entrepreneurial and more likely to take risks than their counterparts in most other countries. It is said that Canadian managers, in particular, view American managers as much more risk-taking than they are. To what extent are these national stereotypes true?

Our results showed no significant difference. Any tendency toward more risk aversion on the part of Canadian managers could be attributed to chance alone. Even the slight negative relationship disappeared when we held other factors constant. So what might have appeared to be a nationality effect is probably due to Canadians having a significantly lower rate of postgraduate education. Only one of the 16 measures of risk showed a negative relationship with nationality.

On the self-perception measure, Canadians rated themselves as less risk-taking compared to their associates than Americans rated themselves.

In summary, while Canadians see themselves as more risk-averse, we have little evidence supporting this viewpoint.

> ***Result:*** Both Canadian and American managers believe that Canadians are more risk-averse; Canadians believe it more strongly. There was no significant evidence that Canadian managers were more risk-averse than American managers.

Although we found no significant difference in risk propensity between American and Canadian managers, there may be differences between other nationality groups. The similarities in language and experience may outweigh any differences between American and Canadian managers. If a company has international operations, it seems reasonable for it to consider the possibility that managers from different countries may differ in their willingness to take risks. By assessing and comparing risk propensities of managers in the various countries in which a company conducts business, it may be better able to match managers to jobs and harmonize local business with headquarters' philosophy.

NOTE ON THE RELATIONSHIP BETWEEN NATIONALITY AND RISK

In the multivariate analyses nationality was a significant explanatory variable for only two of the 16 risk measures. Canadians gambled less than Americans, but they were more risk-taking for BGAMBLE10%. In univariate comparisons Canadians were more risk-averse on IB:LAWSUIT, DEBTRATIO, and SELFRATING, but they were more risk-taking on PGAMBLE10% and PGAMBLE50%. Hence the evidence was very mixed. There does not seem to be any distinct nationality difference in risk propensity between Americans and Canadians.[8]

In a supplementary part of the Risk Portfolio, a series of questions were asked pertaining to perceptions of nationality differences. The most general question asked for a choice between: (a) Americans are less likely to accept risks than Canadians, and (b) Americans are more likely to accept risks than Canadians. Ninety-five percent of the managers thought Americans were more likely to take risks. What is especially surprising is that while 87% of the American managers thought Americans were bigger risk takers, 97% of the Canadian managers thought Americans were bigger risk takers! It seems clear that Canadians believe the stereotype of the "gray, conservative Canadian manager" even more than others do.

Another question asked about entrepreneurship and business initiative. Ninety-one percent of Canadian managers and 92% of American managers thought that Canadians exhibited a lower level of entrepreneurship and business initiative than Americans.

Three other questions asked about attitudes in one's own country in contrast to other countries. On all three questions there was a very significant difference (at the 0.001 level) between Americans and Canadians.

Only 5% of the American managers thought that they were too dependent on foreign technology; 62% of the Canadian managers thought they were too dependent on foreign technology. On willingness to try new products, 99% of American managers thought that people in their country were more willing to try new products than people in other countries; only 68% of the Canadian managers agreed with the statement. Although 86% of the American managers felt that firms in their country spent too little on research and development, 99% of Canadian managers thought that too little was spent on R&D in their country.

Overall, then, there appear to be some very strong differences in *attitudes* between Americans and Canadians on aspects related to risk taking. As far as we could determine, however, this did not seem to translate into actual differences in risk propensity.

RISK AND FINANCIAL CHARACTERISTICS

Do Wealthier Managers Take More Risks?

Managers with more wealth can afford to take more risk. Even if a millionaire loses half his wealth, he will not be destitute. A major loss for a manager who has little wealth may mean carrying a heavy mortgage debt, deferring vacations, missing the opportunity to send his children to private schools, and the like. On the other hand, managers with high levels of wealth have more to lose.

We found that managers with higher wealth did take more risk. In the terms of our focal measure, managers with higher wealth held a significantly greater percentage of their wealth in risky assets. The risk takers had an average wealth of $1.5 million, but the risk averters had an average wealth of only $300,000. This was a major difference. We do not mean to imply a causal direction. We cannot tell whether people were risk takers because they were wealthy or whether they were wealthy because they were risk takers.

NOTE ON THE DEFINITION OF FINANCIAL CHARACTERISTICS

The figure we used for wealth was obtained from the Investment Gambles instrument by asking directly for current net wealth. This figure was checked by subtracting the liabilities from the gross assets in the General Questionnaire. The correlation between the estimates of net wealth obtained in these two ways was 0.90.

Income was obtained by summing the answer to figures given for total income from employment (salary, bonuses, and profit sharing) and total outside income (director's fees, interest, dividends, capital gains or losses).

Even when other factors such as age, education, position, and so on were held constant, wealth still exerted a major effect. There is no doubt that high wealth is related to high risk taking; low wealth is related to low risk taking.

The picture we get of wealth and risk, however, was not strongly supported by the other measures of risk. Four of the other measures showed a positive relationship with wealth and four showed a negative relationship.

There did not seem to be a significant relationship between wealth and self-perception of risk. Wealthy managers and less wealthy managers did not view themselves differently on risk propensity.

In summary, when risk is measured in terms of holdings of risky assets, the relationship between wealth and risk is striking. The risk-taking managers had much higher wealth than the risk-averse managers. This extremely strong positive relationship was supported by about a third of the other measures, was refuted by a third of the other measures, while the remaining third showed no significant effect. Whether you believe that higher wealth is associated with higher risk taking thus depends on what measure of risk you prefer.

> ***Result:*** Managers with more wealth took more risks for some measures of risk. However, they took less risk when other measures were used.

If higher wealth is positively related to higher risk taking, as it was for our focal measure, then choosing people who are financially secure (or making them financially secure) can promote risk taking. Before relying heavily on a claimed relationship between wealth and risk taking, one should check carefully into the risk measure used.

NOTE ON THE RELATIONSHIPS BETWEEN FINANCIAL CHARACTERISTICS AND THE 16 RISK MEASURES

The relationship between risk propensity and wealth has received considerable attention in the literature of economics and finance. In developing a measure of risk aversion for utility functions, Arrow (1971) and Pratt (1964) hypothesized that absolute risk aversion would decrease as wealth increased. That is, the amount a person would accept in lieu of a particular risky gamble would increase (move closer to the actuarial value of the gamble) as wealth increased. Arrow and Pratt also developed a measure of relative risk aversion. They hypothesized that relative risk aversion would increase as wealth increased. This implies that a person would only be willing to stake a lower proportion of his wealth on a particular risky gamble as wealth increased.

Several studies have investigated the hypothesis of increasing relative risk aversion. Cohn and colleagues (1975) found *decreasing* relative risk aversion for assets or income. Lampman (1962) found similar results in a study of portfolio allocation to bonds and cash. Blume and Friend (1975; Friend and Blume, 1975) found *constant* relative risk aversion. More recently, Siegel and Hoban (1982) and Szpiro (1983) have found support for *increasing* relative risk aversion.

Other studies have also related financial characteristics to risk propensity. Ziegler (1977) found that students whose fathers had higher incomes were more inclined to take risks than other students. Dillon and Scandizzo (1978) found that willingness to take risks increased as income increased for small farm owners in Brazil. Blume and Friend (1978) found that investors with higher incomes were more willing to assume risks and held riskier stock portfolios than those with lower incomes. Other studies have shown higher income and wealth to be related to risk-averse behavior. Watts and Tobin (1967) found that cash balances in banks and life insurance premiums increased as disposable income increased. Hammond, Houston, and Melander (1967) found life insurance premiums increased as wealth or income increased. Funk, Rapoport, and Jones (1979) found increased conservatism in savings and betting behavior as people accumulated more capital.

Our study found a significant relationship between wealth and both absolute and relative risk aversion. Wealthier managers not only held more money in riskier categories than poorer managers, they also held a larger percentage of their assets in the riskiest categories (i.e., the measure RISKYASSETS).

The results of the multivariate analysis with all 16 measures gave a mixed picture for wealth. There was a positive relationship with only one other measure (RANK:EV-LO) in addition to RISKYASSETS. There were three negative relationships: PGAMBLE50%, DEBTRATIO, and GAMBLING in the multivariate analyses, although the latter two measures were biased in favor of negative relationships by their functional dependence on wealth (or its close correlate, assets).[9] The univariate analyses added three more positive relationships (BGAMBLE50%, RANK:EV-HI, and SELFINSURED) and one more negative relationship (RESIGNATIONS).[10] On balance, the evidence in our study seems to provide more support for decreasing rather than increasing relative risk aversion. Nonetheless, our results clearly demonstrate how sensitive the relationship between risk and wealth is to the measure of risk used.

The multivariate analyses for income showed that for three of the measures (RISKYASSETS, SELFRATING, and SELFINSURED), income entered into the discriminant function with a positive coefficient. For one measure (PGAMBLE50%) it entered negatively. Univariate analyses added one more positive relationship (SENSATION) and one more negative relationship (RESIGNATIONS). The overall conclusion, then, depends on how much weight is placed on particular measures. Because of past studies, we are placing more weight on the RISKYASSETS measure.

Do Managers with Higher Income Take More Risks?

As with wealth, more income allows one to take more risks. Even if things go wrong, with sufficiently high income bad outcomes can more easily be overcome. With a high enough income a person can withstand major losses of net wealth. With a high wealth level but without correspondingly high income, major losses can be devastating. Hence, it seems more likely that high risk taking will be related to high income than to high wealth.

We found an extremely strong positive relationship between income and risk (as measured by the holding of risky assets). Managers with higher incomes took more risks. Managers in our risk-taking category had an average income of $225,000, while managers in the risk-averse category had an average income of $113,000.

The relationship we found between income and risk was not due to other factors. Even when we held other factors constant, there was a very strong positive relationship between risk and income. There was little relationship with other measures of risk, so there was no strong support or contradiction.

There was a definite difference in the way managers saw their own risk propensity. Managers with higher incomes viewed themselves as more willing to take risks than managers with low incomes viewed themselves.

We conclude, then, that there is a strong positive relationship.

Result: Managers with higher incomes took more risks.

People who can afford to lose take risks. High income provides a definite cushion in case things turn out badly.

RISK AND BUSINESS CHARACTERISTICS

Do CEOs Take More Risks?

Many top executives are at the top because they have taken calculated risks that paid off. The super-cautious managers have probably not distinguished themselves enough to reach the top. The super-reckless have probably made mistakes and fallen off the promotion ladder somewhere. The survivors know which risks to take and which to avoid.

At lower levels, then, we are more likely to find the risk-averse managers. The inherently risk-averse who have not made any mistakes may be slowly moving up or may be mired in dead-end jobs.

The managers who took major risks that did not work out may be still with the company and perhaps chastened, or they may be gone.

Thus, compared with managers at lower levels, top-level managers are likely to be greater risk takers. But is a relationship between position and risk an artifact due to factors such as age, seniority, and firm size? When these factors are held constant, can top-level managers be expected to be greater risk takers?

The results confirm that the managers at the top were greater risk takers. The top third of the managers in our study, consisting of chairmen, presidents, and senior vice-presidents, were significantly more risk-taking than the bottom third which consisted mostly of division managers. Our middle group of managers, mostly vice-presidents, were not significantly more risk-taking than the bottom third.

The other measures of risk provided support for the finding that managers at the top were greater risk takers. For example, they ranked the riskiest personal investment higher, they had taken career risks by resigning more frequently, and they were more inclined toward stimulating experiences. In only one or two instances did top managers show an inclination toward less risk.

In addition, the managers at the top perceived themselves as greater risk takers than managers below them perceived themselves. Their belief in their greater willingness to take risk may have reinforced their tendency to take more risk.

The conclusion is clear-cut.

> ***Result:*** Chief executive officers and chief operating officers took more risks than did lower-level managers.

We have seen in the preceding chapters that very few people are risk takers in all situations. The person who gets to the top knows when to take risks and when to be cautious. The fact that the CEOs in our study are predominantly risk takers means that they are prepared to take risks when the situation calls for it. The lower-level executive who aspires to a top-level position needs to learn which are good risks to take and which are bad risks to be avoided.

NOTE ON THE DEFINITION OF BUSINESS CHARACTERISTICS

Position was a characteristic that influenced the design of the study. We purposefully confined our attention to the top managerial ranks rather than trying to obtain coverage of all ranks. About one-third of the participants were chairmen, presidents, or senior vice-presidents. This made up our top position category. Another group, slightly larger than one-third, were regular vice-presidents. The third group had titles such as assistant vice-president, treasurer, general manager, division manager, or were high-level staff people. The information was obtained by having each executive provide his job title and a brief description of his responsibilities.

Authority was closely related to position. We obtained the characteristic we call "authority" from the question about the annual salary of the highest position for which a manager had primary hiring and firing authority. For categorical analysis we used authority levels of $60,000 and $90,000 as breakpoints to obtain three groups. We checked the suitability of the authority measure by comparing it with information about the managers' budgets and number of managerial personnel under their direction.

Seniority was based on how long a manager had been with his present employer. In addition we computed a measure of the percentage of a manager's career that he had been with his current firm. For this measure the number of years with present employer was divided by the difference between the manager's age and age 21. Three categories were obtained by using breakpoints of 36% and 77%.

Firm size was a factor considered in the design of the study (see Chapter 2). While large firms were overrepresented, we wanted to obtain a spectrum of firm sizes. We used sales revenue as a measure of firm size when such a concept was meaningful; when it was not, we used gross assets. The three categories were firms up to $30 million, from $30 million to $300 million, and over $300 million.

Industry was also a design characteristic. We opted for more in-depth coverage of key industries rather than a broader but more superficial coverage. Overall we studied 35 major industries. For the analysis in this chapter we have grouped them into banking (including trust companies, savings and loans, finance companies, life insurance), venture capital/underwriting, primary (mining, oil, and forestry), chemical/pharmaceutical, manufacturing, and other (transportation, utilities, construction, publishing, leisure, etc.).

Do Managers with Higher Authority Take More Risks?

We can gain further insight into the relationship between risk and position by looking at the data available on authority. For each manager we obtained the highest annual salary for which he had primary hiring and firing authority. In general, managers in the top positions would also have high levels of authority. There may, however, be some differences. Some top-level managers may not be actively involved in company operations. In a few of these cases they may be in figurehead positions. Authority also contributes information on company size since managers in larger companies typically earn more than managers in equivalent positions in smaller companies. Although some managers would not necessarily view the move from the presidency of a $100 million firm to a $500 million firm as a step up, many managers make seemingly lateral moves to attain a higher level of authority.

The argument we made for a higher position being related to greater risk taking can be carried over to authority. Managers with more authority have probably taken risks and had things work out in the past. This experience has reinforced their willingness to take risks. Thus we expect managers with higher authority to take more risks than managers with lower levels of authority.

Just as with position, our expectations were borne out by the data. Managers with higher authority were greater risk takers. This finding was true when authority was considered by itself as well as being true when all other factors were held constant.

Another way to look at the relationship between risk and authority is to observe that those managers who were in the top third on risk taking had an average authority level of over $100,000. In contrast, the managers in the lowest third on risk taking had average authority levels under $75,000.

The other measures of risk added further support. Managers with the highest authority had a higher debt ratio, were more inclined to self-insure, gambled more, and sought more sensation. The only counterevidence was that they had a lower tendency to resign.

The managers with higher authority not only took more risks, but also thought they took more risks. Their self-perception of their risk propensity supports their actual choices.

In summary, the results are very strong. Taken together, both high authority and high position go hand in hand with higher risk taking.

Result: Managers with greater authority took more risks.

As with position, those managers with high authority need to be able to take risks when necessary. The fact that they have more authority means that there is more to lose if things go wrong. Managers who are not prepared to take these risks probably will not get promoted to such positions or will not last long if they do.

NOTE ON THE RELATIONSHIPS BETWEEN POSITION, AUTHORITY, AND SENIORITY AND THE 16 RISK MEASURES

Position showed a positive relationship with risk for two measures (RESIGNATIONS and SENSATION) in addition to RISKYASSETS in the multivariate analyses. There were univariate positive relationships for

RANK:EV-HI and SELFRATING. The only negative relationships were for IB:LAWSUIT and SELFINSURED.[11] Hence the managers at the top did appear to take more risks.[12]

Authority showed even stronger positive relationships than did position. There were six risk measures for which authority entered as a significant positive relationship. These measures are DEBTRATIO, SELFINSURED, GAMBLING, and SENSATION, as well as the two measures focused on in the text, namely RISKYASSETS and SELFRATING. The only negative relationship was a univariate one with RESIGNATIONS. The whole set of measures seems to strongly support a positive relationship between authority and risk taking.

When we defined seniority as percentage of career with current employer, it entered as a significant variable for three of the 16 risk measures. There was a negative relationship between seniority and risk for DEBTRATIO and RESIGNATIONS, while there was a positive relationship for SELFINSURED. The univariate analysis added negative relationships for SENSATION in addition to RISKYASSETS which was discussed in the text. When we defined seniority as years with current employer, we obtained the same results except that the result for SENSATION extended to the multivariate analysis and the univariate analysis added negative relationships for PGAMBLE50% and BGAMBLE10%.

Are Managers with Longer Seniority More Risk-Averse?

Most of us believe that managers with long seniority are unlikely to rock the boat. They are likely to opt for the tried and true. The longer someone is with an organization, the more risk-averse he is likely to become. At least that is the common belief.

We considered seniority in two ways. First, we looked at the number of years a manager had spent with his current firm. Second, we looked at the percentage of a manager's working career that he had spent with his current firm.

We found the expected negative relationship between seniority and risk for our focal measure when we measured seniority as percentage. No relationship was found when seniority was measured as years. When we considered the other risk measures, we found reasonably strong negative relationships. That is, managers with more seniority (measured either as years or percentage) took fewer risks. This result was true for both seniority taken by itself or seniority examined when other factors, such as age, were held constant.

There was no significant relationship between a manager's view of his risk taking and his seniority. More specifically, managers with more seniority did not view themselves as more risk-averse.

> ***Result:*** Managers with more seniority were more averse to risk than managers with less seniority.

Managers who have been with a firm for a large percentage of their career should question themselves when facing risks. Any natural inclinations toward risk aversion should be challenged. That is not to say that years of caution should be thrown aside but that such managers should make sure that they are not lapsing into routine risk-averse actions when something more daring is called for.

Do Managers in Large Firms Take Fewer Risks?

Many people believe that managers in large firms are less inclined to take risk than managers in smaller firms. In large firms managers do not have to commit themselves as much as in a small firm. Furthermore, they are further away from the uncertainties that occur outside the firm, and there are other people around who can take the risks if they do not.

Our results confirmed this belief that managers in large firms were more averse to risk than other managers. Furthermore managers in small firms were more inclined to take risks. This result was true even when other characteristics such as position were held constant. No other measures of risk strongly supported or strongly refuted these relationships with firm size.

Even though managers in large firms took less risk, they did not see themselves as more risk-averse. Although managers in small firms took more risks, they did not see themselves as more risk-taking. The reason for this lack of correspondence may be that managers in large firms are surrounded by other risk-averse managers. Compared to their associates, they do not seem more risk-averse, even though all of them are in fact more risk-averse. Similarly, managers in small firms do not see themselves as more risk-taking, perhaps because they are surrounded by others who are more risk-taking than average.

> ***Result:*** Managers in large firms were more risk-averse than average. Managers in small firms were more risk-taking than average.

To the extent that large firms wish to foster risk taking, they may find it useful to decentralize and allow managers more control in running divisions essentially as small firms. An entrepreneurial spirit can be aided by surrounding uncertain managers with associates who are risk takers and who see themselves as such.

Note on the relationships between firm size and industry and the 16 risk measures

There were not very many supporting or refuting relationships for the hypothesis of less risk taking in larger firms. There were no multivariate relationships in addition to RISKYASSETS.[13] There were only two supporting univariate relationships (negative)—for the measures RESIGNATIONS and BGAMBLE10%. There were no positive relationships of any kind. Hence there was a suggestion that managers in larger firms take less risk, but the results were not strong.

The study of the relationship between risk propensity and industry depends on the industry classifications. While it might have been desirable to subdivide industries further into more than six categories, the number of cases in each category would have been too small for definite conclusions. The clearest result for any industry grouping was for the banking industry. Bankers showed greater risk aversion in the multivariate analyses for four measures (PGAMBLE50%, RANK:EV-HI, RISKYASSETS, and SELFINSURED). There were two additional negative univariate relationships. Bankers were more risk-averse for BGAMBLE50% and RANK:EV-LO. There were two positive relationships (IB: VENTURE and DEBTRATIO), and the latter was probably because loans were more readily available.[14]

Venture capital/underwriter managers had the next highest number of significant relationships. SELFINSURED was positive along with RISKYASSETS, and IB:VENTURE was negative. A univariate positive relationship was found with RESIGNATIONS. One negative univariate relationship was found with IB:LAWSUIT.[15] The results were thus mixed for the venture capital industry. Any overall conclusion must be based on the measures that are given more weight.[16]

Managers in primary industries had three multivariate relationships that were significant. They were more risk-taking on DEBTRATIO but were more risk-averse on PGAMBLE10% and SELFINSURED. The univariate indication of risk taking for RISKYASSETS was discussed in the text. An additional positive univariate result was found for GAMBLING. Hence, as with venture capital, the conclusion concerning the risk propensity of managers in primary industries is based on the relative weight given to each measure.[17]

In the multivariate analyses, manufacturing and chemical/pharmaceutical each had only a single positive coefficient; the former with RANK:EV-LO and the latter with RESIGNATIONS. Manufacturing had two negative univariate relationships while chemical/pharmaceutical had three positive and one negative univariate relationships. The results were not sufficiently strong to conclude that managers in these industries were either more risk-taking or more risk-averse than managers in other industries.

Are Bankers More Risk-Averse?

We considered many different kinds of firms in our study but we need to group them in order to have a large enough sample from which to draw conclusions. We will focus on five main industry groupings: banking, venture capital, primary, manufacturing, and chemical/pharmaceutical. While we have data from many other industries, we will restrict our attention to the five mentioned above. All other industries (e.g., recreational, media) were grouped together.

Some of the common stereotypes were confirmed in our data. Bankers were much more risk-averse than any of the other industry groups. We found this effect even when other factors were held constant. Other risk measures supported strongly the result that bankers were more risk-averse.

On the other hand, venture capitalists and underwriters were much more risk-taking than the other groups. This result also held when all other factors were held constant. The other measures neither supported nor refuted the positive relationship between risk taking and managers in venture capital/underwriter firms.

The results for other industry groupings were mixed. For some measures managers in primary industries were more risk-taking, but for other measures they were less risk-taking. Correspondingly, managers in manufacturing firms and in chemical/pharmaceutical firms showed both risk-taking and risk-averting tendencies on different risk measures.

There were no significant differences from one industry to another in the way managers viewed their own risk propensity.

> ***Result:*** Managers in banking were more risk-averse than average. Managers in venture capital/underwriting industries were more risk-taking than average. No significant differences were found for managers in the primary, manufacturing, or chemical/pharmaceutical industries.

Some interchange of executives between banking and other industries may be useful. The basic risk aversion of bankers clearly has an impact on highly charged risk takers who come to them to get funding for their projects. It may be useful for entrepreneurs to have a more continuing concern about the fiscal side by hiring directly from the banking industry. Similarly banks may gain a competitive advantage in a deregulated system by hiring executives from industries that nurture more aggressive risk takers.

RISK AND SUCCESS

Do Successful Managers Take More Risks?

Success is achieved by taking risks. Nothing can be attained by avoiding risks completely. On the other hand, extreme risk taking is not likely to lead to success. Simply choosing the most risky course of action without balancing expected benefits against costs is reckless. So success is unlikely to result from being extremely risk-averse (ultra-cautious) or by being extremely risk-taking (ultra-reckless). What we would like to know is whether, between these extremes, success is more likely to result from taking risks.

We will address this question by looking at a group of the most successful executives and asking whether these executives are more risk-taking than the rest of the managers in our study.

We identified the most successful managers in two ways. First, we subjectively assessed success by examining position, firm size, and directorships held. This group, called SUCCESS1, consisted of 32 executives. About half of these executives were CEOs and three-quarters held the title "Chairman" or "President." Managers in this group represented three of the five largest banks, three of the five largest insurance companies, and three of the ten largest manufacturing firms in Canada. Second, we used a two-way classification of position and wealth. There were 75 managers in the top category for both position and wealth. We will call this group SUCCESS2.

Using the SUCCESS1 group, we found that the most successful executives were the highest risk takers. They held 51% of their total assets as risky assets compared with 33% for the other executives. In addition, they viewed themselves as being more willing to take business risks than their associates. Clearly success was positively related with risk taking.

Using the SUCCESS2 group, we again found a significant positive relationship between success and risk. The more successful held a greater percentage of risky assets than the less successful.

The results are conclusive.

Result: The most successful executives took more risks.

While success may be due to taking risks, one may feel more able to take risks after achieving success. Especially when we measure risk by the proportion of risky assets held, a high proportion of risky assets may reflect financial security.

NOTE ON THE RELATIONSHIP BETWEEN SUCCESS AND THE 16 RISK MEASURES

The 32 managers in the SUCCESS1 group were significantly more risk-taking (at the 0.05 level) than the remaining managers on three of the 16 measures. They were more willing to go it alone on a joint venture (IB: VENTURE), as well as having a significant positive relationship for the variables RISKYASSETS and SELFRATING, discussed in the text.

The SUCCESS1 group differed from other executives on various dimensions. From the way the category was defined, they differed on nationality (all were Canadians), on income, position, and authority (all were at the highest level), and on firm size (all were in large firms). There were also differences that were not directly designed. The SUCCESS1 group were significantly older, had more dependents, were wealthier, and had longer seniority.

The 75 managers in the SUCCESS2 group included both Americans and Canadians. This group showed significantly greater risk taking than other managers in their preference for risky personal investments (RANK:EV-HI, RANK:EV-LO, and RISKYASSETS) and their desire for a stimulating environment (SENSATION).[18] The greater risk aversion in this group for PGAMBLE50%, DEBTRATIO, and GAMBLING seems inconsistent with the other results. This may be due to the greater amount at stake in the personal gamble among the wealthier SUCCESS2 executives and the functional dependence of the latter two risk measures on wealth.

THE CONSISTENT RISK AVERTERS AND THE CONSISTENT RISK TAKERS

Do the Consistent Risk Averters and the Consistent Risk Takers Differ on Any of the Characteristics?

In Chapter 8 we identified a group of 14 executives who were risk-averting on a majority of the risk measures derived from standardized situations. We also found a group of 12 executives who were risk-taking on a majority of these measures. Neither group showed the opposite risk tendency on any measure. We called these groups the *consistent (relative) risk averters* and the *consistent (relative) risk takers*. We now ask whether these two groups of executives differed on the personal, financial, and business characteristics considered in this chapter. To provide larger sample sizes to conduct this analysis, we extended these groups to include executives who were in the same risk category on a majority of the primary measures, but were in the opposite risk category on at most one measure. The extended groups consisted of 41 and 27 executives, respectively.

We found no significant differences between the consistent risk takers and the consistent risk averters on any of the characteristics. Even though there were no statistical differences, the data did suggest possible differences in firm size and industry. There were more consistent risk takers in smaller firms and in the chemical/pharmaceutical industries and more consistent risk averters in the banking industry.

> ***Result:*** The managers showed a trend toward consistent risk aversion in the banking industry and consistent risk taking in small firms.

These results, for the consistent risk averters and consistent risk takers, are in agreement with our findings from the whole set of executives.

CONCLUSIONS

We found a number of interesting connections between risk propensity and personal, financial, and business characteristics of managers. As we have discussed, some common stereotypes are true, others are not. A summary of the findings of our study are given in Table 10.1.

The personal characteristic that seemed to have the strongest relationship to risk propensity was age, with younger executives more willing to take risks than older executives. There was some evidence for greater risk taking among better educated managers and those with fewer dependents. Although there is a very strong belief that Canadian managers take fewer risks than Americans, we found no evidence to support this view.

Among the financial characteristics income had a strong relationship with risk propensity, and managers with higher incomes took more risks. For wealth there were also strong relationships with risk, but no clear trend emerged for or against taking risks. The conclusion depends upon which measure of risk one prefers.

Each of the business characteristics had a significant relationship to risk with especially strong associations for position, authority, seniority, and the banking industry. Risk taking was related to higher executive position and greater authority. Risk aversion was associated with managers having longer seniority and managers in banking. There was some evidence for greater risk taking among managers in smaller firms and those in the venture capital/underwriting industries.

Table 10.1 Summary of Relationships between Risk Propensity and Personal, Financial, and Business Characteristics

Characteristic		Risk Averters	Risk Takers
Personal	Age	Older managers take less risk	Younger managers take more risk
	Dependents	Managers with more dependents take more risk in some situations and less risk in other situations	
	Education	Managers with high school education or bachelor's degree take less risk	Managers with postgraduate training take more risk
	Nationality	No significant difference between Americans and Canadians	
Financial	Wealth	Managers with more wealth take more risk in some risky situations and less risk in other situations	
	Income	Managers with less income take less risk	Managers with more income take more risk
Business	Position	Managers below the senior VP level take less risk	CEOs and COOs take more risk
	Authority	Managers with less authority take less risk	Managers with more authority take more risk
	Seniority	Managers with longer seniority take less risk	Managers with shorter seniority take more risk
	Firm size	Managers in larger firms take less risk	Managers in smaller firms take more risk
	Industry	Managers in the banking industry take less risk	Managers in the venture capital and underwriting industries take more risk
Success		Less successful managers take less risk	More successful managers take more risk

We also found that more successful managers took more risks than less successful managers. Whether managers became successful because they took risks or whether they took risks once they became successful cannot be determined by our study.

Overall, then, we see that one's willingness to take risks does depend somewhat on one's personal, financial, and business characteristics. In most cases the dependence is in the direction of commonly held views about risk propensity.

RESEARCH CONCLUSIONS

There are four main research conclusions:

1. None of the stereotypical relationships examined in this chapter held for more than half of the 16 risk measures. Therefore, if a desirable property of a risk measure is to explain commonly held observations about the relationship between risk propensity and characteristics of the decision maker, then none of our risk measures fully satisfied it. RISKY-ASSETS had more significant relationships with these characteristics than any other measure, which partially led us to select it as the focus of our discussion. On the other hand, not all stereotypes are true so we cannot expect any risk measure to explain relationships that do not exist in fact.

2. Many significant univariate relationships between a characteristic and risk propensity vanished when other characteristics were included in multivariate analyses. For example, nationality differences in risk propensity disappeared when education level was included as well. Researchers must be careful, then, to use multivariate procedures wherever possible to minimize this danger of misspecifying the effects of interrelated characteristics on risk propensity.

3. Very different relationships between risk propensity and the characteristics were found when different risk measures were used. For example, managers with greater wealth can be shown to be more willing or less willing to take risks than less wealthy managers depending upon which risk measure is used. This very important finding casts considerable doubt on previous studies of risk that purport to show a relationship between (a single measure of) risk and other factors. Our data also highlight how sensitive some findings are to the relative weight one puts on the various risk measures in aggregating disparate and often conflicting relationships.

4. The consistent risk averters and the consistent risk takers were not significantly different on any of the characteristics we examined. The non-statistical trends discussed in the text did provide some ideas for further research.

Chapter 11

Managerial Summary and Implications

Relationships Among Risk Measures and Characteristics

INTRODUCTION

In Chapter 7 we summarized what we had learned from studying risk in the standardized situations in Part Two of the book (discussed in Chapters 3 through 6). These results, including the importance of risk adjustments, are repeated below:

Risk recognition and evaluation

When presented with several important attributes of risky investments, managers focused on only one or two attributes.

The most prominent focus was on the expected return of an investment.

The second most important attribute, in investments involving 10% of personal wealth, was the upside potential gain.

With information available on numerous attributes of investments, managers used two-stage decision thinking; they first used one attribute as a constraint and then used a second attribute as a goal.

The most common two-stage decision thinking used the attributes "chance of major gain" as the constraint and "expected return" as the goal.

When managers did focus on variation in returns, they did not necessarily prefer investments that had lower variation.

When investments have the same level on an important attribute (such as a 10% chance of total loss), this level and the attribute itself can affect the choice.

Risk adjustment

Rather than taking the chances of potential loss, magnitude of loss, and exposure as fixed, the managers tried to adjust the risky situations to make them more attractive.

The managers used a variety of means to try to adjust the risky situations.

The managers used risk adjustments to avoid risks in some situations.

Managers frequently sought additional information before making risky decisions.

Managers frequently delayed their risky decisions.

Managers frequently delegated their risky decisions.

The Risk In-Basket is a very effective way to study risk adjustments in standardized situations.

Risky choice

The managers showed a very different willingness to take risks across the standardized situations.

Managers were more risk-averse when their own money was at stake than when their firms' resources were at stake.

Risk taking was more common in the recognition and adjustment phases of risk than in the choice phase.

Managers were more willing to take risks once in a risky situation than in entering a risky situation.

A manager's willingness to take risks in one standardized situation was only weakly related to his willingness to take risks in seemingly similar situations.

In this chapter we will summarize what we have learned by studying the relationships among the standardized risk measures themselves as well as their relationships with measures of naturally occurring risks and attitudes. In addition we will summarize the relationships between the risk measures and a variety of personal, financial, and business characteristics that have been thought to be related to risk. For more details on any of these topics consult the relevant parts of Chapters 8, 9, and 10. In addition to presenting the general results we will consider the implications of these results for management.

RISK TAKING AND RISK AVERTING

Willingness to take risks can be assessed, but no single measure is sufficient because one's willingness to take risks varies from situation to situation. Up to this point, people have attempted to determine a person's inclination to take risks by using narrow or inappropriate procedures. We have developed and tested a comprehensive Risk Portfolio that allows us to assess the risk inclinations of managers. The measures are based on theories of risk and have been carefully checked for reliability and validity. The risk measures were only weakly associated in different situations, so no single measure can capture the multidimensional nature of risks. It is therefore necessary to use multiple measures as in our Risk Portfolio.

The Risk Portfolio is an effective means of assessing willingness to take risks in a variety of situations. Our study shows the advantages of using a variety of situations to assess risk. A person's naturally occurring choices, such as the amount of debt or the amount of insurance he holds, are obvious candidates for assessing willingness to take risks. However, such choices generally indicate a wide disparity in risk inclination for a given person. A person who seems to be a risk averter when you look at the debt he holds may seem to be a risk taker when you look at his insurance levels. Furthermore, because different people have faced different opportunities, it is hard to compare people who are in different circumstances.

Standardized situations (such as the Risk In-Basket), which can be presented to anyone, allow for direct comparisons. The danger that such situations will not seem real can be overcome by designing situations that are similar to those actually faced by managers. A person's attitudes, including his assessment of his own risk tolerance, provide some information but we have to be more cautious about generalizing from what people say rather than from what they do. It should be clear, then, that the advantages of natural situations, standardized situations, and attitudes can be captured, and the disadvantages can be overcome, by using them together in a carefully designed portfolio.

There are considerable differences in a manager's willingness to take risks from one situation to another. Few managers were consistently risk-averse and fewer still were consistently risk-taking. People who take risks in one situation may be risk-averse in other situations. Hence be careful in trying to generalize from only a few observations of a person. Astronauts who show outstanding physical courage are not necessarily the people to put in charge of an entrepreneurial company.

There is no reason to think that a person should have a uniform risk inclination over all situations. Perhaps each person can be thought of as having an overall aggregate level of tolerable risk. As the risks in one area of life increase (e.g., a marriage breakup or a lawsuit over an auto accident), the risks that are acceptable in other areas decrease. There is no reason to expect everyone's tolerance level to be the same.

While virtually everyone at some time is risk-averse, some people never take risks. Thus, those people who are inclined to be more risk-averse than others are more predictable.

Willingness to take risks does not vary over situations in a random way. There are patterns in how a person's risk inclination changes over situations. We will consider these patterns next.

Risk taking was more predominant in business decisions than in personal decisions. The results of business decisions are more remote and more people are involved, so responsibility for bad outcomes can usually be shared. This finding implies that you should be very careful in trying to generalize to business decisions from knowledge of an individual's willingness to take personal risks and vice versa. Knowing how inclination toward risk differs in business decisions can help you to understand what your associates are likely to do in such situations, and you may even be able to influence them in preferred directions.

Managers tried to avoid threatening situations that had high stakes. People take more risks when the stakes are low. However, when they find themselves in threatening situations, they often will take a very risky alternative to try to break even. Accepting a sure loss is admitting defeat and is not an easy thing to do. Yet the successful military commander and business executive realize that situations do occur when it is best to cut your losses, even if it means losing the battle, so you can get on with winning the war.

Governments or industry-wide organizations can make situations less risky in a wide variety of ways by influencing their perceived riskiness. The chance of loss in many risky situations can be reduced by ensuring that adequate venture capital is available through favorable tax treatment. Governments can announce important policy changes concerning the money supply, environmental regulation, and tax incentives well in advance of their implementation.

Thus firms will not be forced to make hasty, unplanned, and costly expenditures to conform to these changes. Government policy can support industry-wide or joint business-government research and development programs to meet foreign competition in emerging markets of high technology products.

The amount of loss can be limited by guaranteed government loans, grants for research and development projects, and government support for risky ventures. Governments can reduce a firm's exposure to loss by sharing its losses through favorable tax policy, establishing innovative insurance programs to share risks with business, and modifying trade and immigration barriers to increase a firm's import of necessary raw materials and skilled labor and export of finished products. Industry-wide organizations together with government can foster joint ventures among several firms so that no firm's exposure is too great.

The managers were more risk-taking in their attitudes toward risk than in their risk behavior in the natural and standardized situations. Most people think of themselves as more risk-taking than they actually are. While there is some relationship between a person's self-rating of his willingness to take risks and his risk behavior, the relationship is very weak. So do not rely on what a person tells you about his inclination to take risks. Almost invariably the person will think of himself as a bigger risk taker than he really is.

A person who knows his own risk tolerance has a better basis for making his choices match what he really wants. An organization can use a knowledge of its members' willingness to take risks to incorporate a person's preferences in his absence. In a group that is in constant conflict, a knowledge of how each member sees the risks and acts on them may help to sort out differences. In a group that is in constant agreement, a healthy diversity may be created by asking what a hypothetical member with very different risk preferences would choose. A firm can use information about an individual's willingness to take risks in hiring, in selecting people for particular jobs or training programs, and in promotion decisions.

CHARACTERISTICS RELATED TO RISK

Many stereotypes have been built up over the years about how people become more risk-averse as they get older, about how higher education inhibits risk taking, and so forth. Obviously, these beliefs could not be checked until there was a valid way of assessing one's willingness to rake risks. So as part of our study we examined the relationships between risk and a variety of personal, financial, and business characteristics. Here is what we found:

The most successful managers took the most risks. The more rigorously success was defined, the stronger the relationship became. While our data do not imply causality, it seems clear that for most businesses, a person gets to the top by taking risks and having them work out for the best. The person who does not take risks is unlikely to get to the top. However, many people take risks that do not work out and this thwarts their career plans. Hence the risks taken must be carefully chosen and entail a bit of luck too. This finding suggests that top-level executives should nurture deliberative risk taking in lower-level executives. A climate should be created that allows people to survive a few decisions that turn out badly as long as the risks taken are good ones.

Some stereotypes have a solid basis in the facts: Older managers, those who had been with the same firm for a long time, and bankers were more risk-averse. Managers with higher executive positions, greater authority, higher incomes, and those from smaller firms were more risk-taking.

Other stereotypes proved to be false: Higher education did not inhibit risk taking. The managers with postgraduate education took more risks than others. Canadians were not more risk-averse than Americans. Although both Americans and Canadians believed that Canadians were more risk-averse, in fact there was no significant difference between them.

The managers did not always have their own risk inclination pegged correctly. For example, while the more successful executives believed that they were more risk-taking than other managers, those with high seniority did not realize how risk-averse they really were.

Knowing the relationship between one's willingness to take risks and other characteristics allows for a better understanding of yourself and others. For example, knowing what is likely to happen to you (or your associates) as you get older allows you to adjust, if desired. Being able to measure willingness to take risks and being able to predict it based on various characteristics allows one to obtain a preliminary assessment of a person's likely risk behavior before knowing much about him. Thus selection of people for various tasks that require a particular inclination toward risk can be done, if necessary, without even measuring risk itself. In most cases, though, one would want to measure willingness to take risks unless it was impossible to do so.

Although we did not find any relationship between risk inclination and some characteristics that were only examined for special cases (such as nationality), there may be differences in other cases. Finding no differences in willingness to take risks between American and Canadian managers does not mean there are no differences between Americans and Japanese, Germans, or Greeks. It might be useful to test for such differences when conducting operations in a foreign country in order to obtain the best possible match for the company's international operations.

We have been able to examine only a few of the many characteristics that are possibly related to risk. While we have picked some important personal, financial, and business characteristics, other ones may be more useful in particular circumstances. Now that there is a tested way to assess willingness to take risks, the door is open to making those assessments.

In Chapter 12 you will have an opportunity to use part of our Risk Portfolio to make a preliminary assessment of your own willingness to take risks. Such assessments can show how you stack up, both in direct and in relative terms, with other managers. For most of our measures, we are able to say directly whether someone is an absolute risk taker or risk averter. As we have shown in earlier chapters, the managers in our study were predominantly risk averters rather than risk takers. We can also make relative comparisons using our database of top-level managers. Thus we are able to compare anyone's willingness to take risks either with all the managers in our study or with specially selected subgroups.

PART FOUR

Assessing Your Own Willingness to Take Risks

Chapter 12

Assessing Your Own Willingness to Take Risks

INTRODUCTION

You have seen in Chapters 3 through 11 how the managers in our study responded to our portfolio of risky situations. We will now use a selection of situations from this Risk Portfolio to help you assess your own willingness to take both personal and business risks.

Consider first your inclination to take personal risks. We will restrict attention to just three of our measures of personal risk. Two of these measures are taken from standardized situations and one from a naturally occurring situation. These measures will be illustrated by having you answer a few questions.

We begin by asking you to calculate your personal debt ratio. Use page 301 from the General Questionnaire to determine both your personal gross assets and your liabilities.[1] Enter your personal liabilities and gross assets on the top row in Table 12.1. Divide liabilities by gross assets, multiply by 100, and enter this percentage of gross assets held as liabilities in Table 12.1. This will be the first indicator of your willingness to take personal risks.

Next read page 314 from the Personal Investment Gambles questionnaire in the Appendix concerning risking a 50% chance of losing half your personal net wealth in return for possible substantial gain. Recall that your personal net wealth is personal gross assets less per-

Table 12.1 Assessing Your Willingness to Take Personal and Business Risks

Instructions: Read the pages of the Appendix indicated in Chapter 12 and answer the questions. Transfer your answers to the appropriate blanks under the heading "Responses" below, performing the necessary calculations as indicated.

	Risky Situations	Responses	Measures
Personal	Debt Ratio: Questionnaire: General Questionnaire	Gross personal liabilities (pg. 301) $ ____ ÷ Gross personal assets (pg. 301) $ ____ × 100 =	Percentage of gross personal assets held as liabilities ____ %
Personal	Personal Investment Gamble: 50% chance of loss Questionnaire: Investment Choices Under Uncertainty	Smallest possible final net wealth you would require to make the investment (pg. 314) $ ____ ÷ Current net wealth (pg. 314) $ ____ =	Required multiple of net wealth ____
Personal	Risk-Return Rankings: Highest variation in returns Questionnaire: Personal Investment Preferences	Preference rank for alternative with highest variation in returns, venture H (pg. 322) 1 = most preferred 9 = least preferred	____
Business	Business Investment Gamble: 50% chance of loss Questionnaire: Investment Choices Under Uncertainty	Smallest rate of return on the uncertain project you would accept in making the investment (pg. 316) ____ % ÷ Expected (usual) rate of return on capital expenditure (or other) budget (pg. 315) ____ % =	Required multiple of usual rate of return ____
Business	Risk In-Basket: Lawsuit for patent violation Questionnaire: In-Basket Decisions	Lowest chance of winning in court that you would need to recommend taking the case to court (pg. 312): Note: If you would not take the case to court no matter what the chances, enter 100%. If you would take the case to court no matter what the chances, enter 0%.	____ %
Business	Self-Appraisal of Risk Propensity Compared with Other Managers Questionnaire: General Questionnaire	Your own willingness to undertake risky business propositions as compared to other executives at or near your level in your firm (pg. 305): 1 = much less willing to accept risks 7 = much more willing to accept risks	____

sonal liabilities. Make sure that the numbers you use for assets and liabilities here are the same ones you used in calculating your personal debt ratio. Answer the questions on your current net wealth and the gamble on page 314. Remember that there is no right or wrong answer to the gamble question. After you have answered the questions, return to this point in the book.

If you indicated that you would not risk a 50% chance of losing half your net wealth for any amount of gain, check yourself by imagining whether you would take the gamble if winning meant ending up with a very high wealth, say $10 million. If you still would avoid the risk, how about $100 million? Transfer your answers to the gamble and net wealth questions to the second row in Table 12.1.Now, divide the first by the second as indicated to obtain the "required multiple of net wealth" as a second indicator of your willingness to take personal risks. If you rejected the risk even for extremely high gains, write in "1 million" as your required multiple of net wealth.

Next consider the Risk-Return Rankings questionnaire which asks you to rank nine alternative ventures for investing 10% of your personal net wealth. Read pages 317–323 in the Appendix, answering each question. The questionnaire seeks to obtain your overall preference ordering of the nine ventures from best to worst. The pairwise comparisons on pages 319–321 are used to assist you in reaching this overall preference ordering. You can ignore these pairwise comparisons if you wish to give your overall ranking directly. We will concentrate on the investment venture labeled H on page 323, so you might wish to give it special attention.[2]

After you have given your overall ranking, enter your preference rank for venture H in the third row of Table 12.1, using a "1" to indicate most preferred and "9" to indicate least preferred. Then return to this point in the book. This rank will be the third indicator of your willingness to take personal risks.

We will assess your willingness to take business risks from your responses to two standardized risky business situations used in our study and your self-appraisal of willingness to take business risks (an attitudinal measure).

You should begin by reading pages 315–316 from the Business Investment Gambles questionnaire in the Appendix. Give your firm's (or division's) annual capital expenditure budget and the expected (post-tax) annual rate of return on major investments from this budget as requested. Then use these answers to consider the business gamble which risks a 50% chance of zero rate of return on half the capital budget in return for possible substantial gain. If you do not deal with a capital expenditure budget in your firm, give your answers in terms of a budget with which you do customarily deal. If you do not have control over a budget, *imagine* that you did control an annual capital budget of $10 million which had as *assumed* expected post-tax annual rate of return of 15% and answer the business gamble for this hypothetical situation.

As with the personal gamble, if you feel you would not risk a 50% chance of a zero rate of return for any possible significant gain, check this by imagining very high gains such as an annual rate of return of 100% or 500%. If you still would not gamble for any possible rate of return, enter an extremely large rate of return such as 1000 times your expected rate of return.

Transfer your answers to the gamble and expected rate of return questions to the appropriate spaces in Table 12.1. Divide the first by the second to obtain the "required multiple of usual rate of return" as an indicator of your willingness to take business risks.

Next consider the Risk In-Basket which asks you to consider several risky decisions in the role of a hypothetical vice-president. Read pages 307–309 in the Appendix concerning your role as Bill Bickner. Then consider the lawsuit decision described on page 310. We will not consider the other situations in the Risk In-Basket. Take a few minutes now to think about how you would handle the lawsuit described in the letter from the president of multinational's subsidiary.There is no need to write the requested memo.

After you have considered the lawsuit situation, answer the question asked on page 312 of the Appendix. To help determine your answer, you might first wish to decide whether you would settle out of court or take the case to court if there were a 50% chance of winning the case. If you would settle out of court in this circumstance, imagine how high the chance of winning the case would have to be for you to take the case to court. If instead you would take the case to court with a 50% chance of winning, imagine whether you would go to court if the chances of winning were lower. Your overall answer, then, should be the *lowest* chance of winning in court that you would need to recommend taking the case to court. Enter your answer on page 312 and in Table 12.1 in the appropriate blank. If you would not take the case to court no matter what the chances, enter 100%. Conversely, if you would take the case to court no matter what the chances, enter 0%. We will use this response as a second indicator of your willingness to take business risks.

The last measure we will use to help you assess your inclination for business risks is a self-appraisal of your willingness to undertake risky business propositions compared with other executives at or near your level in your firm. Readers who are not managers should compare themselves with other individuals in an appropriate reference group.

To make this self-appraisal, consider question J on page 305 of the General Questionnaire in the Appendix. Mark the position on the scale ranging from "much less willing to accept risks" (1) to "much more willing to accept risks" (7) that best reflects your attitude. You should mark the position that accurately indicates how you see your own risk inclination rather than how you might wish to be seen by others. Translate your mark into a number from one to seven as indicated on the scale and enter it in Table 12.1.

COMPARING YOUR WILLINGNESS TO TAKE RISKS WITH THE RISK-NEUTRAL RESPONSES

How do your answers compare with risk-neutral responses to these questions? We will use this comparison to assess your *absolute* risk propensity.

In Chapters 3, 4, 5, and 8 we saw that the risk theories that provided the foundation for the standardized situations allowed us to determine a risk-neutral response for each situation. For example, we showed that the risk-neutral response for the personal gamble was 1.5 times net wealth.[3] Similar reasoning was used to determine the risk-neutral responses for the other standardized situations as follows: a preference rank of 3.5 (i.e., either 3 or 4) for the alternative with the highest variation in returns, a required multiple of 2.0 times the usual rate of return in the business gamble, and a 50% chance of winning to take the lawsuit to court.

A response lower than these risk-neutral values on any of the four standardized situations means that you are an absolute risk taker in that situation. A response higher than these values means that you are an absolute risk averter in that situation. Thus if you require a return of six times your current net wealth to take the personal gamble, then you are an absolute risk averter, whereas requiring less than 1.5 times your net wealth would make you an absolute risk taker.

The risk-neutral response for the self-appraisal of business risk is the center position of 4.0. Because there is no risk theory underlying our use of debt ratio as a risk measure, we cannot determine a risk-neutral value for this situation. For comparison purposes, however, we will use the same "risk-neutral" value we used in Chapter 9, that is, 50% of total assets held as debt. A response higher than the risk-neutral values for these two measures means that you are an absolute risk taker in that situation. A lower value means that you are an absolute risk averter.

It is perhaps more useful to know how your willingness to take risks compares with the willingness of other managers rather than with the risk-neutral values. In the next section we will compare your responses with those of the managers in our study. This comparison will provide an indication of your *relative* risk propensity. We will use these comparisons to determine your *Personal* and *Business Risk Profiles.*

COMPARING YOUR WILLINGNESS TO TAKE RISKS WITH THE MANAGERS IN THE STUDY

How do your answers compare with those given by the top-level executives in our study? Are you more or less risk-taking than they are?

We first consider your willingness to take personal risks. We will use Table 12.2 to provide a summary of your Personal Risk Profile. Begin by transferring your answers to the three risky personal situations from Table 12.1 to Table 12.2 in the appropriate boxes in the column labeled "Measure." Under the heading "Relative Risk Propensity" we have designated three columns to separate the managers in the study into relative risk groups. The left-most column corresponds to the managers in the study who fell into the most risk-taking third on a given measure of personal risk. The column at the far right corresponds to the most risk-averse third of managers, while the center column corresponds to the risk-neutral third.[4]

Consider your personal debt ratio. If it is over 23%, you are in the most risk-taking third of managers in our study. Having a debt ratio of between 8% and 23% places you in the middle, risk-neutral third of managers. If your debt ratio is under 8%, you are in the most risk-averse third. Check the box in Table 12.2 that corresponds to your personal debt ratio.

Next consider your answer to the Personal Investment Gamble. If you required less than 2.69 times your net wealth to take the gamble, your answer places you in the most risk-taking third of managers in our study. Requiring between 2.69 and 5.16 multiples of net wealth places you in the middle, risk-neutral third. If you required more than 5.16 times your net wealth to take the gamble or if you refused to gamble, you are in the most risk-averse third. Check the box in Table 12.2 that corresponds to your answer for the Personal Investment Gamble.

Finally, consider the Risk-Return Rankings. Ranking the alternative with the highest variation in returns in the top three ranks (1–3) would place you in the most risk-taking third. Giving this alternative one of the four least preferred ranks (6–9) puts you in the most risk-averse third. Ranks 4 or 5 put you in the risk-neutral third. Be sure to put check marks into your relative risk group for each of these three personal risky situations.

Table 12.2 Your Personal Risk Profile

Instructions: Transfer your measures for the risky personal situations in Table 12.1 to the "Measure" column of Table 12.2. Then for each measure put a check (✓) in the column under "Relative Risk Propensity" that corresponds to your answer. Total the number of checks in each column to obtain your Personal Risk Profile.

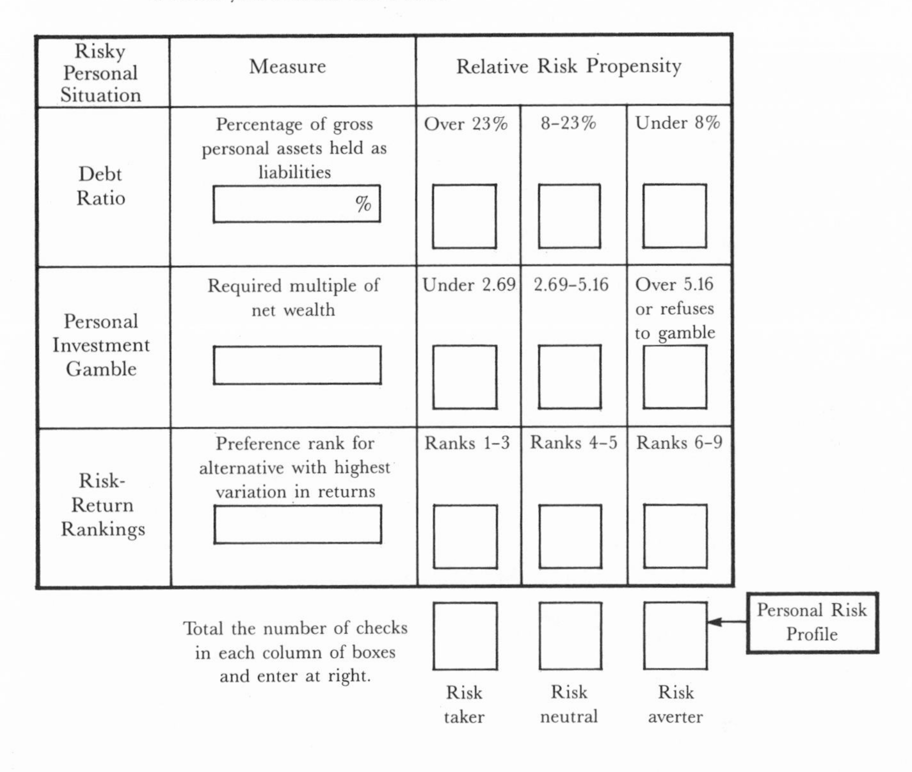

Risky Personal Situation	Measure	Relative Risk Propensity		
Debt Ratio	Percentage of gross personal assets held as liabilities ☐ %	Over 23% ☐	8–23% ☐	Under 8% ☐
Personal Investment Gamble	Required multiple of net wealth ☐	Under 2.69 ☐	2.69–5.16 ☐	Over 5.16 or refuses to gamble ☐
Risk-Return Rankings	Preference rank for alternative with highest variation in returns ☐	Ranks 1–3 ☐	Ranks 4–5 ☐	Ranks 6–9 ☐
	Total the number of checks in each column of boxes and enter at right.	☐ Risk taker	☐ Risk neutral	☐ Risk averter ← Personal Risk Profile

We will now develop your Personal Risk Profile by summarizing how many times out of the three situations you were relatively risk-taking, relatively risk-neutral, and relatively risk-averting. You can total the number of checks in each column of Table 12.2 to obtain your Personal Risk Profile. For example, if you were relatively risk-taking on none of the three measures, relatively risk-neutral on one measure, and relatively risk-averting on two measures, your Personal Risk Profile is denoted "0-1-2."

The triangle in the top of Figure 12.1 provides a diagram of the possible Personal Risk Profiles. The three corners in the triangle correspond to risk profiles for which the three measures of personal risk propensity all fall into the *same* relative risk groups. For example, the lower right corner at point B corresponds to a risk profile for which all three personal risk measures fell into the risk-averse group (i.e., "0-0-3"). An individual with this risk profile could be legitimately called a "consistent risk averter" for personal decisions. Someone

Personal Risk Profile

Risk taker	Risk neutral	Risk averter	Position
1	1	1	A
0	0	3	B
0	1	2	C
0	2	1	D
0	3	0	E
1	2	0	F
2	1	0	G
3	0	0	H
2	0	1	I
1	0	2	J

Instructions: Use the above table to find the letter corresponding to your Personal Risk Profile in Table 12.2. Circle this letter.

Business Risk Profile

Risk taker	Risk neutral	Risk averter	Position
1	1	1	K
0	0	3	L
0	1	2	M
0	2	1	N
0	3	0	O
1	2	0	P
2	1	0	Q
3	0	0	R
2	0	1	S
1	0	2	T

Instructions: Use the above table to find the letter corresponding to your Business Risk Profile in Table 12.3. Circle this letter.

Figure 12.1 Diagram of Personal and Business Risk Profiles

who shows no pattern on his Personal Risk Profile would fall into a *different* relative risk group for each measure. Such a risk profile corresponds to Point A in the center of the triangle.

You can use the table in the upper left of Figure 12.1 to translate your Personal Risk Profile into a letter position on the triangle. Thus if your profile were "0-1-2," it would correspond to point C. As you would expect, having two responses in the risk-averting group would place you close to the completely consistent risk-averting profile (point B). However, the one "risk-neutral" response draws you away from point B in the direction of the completely consistent risk-neutral profile (point E). Find the letter position for your Personal Risk Profile in Table 12.2 and circle it to indicate it is your position.

The *average* Personal Risk Profile for the managers in our study necessarily occurs at point A in the center of the diagram.[5] This is because the risk profiles were defined in terms of how each manager's personal risk measures categorized him *relative to the other managers in the study*. Only a minority of the managers in our study were located at point A as we will illustrate below.

If your Personal Risk Profile is at point A, then you have about the same willingness to take personal risks as the average manager in our study. Twenty-three percent of our managers were located here. If, instead, you are at positions G, H, or I, indicating you are in the most risk-taking third for two or three measures, you are more willing to take risks with your personal wealth than most managers. Thirty-one percent of the managers in our study had Personal Risk Profiles at these locations, including 7% at the consistent risk-taking position H. A Personal Risk Profile at positions B, C, or J indicates you are in the risk-averse third for at least two measures and suggests you are more risk-averse with your personal wealth than most managers. Twenty-three percent of our managers were located at these positions, including 3% at the consistent risk-averting position B. Lastly, you are more neutral toward risk than our managers in risking your personal resources if your position is at D, E, or F corresponding to at least two measures in the relatively risk-neutral group. Another 23% of our managers were located here, including 2% at the consistent risk-neutral position E.

Next we will compare your willingness to take business risks with the managers in our study. Transfer your answers to the three risky business situations from Table 12.1 to Table 12.3, which we will use to summarize your Business Risk Profile. As with the personal risk measures, we have divided the managers into top, middle, and bottom thirds for each of the business risk measures.[6]

You are a relative risk taker on the Business Investment Gamble if you would invest in the risky project even when it had a most favorable rate of return less than 2.66 times the usual rate of return. On the other hand, requiring a favorable rate of return more than 4.07 times the usual rate of return to invest in the risky project would put you into the most risk-averse third.

If you would take the lawsuit to court with less than a 38% chance of winning, you are a relative risk taker. Holding out for at least a 51% chance of winning the case before you would take the

Table 12.3 Your Business Risk Profile

Instructions: Transfer your measures for the risky business situations in Table 12.1 to the "Measure" column of Table 12.3. Then for each measure put a check (✓) in the column under "Relative Risk Propensity" that corresponds to your answer. Total the number of checks in each column to obtain your Business Risk Profile.

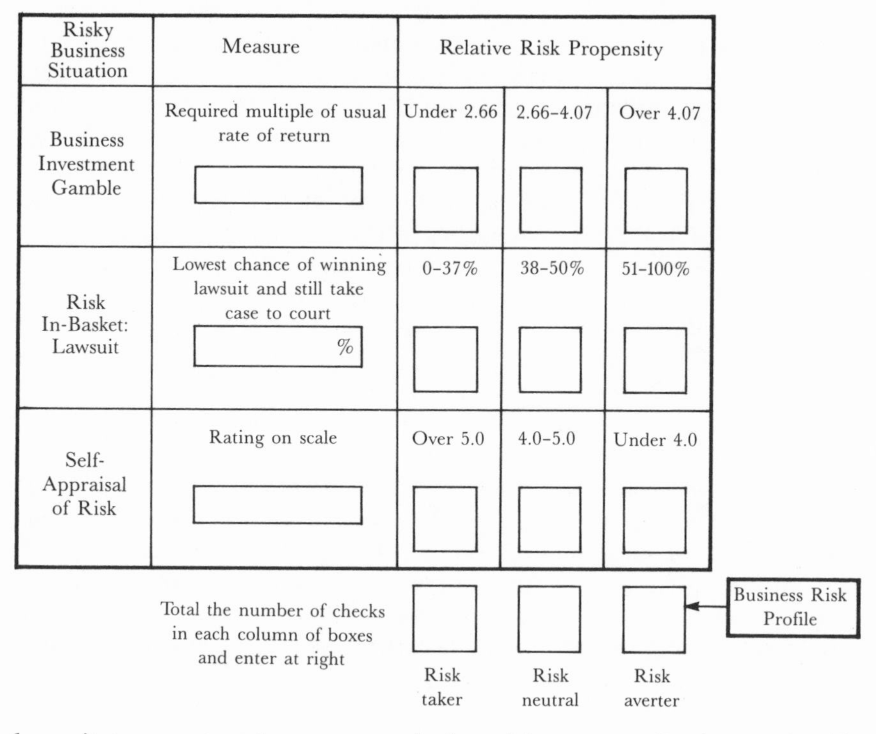

Risky Business Situation	Measure	Relative Risk Propensity		
Business Investment Gamble	Required multiple of usual rate of return	Under 2.66	2.66–4.07	Over 4.07
Risk In-Basket: Lawsuit	Lowest chance of winning lawsuit and still take case to court %	0–37%	38–50%	51–100%
Self-Appraisal of Risk	Rating on scale	Over 5.0	4.0–5.0	Under 4.0
	Total the number of checks in each column of boxes and enter at right	Risk taker	Risk neutral	Risk averter ← Business Risk Profile

lawsuit to court makes you a relative risk averter. Rating yourself above five on the risk self-appraisal scale puts you into the relative risk-taking category, while a score below four makes you a relative risk averter.

Make sure to put a check in the column of Table 12.3 that corresponds to your answer for each of the business risk measures. Once these checks have been entered, total the number of checks in each column to obtain your Business Risk Profile.

The inverted triangle in the bottom of Figure 12.1 provides a diagram of the possible Business Risk Profiles. Again the profiles for which the three risk measures are completely consistent appear at the corners of the triangle. We have inverted the business risk triangle so that the risk-taking and risk-averting corners of both triangles are adjacent to one another. Take your Business Risk Profile from Table 12.3 and use the table in the lower left of Figure 12.1 to find its letter position. Circle this letter to indicate it is your Business Risk Profile.

The average Business Risk Profile for the managers in our study occurs at point K in the center of the diagram and it provides a basis for comparison.[7]

Nineteen percent of our managers had their Business Risk Profiles located at point K. If your Business Risk Profile is here, you are about as willing to take business risks as our managers. If your profile is at positions Q, R, or S, you are more of a risk taker in business decisions than most managers. Twenty-eight percent of the managers were located at these three points, including 3% at the consistent risk-taking position R. You are a risk averter compared with our managers if your Business Risk Profile is at points L, M, or T. Twenty-six percent of the managers were located here, including 3% at the consistent risk-averting position L. You are more neutral to business risks than our managers if your position is at N, O, or P where 27% of the managers are located, including 5% at the consistent risk-neutral position O.

USES OF RISK PORTFOLIOS AND RISK PROFILES

Risk portfolios and their corresponding risk profiles such as the ones constructed in the preceding sections can be used for a variety of purposes. First, they provide an opportunity for an individual to learn about his own willingness to take personal or business risks. An awareness of one's willingness to take personal risks is useful in selecting personal investments, deciding how much debt to hold, and evaluating both insurance and gambling opportunities. Knowing your willingness to take business risks can facilitate evaluation of alternative business ventures. Being aware of your own disposition toward risk allows you to make decisions in risky situations that are consistent with this risk propensity.

Risk profiles can also be used as an evaluation tool. Is a prospective candidate suitable for a job, career, or firm that requires a particular attitude toward risk? Will the candidate be averse to most risks as befits the image of a conservative banker? Will he be willing to take the chances required by the entrepreneurial venture capitalist or oil wildcatter? Will he fit in as an investment partner in a firm of high rollers? More generally, does a candidate have managerial potential as evidenced by a willingness to take risks in some situations? Risk profiles can be used either as self-assessment devices whereby individuals can evaluate their own suitability for a job, career, or firm or as a screening device by organizations.

A third use for risk portfolios is as training devices. Such devices can be used for increasing self-awareness of one's willingness to take risks or for either promoting or discouraging risk taking. Using a risk portfolio in a group setting with participants showing their responses can expand one's views of the variety of ways to respond to risky situations. If a firm wishes to promote risk taking among its managers, the training session can include a positive assessment of risk-taking responses and their importance to the firm. A similar bias in favor of risk aversion can be injected if the firm wishes its managers to avoid risks. The training sessions can also be arranged to encourage either conformity of each individual's risk propensity or diversity among the members' responses.

We will discuss a fourth use of risk portfolios to construct Organizational Risk Profiles for individual firms in the next section.

ORGANIZATIONAL RISK PROFILE FOR A FIRM

By developing an Organizational Risk Profile for a firm we can address several important questions. Do the senior managers in a firm have similar or different propensities toward business risks? Are one or more senior managers out of step with the firm's stated policy concerning business risks? Are the firm's senior managers individually and collectively in step with the prevailing risk disposition in their industry?

We will illustrate the use of an Organizational Risk Profile for one of the corporations that participated in our study. Twenty-three firms had five or more managers who participated in the study. From this group we chose a large primary resources firm for illustration. Its five participants included the chairman and chief executive officer, the president and chief operating officer, a senior vice-president, and two vice-presidents. The Business Risk Profiles for the five executives are displayed in the Organizational Risk Profile for the firm in Figure 12.2.

The chairman and chief executive officer was a consistent risk averter in the three situations. He refused to accept the business investment gamble no matter how favorable the possible return on the risky project. He also would not take the lawsuit to court unless there was at least a 70% chance of winning the case. The chairman rated himself as less willing to take business risks than other executives in his firm. His self-appraisal of his willingness to take business risks was indeed accurate because his answers to the business investment gamble and lawsuit decisions were far more risk-averse than those of the other four participating managers from his firm.

The president and chief operating officer, on the other hand, is located near the "risk taker" corner with two risk-taking and one

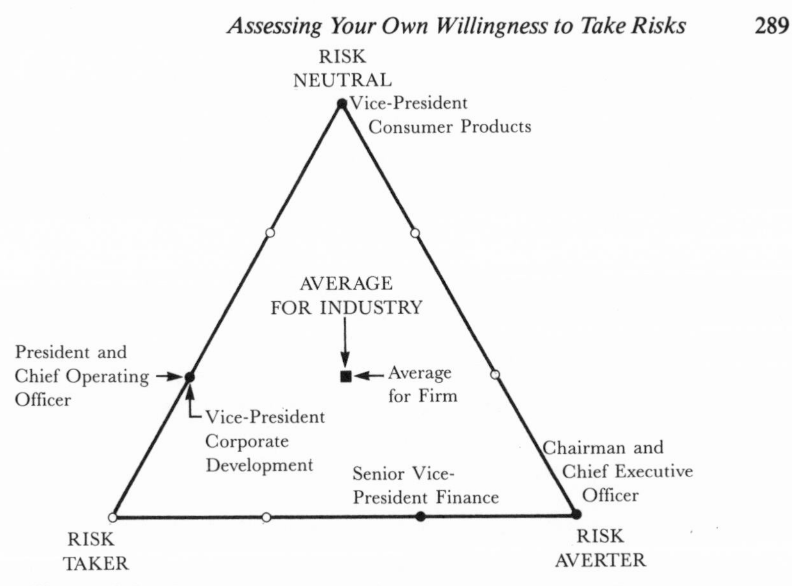

Figure 12.2 Organizational Risk Profile: Large Primary Resources Firm

risk-neutral answers. He would invest in the risky project if it had at least three times the usual rate of return and would take the lawsuit to court with only a 25% chance of success. He rated himself as more willing to take business risks than other managers in his firm. This self-appraisal was true for the lawsuit situation where he gave the most risk-taking response, but he was in the middle of the managers in his willingness to invest in the risky project.

The senior vice-president for finance has a Business Risk Profile similar to that of the chairman. He sees himself as a risk averter compared with other managers in the firm and requires at least five times the usual rate of return to invest in the risky project. His willingness to take the lawsuit to court with a 33% chance of success makes him a risk taker relative to all managers in the study, but places him in the middle of the managers in his firm. The financial vice-president's position near the "risk averter" corner is consistent with the stereotype of the careful and conservative manager who guards the firm's resources.

The Business Risk Profile for the vice-president for corporate development is located at the same position as that of the president. This vice-president is willing to invest in the risky project if it has the potential for only 2.5 times the usual rate of return and he will take the lawsuit to court with only a 30% chance of winning. He also sees himself as more willing to take risks than the firm's other managers.

The vice-president for consumer products is in the risk-neutral group for all three situations. He sees himself as about as willing to take risks as other managers in his firm. This view is confirmed by his answers to the business investment gamble and lawsuit situations which are near the middle of those given by the other managers.

Overall, then, we find quite different inclinations toward business risks among these five top managers in the firm. Two managers are inclined to take risks, two are inclined to avoid risks, and one is neutral to risk. Wide differences among executives such as the risk aversion of the chairman (chief executive officer) and the risk taking of the president (chief operating officer) can form the basis for major conflicts within a firm. Alternatively, such differences can provide a healthy tension that ensures that competing options and policies are examined and debated.

The wide dispersion of the risk profiles in Figure 12.2 demonstrates that a majority of the firm's managers would be out of step with any stated policy toward risk issued by the firm. If conformance to the risk-averse policy of the chairman were desired, major changes in attitude toward risk would be required of the president and both vice-presidents. Conformance to the average risk profile for the firm, located in the center of Figure 12.2, would require more moderate changes in attitude from all five managers.

Deciding the firm's policy regarding risk requires an assessment of the prevalent attitude toward risk in the industry. The average risk profile for the executives in the primary resources firms in our study was also at the center of Figure 12.2. Our designated firm, then, can choose to be more or less willing to take business risks than other firms in the industry with a change in attitude (or in personnel) of a few key managers. A firm may discover that its executives, on average, are less (or more) willing to take risks than managers in other firms in their industry. Such a discrepancy may confirm the firm's desired policy to accept fewer risks than other firms in the industry. Alternatively, it may reveal a previously unknown reluctance to take chances compared with other firms. In the latter case the firm's managers can consider where the Organizational Risk Profile should be relative to the industry and begin to make any necessary changes.

INDIVIDUAL RISK PROFILES

We have illustrated the use of risk profiles based on just a few risk measures. By considering risk measures derived from a wide portfolio of risky situations, we can develop a more comprehensive risk profile that includes both personal and business measures. For example, we can use the standardized situations considered in Chapter 8 and the natural situations and attitudes considered in Chapter 9 to derive 16 risk measures.

These measures can be separated into three relative risk categories, as was done earlier in this chapter. These measures could then form the basis for risk profile "triangles" as in Figure 12.1. Instead of using such triangles, however, we will portray this comprehensive Individual Risk Profile by giving a person's *decile* on each risk measure compared with the managers in our study.[8] See Figure 12.3 for these Individual Risk Profiles for the chairman and president of the large primary resources firm.[9]

Earlier we saw that the chairman fell into the most risk-averse group of managers on the three selected business measures. The profile in Figure 12.3 provides a more detailed comparison of the chairman's risk inclinations with those of other managers. In the lawsuit situation the chairman is in the *ninth decile* which means between 80% and 90% of the managers are more risk-taking than he. In the business investment gamble having a 50% chance of loss the chairman is in the *tenth decile* so he is in the most risk-averse 10% of executives in this situation. The chairman's self-appraisal of his risk disposition places him in the *tenth decile*, so here too only about 10% of the managers see themselves as more risk-averse.

The Individual Risk Profile in Figure 12.3 shows how the chairman's risk propensities compare with our representative sample of hundreds of other managers not only on the three selected business measures, but on all of the risk measures we have focused on throughout the book. In the four standardized business situations displayed on the top of Figure 12.3 we see that the chairman is in the most risk-averse third on all of them. His risk measures fall in the ninth and tenth deciles, confirming our earlier conclusion about his aversion toward business risks. In the four standardized personal situations, however, he tends to be risk-neutral on average, where his risk measures place him mostly in the fifth and sixth deciles. Considering the natural situations which deal primarily with personal finances, we find the chairman again risk neutral and even risk taking in his holding of high risky assets and low life insurance. Likewise the chairman shows risk-neutral or risk-taking attitudes regarding a desire for sensation and a belief in his ability to control his environment. The Individual Risk Profile shows that while risk-averse in his business decisions, the chairman is much more prepared to take risks in his personal decisions compared with other managers.

The Individual Risk Profile shows a different picture for the firm's president. The president is a consistent risk taker in many of the situations. Among the four standardized business situations and the self-appraisal of willingness to take business risks, the president is in the most risk-taking group on all but one, averaging about the third decile. Similarly he is in the most risk-taking group in most of the standardized personal situations and the natural situations where

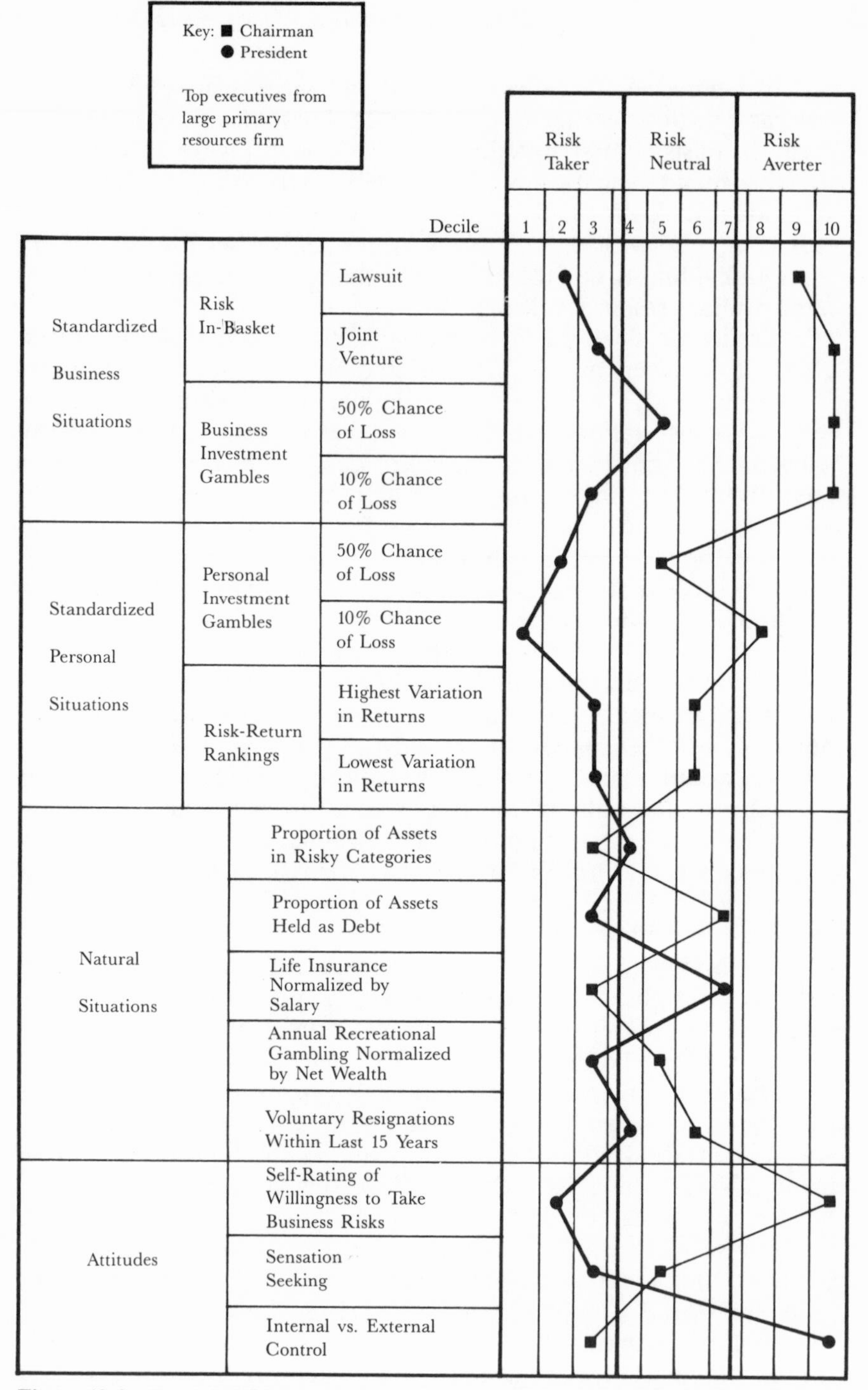

Figure 12.3 Extended Risk Profiles Derived from Standardized Situations, Natural Situations, and Attitudes: Managers within Same Firm

he averages below the fourth decile. Even his position as a relative risk averter on the internal versus external control measure is mitigated by his absolute risk-taking response being overwhelmed by the extreme risk-taking responses of the majority of managers.

Comparing the willingness to take risks of managers in the same firm is easy using the Individual Risk Profiles. The position of the president's profile far to the left of the chairman's for the standardized business situations shows the president is substantially more willing to take business risks than the chairman. Even in the standardized personal situations the president appears much more willing to assume risks. The interpretation of the natural situations and the attitudes (regarding sensation and control) is more equivocal and no trend is apparent.

Individual Risk Profiles can also be used to make insightful comparisons between top executives from different firms. Such comparisons are most useful if the executives head up firms in the same industry. We present the Individual Risk Profiles for the presidents of two pharmaceutical firms in Figure 12.4.[10]

The president of firm A is more willing to take business risks than the president of firm B on the basis of the standardized business situations and the self-appraisal. Only in the joint venture are they equally risk-taking. In an industry like the pharmaceutical industry which requires substantial risk taking firm A would seem to have a distinct advantage with its more entrepreneurial president.

The personal risk dispositions of the two presidents compare very differently in the standardized and natural situations. On the standardized personal investment gambles and Risk-Return Rankings firm A's president is more willing to take personal risks than firm B's president. The reverse is true in the natural situations. Such a discrepancy demonstrates the importance of using a portfolio to measure willingness to take risks. The consistency of willingness to take personal risks in standardized and natural situations of the president in Figure 12.3 makes us more confident that this executive is risk-taking for personal risks.

Risk profiles can be extended in other ways as well. For example, in Chapter 3 we emphasized the risk adjustments used by executives such as gathering information, bargaining, delay, and delegation. Extending the risk profile to include the presence or absence of these modifications would provide useful complementary information on the managers' risk behavior. The focus on investment attributes in Chapter 5 would also add an extra dimension to the risk profiles. Whether the managers focus primarily on loss, gain, or expected return should provide useful insight into how the executives recognize and evaluate risky investments. Additional natural situations such as

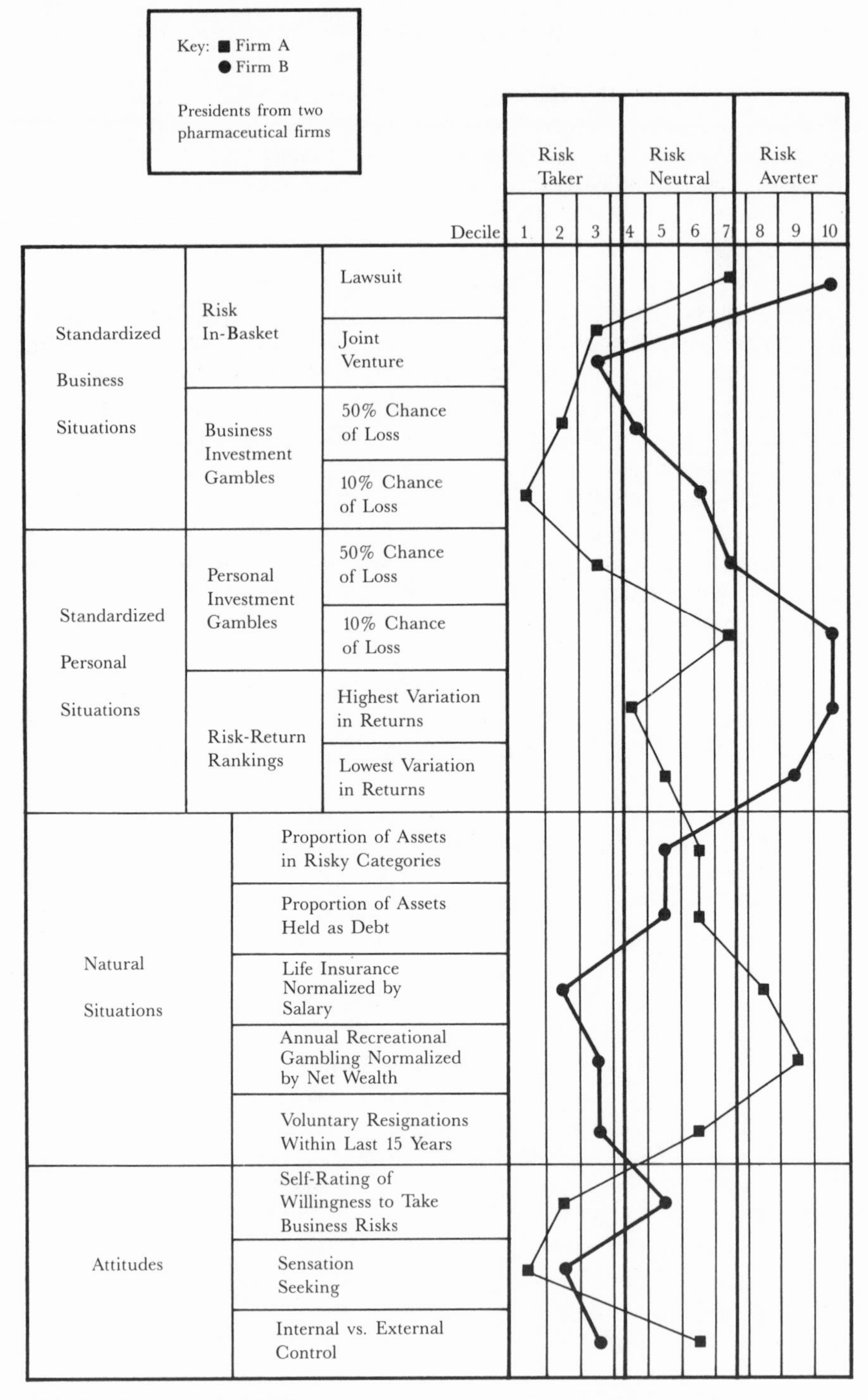

Figure 12.4 Extended Risk Profiles Derived from Standardized Situations, Natural Situations, and Attitudes: Managers in Different Firms

whether the manager personally initiated major changes in his firm's operations can be used to broaden the risk profile, as can additional attitude information such as one's attitude toward losing.

SUMMARY

In this chapter we have shown you how you can make a preliminary assessment of your own willingness to take risks in both personal and business situations. Such assessments are especially useful when they can be compared with those of other managers such as the managers who participated in our study. We have also explored different ways of summarizing these comparisons over the large number of risky situations examined in this book. These summaries provide a useful mechanism for managers to compare themselves with other managers in their own firm. They also establish a framework for developing a risk policy for the firm and for making comparisons with other firms in the industry.

Appendix

Questionnaires in the Risk Portfolio

Questionnaires in the Risk Portfolio

Original Title	*Title Used in the Text*	*Pages in Original Questionnaire*	*Pages Included in Appendix*
General Questionnaire	General Questionnaire	8	8
In-Basket Decisions	Risk In-Basket	16	6
Investment Choices Under Uncertainty	Investment Gambles	11	4
Personal Investment Preferences	Risk-Return Rankings	7	7
Money Wagers	Real Money Wagers	7	2
Societal Attitude Questionnaire	Societal Attitude Questionnaire	4	0

Anticipated time to complete this booklet: 20 minutes

GENERAL QUESTIONNAIRE

NOTE: This questionnaire asks you for information about your personal and business status. We are very much aware that some of the answers you provide should be treated very confidentially. As we stated previously, your answers to all the booklets will be confidential. This booklet, however, will be treated with special care. A code number, not your name, will be used to identify the forms. The master list linking names to code numbers will be known only to the principal researchers. Even with the code numbers, this questionnaire will only be used for the purposes of this study and will be held in the possession of the researchers at all times.

This booklet is for the exclusive use of the Mobius Group. For further information contact:

Professor K. R. MacCrimmon
Faculty of Commerce and Business Administration
University of British Columbia
Vancouver 8, B.C., Canada

I. <u>DEMOGRAPHIC DATA</u>

A. Year of Birth: ________________

B. Marital Status:

[ ] *married* [ ] *separated* [ ] *widowed*

[ ] *single* [ ] *divorced*

C. Number of dependents (wife, children): ___________

D. Citizenship and residence:

1. Citizenship at birth: ________________________________

2. Present citizenship: ________________________________

3. Country of current residence: _________________________

4. Length of residence: _________________________ *years*

5. If country of residence is different from citizenship--

   are you a permanent resident?

   Yes [ ] *No* [ ]

E. Education:

1. Secondary (highest grade completed): ___________________

2. Higher education:

<u>Degree(s)</u>	<u>Specialization</u>
______________	____________________________
______________	____________________________
______________	____________________________

3. Professional/technical qualifications (e.g., C.P.A., C.A., P.Eng., etc.)

   ____

   ____

II. ECONOMIC DATA

A. Income (1972 calendar year, pre-tax):

1. Total income from employment (include only realized income from salary, bonuses, and profit sharing):

$

2. Total outside income (director's fees, interest, dividends, capital gains or losses, etc.):

$

B. Gross assets (current value of personal property, real property, financial assets, stock options, pension plans, insurance policies, etc.):

$

C. Liabilities (mortgages, personal loans, etc.):

$

D. Insurance:

1. Total face value of *life* insurance paid for by

you: $

your company: $

2. Percent of salary covered by *disability* insurance paid for by

you: %

your company: %

3. Do you purchase *travel* insurance at airports before flights?

yes [ ] *no* [ ]

If you do:

On what percentage of your trips do you buy it? %

What amount do you usually buy? $

E. Do you save voluntarily on a systematic basis?

[ ] *yes* [ ] *no*

If you do, what amount do you usually set aside and with what frequency?

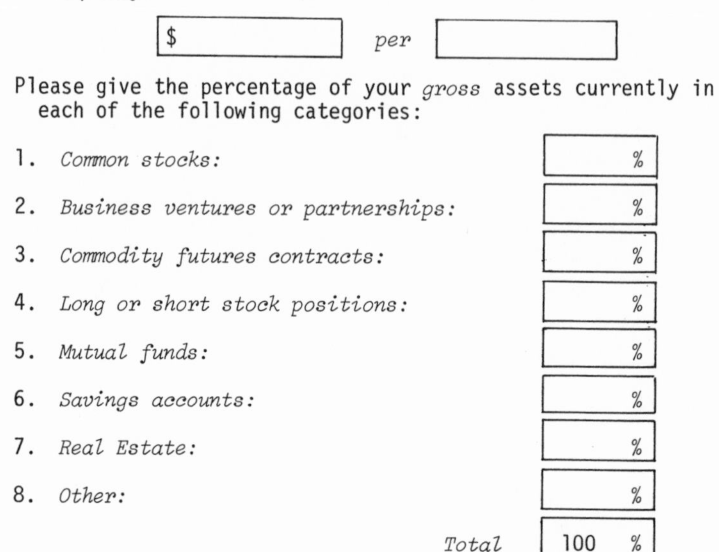

$ ______ *per* ______

F. Please give the percentage of your *gross* assets currently in each of the following categories:

1. *Common stocks:* ______ %
2. *Business ventures or partnerships:* ______ %
3. *Commodity futures contracts:* ______ %
4. *Long or short stock positions:* ______ %
5. *Mutual funds:* ______ %
6. *Savings accounts:* ______ %
7. *Real Estate:* ______ %
8. *Other:* ______ %

Total 100 %

G. Please indicate the number of times in the last 12 months that you have engaged in any of the following activities and also give the average amount wagered per occasion:

1. Gambling in established casinos (Las Vegas, Bahamas, Monte Carlo, etc.)

   Number of times: ______

   Average total wagered per occasion: $ ______

2. Betting on own recreational activities (golf, poker, etc.):

   Number of times: ______

   Average stake per game: $ ______

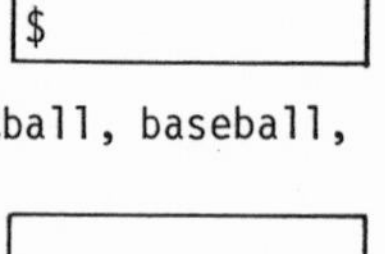

3. Betting on professional sports (e.g., football, baseball, horse racing, etc.):

   Number of times: ______

   Average stake per occasion: $ ______

H. In what recreational activities which some people may consider *hazardous* have you participated in the past 12 months?

____

____

Which of these do *you* consider hazardous?

____

III. <u>JOB INFORMATION</u>

A. Please give your job title and a brief description of your major responsibilities:

Job title: ________________________________

Description: ________________________________

____

____

____

,. How long have you been

With your present employer? __________ *years*

In your present position? __________ *years*

C. How many levels separate you from the chief executive in your firm? [ ]

D. In what functional area of business have you spent most of your career? (e.g., Finance, Marketing, Accounting, Production, etc.)

____

E. Over what corporate resources do you have *primary* decision-making responsibility?

1. Annual operating budget: $
2. Annual capital expenditures budget: $
3. Largest single capital expenditure which you may personally authorize *without* review: $
4. Total number of managerial personnel under your direction:
5. Annual salary of highest position for which you have primary hiring and firing authority:

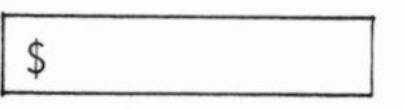

F. How many times in the last *15* years have you voluntarily resigned to take a position with a different employer:

1. *With* another job lined up:
2. *Without* another job lined up:

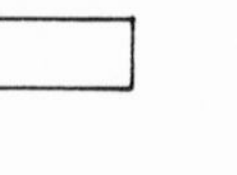

G. When making decisions, do you gather *more* or *less* information than other managers?

less 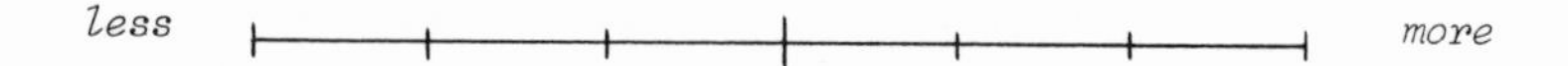 *more*

H. When making decisions, do you take *more* or *less* time deliberating than other managers?

less  *more*

I. What do you mean when you describe a business situation as *"risky?"* What are the important characteristics of a *"risky"* situation?

____

____

____

____

____

J. How would you rate your *own* willingness to undertake risky business propositions as compared to *other* executives at or near your level in *your firm?*

much less willing to accept risks	1	2	3	4	5	6	7	*much more willing to accept risks*

K. How would you rate *your firm's* willingness to undertake risky business propositions as compared to *other firms in the industry?*

much less willing to accept risks								*much more willing to accept risks*

L. When you have been faced with a risky business situation, what specific *actions* have you taken (or recommended the firm take) to *reduce* the risk to your firm? Please be as specific as you can.

____

____

____

____

____

Please turn to the next page.

IV. CHANGES IN YOUR FIRM'S OPERATIONS

Listed below you will find a number of areas in which there could have been *significant changes* in *your company's operations* in the past 5 years. Since the list is fairly general, it may be incomplete. Consequently we have provided room under "Other" for you to include additional *significant* changes in your company's operations. In the box to the right of each of the possible significant changes in company operations, please indicate by using the appropriate letter into which category the change in operations should be classified:

[A] You personally initiated significant change(s) in this area.

[B] You were part of the decision-making group responsible for initiating change(s) in this area.

[C] Significant change(s) in this area occurred in the company but you were not involved in initiating them.

[D] Significant change(s) in this area did not occur in the company in the past 5 years.

Significant Changes in Company Operations	Classification (Please specify) A, B, C, or D
New products, services, or production processes	[ ]
New domestic markets	[ ]
Mergers, acquisitions	[ ]
Major changes in organizational structure	[ ]
Foreign investment, or marketing, decisions	[ ]
Major changes in research and development policy	[ ]
Retrenchments, cutbacks, sell-offs	[ ]

Other: (Please specify)

______________________________	[ ]
______________________________	[ ]
______________________________	[ ]
______________________________	[ ]

Anticipated time to complete this booklet: 45 minutes

IN-BASKET DECISIONS

(Risk In-Basket)

INSTRUCTIONS: In this booklet we ask you to take on the role of the vice-president of a large multinational corporation. You are requested to respond to the letters and memos in his in-basket and then to further specify the decisions you have taken by answering a short questionnaire.

This booklet is for the exclusive use of the Mobius Group. For further information contact:

Professor K. R. MacCrimmon
Faculty of Commerce and Business Administration
University of British Columbia
Vancouver 8, B.C., Canada

I N - B A S K E T   D E C I S I O N S

Please act as if you are Bill Bickner, Vice-President, North American Operations of Multinational Products, Inc. Formerly the president of the Connecticut subsidiary, you have just replaced James Norton, who died last week of a heart attack. Because you were notified of this new appointment only very recently, you have had little time to become acquainted with the job.

Today is Wednesday, March 14. You have arrived in your new office for the first time. It is 7:45 p.m. and you must leave promptly at 8:20 p.m. to catch the 9:30 plane to Mexico City for an important meeting. You will not be back until Thursday, March 22.

The letters and memos in this booklet were left in the in-basket on your desk by Annabel, your secretary. Read through the set of materials and specify whatever action you deem appropriate on each item. Your assistant will take care of the final drafting of the letters; however, every action you wish to take should be carefully specified in the form of memos or wires. Be sure to indicate in the memos or wires to whom they are addressed. Please write them on the blank Memo sheets. (A partial organization chart is given on page   )

You are to use your own experience as the basis for your decisions in the role of Bill Bickner.

NOTE:

THE DAY IS *WEDNESDAY, MARCH 14*. TIME: *7:45 p.m.*

THE TELEPHONE SWITCHBOARD IS *CLOSED*.

WRITE DOWN EVERY ACTION YOU WISH TO TAKE ON ANY ITEM. YOU CANNOT CALL ON ANYONE FOR ASSISTANCE. YOU MUST WORK WITH THE MATERIALS AT HAND. YOU WILL BE OUT OF THE OFFICE FROM 8:20 P.M. UNTIL NEXT THURSDAY, MARCH 22. YOU CANNOT TAKE ANY OF THE MATERIALS WITH YOU ON THE TRIP.

(1) Please read the letters and memos carefully and write your response to each of the four items on the adjacent memo sheets. (Time to complete: 35 minutes)

(2) After you have written responses to the correspondence, please answer parts A and B of the *questionnaire* at the end of this booklet. (Anticipated time to complete: 10 minutes)

MULTINATIONAL PRODUCTS, INC.

MEMORANDUM

TO Mr. Bickner

FROM Annabel

March 14 1973

These are the letters and memoranda that need immediate attention. From past experience I would say that the four problems all fall under your jurisdiction. I know that the meetings in Mexico City will take up much of your time and that you won't have an opportunity to take care of these matters while you are there. I'm sorry that I won't be around tonight to help you.

See you next week.

Annabel

DOMINION INTEGRATED PRODUCTS LTD.
487 WEST 83RD STREET
VANCOUVER 13, CANADA

March 9, 1973

Mr. James Norton, Vice President
Multinational Products, Inc.
North American Headquarters
519 Madison Avenue
New York, N.Y. 10018

Dear Jim:

This is with reference to the PMG case I mentioned in my letter of February 27th. As I indicated, PMG has threatened to sue Dominion Integrated for patent violation. The case has not yet been filed in court, since PMG are waiting to hear our response to their offer to settle out of court. They have proposed that we pay them $300,000 in cash and agree to drop our Duraplast line, which our finance people estimate would involve an additional loss, in present value terms, of about $500,000 (10% of our 1972 profit).

If we do not agree to this proposal, PMG will file their suit, which would, if we lose the case, probably involve a loss of $1,100,000 in damages plus the loss of dropping the Duraplast line. On the other hand, if we win in court, we will incur only a small sum for legal expenses. Our corporate lawyer, Mr. Bell, and our outside law firm agree that the chance of our losing the case in court is 50%.

We have been given one week from today to respond to PMG's settlement offer; I've tried to postpone this deadline, unsuccessfully. What do you recommend?

Please call or wire me as soon as possible. Best regards.

Yours sincerely,

Don

Donald T. Moore
President

DTM/cg

MULTINATIONAL PRODUCTS, INC.

MEMORANDUM

TO Mr. James Norton

Vice-President, North American Operations

FROM Alfred Kaye

Project Coordinator, Southwest Project

March 1 1973

Re: Arizona Proposal, File #69081

Since November of last year my project team, as requested by the Economic Planning Director, has been conducting an investigation of the possibility of investment in the Southwest.

Our investigation has been completed and our interim report has been sent to Economic Planning. As always, the final action rests in your hands. The final report will be sent to you by the end of next week. In this memo, I wish to draw your attention to something unexpected that came up while we were in the process of preparing the final report. We learned that our major competitor ATC has sent a team to Arizona for the same purpose. Their analysis and recommendations have been reported to be the same as ours.

Yesterday, two representatives from ATC came to visit us and made the following proposition: that Multinational Products join up with ATC for a joint venture in order to reduce the destructive effects that always follow market entry by big competitors. They are determined to develop the Southwest market, but the issue of whether to invest alone or go in as a joint venture has not been resolved. Should we prefer to enter into a joint venture, our lawyers have assured me there are no legal (i.e., anti-trust) obstacles to doing so. If we refuse, then ATC will enter and this could mean aggressive competition.

Our new analysis indicates that, in competition with ATC, capturing a large market share would give us an after-tax ROI of 22%, while capturing a small market share would give us a return of 10%. We estimate our chance of getting a large market share to be 1 in 3. If we were to team up with ATC on the terms proposed, our return would be 14% after tax, with the same total investment.

Either way, the investment seems attractive. ATC has asked us for a decision by March 19. Please let us know your decision as soon as possible.

cc: Director, Economic Planning

B. ASSIGNING THE LOWEST ACCEPTABLE CHANCES

1. LETTER FROM DONALD MOORE, DOMINION INTEGRATED

If the chances of winning the court case were 99 out of 100, you would probably recommend taking the case to court. On the other hand, if the chances of winning the court case were 1 out of 100, you would probably recommend accepting the settlement. As the chances were increased, there would be a point at which you would decide to refuse the settlement. What is this switch-over point; that is, what is the *lowest* chance of winning that would prompt you to take the case to court?

What is the lowest chance of winning in court against PMG that you would need to recommend that the case be taken to court?

ANSWER: _______ out of 100

Or check the appropriate box if you

(a) *would not* take the case to court no matter what the chances [ ]

(b) *would* take the case to court no matter what the chances [ ]

Anticipated time to complete this booklet: 20 minutes

INVESTMENT CHOICES UNDER UNCERTAINTY

(Investment Gambles)

INSTRUCTIONS: This booklet contains two sets of questions about hypothetical investment choices to be made under conditions of uncertainty. The first set of questions (on pages) relates to personal investments; the second set of questions (on pages) relates to business investments.

This booklet is for the exclusive use of the Mobius Group. For further information contact:

Professor K. R. MacCrimmon
Faculty of Commerce and Business Administration
University of British Columbia
Vancouver 8, B.C., Canada

PERSONAL INVESTMENT CHOICES

1. Please estimate your *total current net wealth:* $

2. Suppose that you are offered a chance to invest *one-half* your current net wealth in a new venture. If the venture is *successful,* you could end up with a very sizeable gain which could have a significant impact on your life style; if the venture is a *failure,* you could lose your investment and thus end up with only one-half your current wealth. Such a loss might entail liquidating some of your assets, cutting back on some current activities, etc. The *chances* of winning or losing are *50-50.*

   If the possible gain is too low, for example only a small fraction of the possible loss, you might be unwilling to invest one-half your net wealth. You might, however, invest one-half your wealth in such a venture if the possible gain were 20 times larger than the possible loss. By picking numbers between these extremes, you can determine the *smallest* possible gain you would require in deciding to invest.

   QUESTION: *For you to risk one-half your current wealth in a new venture having a 50-50 chance of succeeding, how large would the possible gain from such an investment have to be?*

   Before writing this amount, in dollars, in the box at the bottom of the page, you may find it helpful to use the following *diagram:*

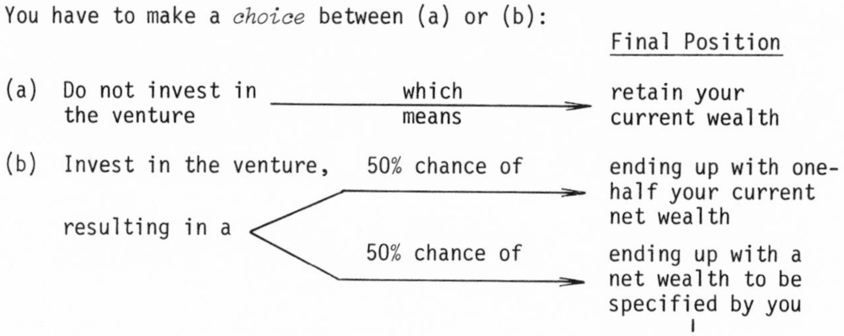

   You have to make a *choice* between (a) or (b):

			Final Position
(a)	Do not invest in the venture	which means →	retain your current wealth
(b)	Invest in the venture, resulting in a	50% chance of →	ending up with one-half your current net wealth
		50% chance of →	ending up with a net wealth to be specified by you

   ANSWER: *Smallest possible final net wealth you would require to make the investment:* $

   NOTE: If this amount is less than 150% of your total net wealth, please review your answer to be sure that it reflects your true preference. If this amount is many times larger than your total net wealth, please ask yourself whether you would take the venture even if the possible gain were a lesser amount. If so, please revise your answer.

BUSINESS INVESTMENT CHOICES

1. What is your firm's (or division's) *capital expenditure budget* this year? * | $ |

2. What is your firm's (or division's) *expected rate of return* on major investments from this budget? | % |

*NOTE: If in your firm you do not deal with a capital expenditure budget, please give, instead, the investment budget that you do customarily deal with (i.e., a major category of funds for which a rate of return is usually calculated). The questions that follow will deal with decisions for allocating this budget.

Type of budget: ____________________

____

Amount:

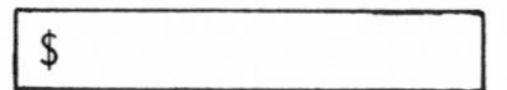

3. Suppose that this year you can invest in standard projects that will yield your firm its expected rate of return, or you can invest *one-half* the budget (specified in your answer to Question 1) in a major project that is subject to considerable *uncertainty*. The project may prove to be *unsuccessful*, in which case you would recoup your investment but would make no profit (hence, a zero rate of return). On the other hand, the project may be very *successful*, yielding a rate of return considerably higher than the average. The *chances* of success or failure are *50-50*.

   If the rate of return from the project (if it is successful) is only slightly higher than average, then you might be unwilling to invest--settling instead for the standard projects with certainty of getting the expected rate of return. However, you might be very willing to invest if the possible yield from the project, if it is successful, were 10 times the average rate of return. By picking rate of return figures between these extremes, you should be able to determine the *smallest* rate of return you would accept and still decide to invest in the uncertain project.

   QUESTION: *For you to invest half your capital expenditure budget in the uncertain project, how large would the possible rate of return have to be?*

   Before writing the required rate of return in the box at the bottom of the page, you may find it helpful to use the following *diagram:*

   You are being asked to specify the *smallest* rate of return on a successful project for which you will take action (b) over action (a):

		Final Position
(a) Invest in the standard projects	which means →	ending up with the current average rate of return
(b) Invest in the uncertain project which will result in a	50% chance of →	ending up with a zero rate of return on the uncertain project and the usual rate of return on the other half of your capital expenditures.
	50% chance of →	ending up with a rate of return *to be specified by you* on the uncertain project and the usual rate of return on the other half of your capital expenditures.

   ANSWER: *Smallest rate of return on the uncertain project you would accept in making the investment:* [%]

   NOTE: If this figure is less than twice as large as your average rate of return, please review your answer to make sure that it reflects your true preference. If the figure in the box is many times larger than your average rate of return, please ask yourself whether you would invest even if the rate of return were lower. If so, please revise your answer.

Anticipated time to complete this booklet: 20 minutes

PERSONAL INVESTMENT PREFERENCES

(Risk-Return Rankings)

INSTRUCTIONS: In this booklet we ask you for your preferences for various pairs of hypothetical personal investments. These investments are ventures that differ in the rate of return that is expected and in the possible variation in the return. There are no right answers--please state your true preferences.

This booklet is for the exclusive use of the Mobius Group. For further information contact:

Professor K. R. MacCrimmon
Faculty of Commerce and Business Administration
University of British Columbia
Vancouver 8, B.C., Canada

PERSONAL INVESTMENT PREFERENCES

We would like to ascertain your preferences for various *combinations* of *rate of return* and *rate of variation* in investment opportunities. Suppose that you are considering the investment of 10% of your current net wealth in a venture whose payoffs are uncertain, but for which the expected *rate of return* and *rate of variation* in return are known quite accurately. You will be asked to compare several such ventures which have different rates of return and rates of variation--although they are identical in all other respects.

Rate of return is a familiar concept, but rate of variation may be an unfamiliar concept. We will illustrate it by an example. Suppose a venture has a rate of return of 20% and a rate of variation of 50%. This combination of return and variation means that there is:

- a 5% chance of a gain of 100% or more on your original investment
- a 27% chance of a gain of 50% or more
- a 66% chance of no loss
- a 27% chance of a loss of 10% or more
- an 8% chance of a loss of 50% or more
- a 1% chance of a loss of all of the original investment.

These figures, and those for the other possible combinations of rate of return and rate of variation, are given in the *table* at the *end* of this *booklet*. In general, the higher the rate of return (for a fixed rate of variation), the *higher* the chance of *gains* and the *lower* the chance of *losses;* this can be seen by looking *down* the *columns* of the table. Also, the higher the rate of variation (for a given rate of return), the *higher* the chance of *large* gains *and large* losses, as can be seen by reading *across* the *rows* of the table.

We would now like you to compare each of several different ventures with one reference venture, called Venture R. This reference venture has the following rate of return and rate of variation characteristics:

Venture R:	Rate of return is 20%
	Rate of variation is 50%

This is the venture described in the example on the preceding page. We want you to compare each of the ventures listed below with Venture R, and decide in which one of the two you would prefer to invest 10% of your current net wealth. You must choose one or the other; you do not have the option not to invest.

Suppose that you have a choice between investing in Venture R or in Venture A:

Venture R		Venture A
Rate of return is 20%	or	Rate of return is 10%
Rate of variation is 50%		Rate of variation is 30%

You can see from the table that with Venture A you have no chance of more than a 100% gain, a 9% chance of more than a 50% gain, a 63% chance of at least coming out ahead, a 24% chance of at least a 10% loss, a 2% chance of at least a 50% loss, and no chance of a total loss of the invested capital. Would you prefer Venture R or Venture A?

I PREFER VENTURE _____

Now suppose instead that the choice is between Venture R and Venture B:

Venture R		Venture B
Rate of return is 20%	or	Rate of return is 30%
Rate of variation is 50%		Rate of variation is 70%

With Venture B, there is a 16% chance of a net gain exceeding 100% of your investment, but also a 13% chance of a net loss exceeding 50% (for the other chances check the table). Would you prefer R or B?

I PREFER VENTURE _____

Suppose instead that the choice is between Venture R and Venture C:

Venture R		Venture C
Rate of return is 20%	or	Rate of return is 15%
Rate of variation is 50%		Rate of variation is 60%

The various gain and loss chances associated with Venture C may be read from the table. Would you prefer R or C?

I PREFER VENTURE _____

Suppose instead that the choice is between Venture R and Venture D:

Venture R		Venture D
Rate of return is 20%	or	Rate of return is 5%
Rate of variation is 50%		Rate of variation is 40%

The gain and loss chances associated with Venture D may be read from the table. Would you prefer R or D?

I PREFER VENTURE _____

Suppose instead that the choice is between Venture R and Venture E:

Venture R		Venture E
Rate of return is 20%	or	Rate of return is 35%
Rate of variation is 50%		Rate of variation is 60%

The gain and loss chances associated with Venture E may be read from the table. Would you prefer R or E?

I PREFER VENTURE _____

Suppose instead that the choice is between Venture R and Venture F:

Venture R		Venture F
Rate of return is 20%	or	Rate of return is 25%
Rate of variation is 50%		Rate of variation is 40%

The gain and loss chances associated with Venture F may be read from the table. Would you prefer R or F?

I PREFER VENTURE _____

Suppose instead that the choice is between Venture R and Venture G:

Venture R		Venture G
Rate of return is 20%	or	Rate of return is 15%
Rate of variation is 50%		Rate of variation is 20%

The gain and loss chances associated with Venture G may be read from the table. Would you prefer R or G?

I PREFER VENTURE _____

Suppose instead that the choice is between Venture R and Venture H:

Venture R		Venture H
Rate of return is 20%	or	Rate of return is 25%
Rate of variation is 50%		Rate of variation is 80%

The gain and loss chances associated with Venture H may be read from the table. Would you prefer R or H?

I PREFER VENTURE _____

RANKING OF VENTURES

Now that you have become familiar with Ventures A through H separately, we would like you to compare them with each other directly. Please rank the 9 ventures (R, A, B, C, D, E, F, G, and H) in order of your preference on the list called "Ranking" below.

It may be helpful to use the following procedure. First, write in Box 1 the ventures you *preferred* to R. Then write in Box 2 the ventures you *did not prefer* to R. Next rank, in terms of your preferences, the ventures you have written in Box 1 and write them in this order at the top of the "Ranking" list. Then write "R" in the next position on the list. Finally, rank the ventures you have written in Box 2 and place them in order below R in the list.

Ventures preferred to R

Box 1 [   ]

[R]

Ventures not preferred to R

Box 2 [   ]

Ranking

Most preferred _____

_____

_____

_____

_____

_____

_____

_____

Least preferred _____

RATE OF RETURN	GAIN AND LOSS POSSIBILITIES	RATE OF VARIATION									
		10%	20%	30%	40%	50%	60%	70%	80%	90%	100%
5%	Gain of 100% or more	nil	nil	nil	1%	3%	5%	9%	12%	15%	17%
	Gain of 50% or more	nil	1%	7%	13%	18%	23%	26%	29%	31%	33%
	No loss	69%	60%	56%	55%	54%	53%	53%	52%	52%	52%
	Loss of 10% or more	7%	23%	31%	35%	38%	40%	42%	43%	44%	44%
	Loss of 50% or more	nil	nil	3%	8%	14%	18%	21%	24%	27%	29%
	Total loss	nil	nil	nil	nil	2%	4%	7%	10%	12%	15%
10%	Gain of 100% or more	nil	nil	nil	1%	4%	7%	9%	13%	16%	18%
	Gain of 50% or more	nil	2%	9%	16%	21%	25%	28%	31%	33%	34%
	No loss	84%	69%	63%	60%	58%	57%	55%	54%	54%	54%
	Loss of 10% or more	2%	16%	24%	31%	35%	37%	38%	40%	42%	42%
	Loss of 50% or more	nil	nil	2%	7%	12%	16%	19%	23%	25%	27%
	Total loss	nil	nil	nil	nil	1%	3%	5%	8%	11%	14%
15%	Gain of 100% or more	nil	nil	nil	2%	4%	8%	11%	14%	17%	20%
	Gain of 50% or more	nil	4%	12%	19%	24%	28%	31%	32%	34%	36%
	No loss	93%	77%	69%	65%	62%	60%	58%	57%	57%	56%
	Loss of 10% or more	1%	11%	20%	26%	31%	34%	36%	38%	39%	40%
	Loss of 50% or more	nil	nil	1%	5%	10%	14%	17%	21%	24%	26%
	Total loss	nil	nil	nil	nil	1%	3%	5%	7%	10%	12%
20%	Gain of 100% or more	nil	nil	nil	2%	5%	9%	12%	16%	18%	21%
	Gain of 50% or more	nil	7%	16%	23%	27%	31%	33%	35%	37%	39%
	No loss	98%	84%	76%	69%	66%	63%	62%	60%	59%	58%
	Loss of 10% or more	nil	7%	16%	23%	27%	31%	33%	35%	37%	38%
	Loss of 50% or more	nil	nil	1%	4%	8%	12%	16%	18%	21%	24%
	Total loss	nil	nil	nil	nil	1%	2%	4%	7%	9%	12%
25%	Gain of 100% or more	nil	nil	1%	3%	7%	11%	14%	17%	20%	23%
	Gain of 50% or more	1%	11%	20%	26%	31%	34%	36%	38%	39%	40%
	No loss	99%	88%	80%	74%	69%	67%	64%	62%	61%	60%
	Loss of 10% or more	nil	4%	13%	18%	24%	28%	31%	33%	34%	36%
	Loss of 50% or more	nil	nil	1%	3%	7%	11%	14%	17%	20%	23%
	Total loss	nil	nil	nil	nil	1%	2%	4%	6%	8%	12%
30%	Gain of 100% or more	nil	nil	1%	4%	8%	12%	16%	19%	22%	24%
	Gain of 50% or more	2%	16%	25%	31%	34%	37%	38%	40%	41%	42%
	No loss	100%	93%	84%	77%	73%	69%	66%	65%	63%	62%
	Loss of 10% or more	nil	2%	9%	16%	21%	25%	28%	31%	32%	34%
	Loss of 50% or more	nil	nil	nil	2%	5%	9%	13%	16%	18%	21%
	Total loss	nil	nil	nil	nil	nil	2%	3%	5%	8%	10%
35%	Gain of 100% or more	nil	nil	1%	5%	10%	13%	17%	21%	24%	26%
	Gain of 50% or more	7%	23%	31%	35%	38%	40%	42%	43%	44%	44%
	No loss	100%	96%	88%	81%	76%	72%	69%	67%	65%	64%
	Loss of 10% or more	nil	1%	7%	13%	18%	23%	26%	29%	31%	33%
	Loss of 50% or more	nil	nil	nil	2%	4%	8%	11%	14%	17%	20%
	Total loss	nil	nil	nil	nil	nil	1%	3%	4%	7%	9%
40%	Gain of 100% or more	nil	nil	2%	7%	12%	16%	19%	23%	25%	27%
	Gain of 50% or more	16%	31%	37%	40%	42%	44%	44%	45%	46%	46%
	No loss	100%	98%	91%	84%	79%	75%	72%	69%	68%	65%
	Loss of 10% or more	nil	1%	4%	11%	16%	20%	24%	27%	29%	31%
	Loss of 50% or more	nil	nil	nil	1%	4%	7%	10%	13%	16%	18%
	Total loss	nil	nil	nil	nil	nil	1%	2%	4%	6%	8%

Note: Heavy box denotes venture H.

Anticipated time to complete this booklet: 15 minutes

MONEY WAGERS

(Real Money Wagers)

INSTRUCTIONS: In this booklet you will be presented with three *sets* of wagers. Each set consists of five separate wagers. One of the options in each set guarantees that you will receive $10; the other four options in each set are actual *wagers* in which *you can win or lose.* We would like you to study the *options in each set* and then *rank them* in order, from most preferred to least preferred. Finally, we would like you to *rank the sets* by comparing only the first choice from each set.

These wagers involve *real money;* they are not hypothetical. During the interview, there is a chance that you will be selected to play out one of the options that you like. If you are selected and you win, we will pay you on the spot. If you lose, we will expect immediate payment from you. Please read carefully the additional instructions on the next page for further details.

This booklet is for the exclusive use of the Mobius Group. For further information contact:

Professor K. R. MacCrimmon
Faculty of Commerce and Business Administration
University of British Columbia
Vancouver, B.C., Canada, V6T 1W5

SET A

Please mark your preference order in the box beside each option. Put the number "1" for your most preferred option, "2" for your next most preferred option, and so on, down to "5" for the option you least prefer in this set.

1. You receive $10 for sure. RANK ☐

2. You will receive $13.20 if at least 1 of the 5 randomly chosen stocks is favourable.
   However, you must pay $20 if none of the 5 stocks is favourable.

   Chance of winning: 90% RANK ☐

3. You will receive $28.50 if at least 2 of the 5 randomly chosen stocks are favourable.
   However, you must pay $20 if none or only 1 of the 5 stocks is favourable.

   Chance of winning: 62% RANK ☐

4. You will receive $89 if at least 3 of the 5 randomly chosen stocks are favourable.
   However, you must pay $20 if only 2 or fewer of the 5 stocks are favourable.
   Chance of winning: 28% RANK ☐

5. You will receive $414 if at least 4 of the 5 randomly chosen stocks are favourable.
   However, you must pay $20 if only 3 or fewer of the 5 stocks are favourable.

   Chance of winning 7% RANK ☐

All of the above wagers have expected winnings of $10.

Notes

CHAPTER 2. STUDYING RISK

1. There were 19 executives who had nationalities other than American or Canadian. For another 19 executives nationality and country of residence were not identical so we did not label them as either American or Canadian.
2. The other comparison groups were: same function, same firm size, same nationality, same income, same age group, and same educational level.
3. We included some other managers from the main study who wished to participate in the follow-up so that two-thirds of this group were at the vice-president level or above.
4. All figures have been converted to 1985 dollars based on published figures on pay increases of top executives.

CHAPTER 3. RISK IN-BASKET

1. Although the expected value of the risky alternative in the union dispute was intended to be equal to the sure alternative, the expected value is ambiguous.

2. Non-monetary consequences could have a major influence in all four situations. The lawsuit could lead to a possible entanglement in a protracted litigation for management. The impact of stopping supply to the competitor of a major customer could have repercussions on other customers. A strike as a result of the time-and-motion study would have impacts on employees and customers beyond the financial losses. Cooperation with a competitor has implications for future dealings. Other issues such as the potential controllability of key uncertain events and attitudes regarding the decision contexts could also play a role in the situations. One must be careful, then, in interpreting the sure and the uncertain alternatives as having the same expected value, based on a calculation involving only the financial outcomes.
3. For the ratings, the locations on the scale between the risky action and the sure action were assigned the numbers zero to ten. The executive's placement of an *X* on this continuum was assigned the corresponding number, rounded to the nearest 0.5. Scales for two of the situations were designed with the risky alternative at the high end of the scale. The other two scales had the risky alternative at the low end. The switch was intended to reduce the chance of a routinized response. For the purposes of presentation, all data presented in this chapter have been transformed so that higher values correspond to an inclination toward the risky action.
4. One coder was 28 years of age, married, had obtained a graduate degree in business administration, and had previously been employed as an account executive. The other coder was 36 years of age, married, had obtained a degree in business administration, and had been previously employed in retail sales.
5. When the coding categories are only nominal, an analysis using the "degree of agreement" is appropriate.
6. The degree of agreement was moderately low (0.27 to 0.38) when eight categories were considered, but improved to a range of 0.49 to 0.59 when the eight risk categories were collapsed to four and the nonaction response was included.
7. The combined memo risk score was an average of the coders' scores unless one or both coders indicated a nonaction response. When only one coder indicated a nonaction response, the other coder's score was used. When both coders judged the memo to have a nonaction response, the executive's response was excluded from analysis of the overall memo risk score. In the four situations, there were 19, 38, 4, and 24 written memos, respectively, excluded from combined coding on the memo risk score.
8. The six codes used were: (1) no mention made of collecting information or bargaining; (2) collecting information mentioned, but executive will do without it; (3) desire expressed to collect information, but no action specified to obtain it; (4) action specified to collect some information; (5) action specified to collect much information; (6) action specified to

bargain or present new alternative, perhaps in addition to collecting information.

9. The degree of agreement was at least 0.37 for all four situations. When the six information categories were collapsed to three (do not collect information, collect information, bargain), the degree of agreement improved substantially for all but the union dispute situation.
10. All 464 executives were coded for the combined memo information score.
11. The seven codes used were: (1) no mention made of delay or delegation; (2) delay mentioned but rejected; (3) temporary delay action specified; (4) indefinite delay action specified; (5) delegate decision with recommendation; (6) delegate decision without recommendation; (7) delegate implementation, but decision specified.
12. The degree of agreement ranged from 0.50 to 0.68.
13. The combined delay code was assigned the value one if either coder specified delay. Otherwise a value of zero was assigned. Cases in which both coders mentioned delegation were excluded from the coding on the combined delay score. The exclusion was done because it was not clear whether the absence of a delay code was a result of the presence of a delegation code. This coding excluded 45, 54, 43, and 20 executives from the four situations, respectively. The combined delegation code was assigned the value one if either coder specified delegation. Otherwise a value of zero was assigned except for cases in which both coders mentioned delay which were excluded. This coding of the combined delegation score excluded 97, 89, 82, and 132 executives, respectively, from the four situations.
14. Chi-squared goodness of fit test for binomial model with $p=0.63$ and $n=4$ with 0.001 significance level.
15. We found that significantly more executives (14) than expected by chance (4) specified collecting information in all four situations. The test used here and elsewhere in this section was chi-squared based on a binomial model with a significance level of 0.001.
16. Significant differences were found in the percentages of executives who attempted to bargain between the lawsuit/union dispute situations and the customer threat/joint venture situations (binomial test, 0.001 level).
17. Significant differences were found in the percentages of executives who delegated the decision between the lawsuit/union dispute situations and the customer threat/joint venture situations (binomial test, 0.001 level).
18. The binomial test used here and elsewhere in this section was based on $p=0.5$ and a significance level of 0.001.
19. The probability premium is defined as the difference between the probability equivalence and the break-even probability in each situation.
20. Since we cannot accurately calculate the break-even probability in the union dispute situation, we assume it to be 0.40, the probability of no strike specified in the letter, for the purposes of comparison.

21. The memos in the customer threat provided strong evidence that nonquantitative factors were important. Most executives thought that it was improper for the customer to threaten to withdraw his business. They were unwilling to give in to such a threat and hence took the action that we label as "risky" (i.e., they rejected the threat)—but not necessarily for riskiness reasons.
22. The binomial test used here was based on $p = 0.5$ and a significance level of 0.001.
23. A t-test of the difference in means was used with a 0.001 significance level. The difference between the lawsuit and union dispute situations is only statistically significant for the memo risk score (t-test, $\alpha < 0.01$).
24. When we averaged the mean responses across the two most threatening situations (i.e., lawsuit and customer threat), they were statistically more risk-taking than the mean response for the opportunity situation (i.e., joint venture). This result held for all three response modes. Because the union dispute involves both gains and losses, it was not clear whether it was perceived more as a threat or an opportunity. Including this situation as a threat or as an opportunity led to the same result. Therefore the evidence supported greater risk taking in threat situations than in opportunity situations.
25. The analyses were also performed with the risk rating and the probability premium as the measure of risk propensity, but they gave almost identical results and will not be described.
26. The original six-point scale was collapsed to three points: (1) no extra information to be collected, (2) extra information to be collected, and (3) attempts to negotiate and collect information. A one-way analysis of variance was used with a significance level of 0.001. We also constructed separate dichotomous variables for the presence or absence of actions to collect information and for the presence or absence of actions to bargain. We found significant relationships between collecting information and the memo risk score in the customer threat and joint venture situations and between bargaining and the memo risk score in the lawsuit and customer threat situations.
27. The results of the analyses for delay and delegation were based on t-tests with a significance level of 0.001. (The relationship between memo risk and delegation for the union dispute was significant only at the 0.05 level.)

CHAPTER 4. INVESTMENT GAMBLES

1. The actuarially fair amount is calculated as follows: 50% times one-half of net wealth plus 50% of the unknown level of net wealth has to equal current net wealth. Hence the unknown level of wealth has to be one and one-half times current net wealth. We state the outcomes in terms

of final position (in net wealth multiples) to relate more directly to the relevant risk theory.

2. Risk taking for gambles over some wealth interval is indicated when a straight line, drawn between the two wealth levels defining the interval, lies completely above the curve. Correspondingly, risk aversion over some wealth interval is indicated when a straight line, drawn between the endpoints of the interval, lies completely below the curve.
3. The measures of risk aversion in utility theory are local measures, applying to a specific wealth level. Since actual gambles cover an interval, we are using an interval focus and hence have an ambiguous region P to Q, in which a person may be labeled as risk-averting or risk-taking depending on which other outcomes are considered.
4. After the executive provided his gain equivalence multiple, he was asked a question to make sure that he would not accept the gamble if the multiple was less than he had specified. That is, we were checking to make sure that he was not overstating his gain equivalence.
5. If the executive did not have control over a capital expenditure budget, he was asked to specify a normal rate of return on a comparable investment budget. He then was asked to consider the risky venture in terms of that budget.
6. For the 492 executives who did provide a personal net wealth figure, we also derived personal net wealth from information they provided on assets and liabilities in another questionnaire. The correlation between the two figures was 0.90 so we have a basis for thinking that they responded consistently to this question.
7. When the probability of loss decreases, one expects the gain equivalence to decrease as well, i.e., you do not require as much to enter a gamble where the odds are better. Thus as the probability of loss changes from 0.50 to 0.40 to 0.30 to 0.10, consistent behavior requires that the gain equivalence decrease each time. Forty-seven executives for personal gambles and 59 executives for business gambles had non-monotonic equivalences. When two adjacent gain equivalences were tied this was not deemed serious enough to remove. The most common violation of monotonicity occurred when the gain equivalence for the gamble with the 30% chance of loss was larger than the gain equivalence for the gamble with the 40% chance of loss.
8. Many of the gain equivalences were even multiples of net wealth. That is, an executive was much more likely to require 5 times net wealth than to require 5.2 times net wealth. In all, for the personal gambles, 24% of the multiples were exact integers of net wealth, 13% were exact half multiples, and 6% were exact quarter multiples. (The business gambles were about the same.)
9. The absence of an expected return occurred most frequently for executives in banking and venture capital industries. Even though most of these executives had control over major assets, many did not have capital expenditure (or similar) budgets.

10. The large number of responses indicating that the executive would not participate in the risky gamble no matter what the gain prospects may indicate a lack of consideration of really large multiples such as 100 or 1000. Although it would be desirable to have these discriminations, the analysis we conduct using probability premiums is not sensitive to these differences.
11. We have labeled a person as significantly risk-averse if his premium is greater than 0.10, as significantly risk-taking if his premium is less than −0.10, and as risk-neutral if his premium is between −0.10 and 0.10.
12. Table 4.2 shows that gambles with intermediate chances of loss (that is, between 10% and 50%) were refused proportionately.
13. Risk-neutral segments occurred in only six preference curves. These executives were removed from the analysis to facilitate the comparison of risk-taking and risk-averse segments.
14. A sign test confirmed that the executives were more risk-averse for personal wealth than for business wealth at the 1% significance level.
15. The mean probability premiums for the personal and business questions were 0.32 and 0.21, respectively. They were significantly different at the 0.001 level of significance using a *t*-test for difference in means.
16. The difference in the probability premiums for the personal and business gambles with a 50% chance of loss was calculated. The mean value of this difference for executives who thought they were more risk-averse for personal gambles was significantly higher than the mean value for executives who thought they were more risk-averse for business gambles. A *t*-test for difference in means showed a significant difference at the 1% level.
17. In this comparison 83% of the 285 executives were more risk-averse for personal rather than business wealth, 16% were more risk-averse for business, and 1% were equally risk-averse. The median probability premiums were 0.40 and 0.19 in the personal and business investments, respectively.
18. The Pearson correlations among the four personal probability premiums ranged from 0.65 to 0.94; the correlations among the four business premiums ranged from 0.67 to 0.94. The correlations between the personal and the business premiums were lower, ranging from 0.24 to 0.42. The correlation coefficients for the questions involving 50%, 40%, 30%, and 10% chances of loss were 0.42, 0.42, 0.35, and 0.33, respectively.
19. We derived Figure 4.5 using a Guttman-Lingoes smallest space analysis for two dimensions assuming weak monotonicity. The data for this analysis were the pairwise correlations among the measures for the 285 managers who had all eight measures. The measures of goodness of fit were quite good; the coefficient of alienation was 0.0013 and Kruskal's stress statistic was 0.0007.

CHAPTER 5. RISK-RETURN RANKINGS

1. Alternatives S, R, A, B, C, D, E, F, and G in Chapter 5 were labeled alternatives G, H, F, A, E, R, D, B, and C in the Personal Investment Preferences (Risk-Return Rankings) instrument in the Appendix.
2. In more technical terms, we have gone from two discrete outcomes to a continuous distribution of outcomes.
3. Nine alternatives can be ordered in $9! = 9 \times 8 \times 7 \ldots \times 1 = 362{,}880$ ways.
4. Several other measures of risk propensity were also considered. One risk measure was the Spearman correlation between the observed ranking and a focal ranking that ordered the ventures from least to most risky. In order to maintain conceptual independence of the measures, ventures R and S were excluded from this ranking. This focal ranking was ABCDEFG, and it was based on a joint consideration of the probabilities of any, partial, or total loss. This risk measure had a correlation of 0.60 with the preference rank for S and also with the preference rank for R after they were suitably rescaled.

   We also considered three other risk measures: (1) the Spearman correlation between the observed ranking and the focal ranking SABCDEFGR which extended the riskiness ranking to include ventures S and R, (2) the difference in preference ranks for ventures S and R, and (3) preference for variation in returns defined as the coefficient of standard deviation in the regression model for preference ranks as a linear combination of expected return and standard deviation. The correlations between the preference rank for venture S and these three measures ranged from 0.75 to 0.88. For venture R they ranged from 0.75 to 0.89.

   The high correlations among the alternative risk measures and the ease of describing the preference ranks for ventures S and R led us to chose the latter as our risk measures in the Risk-Return Rankings.
5. These results are based on correlations between risky asset holdings and the ranking of ventures S and R, significantly different from zero at the 0.05 level.
6. Only 41 executives had extremely variable risk preferences in that they liked (disliked) both S and R.
7. There are four rankings that are a perfect fit with the expected return criterion because two pairs of alternatives (A and R, G and S) each have the same expected return.
8. We actually used ten minus preference rank as the dependent variable so that positive coefficients on attributes such as expected return and chance of significant gain would indicate that executives preferred higher values of these attributes. All 464 executives with complete rankings were included in the analysis. In this and other regression analyses described in this chapter we assumed that the preference ranks were intervally scaled measurements.

9. The expected return model was 0.69+21.55 [expected return]. It explained 58% of the variation in the preference ranks compared with 58.5% for the two-variable model.
10. We used a 5% significance level.
11. The safest venture, S, has the lowest expected gain and the lowest expected loss, so we may think of it as the low-return, low-risk option. This consideration reinforced our selection of S as the "safest" option. Similarly the riskiest venture, R, has the highest expected gain and the highest expected loss, so we may think of it as the high-return, high-risk option. Thus it was the "riskiest" venture.

CHAPTER 6. REAL MONEY WAGERS

1. In contrast, a risk-neutral person would be indifferent between any changes in gains and losses as long as the expected payoff remained the same.
2. When the actual probabilities of obtaining the best outcome are rounded to four decimal places, the expected payoffs of the uncertain wagers deviate from $10 by no more than 1%. When the probabilities are rounded to two decimal places, as reported on the questionnaire, the expected payoffs do not deviate from $10 by more than 2% except in wagers A4 (expected payoff = $10.52) and A5 ($10.38) in set A and wager B5 ($8.60) in set B. The impact of these deviations will be addressed later in the chapter.
3. Wager numbers in set B were reversed in the questionnaire from the way they are reported in Table 6.1 to counteract the potential order effect of the position of the sure alternative.
4. In alternative B2, loss is viewed as opportunity loss since both payoffs are positive.
5. We presented a list of prices of 100 stocks on the New York Stock Exchange on a specified date. The instructions stated that five of these stocks would be chosen at random and the number of "favorable" stocks in this group would determine whether the executive received the best or worst outcome. A favorable stock was one whose price had a fractional part of 1/4, 1/2, or 3/4. Correspondingly, unfavorable stocks were those whose prices were whole number or had fractional parts of 1/8, 3/8, 5/8, or 7/8. These were 38 favorable stocks (out of 100) and so probabilities could be generated by standard binomial calculations.

   The event associated with the best outcome in the uncertain wagers was the presence of a minimum number of favorable stocks in the set of five randomly chosen stocks. This minimum ranged from one to four for the different uncertain wagers.

   The event associated with obtaining the best of the two outcomes was described in two forms. First, the minimum number of favorable stocks from the five randomly chosen stocks was stated. Second, the probability that such a minimum number of favorable stocks would occur was calculated based on a binomial distribution where the chance that any single stock was favorable was assumed to be 3/8. This probability was expressed in terms of the "chances of winning" (a percentage rounded to two digits.).

6. Due to an error, the chance that any executive would play out a wager was sometimes 1/6 rather than 1/3 as mentioned in the instructions.
7. Wager C5 is less risky than wager B5 on both the expected loss and standard deviation, but each wager is most preferred by only 6% and 3% of the executives, respectively.
8. We used a 1% significance level. If an executive noticed that wagers A4 and A5 had expected payoffs slightly above $10 and wager B5 had an expected payoff somewhat below $10, this could influence his ranking. Attention to slight differences in expected payoff could reduce preference for decreasing variation in set A and increase it in set B. Although the data might change somewhat if this potential bias were accounted for, we do not believe the general conclusion would change.

CHAPTER 8. COMPARISON OF RISK MEASURES IN STANDARDIZED SITUATIONS

1. One exception is the business gambles where only 317 out of 509 executives provided all necessary responses. Many executives did not have a capital expenditure (or other) budget under their control. Others did not state the usual rate of return on this budget. These omissions occurred disproportionately for executives in the financial industries.
2. A paired *t*-test of the difference in mean probability premiums was used with a 0.001 significance level. The personal and business gambles were compared twice—first when the chance of loss was 50% and second when the chance of loss was 10%. Both tests exceeded the stated significance level.
3. The probability premiums were different at a 0.001 significance level using a *t*-test of the difference in means. Separate tests were performed for the Risk In-Basket, the Personal Investment Gambles, and the Business Investment Gambles.
4. The Business Investment Gambles involve risking the usual rate of return on half the capital expenditure budget, whereas the joint venture involves only gains and the lawsuit involves a possible one-time major loss that could be attributed to parties other than the executive (e.g., the litigant, courts, or prior management).
5. John deLorean was a successful executive who quit his top-level job at General Motors to start his own automobile company. He was put on trial, but acquitted, for allegedly dealing in drugs to obtain funds for

his struggling company. Paul Volcker was Chairman of the Federal Reserve Board under President Reagan. He was known for his cautious, tight-money policies.

6. The only other correlations significantly different from zero beyond the 0.05 level are 0.13 (PGAMBLE50%, RANK:EV-LO), 0.11 (BGAMBLE50%, RANK:EV-HI), and 0.10 (PGAMBLE50%, RANK:EV-HI).
7. An identical factor analysis was conducted based on the pairwise correlations and similar results were obtained.
8. Three and four factor models were tried, but problems with estimating communalities prevented finding the factor loadings.
9. The eight risk measures could be combined into four principal components accounting for 77% of the variation in the measures. The first three components loaded heavily on the Investment Gambles measures, the Risk-Return Rankings measures, and the Risk In-Basket measures, respectively. The last component had lower loadings on several measures across instruments.
10. The correlations between the risk measures provide stronger support for this finding. Four of the six correlations between pairs of personal measures are significant at the 0.001 level. The remaining two correlations are significant at the 0.05 level. Of the six possible correlations between pairs of business measures only two are significant beyond the 0.05 level. Both of these correlations are for situations drawn from the same questionnaire.
11. The position of the lawsuit measure above the business gamble measure with a 10% chance of loss may be due to its higher chance of loss rather than a comparison of the stake.
12. Using the correlations in the "Note on Relationships Among Risk Measures in Standardized Situations" (page 197) produced a spatial representation similar to Figure 8.2
13. The groups did not have exactly one-third of the executives in each category because there were too many identical responses near the break points. The joint venture had the most uneven division into groups with 36.6% relatively risk-taking, 35.0% relatively risk-neutral, and 28.4% relatively risk-averting.
14. Fourteen cases were observed versus the expected 2.6 cases.
15. Twelve cases were observed versus the expected 4.8 cases.
16. We used a random model that assumed no relationships among the manager's responses across situations to derive an expected number. This expected number was compared with the actual number of executives found in each group using a chi-squared test.
17. All chi-squared tests for relative risk averters were significant at a 0.005 level.
18. The significance levels for relative risk takers were 0.0001 for the personal decisions and threats, 0.025 for the business decisions, and greater than 0.05 for the opportunities and all combination of attributes.

CHAPTER 9. MEASURING RISK IN NATURAL SITUATIONS AND ATTITUDES

1. When real estate is considered as a risky asset, the proportion of executives holding 90% or more of their assets in the riskiest categories increases to 29%.
2. Two executives claimed that their debt exceeded gross assets. These two observations were excluded from the debt ratio measure.
3. Three managers held life insurance worth between 15 and 44 times salary. To eliminate the inordinate influence of these observations on the analyses, we removed them.
4. A majority of executives said they had not participated in the listed gambling categories within the past year, including 87%, 54%, and 69%, respectively, on casino gambling, recreational sports, and professional sports. For each gambling activity about 10% of the executives had wagered an average of $30 or more with the maximum average bet exceeding $300 for only 4%, 1%, and 1% of the executives in the three categories, respectively. Among those who wagered, the typical bet per occasion was $150, $15, and $30, respectively.
5. One executive reported wagering 17% of his wealth within one year (i.e., $45,000 out of $270,000). Because this percentage was about twice as high as the next highest, we removed this executive so as not to bias the analyses with this single extreme observation.
6. The following risk-neutral values were also examined and a majority of executives were still risk-averting: 20%, 33%, 50%, and 67% of total assets held in riskiest categories; 20%, 33%, 50%, and 67% of total assets held as debt; life insurance of one, two, and three times annual salary; 1%, 0.5%, and 0.1% of wealth wagered annually on recreational gambles; one, two, and three voluntary resignations within a 15-year period.
7. Younger executives also have lower annual salaries. Together with higher life insurance holdings, the ratio of life insurance to salary is even higher.
8. The correlations ranged from 0.08 to 0.16 in absolute value and were significantly different from zero at less than a 5% level.
9. We asked the executives to consider what significant changes had occurred in their firms' operations within the past five years in seven fundamental areas. These seven areas were: (1) new products, services, or production processes, (2) new domestic markets, (3) mergers and acquisitions, (4) organizational structure, (5) foreign investment or marketing decisions, (6) research and development policy, and (7) retrenchments, cutbacks, or sell-offs.

   For each of these areas and any additional ones specified by the executive, he was asked to specify his role in the change. Four roles were listed: (1) personally initiated significant changes in the area, (2) part of the decision-making group responsible for initiating change in the area,

(3) significant change in the area occurred in the company, but executive was not personally involved in initiating change, and (4) significant changes in the area did not occur in the company within the past five years.

10. The wording of two items was changed slightly from the Zuckerman et al. form to make them more suitable for executives.
11. Defined as "1" if sensation seeking and "0" if sensation averting.
12. This score is $\alpha_s = k\bar{r}/(1+(k-1)\bar{r})$ where k is the number of items and $\bar{r}$ is the average correlation between pairs of items.
13. This score is $G_S = 2r^*/(1+r^*)$ where $r^* = 2[\text{cov}(X, Y) - \sigma_X^2 - \sigma_Y^2]$ and X and Y are the first half and second half measures, respectively.
14. We used a t-test with a 0.01 significance level to test whether the average response was significantly greater than the value of 4.0 representing no difference between the manager and his peers.
15. The correlation between the self-rating and sensation measures of $r=0.22$ was statistically different from zero at a 0.001 level. The correlations between the control measure and the self-rating and sensation measures were 0.11 and 0.13, respectively, for 362 managers who had all eight secondary measures. These latter correlations were significantly different from zero at between 0.01 and 0.02 levels.
16. The correlations ranged from 0.07 to 0.13 and were significantly greater than zero at less than a 5% level.
17. The self-rating was positively associated with debt ratio ($r=0.10$) and resignations ($r=0.12$) and negatively associated with life insurance holdings ($r=-0.12$), but the significance levels were greater than 0.1%. The correlation between sensation and resignations was $r=0.14$ with a similar significance level.
18. The measures RESIGNATIONS and GAMBLING each label substantially more than a third of the executives as relatively risk-averse whereas the measures I/E:CONTROL and SELFRATING each label substantially less than a third of the executives as relatively risk-averse. However the probabilities of an executive being labeled relatively risk-averse (or relatively risk-taking) average out to close to one-third when averaged over all eight measures.
19. This analysis was repeated defining consistent risk averters (takers) as executives classified as risk-averting (taking) on a majority of the 8 combined natural situation and attitude measures. The results were similar.
20. When we used a majority of at least nine of the combined set of 16 measures to define the categories, equivalent results were obtained for consistent risk averters. There were also more consistent risk takers than expected by chance (chi-squared, 0.01 level). This was likely due to the existence of a group of consistent risk takers based on the 8 standardized measures which comprised half of the measures in this new analysis.

CHAPTER 10. CHARACTERISTICS RELATED TO RISK

1. Carl Chapman and David Drew are hypothetical individuals, constructed to be extreme cases on each of the dimensions. However, they are each very close to actual individuals in the study.
2. For a thorough analysis of all measures and for technical detail, see MacCrimmon and Wehrung (1985b).
3. For simplicity in the discussion we have dropped the term "relative," but the reader should remember that the categories were defined strictly in relative terms with no reference to a risk-neutral point. For the measure RESIGNATIONS we did not break the data into three equal groups because it could not be done. Instead we divided the executives in those who had voluntarily resigned one or more times (the risk takers) and those who had never voluntarily resigned (the risk averters).
4. We used the top third and bottom third on risk propensity for our categories wherever possible, so again we are using a relative concept of risk. We used two categories for RESIGNATIONS as mentioned in note 3 above. For IB:LAWSUIT and BGAMBLE10% no significant discriminant functions were found when we used top third and bottom third. In Chapter 10 we report the results found for these two risk measures using top half and bottom half on risk propensity as our two categories.
5. Note that our main study is cross-sectional, so we are addressing the question of whether at one point in time, the older managers are more risk-averse than the younger managers. We are not directly answering the question of whether people grow more risk-averse as they get older.
6. The negative relationship between age and risk was also supported by the risk measures concerning attitude toward losing and initiating changes in the firm introduced in Chapter 9. Younger managers personally initiated significantly more changes and hated to lose at anything more than older managers.
7. In the univariate analyses managers with a university or postgraduate education also personally initiated significantly more changes than managers with only a high school education.
8. Two of the risk measures introduced in Chapter 9 did show Canadians to be more risk-averse. Compared with American managers, Canadians tended to collect more information before making a decision and they did not mind losing if little was at stake.
9. RISKYASSETS is also functionally dependent on total assets, but this dependence would lead to a bias in favor of a negative relationship rather than the positive one obtained.
10. We also found that wealthier managers personally initiated more significant changes in their firms' operations than did less wealthy managers.
11. Their greatest risk aversion on IB:LAWSUIT may be related to a desire to stay out of protracted litigation borne of such experience as chief officers.

12. We also found that the most senior executives personally initiated more significant changes in their firms' operations than did more junior managers. This result held for managers with greater authority as well.
13. We did find some support for less risk taking in larger firms when we considered attitudes toward losing. Executives who worked for larger firms did not mind losing if little was at stake, whereas managers in smaller firms hated to lose at anything.
14. We found further support for greater risk aversion among managers in the banking industry in that these executives took more time deliberating decisions and they did not mind losing if little was at stake.
15. In both the in-basket situations the executives in the venture capital industry indicated lower risk taking than other executives—perhaps because of prior experiences with joint ventures and lawsuits.
16. Managers in the venture capital industry also took more time deliberating decisions and collected more information than managers in other industries.
17. Managers in the primary industries also took more time deliberating decisions than managers in other industries.
18. The most successful managers also initiated significantly more changes in their firms' operations than other managers. This result was true regardless of which definition of success was used. In particular, we found that executives in the SUCCESS1 group personally initiated an average of 55% of the significant changes in their firms compared with an average of 30% for the remaining executives. This result is not surprising given that position was a significant explanatory variable for CHANGES and it also played a major role in the definition of both groups of successful managers.

CHAPTER 12. ASSESSING YOUR OWN WILLINGNESS TO TAKE RISKS

1. Whether you use "individual" or "family" assets and liabilities is immaterial in this questionnaire as long as the same definition is used to consider net wealth in the Personal Investment Gamble.
2. This venture was called R in Chapters 5 and 8.
3. In this case the expected value of the gamble [i.e., .5 (half of net wealth) + .5 (one and one-half times net wealth)] is the same as not accepting the gamble and maintaining one's current net wealth.
4. For the debt ratio and the Personal Investment Gamble measures we could divide the executives into three approximately equal groups. This was not possible for the Risk-Return Rankings measure because the preference ranks were discrete. As a result, 38.8% of the managers fell into the risk-taking "third," 30.4% in the risk-neutral "third," and 30.8% in the risk-averting "third."

5. The average Personal Risk Profile was defined as the sum of the individual Personal Risk Profiles divided by the number (383) of managers for whom all measures were available. This average Personal Risk Profile is "1.10-0.95-0.95." It does not correspond exactly to the risk profile "1-1-1" at point A because we could not break each personal risk measure into three exactly equal groups.
6. We could divide the managers into three approximately equal groups for the Business Investment Gamble and the lawsuit measures. For the self-appraisal of risk propensity the distribution of responses over the ratings did not allow this. Consequently 24.7% of the managers made up the risk-taking "third," 45.8% the risk-neutral "third," and 29.5% the risk-averting "third."
7. The average Business Risk Profile was based on 287 managers for whom all business risk measures were available. This profile is "0.99-1.05-0.96" rather than "1-1-1" at point K because all business risk measures could not be divided into three equal groups.
8. The deciles indicate what percentage of the managers had risk measures indicating greater risk taking than a given manager. For example, a manager scoring in the fifth decile on a risk measure indicated that at most 50% of the executives were more risk-taking than he. Scoring in the first decile indicated that at most 10% of the managers were more risk-taking than he.
9. The chairman did not give answers for the Risk-Return Rankings or the voluntary resignation question. We recorded his position at the fifth decile for these measures.
10. The president from firm A did not answer the voluntary resignation question. We recorded his position at the fifth decile for this measure.

References

ALDERFER, C. P., AND BIERMAN, H., JR. (1970), "Choices with risk: Beyond the mean and variance," *Journal of Business*, *43*:341–353.

ANDERSON, N. H., AND SHANTEAU, J. C. (1970), "Information integration in risky decision making," *Journal of Experimental Psychology*, *84*:441–451.

ANDERSON, R. M. (1969), "Handling risk in defense contracting," *Harvard Business Review*, *47*:90–98.

ARNOLD, S. J., WHITE, J. S., AND TIGERT, D. J. (1972), "Canadians and Americans: A comparative analysis," Working paper No. 72-23, Toronto: University of Toronto, Faculty of Management Studies.

ARROW, K. J. (1951), *Social Choice and Individual Values*, New York: Wiley.

ARROW, K. J. (1971), *Essays in the Theory of Risk-Bearing*, Chicago: Markham.

ARROW, K. J. (1982), "Risk perception in psychology and economics," *Economic Inquiry, 20*:1–9.

ASCHENBRENNER, K. M. (1978), "Single-peaked risk preferences and their dependability on the gambles' presentation mode," *4*:513–520.

ATKINSON, J. W. (1957), "Motivational determinants of risk-taking behavior," *Psychological Review*, *64*:359–372.

ATKINSON, J. W., BASTIAN, J. R., EARL, R. W., AND LITWIN, G. H. (1960), "The achievement motive, goal setting, and probability preferences," *Journal of Abnormal and Social Psychology*, *60*:27–36.

Atkinson, J. W., and Feather, N. T. (eds.) (1966), *A Theory of Achievement Motivation*, New York: Wiley.

Baird, I. S., and Thomas, H. (1985), "Toward a contingency model of strategic risk taking," *Academy of Management Review*, *10*:230–243.

Baker, H. K., and Haslem, J. A. (1974), "The impact of investor socioeconomic characteristics on risk and return preferences," *Journal of Business Research, 2*:469–476.

Baker, W. G., III (1970), "Personality correlates of stock market speculation," Ph.D. dissertation, University of Oklahoma.

Banker, P. (1983), "You're the best judge of foreign risks," *Harvard Business Review, 61*:157–165.

Barnett, A., and Lofasco, A. J. (1983), "After the crash: The passenger response to the DC-10 disaster," *Management Science, 29*:1225–1236.

Baron, R. A. (1968), "Authoritarianism, locus of control, and risk taking," *Journal of Psychology, 68*:141–143.

Bassler, J. F. (1972), "The consistency of risk attitudes in decision making under uncertainty," Ph.D. dissertation, Carnegie-Mellon University.

Bassler, J. F., MacCrimmon, K. R., and Stanbury, W. T. (1973), "Risk attitudes of U.S. and Canadian top managers," paper presented at the meeting of the Fourth International Conference on Subjective Probability, Utility and Decision Making, Rome.

Bassler, J. F., MacCrimmon, K. R., Stanbury, W. T., and Wehrung, D. A. (1978), "Multiple criteria dominance models: An empirical study of investment preferences," in S. Zionts (ed.), *Multiple Criteria Problem Solving*, Berlin: Springer-Verlag, 494–508.

Bauer, R. A. (1960), "Consumer behavior as risk taking," *Proceedings of the American Marketing Association*, 389–398.

Baumol, W. J. (1963), "An expected gain-confidence limit criterion for portfolio selection," *Management Science*, *10*:174–182.

Becker, G. M., DeGroot, M. H., and Marschak, J. (1963a), "An experimental study of some stochastic models for wagers," *Behavioral Science*, *8*:199–202.

Becker, G. M., DeGroot, M. H., and Marschak, J. (1963b), "Stochastic models of choice behavior," *Behavioral Science*, *8*:41–55.

Becker, G. M., DeGroot, M. H., and Marschak, J. (1964), "Measuring utility by a single-response sequential method," *Behavioral Science*, *9*:226–232.

Bell, D. E. (1982), "Regret in decision making under uncertainty," *Operations Research*, *30*:961–981.

Bell, D. E. (1983), "Risk premiums for decision regret," *Management Science*, *29*:1156–1166.

Bell, D. E. (1985), "Disappointment in decision making under uncertainty," *Operations Research, 33*:1–27.

Bell, D. E., and Raiffa, H. (1982), "Marginal value and intrinsic risk aversion," in H. Kunreuther (ed.), *Risk: A Seminar Series*, Laxenburg, Austria: International Institute for Applied Systems Analysis, 325–350.

BERNOULLI, D. (1738), "Exposition of a new theory on the measurement of risk," *Comentarii Academiae Scientiarum Imperiales Petropolitanae*, *5*:175–192 (Translated in *Econometrica*, 1954, *22*:23–36).

BETTMAN, J. R. (1973), "Perceived risk and its components: A model and empirical test," *Journal of Marketing Research*, *10*:184–190.

BETTMAN, J. R., AND JACOBY, J. (1976), "Patterns of processing in consumer information acquisitions," in B. B. Anderson (ed.), *Advances in Consumer Research, Vol. III*, Chicago: Association for Consumer Research, 315–320.

BETTMAN, J. R., AND KAKKAR, P. (1977), "Effects of information presentation format on consumer information acquisition strategies," *Journal of Consumer Research*, *3*:233–240.

BIAMONTE, E. (1982), "Controlling the risks from liquefied natural gas," *Geneva Papers on Risk and Insurance*, *7*:75–88.

BLUM, S. H. (1976), "Investment preferences and the desire for security: A comparison of men and women," *Journal of Psychology*, *94*:87–91.

BLUME, M. E., AND FRIEND, I. (1975), "The asset structure of individual portfolios and some implications for utility functions," *Journal of Finance*, *30*:585:603.

BLUME,M. E., AND FRIEND, I. (1978), *The Changing Role of the Individual Investor*, New York: Wiley.

BOISSONNADE, A. C., AND SHAH, H. C. (1984), "Seismic vulnerability and insurance studies," *Geneva Papers on Risk and Insurance*, *9*:223–254.

BONOMA, T. V., AND JOHNSTON, W. J. (1978), "Locus of control, trust, and decision making," *Decision Sciences*, *9*:39–56.

BONOMA, T. V., AND SCHLENKER, B. R. (1978), "The SEU calculus: Effects of response mode, sex, and sex role on uncertain decisions," *Decision Sciences*, *9*:206–227.

BORCH, K. H. (1963), "A note on utility and attitudes to risk," *Management Science*, *9*:697–701.

BOSSONS, J. (1973), "The distribution of assets among individuals of different age and wealth," in R. Goldsmith (ed.), *Institutional Investors and Corporate Stock*, New York: National Bureau of Economic Research.

BOWMAN, E. H. (1982), "Risk seeking by troubled firms," *Sloan Management Review*, *23*:33–42.

BRICHACEK, V. (1968), "Comparative analysis of decision processes," *Ceskoslovenska Psychologie*, *12*:456–460.

BRIM, O. G., JR., AND HOFF, D. B. (1957), "Individual and situational differences in desire for certainty," *Journal of Abnormal and Social Psychology*, *54*:225–229.

BROCKHAUS, R. H. (1980), "Risk taking propensity of entrepreneurs," *Academy of Management Journal*, *23*:509–520.

BROWN, R. (1965), *Social Psychology*, New York: Free Press of Glencoe.

Chew, S. H., and MacCrimmon, K. R. (1979a), "Alpha-nu choice theory: A generalization of expected utility theory," Working paper, Faculty of Commerce, University of British Columbia.

Chew, S. H., and MacCrimmon, K. R. (1979b), "Alpha-utility theory, lottery composition and the Allais paradox," Working paper, Faculty of Commerce, University of British Columbia.

Clarkson, G. P. E. (1962), *Portfolio Selection: A Simulation of Trust Investment*, Englewood Cliffs, N.J.: Prentice Hall.

Coet, L. J., and McDermott, P. J. (1979), "Sex, instructional set, and group make-up: Organismic and situational factors influencing risk-taking," *Psychological Reports*, *44*:1283–1294.

Cohen, B. L., and Lee, I. S. (1979), "A catalog of risks," *Health Physics*, *36*:707–722.

Cohen, J., and Hansel, M. (1956), *Risk and Gambling*, New York: Philosophical Library.

Cohn, R. A., Lewellen, W. G., Lease, R. C., and Schlarbaum, G. G. (1975), "Individual investor risk aversion and investment portfolio composition," *Journal of Finance*, *30*:605–620.

Cooley, P. L. (1977), "Multidimensional analysis of institutional investor perception of risk," *Journal of Finance*, *32*:67–78.

Coombs, C., H., and Pruitt, D. G. (1960), "Components of risk and decision-making: Probability and variance preferences," *Journal of Experimental Psychology*, *60*:265–277.

Coombs, C. H. (1964), *A Theory of Data*, New York: Wiley.

Coombs, C. H., and Huang, L. C. (1970), "Tests of a portfolio theory of risk preference," *Journal of Experimental Psychology*, *85*:23–29.

Cox, D. F., and Rich, S. U. (1964), "Perceived risk and consumer decision making," *Journal of Marketing Research*, *1*:32–39.

Cox, D. F. (1967a), "Risk handling in consumer behavior—An intensive study of two cases," in D. F. Cox (ed.), *Risk Taking and Information Handling in Consumer Behavior*, Boston: Division of Research, Graduate School of Business, Harvard University, 34–81.

Cox, D. F. (ed.) (1967b), *Risk Taking and Information Handling in Consumer Behavior*, Boston: Division of Research, Graduate School of Business, Harvard University.

Cramer, R. H., and Smith, B. E. (1964), "Decision models for the selection of research projects," *Engineering Economist*, *9*:1–20.

Crum, R. L., Laughhunn, D. J., and Payne, J. W. (1980), "Risk preference: Empirical evidence and its implications for capital budgeting," in F. G. J. Derkinderen and R. L. Crum (eds.), *Risk, Capital Costs, and Project Financing Decisions*, Boston: Martinus Nijhoff Publishing, 14–36.

Crum, R. L., Laughhunn, D. J., and Payne, J. W. (1981), "Risk-seeking behavior and its implications for financial models," *Financial Management*, *10*:20–27.

CUMMINGS, L. L., HARNETT, D. L., AND STEVENS, O. J. (1971), "Risk, fate, conciliation and trust: An international study of attitudinal differences among executives," *Academy of Management Journal, 14*:285–304.

CUNNINGHAM, S. (1966), "Perceived risk as a factor in diffusion of new product information," in *Science, Technology, and Marketing*, 698–721.

CUNNINGHAM, S. M. (1967), "The major dimensions of perceived risk," in D. F. Cox (ed.), *Risk Taking and Information Handling in Consumer Behavior*, Boston: Division of Research, Graduate School of Business, Harvard University, 82–108.

DAVIDSON, D., SUPPES, P., AND SIEGEL, S. (1957), *Decision Making: An Experimental Approach*, Stanford, Calif.: Stanford University Press.

DICKSON, G. C. A. (1982), "A comparison of attitudes towards risk among business managers," *Geneva Papers on Risk and Insurance, 7*:89–97.

DILLON, J. L., AND SCANDIZZO, P. L. (1978), "Risk attitudes of subsistence farmers in northeast Brazil: A sampling approach," *American Journal of Agricultural Economics, 60*:425–435.

DOWIE, J. A. (1976), "On the efficiency and equity of betting markets," *Economica, 43*:139–150.

DRWAL, R. L. (1980), "Delta questionnaire for measuring locus of control," *Polish Psychological Bulletin, 11*:269–282.

DYER, J. S., AND SARIN, R. K. (1982), "Relative risk aversion," *Management Science, 28*:875–886.

EDWARDS, W. (1953), "Probability preferences in gambling," *American Journal of Psychology, 66*:349–364.

EDWARDS, W. (1954), "Variance preferences in gambling," *American Journal of Psychology, 67*:441–452.

EDWARDS, W. (1965), "Optimal strategies for seeking information: Models for statistics, choice reaction times, and human information processing," *Journal of Mathematical Psychology, 2*:312–329.

EDWARDS, W., AND SLOVIC, P. (1965), "Seeking information to reduce the risk of decisions," *American Journal of Psychology, 78*:188–197.

EISNER, R., AND STROTZ, R. H. (1961), "Flight insurance and the theory of choice," *Journal of Political Economy, 69*:355–368.

FARQUHAR, P. H. (1984), "Utility assessment methods," *Management Science, 30*:1283–1300.

FINNEY, P. D. (1978), "Personality traits attributed to risky and conservative decision makers: Cultural values more than risk," *Journal of Psychology, 99*:187–197.

FISCHHOFF, B., HOHENEMSER, C., KASPERSON, R. E., AND KATES, R. W. (1978), "Handling hazards," *Environment, 20*:16–37.

FISCHHOFF, B., SLOVIC, P., LICHTENSTEIN, S., READ, S., AND COMBS, B. (1978), "How safe is safe enough? A psychometric study of attitudes towards technological risks and benefits," *Policy Sciences, 9*:127–152.

FISCHHOFF, B., SLOVIC, P., AND LICHTENSTEIN, S. (1979), "Weighing the risks," *Environment*, *21*:17–20, 32–38.

FISCHHOFF, B., LICHTENSTEIN, S., SLOVIC, P., DERBY, S., AND KEENEY, R. (1981), *Acceptable Risk*, New York: Cambridge University Press.

FISHBURN, P. C. (1977), "Mean-risk analysis with risk associated with below-target returns," *American Economic Review*, *67*:116–126.

FISHBURN, P. C., AND KOCHENBERGER, G. (1979), "Concepts, theory and techniques: Two-piece Von Neumann-Morgenstern utility functions," *Decision Sciences*, *10*:503–518.

FISHBURN, P. C. (1979), "Foundations of mean-variance analyses," *Theory and Decision*, *10*:99–111.

FISHBURN, P. C. (1982a), "Foundations of risk measurement. II: Effects of gains on risk," *Journal of Mathematical Psychology*, *25*:226–242.

FISHBURN, P. C. (1982b), "Nontransitive measurable utility," *Journal of Mathematical Psychology*, *26*:31–67.

FISHBURN, P. C. (1983), "Transitive measurable utility," *Journal of Economic Theory*, *31*:293–317.

FISHBURN, P. C. (1984a), "Multiattribute nonlinear utility theory," *Management Science*, *30*:1301–1310.

FISHBURN, P. C. (1984b), "Foundations of risk measurement. I: Risk as probable loss," *Management Science*, *30*:396–406.

FITZPATRICK, M. (1983), "The definition and assessment of political risk in international business: A review of the literature," *Academy of Management Review*, *8*:249–254.

FOSTER, H. D. (1984), "Reducing vulnerability to natural hazards," *Geneva Papers on Risk and Insurance*, *9*:27–56.

FREDERIKSEN, N., SAUNDERS, D. R., AND WAND, B. (1957), "The in-basket test," *Psychological Monographs: General and Applied*, *71*:438.

FREDERIKSEN, N. (1962), "Factors in in-basket performance," *Psychological Monographs*, *76*:1–25.

FRIED, L. S., AND PETERSON, C. R. (1969), "Information seeking: Optimal vs. fixed stopping," *Journal of Experimental Psychology*, *80*:525–529.

FRIEDMAN, B. (1974), "Risk aversion and the consumer choice of health insurance option," *Review of Economics and Statistics*, *56*:209–214.

FRIEDMAN, M., AND SAVAGE, L. J. (1948), "The utility analysis of choices involving risk," *Journal of Political Economy*, *56*:279–304.

FRIEDMAN, M., AND SAVAGE, L. J. (1952), "The expected-utility hypothesis and the measurability of utility," *Journal of Political Economy*, *60*:463–475.

FRIEND, I., AND BLUME, M. E. (1975), "Demand for risky assets," *American Economic Review*, *65*:900–922.

FUNK, S. G., RAPOPORT, A., AND JONES, L. V. (1979), "Investing capital on safe and risky alternatives: An experimental study," *Journal of Experimental Psychology: General*, *108*:415–440.

GILL, R. W. T. (1979), "The in-tray (in-basket) exercise as a measure of management potential," *Journal of Occupational Psychology*, *52*: 185-197.

GOODING, A. E. (1975), "Quantification of investors' perceptions of common stocks—Risk and return dimensions," *Journal of Finance*, *30*:1301-1316.

GRAYSON, C. J. (1960), *Decisions under Uncertainty: Drilling Decisions by Oil and Gas Operators*, Boston: Division of Research, Graduate School of Business, Harvard University.

GREEN, P. E. (1963), "Risk attitudes and chemical investment decisions," *Chemical Engineering Progress*, *59*:35-40.

GREEN, P. E., HALBERT, M. H., AND MINAS, J. S. (1964), "An experiment in information buying," *Journal of Advertising Research*, *4*:17-23.

GREENE, M. R. (1963), "Attitudes toward risk and a theory of insurance consumption," *Journal of Insurance*, *30*:165-182.

GREENE, M. R. (1964), "Insurance mindedness—Applications for insurance theory," *Journal of Risk and Insurance*, *31*:27-38.

GRETHER, D. M., AND PLOTT, C. R. (1979), "Economic theory of choice and the preference reversal phenomenon," *American Economic Review*, *69*:623-638.

GREY, R. J., AND GORDON, G. G. (1978), "Risk-taking managers: Who gets to the top?" *Management Review*, *67*:8-13.

GUILFORD, J. P., CHRISTENSEN, P. R., BOND, N. A., AND SUTTON, M. A. (1953), "A factor analysis study of human interest," Research Bulletin 53-11, Human Resources Research Center, Lackland Air Force Base, San Antonio, Texas.

HADAR, J., AND RUSSELL, W. R. (1969), "Rules for ordering uncertain prospects," *American Economic Review*, *59*:25-34.

HALTER, A. N., AND BERINGER, C. (1960), "Cardinal utility functions and managerial behavior," *Journal of Farm Economics*, *42*:118-132.

HALTER, A. N., AND DEAN, G. W. (1971), *Decisions Under Uncertainty with Research Applications*, Cincinnati: South-western Publishing Co.

HAMILTON, J. O. (1974), "Motivation and risk taking behavior: A test of Atkinson's theory," *Journal of Personality and Social Psychology*, *30*:856-864.

HAMMOND, J. D., HOUSTON, D. B., AND MELANDER, E. R. (1967), "Determinants of household life insurance premium expenditures: An empirical investigation," *Journal of Risk and Insurance*, *34*:397-408.

HAMMOND, J. S. (1967), "Better decisions with preference theory," *Harvard Business Review*, *45*:123-141.

HANCOCK, J. G., AND TEEVAN, R. C. (1964), "Fear of failure and risk-taking behavior," *Journal of Personality*, *32*:200-209.

HEADEN, R. S., AND LEE, J. F. (1974), "Life insurance demand and household portfolio behavior," *Journal of Risk and Insurance*, *41*:685-698.

HERSHEY, J. C., AND SCHOEMAKER, P. J. H. (1980a), "Risk taking and problem context in the domain of losses: An expected utility analysis," *Journal of Risk and Insurance*, *47*:111–132.

HERSHEY, J. C., AND SCHOEMAKER, P. J. H. (1980b), "Prospect theory's reflection hypothesis: A critical examination," *Organizational Behavior and Human Performance*, *25*:395–418.

HERSHEY, J. C., KUNREUTHER, H. C., AND SCHOEMAKER, P. J. H. (1982), "Sources of bias in assessment procedures for utility functions," *Management Science*, *28*:936–954.

HERSHEY, J. C., AND SCHOEMAKER, P. J. H. (1984), "Probability vs. certainty equivalence methods in utility measurement: Are they equivalent?" Working paper, Center for Decision Research, Graduate School of Business, University of Chicago.

HIGBEE, K. L., AND STREUFERT, S. (1969), "Perceived control and riskiness," *Psychonomic Science*, *17*:105–106.

HIGBEE, K. L. (1971), "Expression of 'Walter Mitty-ness' in actual behavior," *Journal of Personality and Social Psychology*, *20*:416–422.

HIGBEE, K. L., AND LAFFERTY, T. (1972), "Relationships among risk preferences, importance and control," *Journal of Psychology*. *81*:249–251.

HOGAN, W. W., AND WARREN, J. M. (1974), "Toward the development of an equilibrium capital market model based on semivariance," *Journal of Financial and Quantitative Analysis*, *9*:1–11.

HOPKINS, M. E., LO, L., PETERSON, R. E., AND SEO, K. K. (1977), "Japanese and American managers," *Journal of Psychology*, *96*:71–72.

HOWARD, R. A. (1984), "On fates comparable to death," *Management Science*, *30*:407–422.

HUNSAKER, P. L. (1975), "Incongruity adaptation capability and risk preference in turbulent decision-making environments," *Organizational Behavior and Human Performance*, *14*:173–185.

HUTCHISON, S. L., JR., AND CLEMENS, F. W. (1980), "Advisement to take risk: The elderly's view," *Psychological Reports*, *47*:426.

HUTCHISON, S., AND LILIENTHAL, R. (1980), "Advisement to take risk: A study of attitudes toward the old," *International Journal of Behavioral Development*, *3*:19–26.

JACKSON, B. B. (1980), "Manage risk in industrial pricing," *Harvard Business Review*, *58*:121–133.

JACKSON, D. N., HOURANY, L., AND VIDMAR, N. J. (1972), "A four-dimensional interpretation of risk taking," *Journal of Personality*, *40*:483–501.

JACOBY, J. (1976), "Consumer psychology: An octennium," *Annual Review of Psychology*, *27*:331–358.

JANIS, I., AND MANN, L. (1977), *Decision Making: A Psychological Analysis of Conflict, Choice, and Commitment*, New York: Free Press.

JOY, O. M., AND BARRON, F. W. (1974), "Behavioral risk constraints in capital budgeting," *Journal of Financial and Quantitative Analysis*, *9*:763.

KAHNEMAN, D., AND TVERSKY, A. (1979), "Prospect theory: An analysis of decision under risk," *Econometrica, 47*:263–291.

KAHNEMAN, D., AND TVERSKY, A. (1982), "The psychology of preferences," *Scientific American, 246*:160–173.

KAHNEMAN, D., SLOVIC, P., AND TVERSKY, A. (1982), *Judgment Under Uncertainty: Heuristics and Biases*, London: Cambridge University Press.

KATAOKA, S. (1963), "A stochastic programming model," *Econometrica, 31*:181–196.

KATES, R. W. (1978), *Risk Assessment of Environmental Hazard*, Chichester, U.K.: Wiley.

KEENEY, R. L., AND RAIFFA, H. (1976), *Decisions with Multiple Objectives: Preferences and Value Tradeoffs*, New York: Wiley.

KEENEY, R. L. (1980), *Siting Energy Facilities*, New York: Academic Press.

KEENEY, R. L., SARIN, R. K., AND WINKLER, R. L. (1984), "Analysis of alternative national ambient carbon monoxide standards," *Management Science, 30*:518–528.

KNOWLES, E. S. (1976), "Searching for motivations in risk-taking and gambling," in W. R. Eadington (ed.), *Gambling and Society: Interdisciplinary Studies on the Subject of Gambling*, London: Charles C. Thomas.

KOGAN, N., AND WALLACH, M. A. (1964), *Risk Taking: A Study in Cognition and Personality*, New York: Holt, Rinehart and Winston.

KOGAN, N., AND WALLACH, M. A. (1967), "Risk taking as a function of the situation, the person, and the group," in G. Mandler (ed.), *New Directions in Psychology, III*, New York: Holt, Rinehart and Winston.

KUNREUTHER, H. (1968), "The case for comprehensive disaster insurance," *Journal of Law and Economics, 11*:133–163.

KUNREUTHER, H. (1976), "Limited knowledge and insurance protection," *Public Policy, 24*:241–246.

KUNREUTHER, H., GINSBEY, R., MILLER, L., SAGI, P., SLOVIC, P., BORKAN, B., AND KATZ, N. (1978), *Disaster Insurance Protection: Policy Lessons*, New York: Wiley.

KUNREUTHER, H. (1979), "The changing societal consequences of risks from natural hazards," *The Annals of the American Academy of Political and Social Science, 443*:104–116.

KUNREUTHER, H., AND LATHROP, J. (1981), "Siting hazard facilities: The case of LNG terminals," *Risk Analysis, 1*:289–302.

KUNREUTHER, H., LINNEROOTH, J., LATHROP, J., ATZ, H., MACGILL, S., MANDL, C., SCHWARTZ, M., AND THOMPSON, M. (1983), *Risk Analysis and Decision Processes: The Siting of LEG Facilities in Four Countries*, New York: Springer-Verlag.

KUNREUTHER, H., LINNEROOTH, J., AND VAUPEL, J. W. (1984), "A decision-process perspective on risk and policy analysis," *Management Science, 30*:475–485.

LAMPMAN, R. (1962), *Share of Top Wealth-Holders in National Wealth, 1922-1956*, Princeton: Princeton University Press.

LAUGHHUNN, D. J., PAYNE, J. W., AND CRUM, R. (1980), "Managerial risk preferences for below target returns," *Management Science*, *26*:1238-1249.

LAVE, L. (1971), "Risk, safety and the role of government," in *Perspectives on Benefit-Risk Decision Making*, Colloquium of the Committee on Public Engineering Policy, Washington: National Academy of Engineering.

LEFCOURT, H. M. (1965), "Risk taking in Negro and white adults," *Journal of Personality and Social Psychology*, *2*:765-770.

LEFCOURT, H. M., AND LADWIG, G. W. (1965), "The American Negro: A problem in expectancies," *Journal of Personality and Social Psychology*, *1*:377-380.

LEFCOURT, H. M., AND STEFFY, R. A. (1970), "Level of aspiration, risk-taking behavior, and projection test performance: A search for coherence," *Journal of Consulting and Clinical Psychology*, *34*:193-198.

LEVINGER, G., AND SCHNEIDER, D. J. (1969), "Test of the 'risk is a value' hypothesis," *Journal of Personality and Social Psychology*, *11*:165-169.

LIBBY, R., AND FISHBURN, P. C. (1977), "Behavioral models of risk taking in business decisions: A survey and evaluation," *Journal of Accounting Research*, *15*:272-292.

LICHTENSTEIN, S. (1965), "Bases for preferences among three outcome bets," *Journal of Experimental Psychology*, *69*:162-169.

LICHTENSTEIN, S., AND SLOVIC, P. (1971), "Reversals of preference between bids and choices in gambling decisions," *Journal of Experimental Psychology*, *89*:46-55.

LICHTENSTEIN, S., AND SLOVIC, P. (1973), "Response-induced reversals of preference in gambling: An extended replication in Las Vegas," *Journal of Experimental Psychology*, *101*:16-20.

LICHTENSTEIN, S., SLOVIC, P., FISCHHOFF, B., LAYMAN, M., AND COMBS, B. (1978), "Judged frequency of lethal events," *Jounral of Experimental Psychology: Human Learning and Memory*, *4*:551-578.

LIVERANT, S., AND SCODEL, A. (1960), "Internal and external control as determinants of decision making under conditions of risk," *Psychological Reports*, *7*:59-67.

LOOMES, G., AND SUGDEN, R. (1982), "Regret theory: An alternative theory of rational choice under uncertainty," *Economic Journal*, *92*:805-824.

LOPES, L. L. (1983), "Some thoughts on the psychological concept of risk," *Journal of Experimental Psychology: Human Perception and Performance*, *9*:137-144.

LORANGE, P., AND NORMAN, V. D. (1971), "Risk preference and strategic decision making in large Scandinavian shipping enterprises," Bergen: Institute for Shipping Research.

LORANGE, P., AND NORMAN, V. D. (1973), "Risk preference in Scandinavian shipping," *Applied Economics*, *5*:49–59.

LUCE, R. D. (1980), "Several possible measures of risk," *Theory and Decision*, *12*:217–228.

MACCRIMMON, K. R. (1968), "Some normative and descriptive aspects of the decision theory postulates," in K. Borch and J. Mossin (eds.), *Risk and Uncertainty*, London: MacMillan, 3–23.

MACCRIMMON, K. R. (1973), "An overview of multiple objective decision making," in J. Cochrane and M. Zeleny (eds.), *Multiple Criteria Decision Making*, Columbia, S.C.: University of South Carolina Press, 18–44.

MACCRIMMON, K. R., AND LARSSON, S. (1979), "Utility theory: Axioms versus paradoxes," in M. Allais and O. Hagen (eds.), *Expected Utility and the Allais Paradox*, Dordrecht, Holland: Reidel Publishing Co., 333–409.

MACCRIMMON, K. R., STANBURY, W. T., AND WEHRUNG, D. A. (1980), "Real money lotteries: A study of ideal risk, context effects, and simple processes," in T. S. Wallsten (ed.), *Cognitive Processes in Choice and Decision Behavior*, Hillsdale, N.J.: Erlbaum, 155–177.

MACCRIMMON, K. R., AND WEHRUNG, D. A. (1984), "The Risk In-Basket," *Journal of Business*, *57*:367–387.

MACCRIMMON, K. R., AND WEHRUNG, D. A. (1985a), "Assessing risk propensity," in Proceedings of Second International Conference on Foundations of Utility and Risk Theory, Venice, Italy, June 1984, Dordrecht, Holland: Reidel Publishing Co., forthcoming.

MACCRIMMON, K. R., AND WEHRUNG, D. A. (1985b), "Relationships between risk propensity and characteristics of top-level managers," Working paper, Faculty of Commerce, University of British Columbia.

MACCRIMMON, K. R., AND WEHRUNG, D. A. (1985c), "A portfolio of risk measures," *Theory and Decision*, forthcoming.

MACHINA, M. J. (1982), "Expected utility analysis without the independence axiom," *Econometrica*, *50*:277–323.

MACHOL, R. E., AND LERNER, E. M. (1969), "Risk, ruin and investment analysis," *Journal of Financial Quantitative Analysis*, *4*:473–492.

MAEHR, M. L., AND VIDEBECK, R. (1968), "Predisposition to risk and persistence under varying reinforcement-success schedules," *Journal of Personality and Social Psychology*, *9*:96–100.

MANTIS, G., AND FARMER, R. N. (1968), "Demand for life insurance," *Journal of Risk and Insurance*, *35*:247–256.

MAO, J. C. T. (1970), "Models of capital budgeting, E-V vs. E-S," *Journal of Financial and Quantitative Analysis*, *4*:657–675.

MARKOWITZ, H. M. (1952), "Portfolio selection," *Journal of Finance*, *7*:77–91.

MARKOWITZ, H. M. (1959), *Portfolio Selection*, New York: Wiley.

MARSCHAK, J. (1950), "Rational behavior, uncertain prospects, and measurable utility," *Econometrica*, *18*:111–141.

Martin, J. W. (1978), "A study of practicing CPAs' risk profiles to determine attributes relevant to the certified public accountant's personality and practice," Ph.D. dissertation, University of Alabama.

Mascarenhas, B. (1982), "Coping with uncertainty in international business," *Journal of International Business Studies*, *13*:87–98.

McCahill, F. X., Jr. (1971), "Avoid losses through risk management," *Harvard Business Review*, *49*:57–65.

McClelland, D. C., Atkinson, J. W., Clark, R. A., and Lowell, E. L. (1953), *The Achievement Motive*, New York: Appleton-Century-Crofts.

McCord, M., and de Neufville, R. (1983), "Experimental demonstration that expected utility decision analysis is not operational," in B. Stigum and F. Wenstop (eds.), *Foundations of Utility and Risk Theory*, Dordrecht, Holland: Reidel Publishing Co.

McInish, T. H. (1982), "Individual investors and risk-taking," *Journal of Economic Psychology*, *2*:125–136.

Meyer, H. H., Walker, W. B., and Litwin, G. H. (1961), "Motive patterns and risk preferences associated with entrepreneurship," *Journal of Abnormal and Social Psychology*, *63*:570–574.

Meyer, R. F., and Pratt, J. W. (1968), "Consistent assessment and fairing of preference functions," *IEEE Transactions on Systems Science and Cybernetics*, *SSC-4*:270–278.

Miller, D., Kets de Vries, M. F. R., and Toulouse, J. M. (1982), "Top executive locus of control and its relationship to strategy-making, structure, and environment," *Academy of Management Journal*, *25*:237–253.

Mosteller, F., and Nogee, P. (1951), "An experimental measurement of utility," *Journal of Political Economy*, *59*:371–404.

Neter, J., and Williams, C. A., Jr., (1971), "Acceptability of three normative methods of insurance decision-making," *Journal of Risk and Insurance*, *38*:385–408.

Neter, J., and Williams, C. (1973), "Performance of the expected utility method and two other normative methods in insurance decision making," *Decision Sciences*, *4*:517–532.

Newman, J. M. (1977), "Comparison of I-E scale and a specific locus of control measure in predicting risk-taking behavior under novel task conditions," *Psychological Reports*, *40*:1035–1040.

Newman, O. (1972), *Gambling: Hazard and Reward*, Atlantic Highlands, N.J.: Athlone Press/Humanities Press.

O'Connor, M. F., Peterson, C. R., and Palmer, T. J. (1972), "Stakes and probabilities in information purchase," *Organizational Behavior and Human Performance*, *7*:43–52.

Oldman, D. (1974), "Chance and skill: A study of roulette," *Sociology*, *8*:407–426.

Olson, M. C. (1976), *Unacceptable Risk*, New York: Bantam Books.

Otway, H. J. (1975), "Risk assessment and societal choices," RM-75-2,

Laxenburg, Austria: International Institute for Applied Systems Analysis.

Otway, H. J., and Pahner, P. D. (1976), "Risk assessment," *Futures*, *8*:122–134.

Payne, J. W., and Braunstein, M. L. (1971), "Preferences among gambles with equal underlying distributions," *Journal of Experimental Psychology*, *87*:13–18.

Payne, J. W. (1973), "Alternative approaches to decision making under risk: Moments versus risk dimensions," *Psychological Bulletin*, *80*:439–453.

Payne, J. W., and Braunstein, M. L. (1978), "Risky choice: An examination of information acquisition behavior," *Memory and Cognition*, *6*:554–561.

Payne, J. W., Laughhunn, D. J., and Crum, R. L. (1980), "Translation of gambles and aspiration level effects in risky choice behavior," *Management Science*, *26*:1039–1060.

Payne, J. W., Laughhunn, D. J., and Crum, R. L. (1981), "Further tests of aspiration level effects in risky choice behavior," *Management Science*, *27*:953–958.

Payne, J. W., Laughhunn, D. L., and Crum, R. (1984), "Multiattribute risky choice behavior: The editing of complex prospects," *Management Science*, *30*:1350–1361.

Peter, J. P., and Ryan, M. J. (1976), "An investigation of perceived risk at the brand level," *Journal of Marketing Research*, *13*:184–188.

Peters, T. J., and Waterman, R. H., Jr. (1982), *In Search of Excellence*, New York: Harper and Row.

Pitz, G. F., and Reinhold, H. (1968), "Payoff effects in sequential decision-making," *Journal of Experimental Psychology*, *77*:249–257.

Pitz, G. F. (1969a), "The influence of prior probabilities on information seeking and decision making," *Organizational Behavior and Human Performance*, *4*:213–226.

Pitz, G. F. (1969b), "Use of response times to evaluate strategies of information seeking," *Journal of Experimental Psychology*, *80*:553–557.

Pollatsek, A., and Tversky, A. (1970), "A theory of risk," *Journal of Mathematical Psychology*, *7*:540–553.

Popielarz, D. T. (1967), "An explanation of perceived risk and willingness to try new products," *Journal of Marketing Research*, *4*:368–372.

Pratt, J. W. (1964), "Risk aversion in the small and in the large," *Econometrica*, *32*:122–136.

Pruitt, D. G. (1962), "Pattern and level of risk in gambling decisions," *Psychological Review*, *69*:187–201.

Pyle, D. H., and Turnovsky, S. J. (1970), "Safety-first and expected utility maximization in mean-standard deviation portfolio analysis," *Review of Economics and Statistics*, *52*:75–81.

Quiggin, J. (1982), "A theory of anticipated utility," *Journal of Economic Behavior and Organization*, *3*:323–343.

QUIRK, J. P., AND SAPOSNICK, R. (1962), "Admissibility and measurable utility functions," *Review of Economic Studies*, *29*:140–146.

RAIFFA, H. (1968), *Decision Analysis: Introductory Lectures on Choices Under Uncertainty*, Reading, Mass: Addison Wesley.

RAMSEY, F. P. (1926), "Truth and probability," in *The Foundations of Mathematics and Other Logical Essays*, New York: Harcourt, Brace. 1931.

RANYARD, R. H. (1976), "Elimination by aspects as a decision rule for risky choice," *Acta Psychologica*, *40*:299–310.

REINGEN, P. H. (1976), "Do subjects understand the choice dilemma questionnaire?" *Journal of Social Psychology*, *99*:303–304.

REUM, W. R., AND STEELE, T. A., III (1970), "Contingent payouts cut acquisition risks," *Harvard Business Review*, *48*:83–91.

RIM, Y. (1963), "Risk taking and need for achievement," *Acta Psychologica*, *21*:108–115.

ROSELIUS, T. (1971), "Consumer rankings of risk reduction methods," *Journal of Marketing*, *35*:56–61.

ROSS, I. (1974), "Perceived risk and consumer behavior: A critical review," in M. J. Schlinger (ed.), *Advances in Consumer Research, Vol. II*, Urbana, Ill.: Association for Consumer Research, 1–19.

ROTTER, J. B., SEEMAN, M., AND LIVERANT, S. (1962), "Internal vs. external control of reinforcements: A major variable in behavior theory," in N.F. Washburne (ed.), *Decisions, Values and Groups, 2*, London: Pergamon Press.

ROTTER, J. B. (1966), "Generalized expectancies for internal versus external control of reinforcement," *Psychological Monographs*, *80*:1–28.

ROY, A. D. (1952), "Safety first and the holding of assets," *Econometrica*, *20*:431–449.

ROYDEN, H. L., SUPPES, P., AND WALSH, K. (1959), "A model for the experimental measurement of the utility of gambling," *Behavioral Science*, *4*:11–18.

SARIN, R. K. (1982), "Strength of preference and risky choice," *Operations Research*, *30*:982–997.

SAVAGE, L. J. (1954), *The Foundations of Statistics*, New York: Wiley.

SCHAEFER, R. E (1978), "What are we talking about when we talk about 'risk'? A critical survey of risk and risk preference theories," RM-78-69, Laxenburg, Austria: International Institute for Applied Systems Analysis.

SCHLAIFER, R. (1971), *Computer Programs for Elementary Decision Analysis*, Boston: Division of Research, Graduate School of Business, Harvard University.

SCHOEMAKER, P. J. H., AND KUNREUTHER, H. (1979), "An experimental study of insurance decisions," *Journal of Risk and Insurance*, *46*:603–618.

SCHOEMAKER, P. J. H. (1979), "The role of statistical knowledge in gambling decisions: Moment vs. risk dimension approaches," *Organizational Behavior and Human Performance*, *24*:1–17.

SCHOEMAKER, P. J. H. (1980), *Experiments on Decisions under Risk: The Expected Utility Hypothesis*, Boston: Martinus Nijhoff Publishing.

SCHOEMAKER, P. J. H. (1984), "An experimental test of expected utility theory: Preferences for information," Working paper, Center for Decision Research, Graduate School of Business, University of Chicago.

SHARPE, W. F. (1964), "Capital asset prices: A theory of market equilibrium under conditions of risk," *Journal of Finance*, *19*:425–442.

SHEPARD, D. S. AND ZECKHAUSER, R. J. (1984), "Survival versus consumption," *Management Science*, *30*:423–439.

SHETH, J. S. AND VENKATESAN, M. (1968), "Risk-reduction processes in repetitive consumer behavior," *Journal of Marketing Research*, *5*:307–310.

SHURE, G. H., AND MEEKER, R. J. (1967), "A personality/attitude schedule for use in experimental bargaining studies," *Journal of Psychology*, *65*:233–252.

SIEGEL, F. W., AND HOBAN, J. P., JR. (1982), "Relative risk aversion revisited," *Review of Economics and Statistics*, *64*:481–487.

SLOVIC, P. (1962), "Convergent validation of risk taking measures," *Journal of Abnormal and Social Psychology*, *65*:68–71.

SLOVIC, P. (1964), "Assessment of risk taking behavior," *Psychological Bulletin*, *61*:220–233.

SLOVIC, P., LICHTENSTEIN, S., AND EDWARDS, W. (1965), "Boredom-induced changes in preferences among bets," *American Journal of Psychology*, *78*:208–217.

SLOVIC, P. (1966), "Risk-taking in children: Age and sex differences," *Child Development*, *37*:169–176.

SLOVIC, P., AND LICHTENSTEIN, S. (1968), "Relative importance of probabilities and payoffs in risk taking," *Journal of Experimental Psychology Monograph*, *78*:1–18.

SLOVIC, P. (1969), "Analyzing the expert judge: A descriptive study of a stock-broker's decision processes," *Journal of Applied Psychology*, *53*:255–263.

SLOVIC, P. (1972), "Information processing, situation specificity, and the generality of risk-taking behavior," *Journal of Personality and Social Psychology*, *22*:128–134.

SLOVIC, P., AND FISCHHOFF, B. (1976), "How safe is safe enough? Determinants of perceived and acceptable risk," in L. Gould and C. A. Walker (eds.), *Too Hot to Handle: Social and Policy Issues in the Management of Radioactive Wastes*, New Haven: Yale University Press.

SLOVIC, P., FISCHHOFF, B., AND LICHTENSTEIN, S. (1978), "Accident probabilities and seat belt usage: A psychological perspective," *Accident Analysis and Prevention*, *10*:281–285.

SLOVIC, P., LICHTENSTEIN, S., AND FISCHHOFF, B. (1979), "Images of disaster: Perception and acceptance of risks from nuclear power," in G. Goodman and W. Rowe (eds.), *Energy Risk Management*, London: Academic Press.

SLOVIC, P., FISCHHOFF, B., AND LICHTENSTEIN, S. (1980), "Perceived risk," in R. C. Schwing and W. A. Albers Jr. (eds.), *Societal Risk Assessment: How Safe is Safe Enough?* New York: Plenum.

SLOVIC, P., FISCHHOFF, B., AND LICHTENSTEIN, S. (1981), "Characterizing perceived risk," in R. W. Kates and C. Hohenemser (eds.), *Technological Hazard Management*, Cambridge: Oelgeschlager, Gunn, and Hain.

SLOVIC, P., AND LICHTENSTEIN, S. (1983), "Preference reversals: A broader perspective," *American Economic Review*, *73*:596–605.

SPENCE, H. E., ENGEL, J. F., AND BLACKWELL, R. D. (1970), "Perceived risk in mail-order and retail store buying," *Journal of Marketing Research*, *12*:364–369.

SPETZLER, C. S. (1968), "The development of a corporate risk policy for capital investment decisions," *IEEE Transactions on Systems Science and Cybernetics*, *SCC-4*:279–300.

SRINIVASULU, S. L. (1981), "Strategic response to foreign exchange risks," *Columbia Journal of World Business*, *16*:13–23.

STARBUCK, W. H., AND BASS, F. M. (1967), "Experimental study of risk-taking and the value of information in a new product context," *Journal of Business*, *40*:155–165.

STARR, C. (1969), "Social benefit versus technological risk," *Science*, *165*:1232–1238.

STARR, C., AND WHIPPLE, C. (1984), "A perspective on health and safety risk analysis," *Management Science*, *30*:452–463.

STONE, B. K. (1973), "A general class of three-parameter risk measures," *Journal of Finance*, *28*:675–685.

STONER, A. F. J. (1961), "A comparison of individual and group decisions involving risk," master's thesis, M.I.T.

SVENSON, O. (1984), "Managing the risks of the automobile: A study of a Swedish car manufacturer," *Management Science*, *30*:486–502.

SWALM, R. O. (1966), "Utility theory: Insights into risk taking," *Harvard Business Review*, *44*:123–136.

SZPIRO, G. G. (1983), "The hypotheses of absolute and relative risk aversion: An empirical study using cross-section data," *Geneva Papers on Risk and Insurance*, *8*:336–349.

TAYLOR, R. N., AND DUNNETTE, M. D. (1974), "Influence of dogmatism, risk-taking propensity, and intelligence on decision-making strategies for a sample of industrial managers," *Journal of Applied Psychology*, *59*:420–423.

TEGER, A. I., AND PRUITT, D. B. (1967), "Components of group risk taking," *Journal of Experimental Social Psychology*, *3*:189–205.

TELSER, L. (1955), "Safety first and hedging," *Review of Economic Studies*, *23*:1–16.

TORRANCE, E. P., AND ZILLER, R. C. (1957), "Risk and life experience: Development of a scale for measuring risk taking tendencies," Research report 57-23, United States Air Force.

TVERSKY, A., AND KAHNEMAN, D. (1981), "The framing of decisions and the psychology of choice," *Science*, *211*:453-458.

VLEK, C., AND STALLEN, P. J. (1981), "Judging risks and benefits in the small and in the large," *Organizational Behavior and Human Performance*, *28*:235-271.

VON NEUMANN, J., AND MORGENSTERN, O. (1947), *Theory of Games and Economic Behavior*, Princeton: Princeton University Press.

VROOM, V. H., AND PAHL, B. (1971), "Relationship between age and risk taking among managers," *Journal of Applied Psychology*, *55*:399-405.

WALLACH, M. A., AND CARON, A. J. (1959), "Attribute criteriality and sex-linked conservatism as determinants of psychological similarity," *Journal of Abnormal Social Psychology*, *59*:43-50.

WALLACH, M. A., AND KOGAN, N. (1959), "Sex differences and judgment processes," *Journal of Personality*, *27*:555-564.

WALLACH, M. A., AND KOGAN, N. (1961), "Aspects of judgment and decision making: Interrelationships and changes with age," *Behavioral Science*, *6*:23-26.

WALLACH, M.A., AND WING, C. W., JR. (1968), "Is risk a value?" *Journal of Personality and Social Psychology*, *9*:101-106.

WATSON, S. R., AND BROWN, R. V. (1978), "The valuation of decision analysis," *Journal of the Royal Statistical Society, A*, *141*:69-78.

WATTS, H. W., AND TOBIN, J. (1967), "Consumer expenditures and the capital account," in D. D. Hester and J. Tobin (eds.), *Studies of Portfolio Behavior*, New York: Wiley, 1-39.

WEHRUNG, D. A., MACCRIMMON, K. R., AND BROTHERS, K. M. (1984), "Utility assessment: Domains, stability, and equivalence procedures," *INFOR*, *22*:98-115.

WEHRUNG, D. A., AND MACCRIMMON, K. R. (1985), "Expected gain and expected loss: A linear model of investment preferences," Working paper, Faculty of Commerce, University of British Columbia.

WEINSTEIN, E., AND MARTIN, J. (1969), "Generality of willingness to take risks," *Psychological Reports*, *24*:499-501.

WEINSTEIN, M. S. (1969), "Achievement motivation and risk preference," *Journal of Personality and Social Psychology*, *13*:153-172.

WILLEMS, E. P. (1969), "Risk is a value," *Psychological Reports*, *24*:81-82.

WILLIAMS, C. A. (1966), "Attitudes toward speculative risks as an indicator of attitudes toward pure risk," *Journal of Risk and Insurance*, *33*:577-586.

WILLIAMS, L. K. (1960), "The measurement of risk taking propensity in an industrial setting," Ph.D. dissertation, University of Michigan.

Wilson, R. (1979), "Analyzing the daily risks of life," *Technology Review*, *81*:40–46.

Yaari, M. E. (1969), "Some remarks on measures of risk aversion and on their uses," *Journal of Economic Theory*, *1*:315–329.

Ziegler, L. D. (1977), "A study of differences in risk taking propensity between business and education students and practitioners," Ph.D. dissertation, University of Akron.

Zuckerman, M., Kolin, E. A., Price, L., and Zoob, I. (1964), "Development of a sensation-seeking scale," *Journal of Consulting Psychology*, *28*:477–482.

Zuckerman, M. (1971), "Dimensions of sensation seeking," *Journal of Consulting and Clinical Psychology*, *36*:45–52.

Zuckerman, M. (1974), "The sensation seeking motive," in A. Maher (ed.), *Progress in Experimental Personality Research, Vol. 7*, New York: Academic Press.

Zuckerman, M. (1978), "The search for high sensation," *Psychology Today*, February, 39–46, 95–99.

Index

Note: References to the main text appear in roman type
References to the technical notes appear in italics
References to the endnotes are followed by an "n"